THE GATEKEEPERS

THE GATEKEEPERS

*Inside the Admissions Process
of a Premier College*

JACQUES STEINBERG

Viking

VIKING
Published by the Penguin Group
Penguin Putnam Inc., 375 Hudson Street, New York, New York 10014, U.S.A.
Penguin Books Ltd, 80 Strand,
London WC2R 0RL, England
Penguin Books Australia Ltd, 250 Camberwell Road, Camberwell,
Victoria 3124, Australia
Penguin Books Canada Ltd, 10 Alcorn Avenue,
Toronto, Ontario, Canada M4V 3B2
Penguin Books India (P) Ltd, 11 Community Centre, Panchsheel Park,
New Delhi—110 017, India
Penguin Books (N.Z.) Ltd, Cnr Rosedale and Airborne Roads, Albany,
Auckland, New Zealand
Penguin Books (South Africa) (Pty) Ltd, 24 Sturdee Avenue,
Rosebank, Johannesburg 2196, South Africa

Penguin Books Ltd, Registered Offices:
Harmondsworth, Middlesex, England

First published in 2002 by Viking Penguin,
a member of Penguin Putnam Inc.

3   5   7   9   10   8   6   4

Library of Congress Cataloging-in-Publication Data

Steinberg, Jacques.
The gatekeepers : inside the admissions process of a premier college / Jacques Steinberg.
p.   cm.
Includes bibliographical references.
ISBN 0-670-03135-6
1. Universities and colleges—United States—Admission—Case studies.   2. Wesleyan
University (Middletown, Conn.)—Admission.   I. Title.

LB2351.2 .S72 2002
378.1'61—dc21   2002016884

This book is printed on acid-free paper. ∞

Printed in the United States of America
Set in Galliard
Designed by Jaye Zimet

For Sharon,
who said, Yes!

and

In memory of Karen Avenoso,
who taught me so much

CONTENTS

INTRODUCTION

Colleges make their admissions decisions behind a cordon of security befitting the selection of a pope. The reasons why one applicant was accepted, while another was rejected, are closely held by the few people permitted in the room at the time the choices are made. And soon after issuing their one-word rulings—*yes, no* or *maybe*—admissions officers usually feed the evidence of their deliberations into Iran-Contra–era document shredders. The raw materials that fuel such discussions—test scores, race, social class, grades, athletic ability, family connections—are considered far too combustible to be combined in front of the applicants themselves, let alone a wider audience.

To penetrate this mysterious culture, I spent eight months, from the fall of 1999 until the spring of 2000, as an observer inside the admissions office of one of the most selective colleges in the country, Wesleyan University in Middletown, Connecticut. I then mined that experience to write a series of articles that appeared on the front page of *The New York Times*. As part of my research, I peered over the shoulders of the Wesleyan admissions staff as they sorted and evaluated ten times as many applications as there were seats available in the Class of 2004. At the moment that these sentries were turning back most of the teenagers massed at the university's front gate, so, too, were their colleagues at Harvard, Yale, Stanford and dozens of other elite educational institutions. Each received a record number of applications in the winter of 2000. And each would whittle its lists of applicants down in strikingly similar ways.

The Gatekeepers grew out of that newspaper series. Specifically, it tells the story of one admissions officer, Ralph Figueroa, and the high school seniors whose cases he and his colleagues considered that year. My goal in writing this book is to allow any outsider—including those teenagers hoping to gain access themselves—to follow along as actual applications pass through each stage of an entire admissions cycle at an elite private college. None of the applicants' names have been changed, nor have the details of their lives.

The story told here begins in classrooms and homes across the country, as the applicants huddle anxiously with their guidance counselors and parents in their junior year before scrambling to take the SAT and to compose their college essays. The narrative then travels behind the closed doors of the admissions office, as well as the officers' homes, as the applications of those same students are debated, often heatedly. Finally, the applicants receive responses from Wesleyan and other colleges, and face decisions of their own. As they try to imagine their lives four years into the future, and well beyond that, they embark on visits to Wesleyan and some of its most formidable competitors, including Stanford, Brown, Harvard, Yale, Cornell, Vassar and the University of Chicago. In a postscript, the applicants reflect on the whole nerve-wracking experience, from the vantage point of their first two years of college. Some attend Wesleyan; others do not.

In granting me such privileged access, Ralph Figueroa and his colleagues have enabled me to describe the high drama of selective college admissions in a way that no "how to" book ever could. Although Wesleyan and other colleges have adapted numerous techniques from social science to help them sift each year's freshman class, their judgments are just as often intuitive and idiosyncratic. It's actually quite a messy process, and only by watching admissions officers wrestle with the attributes of an actual candidate can an outsider grasp the various, sometimes competing, institutional priorities in play. Similarly, only by listening closely to teenagers and their parents can one appreciate why so many applicants from so many different backgrounds came to concentrate their pleas for acceptance on such a small collection of private colleges in the late twentieth century. By then the prize that those families were pursuing, the first-class private education described in the brochure for the American Dream, had become at once more accessible, and more elusive, than ever.

* * *

Among the questions that have informed the reporting of this book is one that has stumped me for nearly twenty years, ever since I applied to my own dream college: How had I managed to get in, when so many others had not?

I knew I wanted to attend Dartmouth College since at least the age of thirteen. I'm not sure if I was aware then that Dartmouth was part of the Ivy League, for my immediate concern was the appeal of its campus. It was located in Hanover, New Hampshire, a twenty-five-mile drive from the summer camp that my brother and I had attended for nearly a decade. One summer, eight bunkmates and I spent four rainy days and nights on the Appalachian Trail, attempting to hike up and over the range of mountains that lay like an obstacle course between Camp Walt Whitman and Dartmouth. Once we finally arrived in Hanover and sought shelter in a shop called the Ice Cream Machine, none of us wanted to leave. Attending Dartmouth, I figured, would be like finding refuge in that shop.

One morning during my senior year of high school, my parents and I rose at dawn and drove four hours from our home in southeastern Massachusetts to Hanover. Once on the Dartmouth campus, we scaled the thick granite steps of McNutt Hall to attend a general information session led by an admissions officer, the first admissions officer whom I had ever seen. Sitting in a hard-back chair on carpeting that was as well tended as a putting green, I counted more than one hundred other applicants in the audience, each of whom looked as nervous as I was. By then, I knew all about the Ivy League and where Dartmouth stood in the nation's academic pantheon, at least as scored by *U.S. News & World Report*. As I gazed up at a towering oil portrait of a balding man wearing a severe expression—*You don't have a prayer*, he seemed to be saying to me—I wondered how I would ever be able to distinguish myself in this company, particularly since Dartmouth discouraged on-campus interviews. My mother, however, had already considered the problem, and at the conclusion of the admissions officer's talk, grabbed me by the elbow and dragged me to the front of the room.

"We're the *Steinbergs*," she told the officer, a smile on her face and her eyes piercing his meaningfully. From the gravity of her tone, the officer must have thought he was about to have an audience with one of the Kennedys, rather than with the son of a Jewish anesthesiologist and his wife, a nurse who had abandoned her profession because she grew woozy at the sight of blood.

When the thick letter filled with good news arrived from Hanover a few months later, my mother was half-convinced that her introduction had made a difference. At the very least, she figured, the officer must have noted the depth of this particular mother's love for her son. For my part, I was both gratified and mystified by Dartmouth's interest in me. In 1983, the year I applied, nearly nine thousand applicants had sought about one thousand seats in the freshman class. And most of those accepted had better SAT scores than I did.

Had my essay pushed me over the top? Asked to reflect on something I had read recently, I chose a column that Russell Baker had published one Sunday in *The New York Times Magazine,* in which he described having his credit cards stolen by someone who had then spent thousands of dollars on first-class airline tickets. Baker had written: "In today's world, you are not who you are named; you are what you are numbered." That sentiment certainly spoke to me, a seventeen-year-old obscured by a haze of standardized test scores, and I said as much in my essay. Had the admissions committee, despite its insistence that I take all those tests, secretly agreed with me?

What about my high school? The same year I was accepted by Dartmouth, a friend from my hometown was rejected, even though she had attended one of the top prep schools in New England and had better SAT scores than I did. Her school sent a half dozen graduates to Dartmouth each year. I attended a public high school in a small town, and only about half my classmates even applied to college. The last person I was aware of who went to Dartmouth from my high school had graduated years earlier, and he was a star quarterback. I wrote for the newspaper. Had I gained an edge over my private-school peers sheerly by virtue of demographics?

The college admissions process rarely affords an opportunity to answer such questions. How many among us even get the chance to meet an admissions officer? My curiosity lay dormant for more than a decade but was suddenly awakened in the fall of 1999. By then, I had become an education writer for *The New York Times.* And after four years covering the New York City public schools, I was being promoted to the national education beat. Higher education was now part of my portfolio.

One of my first assignments was to cover the annual meeting of the National Association for College Admission Counseling, or NACAC. When these gatherings first began in the 1940s, they were intimate, clubby affairs that drew just a handful of college admissions officers and high school guidance counselors, most of whom had elbow patches on their tweedy blazers. But over the half century that followed, the meetings evolved into a must-attend extravaganza for the many men and women whose jobs now fell into the broad category of selective college admissions. The forums offered professionals on both sides of the admissions equation an opportunity for frank conversation at a neutral site. Few teenagers or their parents were made aware that these summits were taking place. Thus the college admissions season opened each September at NACAC (or *KNACK ack*) with all the pomp, pageantry, excess and anxious anticipation of the Olympics—but without the primary competitors. The year that I visited, nearly fifteen hundred admissions officers and another fifteen hundred guidance counselors were in attendance. The setting was Disney World.

The growth in the scale and importance of this annual affair paralleled the dramatic changes that had taken place in the college admissions process over the same half century. Up until the late 1950s, admission to elite colleges was usually reserved for those applicants who were fortunate enough to have been born into the right family or to have attended a particular private or public high school. In many cases, a college set aside a certain number of seats for the graduates of a small collection of feeder schools within easy driving distance, and then decided who would fill those seats in consultation with headmasters or principals. A college dean sealed the transaction with a handshake. Harvard, for example, drew heavily on the graduating class at Phillips Exeter Academy in New Hampshire, while Yale relied on Phillips Andover in Massachusetts. It was unusual for an applicant to apply to more than three or four colleges. And for the most part, blacks, Jews and women need not have bothered trying. Indeed, for much of the nation's history prior to World War II, relatively few Americans graduated from high school, let alone went on to college.

The civil rights movement helped pry open the gates that protected those long-exclusive institutions, which were headquartered, for the most part, in the northeast. In an effort to diversify their campuses in the 1960s and early 1970s, the nation's best colleges began embarking on cross-country searches for the most qualified black, Hispanic and, eventually, female applicants. Suddenly, the children of families that had been previously shut out of these institutions were being enthusiastically ushered through the front door, sometimes ahead of applicants who had taken their place in line much earlier. By 1978, the Supreme Court's *Bakke* decision was widely interpreted as giving public universities, as well as private colleges, permission to consider race "a plus" in their admissions decisions.

That many of the students now being accepted could not afford to pay full tuition became relatively moot: colleges adopted so-called need-blind admissions policies that promised students that they would only have to pay what they could afford, at least as calculated by the universities. To help offset their financial losses, particularly as high school enrollments declined in the 1970s and energy prices rose, the colleges initiated an equally intense search for other customers who could pay full price, whether from the United States or abroad.

After inherited privilege was dislodged as a primary credential for elite college admission, the SAT—an aptitude test that was originally intended for limited use as a screener of scholarship applications at Harvard—was enlisted to fill the void, creating the foundation for the establishment of a meritocracy and sending several million students a year scurrying to sharpen their no. 2 pencils. But SAT scores could not be evaluated in a vacuum. For a variety of reasons, not always attributable to intelligence, some students scored better than peers who were otherwise academically outstanding. The process of admitting students to college became, as a result, a much more complicated enterprise, prompting universities to expand their admissions staffs and codify criteria for entry. In seeking to ensure that the communities behind their ivy walls were well stocked with citizens of diverse talents, colleges came to value some applicants' extracurricular and cultural experiences as much as, if not more than, their academic accomplishments. Tuba players were suddenly courted as assiduously as quarterbacks. And teenagers began responding in kind, loading up on the sorts of outside activities in which they thought the colleges would want them to engage.

In many instances, colleges relied on admissions committees to screen such résumés, and the vote of the majority often ruled. Thus, the process of distributing precious seats at Ivy League and other elite institutions became more democratic, as did the distribution of the primary perk that usually accompanied those coveted slots: entrée, upon graduation, to the best corporations and graduate schools in America. Little wonder that applicants who had come to consider those seats a birthright grew angry that they now had to compete for them.

Throughout the 1980s and 1990s, the mailboxes of elite colleges like the Ivies, as well as smaller liberal arts colleges that were previously less competitive, began to bulge with applications, sometimes at rates double and triple those of only a few years earlier. It wasn't just that more students were now graduating from high school annually, or that more minority students and students from impoverished backgrounds were applying to such colleges; so were more affluent students whose parents had recently reached the ranks of the upper middle class. Many of these nouveau riche parents had themselves been educated at the nation's finest public universities, but having attained financial security without necessarily gaining social status, they had decided that their children deserved better. On the eve of the NACAC conference in the fall of 1999, Farrar, Straus and Giroux published *The Big Test: The Secret History of the American Meritocracy,* in which the author, Nicholas Lemann, wrote:

> Here is what American society looks like today. A thick line runs through the country, with people who have been to college on one side of it and people who haven't on the other. This line gets brighter all the time. Whether a person is on one side of the line or the other is now more indicative of income, of attitudes, and of political behavior than any other line one might draw: region, race, age, religion, sex, class. As people plan their lives and their children's lives, higher education is the main focus of their aspirations (and the possibility of getting into the elite end of higher education is the focus of their very dearest aspirations).

With parents and children finding the pursuit of their higher-education dreams to be increasingly competitive, a cottage industry sprang up to help them. Stanley H. Kaplan's test-preparation courses—which had begun luring families as early as the 1950s with the promise that the SAT could be coached, contrary to the test's billing as an IQ-style aptitude test—became so wildly popular in the 1980s that several competitors arose, most notably the Princeton Review. Like well-paid psychologists, college consultants also began hanging out their shingles, offering to give middle-class students at public high schools the sort of strategic edge that previously had been reserved for students at elite private schools. Meanwhile, the lucrative literary genre of college guidebooks was born, which offered detailed portraits and rankings of the nation's top colleges. Other books claimed to explain, definitively, how to get in. (At least one was called *Getting In.*) As it became clear that money was giving some applicants an implicit advantage, jeopardizing the fledgling meritocracy, the colleges began adjusting the admissions process to raise the bar—in terms of test scores and grades—that they would expect students of means to vault. Critics soon saw a double standard that, they said, was equally threatening to the meritocracy. An impoverished applicant whose academic profile might be slightly inferior to a rich applicant's was, in many instances, now considered the more desirable of the two.

Meanwhile, the admissions ritual started taking place earlier and earlier. During the late 1970s and early 1980s, universities let it be known that they wanted applicants to take as many college-level, Advanced Placement courses in high school as they could handle, the better to prepare them for the work that lay ahead. That meant students would have to begin taking some high school level courses in middle school, which many, indeed, did. Around that time, more colleges also began encouraging those applicants who felt certain about their first choice to apply to college early, in the fall of senior year, with an ofttimes binding decision due from the college in December, rather than April, the traditional month for acceptances. Like their focus on the SAT and AP courses, the colleges' increasing emphasis on the early-decision process began further encroaching on the high school experience. By the late 1990s, some colleges, including Wesleyan, were admitting as much as 40 percent of the following year's freshman class before most students had even applied. Soon, students as young as those in the sixth grade were reporting that the pressure of preparing for college had become unbearable.

With more of those early applications due in November, the NACAC convention, which was always held in September, took on increasing significance. As I arrived at the Swan and Dolphin Resort in Orlando in the fall of 1999, I felt as if I had finally picked the lock on the admissions office door. In a hall illuminated by faux skylights and decorated with giant pastel flowers, representatives of nearly 450 colleges stood shoulder to shoulder behind long rows of tables that seemed to go on forever. High school counselors—from public and private institutions, as well as those hired individually by families—passed before them like slow-moving barges trying to dock, but often getting swept along by the tide. So that no college had an unfair advantage, they were arranged alphabetically. Each draped its wool or nylon banner over a folding rectangular table that measured no more than six feet long.

Virtually the only exception was Harvard: its booth was double the size of the others—the better to accommodate the crowd that always seemed to surround Bill Fitzsimmons, the university's longtime dean of admissions. He looked the part, dressed in pressed chinos, a starched white button-down shirt open at the neck, and blue blazer. His advice was in such demand that he was forever sucking on Halls cough drops to preserve his voice. Fitzsimmons's fans kept spilling over into the gallery next door, which was occupied by a more obscure competitor, Harvey Mudd College, of Claremont, California.

As they pushed their way toward the Harvard, Princeton, Dartmouth, Stanford and Yale booths, among many others, the guidance counselors brandished pens in one hand and stacks of their business cards in the other. Once they were within range, they scribbled the names of their favorite high school seniors on the backs of the cards and pressed them into the hands of the admissions officers. The counselors hoped that putting an applicant's name before an officer so early might pay dividends later in the year. In turn, representatives of colleges with more regional reputations (like Harvey Mudd) hoped that by traveling to NACAC they might get an opportunity to whisper the names of their institutions into the ears of influential guidance counselors from other parts of the country.

Underscoring just how big a business the admissions process had become, representatives from several hundred companies were gathered in an adjoining space in similarly sized booths, marketing their wares to high schools (and, by extension, to students) as well as to the colleges. The College Board, which administered the SAT, sent twenty-nine statisticians and other employees to that year's convention, at a time when a small but increasing number of liberal arts colleges were questioning the test's value, with some even dropping it as an admissions requirement. Kaplan Inc., which had grown in proportion to the SAT and was now owned by the Washington Post Company, dispatched ten representatives to NACAC. *U.S. News & World Report,* whose rankings of the nation's top colleges had expanded to include graduate schools and hospitals, sent thirteen researchers and salespeople. By now, however, the overt commercial presence was not necessarily welcome. In an address to the meeting's general assembly, Bruce Poch, a vice president and longtime dean of admissions at Pomona College, in California, said: "I am distressed by the direction taken by NACAC at this conference, which to my eye and to the eyes of many others seems to represent a transformation from a professional conference to a four-day infomercial."

I elbowed my way through the crowd, clutching a list of influential deans compiled by my editor. Fitzsimmons, who had worked at Harvard since 1972, was one, of course, as was Bill Hiss, who had served almost as long at Bates College, a small liberal arts school in Lewiston, Maine, 140 miles north of Harvard Yard. Soon after I met Hiss, who was now a Bates vice president, and Wylie Mitchell, his successor as dean of admissions, they pitched me a proposition: Would I be interested in spending the next nine months as a spectator with a front-row seat in the Bates admissions office, as they selected the Class of 2004?

It was a tempting offer, not least because of its timing. The previous spring, my editor, Ethan Bronner, had reported on the front page of the *Times* that the selection of the Class of 2003 had been the most competitive ever at several dozen highly selective colleges; the academic year just beginning was already promising to break most of those records. Like a river of champagne flowing down one of those pyramids of glasses so beloved at weddings, the excess of applicants to the Ivies was raining down on the next tier, too, including schools like Bates and its neighbors Bowdoin and Colby, as well as Middlebury, Williams, Amherst and Swarthmore. Below them, colleges and universities that were once dismissed by some of the best students as safety schools—including Skidmore in upstate New York and Muhlenberg in Pennsylvania's Lehigh Valley—were beneficiaries as well, and now found themselves in the position of rejecting students from some of the premier high schools in the country. Hedging their bets, students whose parents and high schools would permit them to do so were submitting applications to a dozen or more colleges, further clogging the pipeline.

Bates made its admissions decisions by consulting a time-tested template. Its admissions criteria were similar to those that had long guided the fifty or so other colleges that reject more students than they accept each year. But it differed in one critical respect: it was still one of the relatively few elite colleges that did not require an applicant to submit an SAT score. While its deliberations were surely worth watching, Bates was too anomalous in its policies to be relevant to most of the high school seniors applying to highly selective colleges. And so my editor and I decided to turn Bates down.

But, having already spent considerable time daydreaming about the prospect of being knee deep in actual applications, I couldn't let go of the idea behind Bates's proposal. And so I began seeking out another top college that would let me audit its admissions process. Ultimately my criteria were, of course, as subjective as those of the admissions officers and the applicants themselves. Among my parameters was that the school be within two hours' drive from Manhattan, so that I could still report for the *Times* on other areas of education. And while I would interview admissions officers throughout the Ivy League, I hoped to establish my base camp elsewhere. I knew that the admissions officers under the most pressure were those working at colleges that had caught fire almost overnight—colleges that had neither the time nor the means to bulk up their admissions staffs in response to their sudden popularity.

More than anything, I wanted to learn how admissions officers dealt with having to make impossible choices. And I wanted to see how they grappled with the always elusive definition of what constituted "merit." That fall, one of the rubrics that had underpinned that definition for more than a generation, affirmative action, was being chipped away at public institutions in California, Florida, Texas and other states.

Most of the dozen or so colleges I approached refused, fearing my presence would somehow compromise the process. And they were understandably concerned about having the mechanics of how they made their most sensitive decisions revealed to a large audience, one that would include trustees and wealthy alumni. Someone was bound to disagree with a particular choice, and donations might suffer as a result. While a number of other institutions were game, I was warned by several guidance counselors that the deans of those colleges were capable of presenting me with a highly sanitized version of their normal admissions procedures.

And then there was Wesleyan. Founded by Methodist ministers and the fathers of a small Connecticut town in 1831, Wesleyan had long ago matured into a liberal arts powerhouse, if not necessarily a force on the football field. Few colleges could challenge its reputation for excellence, though one loomed only twenty-seven miles to the southwest, in New Haven.

Wesleyan was particularly well known for its stellar writing and literature programs. The university's alumni include Sebastian Junger, an anthropology major who later wrote *The Perfect Storm;* Robin Cook, a chemistry major and the best-selling author of *Coma* and other medical mysteries; Alex Kotlowitz, who wrote *There Are No Children Here;* and the suspense writer Robert Ludlum. John Perry Barlow, a lyricist for the Grateful Dead, had gone there, too. Wesleyan also had a renowned film studies department whose archives housed the papers of Martin Scorsese, Frank Capra and Clint Eastwood, among others. In recent years, Wesleyan's faculty had included the vibraphonist Jay Hoggard, who was also an alumnus; the jazz saxophonist Anthony Braxton; the nature writer Annie Dillard; and Phyllis Rose, the memoirist and author of the critically acclaimed book *The Year of Reading Proust.*

Meanwhile, Wesleyan's countercultural climate had survived the 1960s relatively intact. Perhaps only at the University of California at

Berkeley were students working harder to keep the hippie ethos alive. Indeed, at Wesleyan, "affirmative action" was defined broadly enough to include some preference for students with conservative leanings. "It'd be nice to have some antiabortionists on campus," one former admissions officer told me.

One of the few elements that was preventing Wesleyan from attaining the strata of the elite elite, at least as far as some applicants were concerned, was its campus. While laid out across a series of rolling hills that offered breathtaking views of the Connecticut River, Wesleyan had no main gate and no central quadrangle. The college almost crept up on applicants and their parents as they made their way up the hill from Middletown's fraying downtown. Though the architects of the Lincoln Memorial and the original Pennsylvania Station had designed some of its buildings, the overall crazy-quilt quality detracted from the whole. At Wesleyan, a medieval-style castle (the old gym) stood across from a modern, concrete-covered arts center that was laid out like Stonehenge. A shortage of cash in the 1980s and 1990s—partly a result of Wesleyan's relatively late entry into the alumni fund-raising game—had left a layer of dirt accumulated on the surface of many of its brownstone buildings, which were constructed more than a century earlier from nearby quarries. In some places, the campus looked as if it needed a bath.

Nonetheless, Wesleyan clearly fit the definition of a hot school with an overworked admissions office. When Maureen Dowd, then a reporter for the *Times*'s Metropolitan section, visited Wesleyan for several articles during the 1985–1986 school year, the college received forty-nine hundred applications, a number that dipped to forty-four hundred in 1990. Over the next ten years, that figure would grow by more than 50 percent, to nearly seven thousand. Over the same period, the admissions staff wading through that pile of applications grew by only one member and now stood at ten. (As it embarked on its search for the Class of 2004, the staff was actually short one person, as the college administration sought a replacement for the longtime dean of admissions, who had recently been promoted to a vice president's job.) In practical terms, that meant that because every application was read by at least two officers, each officer was responsible for dealing with nearly fifteen hundred applications—mostly in the eight weeks between early January and early March. Little wonder that faculty members and seniors were occasionally enlisted to give an application its first read, to help lighten the burden.

Unlike Bates, Wesleyan did require SAT scores, and like almost every other selective college, it interpreted those scores differently for each applicant, based on that applicant's race, the educational attainment of his or her parents, the quality of his or her high school, and those extracurricular skills that he or she might bring to campus. Wesleyan also assigned numerical ratings to applicants in amorphous categories like "commitment" and "intellectual curiosity." Dartmouth, Williams, Michigan and many other colleges compiled similar ratings, and I was curious to see the calculations that went into such assessments.

A Wesleyan administrator polled the members of the admissions staff and found none opposed to the idea of my series. As was the case when Maureen Dowd visited thirteen years earlier, Wesleyan was a college that cultivated a reputation of being more open than its competitors: it hoped that a public examination of its admissions practices, however controversial, would lift the veil of mystery from the process and perhaps raise Wesleyan's profile in the bargain. Apart from one admissions officer who asked not to be mentioned by name in the newspaper, my access would be unfettered, and I would be able to read any application or observe any deliberation. Since I would be present for hundreds of decisions over the course of many days, the admissions officers would not know which applicants in particular I was following. Thus, the chances that I would influence the outcome were minimized. After the decision letters were sent out, I was free to contact the applicants directly. At no point would Wesleyan be permitted to review what I was writing. The high school guidance counselors whom I consulted assured me that Wesleyan would keep its word on these terms.

Wesleyan and I agreed that for my benefit, and for that of the readers, I should shadow a single officer as my guide. Four of the possible candidates were effectively disqualified because they had just arrived and would be learning their jobs. I'd like to say I used a scientific method to pick from among the five veterans, one of whom was acting as dean. But because I was determined to spend long periods of time with an admissions officer reading applications at his or her home—a crucial part of the process that I had never seen described in print—my criteria boiled down to one: the admissions officer tapped could not have a dog or a cat, because I was allergic.

That pretty much narrowed the field to Ralph Figueroa. A native Californian, Ralph had worked as an admissions officer at Wesleyan for five years, and at Occidental College in Los Angeles for the previous three years. Prior to that, Ralph was a lawyer. As it turned out, his résumé was as representative as anyone else's of the typical admissions officer. There is no prototype or formal training for such a unique line of work. Wesleyan, like most colleges, considered the perspective of its faculty to be too narrow to entrust them with exclusive authority to select a class, though professors were regularly consulted during the process. To Wesleyan, it was an admissions officer's life experiences—the broader and further afield the better—that gave him or her the essential tools to assemble a class.

Thus, the previous occupations of Ralph's colleagues at Wesleyan included food stamp interviewer, resident administrator in a psychiatric halfway house, high school English teacher, management trainee at Sears and sometime dogcatcher. There was even one admissions officer who, his colleagues half believed, was in the witness protection program, given his secrecy about the most basic details of his life.

It was only after the newspaper series was completed that I began to consider expanding my notes into a book. After doing some research on what had been published on the subject in recent years, I discovered that few outsiders had been granted the opportunity that I had: the access and time necessary to support a work of narrative nonfiction examining the workings of an admissions office. The definitive work is probably *How an Ivy League College Decides on Admissions,* by Katharine Kinkead, which began as a *New Yorker* article. It was set at Yale and was later published as a slim volume by Norton. But Kinkead completed her research in 1961, and much has changed in the world of college admissions in the four decades since, not the least of which is that women now attend Yale and nearly every other college. The handful of books of a similar nature that have appeared in recent years have usually changed the names and identifying details of the students under discussion, just as Ms. Kinkead did.

Because of the openness of Wesleyan and its applicants, the story told here carries no such restrictions. All the students interviewed have not only permitted me to refer to them by name, but also have allowed me to quote from their applications and academic transcripts. Entrusted with such precious material, I have made a conscious decision not to write yet another volume for the buckling shelf of books that promise to reveal the secret password for gaining entrance to a top college. As far as I can tell, no such formula exists. Instead, it is my hope that the tales within *The Gatekeepers* will convey a real-life sense of what it is like to be an admissions officer at a time when more American families than ever are intent on passing muster with such people. Given what is at stake, or at least perceived to be so, the job of an admissions officer at an elite private college has become one of the most powerful, stressful and least understood occupations in the nation. In one sense, it is surely depressing—for those teenagers who will be applying to future freshman classes, and others, like me, who passed through college years earlier—to watch Ralph Figueroa and others struggle to fit so many talented candidates into so few available slots. One can't help but tighten in anger at the logic behind some of the decisions they make, and the idea that such hard calls have to be made at all. But, at the same time, I hope the reader will find it heartening to discover that Ralph and his colleagues give serious and careful consideration to nearly every request brought before them, and that in making their final determinations, they regularly plumb the depths of those applicants, probing far below the surface of test scores and grades.

THE GATEKEEPERS

One
THE TORTILLA TEST

The lime-green Saturn raced along the winding roads of northern New Jersey, past trees strung with leaves that glowed tangerine, gold and maroon. But the driver was too preoccupied to notice the glorious foliage, his eyes continually darting to the passenger seat. There he had laid out travel directions printed from the Internet, along with a well-worn road atlas pocked with green asterisks spread across a half dozen states. Each designated a community that he had visited previously.

On that bracing morning in early November of 1999, Ralph Figueroa was beginning his fifth year as an admissions officer at Wesleyan University, in Middletown, Connecticut, one of the nation's premier liberal arts colleges. But from the vantage point of a passing driver, Ralph was just another motorist wearing a gray wool suit, white starched shirt and deep red tie. He sat hunched over the wheel of a rental car that was too small to contain his body, which unfolded to more than six feet and weighed well over two hundred pounds. With his thick, blown-back black hair, which he had neatly arranged at a Courtyard by Marriott just after daybreak, Ralph looked like someone on his way to sell a $350 vacuum cleaner, rather than the product of a $35,000-a-year education that came with the unwritten guarantee of a happy and meaningful life.

At ten-thirty, a few minutes early as usual, Ralph pulled up in front of Northern Valley Regional High School in Demarest, a boxy, tan-brick public school that looked nothing like the private Tudor-style academy that he had left a half hour before. This was his second sales call of the day, and one of four visits that he had scheduled within a fifty-mile radius. He had allotted just six hours for the day's work, so he would have to speak quickly. As he moved purposefully past green-tiled walls and gray lockers on the way to the guidance office, he fumbled to pin on a plastic badge embossed with his name and that of WESLEYAN in big letters.

The popular image of university admissions officers is not unlike that of Hollywood studio executives. Both are assumed to spend most days sitting imperiously behind desks well out of reach of the general public, from which they deign to approve only a fraction of the endless series of pitches that are presented to them in rapid-fire succession. But to the handful of seniors and juniors who sat around a conference table that autumn morning listening to this smiling emissary on leave from his ivory tower, the message was unmistakable: Wesleyan Wants *You!* The university's gates, it seemed, had been flung wide open. And here, before their very eyes, was one of the gatekeepers who could escort them in.

From his seat beneath a giant map of the United States that a guidance counselor had labeled "College Acceptances"—so far, it had only one pin pushed into it, in the vicinity of Wilkes University in the Pocono Mountains—Ralph belied the familiar notion of admissions officer as intimidator. His voice was as soothing as a pediatrician's. He urged them to call him Ralph, not Rafael, his given name, and certainly not Mr. Figueroa.

The pitch Ralph delivered to his small audience seemed to promise that Wesleyan could fulfill virtually anyone's fantasy of higher education, if only the students would give the university the chance. And just to make sure that the students kept a vivid snapshot of the Connecticut campus projected on the screens in their minds, the university had sent along piles of posters of a Wesleyan landmark, Foss Hill, photographed on a fall day as beautiful as this one.

Even a devoted alumnus might not have noticed that the creaky football bleachers had been digitally removed, as had the many patches of brown dead turf. Instead, the late-fall grounds had the freshly tended appearance of the infield at Fenway Park. While the poster made a good first impression, some applicants would be disappointed when they saw the real thing. The curriculum, as described by Ralph, sometimes received a similar gloss.

"One of the first things to remember about the university is that there are no requirements," Ralph told the assembled group, tantalizing them with the prospect of never again having to take a dreaded subject like math or chemistry. "Wesleyan stresses a real-world approach."

Moreover, Ralph explained, while other institutions had begun only recently to appreciate and celebrate the differences among students, "We started our focus on diversity in 1965."

"That's the year I was born," he said, before adding that thirty-four years was indeed "a long time ago."

Almost immediately, the students' hands shot up. Would there be opportunities at Wesleyan to perform in a musical? one girl asked.

"Wesleyan does a *lot* of theater," Ralph responded. He mentioned that a first-string quarterback had played the lead in a recent production of *Sweeney Todd,* and that Wesleyan had a disproportionate share of alumni working in Hollywood. They included the writer of *Batman Forever,* the director of *American Pie* and the actor William Christopher, who, Ralph assured his listeners, would be well known to their parents as Father Mulcahy on *M*A*S*H.*

Just then a girl interrupted: Was the biology department any good?

"The physical sciences faculty does more research than just about any other liberal arts college," Ralph said. "Haverford beat us," he added. "But don't tell anyone."

Was there enough time for students at Wesleyan to study and to play sports?

"We want students to be scholar-athletes," Ralph said. Nearly two-thirds of Wesleyan undergraduates played an intramural or team sport. "The only thing that students do more of than sports at Wesleyan is community service."

How's the food?

One of the high school seniors, who had already visited a friend on the Wesleyan campus, answered before Ralph could. "There's always free frozen yogurt in the cafeteria," she said, describing the unique donation of a wealthy alumnus with a sweet tooth.

"Ice cream, too," Ralph added, sounding like Willie Wonka beckoning kids to the chocolate factory.

How fast are the Internet connections?

"Very fast," Ralph said.

Were there cable television jacks in the dorm rooms?

Ralph smiled. "There actually are," he said.

Only two questions drew answers that dimmed the Technicolor portrait that Ralph was painting that morning. But, then, an admissions officer from almost any other college would have had to give the same responses, if he or she was being honest.

One was posed by a serious-looking boy, who inquired: "Do you have any Nobel Prize winners on the faculty?"

"We don't have any Nobels," Ralph admitted, momentarily taken aback. "But we do have professors who have won Guggenheim and MacArthur and other grants."

The boy had been advised by his father, a Yale-educated ophthalmologist, to ask Ralph this question, and was obviously unimpressed.

The other tough question was a follow-up to Ralph's earlier point about diversity. "Do the races mix?" he was asked.

"Yes and no," Ralph answered. Wesleyan had acquired nicknames like "PCU" and "Diversity U" by attracting and admitting more black and Hispanic students than nearly any other top school, Ralph told his audience. "People think it's a place where students are holding hands and singing 'Kumbaya.'"

But, he had to acknowledge, "There is a tension. It's a process to address these issues and forge a community. Students will mix together one moment, only to segregate afterward."

And then, nearly an hour after his sales call had begun, it was over.

After making a note to contact the campus rabbi on behalf of one student, and passing out business cards with his e-mail address to several others, Ralph was back in his rental car and on his way to the next group of potential customers: a high school in the neighboring community of Ridgewood. He had spoken too long, and as he turned right onto Oradell Avenue, he was going to have to rush to make it on time.

But in all the talking he had done at Northern Valley Regional High, Ralph had neglected to mention a fact that the students surely would have found relevant: Wesleyan had just come off a year in which it had attracted a record number of applicants. Nearly 7000 students had sought the 715 spots available in the freshman class—almost 10 applicants for each seat. Though the university had offered admission to more than 715, because some of those accepted would invariably choose to go elsewhere, Wesleyan had still rejected 7 of every 10 who applied. The median SAT score of those admitted—a combined 1370 on a scale of 1600—was not only the highest in Wesleyan's history, but also higher than that of all but a handful of other colleges.

And as Ralph spoke, two months before all applications were due, there were already indications that this year would be even more competitive, with thousands more students projected to graduate from American high schools than in the previous school year. Rather than spend six weeks of the fall on the road courting applicants, as Ralph and his eight other colleagues from the admissions office were doing, they could easily have stayed home and still assembled a stellar class—several classes, in fact, given the pool of highly qualified applicants. But like a politician wading into a room full of strangers, Ralph and his colleagues were not going to rest until they had given every last college applicant a reason to cast a vote for Wesleyan.

Ralph had a particular voter in mind. He was hoping to seize the imagination of that elusive senior who hadn't given Wesleyan much thought, if he or she had given it any thought at all, but who appeared to have credentials so impeccable as to fairly sail through the admissions process. Ralph knew, though, that in his quest to find such a prize he was inviting most of his listeners to submit a fifty-five-dollar application fee sheerly for the privilege of being rejected.

"You realize that, further down the line, a lot of these kids will end up applying and being denied," Ralph said later. "But you can't really think about that at this stage. This stage is about figuring out which students should be considering Wesleyan, which students really need to have us on their radar screens. At this stage, I want everyone who could possibly benefit from Wesleyan to have that chance. They'll never get in if they don't try."

That may seem like a cute way to do business, but at the very moment that Ralph and his colleagues were fanning across the country and around the world, admissions officers from four dozen other highly selective colleges—including Harvard and Haverford, Swarthmore and Stanford, Princeton and Pomona—were spending tens of thousands of dollars, and hundreds of hours, on similar expeditions. Like Wesleyan, each had received a record or near-record number of applicants the previous winter. Nonetheless, each was intent on assembling a class that was a little bit better than last year's—and, if possible, a little bit better than almost every other institution's. As Ralph and his colleagues saw it, so worthy was the goal of putting together such a community that it justified the difficult and sometimes cruel practicalities that were required to make it happen.

In recent years, the elite colleges had become something like combatants in a global arms race, a contest in which strength would be measured by stockpiles of candidates arranged by test scores, grade point averages, outside interests and skin color. None of the institutions was willing to be the first to stand down and pronounce itself content with its lot.

"No one is staying static," said Barbara-Jan Wilson, who had left the deanship of the Wesleyan admissions office over the previous summer to become the university's vice president for university relations, which meant she had gone from sweet-talking applicants to sweet-talking donors.

"Schools under us are trying to pick off the kids in our applicant pool," she explained, ticking off college names like Trinity, Bates, Muhlenberg and Connecticut. "Meanwhile, we're trying to pick off Brown's kids and Yale's kids."

"Maybe we're just keeping up with the Joneses," she added. "But it's bigger than that."

In truth, Wesleyan was part of a distinct minority within the academy that fall: one of only about fifty American colleges that reject more students than they accept. The lion's share of the nation's two thousand four-year colleges take almost anyone who applies. Yet each year, an increasing number of American teenagers flood those brand-name institutions with a disproportionate number of applications. One explanation for this, apart from the larger student population, surely lies with their parents, who were impressing ever more strongly on their offspring that a blue-chip education is the key to a successful life. First- and second-generation Americans, whose own parents had been content to see them graduate from any college, were now advising their own children and grandchildren that only a marquee name would be acceptable. In addition, elaborate online tours were now making it possible for students and parents from as far away as Wyoming and New Mexico to roam the academic epicenter of the northeast without ever leaving home.

A university is only as good as its students, so why shouldn't Ralph seek to lure the best that were out there? Those turned back from the Wesleyan gate would surely find a place elsewhere, a fact in which Ralph took great comfort. More important, since Harvard and Yale and Brown were rejecting more applicants than ever, Wesleyan had a real shot at getting some students whom it might have lost to the Ivies a decade ago—if only enough of them knew Wesleyan's name and philosophy, and could be persuaded to choose Wesleyan over its more immediate competitors, including Williams and Amherst.

Other than those fortunate enough to be accepted, the most immediate beneficiaries of all this wooing would be Wesleyan's professors. Like gardeners, the university's faculty members needed fertile minds in which to plant the seeds of knowledge, and when they weren't satisfied with the quality in a given year—if there were too few Russian majors or not enough budding microbiologists, for example—the professors were never shy about telling the administration. Also paying close attention to Ralph's efforts were the university's alumni, who were particularly gratified when Wesleyan snared a hot prospect—academic, as well as athletic—from a competitor. That swelling pride was often all it took to nudge a willing alumnus to contribute upward of a million dollars to his alma mater, which in turn made it possible for the institution to seek to attract even better applicants.

But in building its arsenal of top students—with "top" variously defined as those who checked "valedictorian" on their applications; those with decent test scores who identified themselves as black or Hispanic; or those who played the bassoon—Wesleyan was also seeking to impress demanding audiences far from its Connecticut campus.

For the last two decades, much of the pressure on admissions officers like Ralph had been applied by a group of observers who had assigned themselves the task of rating universities as if they were sports teams or stocks. Chief among the unofficial evaluators was *U.S. News & World Report*. In 1985 the magazine, long obscured by the more widely read *Time* and *Newsweek,* stumbled upon a niche by developing its own formula to handicap the top educational institutions in America. One crucial component in the magazine's assessment was the percentage of applicants that an institution accepted—the lower the better, as the editors believed. *U.S. News* also tabulated the percentage of accepted students who chose to matriculate at that institution, a number it wanted to be as high as possible.

At once responding to and stoking Americans' obsession with elite colleges, *U.S. News*'s annual education issue had become essential reading for teenagers, joined on their bookshelves by similar book-length guides published by such disparate companies as *The Yale Daily News,* Barron's, Peterson's and the test-prep upstart Princeton Review. All compiled admissions statistics liked those that filled *U.S. News.* Edward B. Fiske, a one-time education editor of *The New York Times* (and a 1959 Wesleyan graduate), had, with his annual *Fiske Guide to Colleges,* assumed the mythic status of a Broadway theater reviewer, his recommendations so influential that they could determine how tens of thousands of students might perceive a college for an entire year and beyond.

If Ralph had stayed home that fall, and Wesleyan's numbers fell, its rankings in these publications could plummet. And as a study coauthored by a Cornell professor in 2000 suggested, after an institution's standing in *U.S. News* fell, so, at times, did the number and quality of its applicants.

"I am an agent of the institution," Ralph said in an interview that fall. "And as an agent of the institution, I am trying to get as many students to apply to the institution as I can. Yet I like to focus on the more human perspective: there are going to be students who discover Wesleyan who wouldn't have otherwise."

Whatever was motivating Ralph, his journey remained forever uphill, the summit always seeming to move higher. That was evident as he wearily took stock at the end of that day he spent in northern New Jersey. At the first three high schools he had visited, each of which was considered among the better-performing in the state, fewer than ten students had turned out to see him. And while nineteen juniors and seniors filled a conference room at his final stop, a relatively new public school called the Bergen Academies, the students had been required to attend by their guidance counselor.

Asked later by another visitor if Ralph's talk had swayed them in any way, most of those he met that day listed first choices that were not Wesleyan. One boy with a high SAT score at Dwight-Englewood School, a respected prep school, said he was seeking early admission to Connecticut College because he "had a feeling" about the place. Another girl said she'd consider Wesleyan "if I don't get into Hopkins." Students at Bergen Academies ranked Princeton and Brown, as well as Vassar and Rutgers, ahead of Wesleyan.

Almost all of the students, though, promised Ralph that they would apply to Wesleyan, and experience had taught him that such students usually did. Wesleyan's numbers might well be up this year, and that would mean he was doing a critical part of his job well.

Still, the more successful he was in the fall, the more applications he would have to read in the winter. And that would only make it harder to make his final selections in the spring.

Between his third and fourth appointments in New Jersey, Ralph was offered the chance to eat at the toniest restaurant that he could find in affluent Bergen County, courtesy of *The New York Times*. A free lunch was the least that a reporter could offer him that day, the first of many on which the reporter would shadow Ralph as he went about his work. The admissions officer made his choice without hesitation: Fuddruckers. That his first choice would be to eat a burger off a tray at a cafeteria-style chain would not have surprised those who knew Ralph best, and not just because of his notorious love of greasy food.

At age thirty-four, Ralph had been perfectly content to take a job that paid him an annual salary of $42,000, only a little more than what a student without financial aid paid for a year at Wesleyan. And at that point, he had seven years' experience in the field. Even his wife, Natalie, earned more, and she was a public school teacher. The truth was, luxury items meant little to Ralph, as evidenced by his refusal to part with the battered, eleven-year-old blue Honda Accord that sat in his driveway most days, while he walked the mile or so to campus.

It was fairly remarkable, in any event, that a first-generation Californian whose parents were born in Mexico would be tapped to traipse through suburban New Jersey on behalf of one of the nation's most elite northeastern colleges. As recently as a generation earlier, Ralph's job would have probably been filled by a white male of some privilege, someone whose own admission to the college he was representing, or to a similar one, had been handed down like a family crest. Ralph owed his job, at least in part, to the concerted efforts made, beginning in the 1960s, by elite colleges to integrate their student bodies, as well as to the attempts by those same colleges to diversify their admissions offices, which came later.

But in Ralph's case, the answer to the question of how a talented, bilingual man like him had ended up doing a job like this was more complicated. In fact, Ralph Figueroa had been training to become a college admissions officer from an early age, even if that didn't become obvious to him until he reached his midtwenties.

For much of his young life, Ralph had just assumed he would follow in the footsteps of his father, William, a lawyer in Los Angeles in civil practice. When he began work in the mid-1950s, Bill was one of only a half dozen Mexican American lawyers in Los Angeles County, and for nearly four decades, he used his degree from Loyola Law School in Los Angeles to ensure that poor Mexican Americans had someone at their side when they went up against a landlord or the city.

Bill's clients could rarely pay him, so he would typically ask them: "What do you do?" Thus a local plumber who had no legs, and could therefore navigate cramped spaces with the dexterity of an acrobat, became a regular fixture under the kitchen sink of the family's first home, a three-bedroom in the middle-class community of Santa Fe Springs. A mason paid off his legal bills by building the family a concrete patio. Tree trimmers, landscapers, fence builders and car mechanics were always arriving unannounced. Sometimes, because Bill was too kind to refuse such gifts, the family got stuck with items it didn't even need, like the wrought-iron bars that a welder laid over the house's first-floor windows. "I think my father knew that some of these people needed to do something," Ralph said.

At one point, Bill had been offered the opportunity to join one of the biggest law firms in California, Manatt, Phelps & Phillips, but declined. He would miss being his own boss, he said, and believed his talents could be put to better use in his own community.

Ralph, the sixth of seven siblings, and the third and youngest son, had always had a great deal in common with his father. In his midthirties, Ralph, with his heavy eyebrows and dense, wavy hair, bore an uncanny physical resemblance to his father at a similar age, as could be seen in now-yellowed photographs that his mother had clipped from newspapers in the 1950s and 1960s, whenever Bill was elected to some position in the Mexican-American Lawyers Association or the United Way. Bill and Ralph also shared a love of poetry, particularly Thomas Gray's "Elegy Written in a Country Churchyard," which Bill could recite nearly from memory, including the following: "Full many a flower is born to blush unseen / And waste its sweetness on the desert air." Both Figueroas also loved jazz, particularly the clarinetist Artie Shaw, and both played the saxophone. Ralph would always envy his father's tone and intonation, which came more naturally than his own.

Almost as if it had been preordained, Ralph had graduated from the law school at the University of California in Los Angeles, after attending Stanford University in the late 1980s. Unlike his father, he would no doubt feel welcome at any law firm in California, and maybe in the entire country. But as he began to look for legal work after his law school graduation in the winter and spring of 1992, Ralph felt a startling tug in a different direction. He wondered if the parent whose career he was meant to follow was his mother.

Bertha Figueroa had studied to be a teacher at Los Angeles State College (since renamed California State University at Los Angeles) in the late 1950s. Only hours after she had completed her last final exam, Bertha was rushed to the hospital, where her first child, Ana Luisa, was born. Two days later, Bertha was scheduled to graduate, but instead, as *The East Los Angeles Citizen* noted under a photograph of Bertha wearing a mortarboard and cradling a swaddled baby: "Husband William accepted 'power of attorney' and attended graduation ceremonies in her place."

Despite her training, Bertha thought that she, too, would follow her husband into law. The fall after her first child was born, she enrolled in Loyola Law School, at Bill's urging. "I wanted her to be my partner," Bill explained. But a year later, after giving birth to her second child, Bertha found that her heart wasn't in it. Ralph would not learn of his mother's flirtation with the legal profession until he himself was in law school. When he complained to her about a contracts class, she said, matter-of-factly, "Oh, I used to hate contracts, too."

In 1970, when Ralph was five, Bertha began studying at California State University in Los Angeles, where she soon earned a master's in bilingual education. She then took a job teaching Spanish at Sierra High School in the Whittier public school district, near where the family lived.

But Bertha didn't teach for long, for she had quickly become consumed by a gnawing observation: few Mexican American parents whose children attended Los Angeles–area public schools were preparing those children to apply to college, let alone to do the work once they got there. Both Bertha and her husband had been born in Mexico to parents who had not graduated from high school and who had moved their families to the United States when their children were small. Bertha and Bill had made it to college, in large part, because their parents regularly lamented that they had missed out on obtaining a formal education. Many of the students Bertha was meeting in her job, the children of migrant workers and welfare recipients, were not receiving such encouragement at home.

And so Bertha soon took a job as the assistant director of Expanded Horizons, a fledgling districtwide program that sought to give Mexican American children all of the skills, both educational and practical, that they needed to attend college. In 1967, the year before the district piloted the program at Pioneer High School, only three Mexican American students at the school, of a graduating class of more than three hundred, took the SAT. At the end of the first year of the program, the number of students who took the SAT jumped to twenty-one, while two years later, when Bertha joined the program, the total had risen to seventy-six. By the early 1980s, those statistics had attracted the attention of President Ronald Reagan and his education secretary, Terrell Bell, who later wrote an influential report on the state of American education, "Nation at Risk." Both the president and Mr. Bell spent the better part of a day at Pioneer High School to learn why Mrs. Figueroa, by then the director of

Expanded Horizons, was so successful. Ralph, who attended a school in the same district, California High, even appeared on a panel with Mr. Reagan.

What the president was told was that Bertha wasn't satisfied with browbeating impoverished children into taking college entrance exams, filling out financial aid forms and carefully planning their essays, when these students didn't even have a clue where they could apply, or how high they were entitled to reach, now that so many of the nation's colleges were looking to diversify. Bertha figured there was only one way to give them a crash course on college admissions, in a way she couldn't fully accomplish during school hours.

Several times each fall, she and Bill would borrow a bus from the district and pile in whichever of their seven children happened to be around. The family would then pick up three to four dozen local teenagers and escort them to every area college that would see them, including UCLA, USC, Pomona, Occidental and Caltech. When some teachers scoffed that Bertha was wasting her time, considering that some of her most prized pupils had abysmal grades and SAT scores, Bertha calmly responded: "You can't play God and say they won't make it. You never know what's going to turn these kids on."

Bertha and Bill also believed that if these children were willing to work so hard to get into college, they should be rewarded with some downtime. And so, each summer, the Figueroas would again load a group onto a bus and drive eight hours to Yosemite National Park. In a Latino version of *The Partridge Family,* Mary, the second-eldest daughter, would lead the singing, while Bill taught everyone to fish. He also cooked them elaborate breakfasts of hash browns and ham and eggs on a portable gas stove.

Ralph's mother has no trouble ticking off the names of the doctors, lawyers and even judges she nurtured in her program. The most popular career choice, though, was teaching. One graduate of the Figueroa family college bus tour, Javier Gonzalez, was selected as the California Teacher of the Year in 1996. At the time, Javier, a math teacher, wrote to Bertha: "Please know that who I am today has to do with the influence you have had on me and my way of thinking."

Though he wasn't conscious of it, Ralph, too, was profoundly influenced by those bus rides, which he took for granted during his childhood and adolescence. When Bertha left the Expanded Horizons program in 1995 to work for the Los Angeles County Office of Education, Ralph couldn't be at the farewell party for he had just left his first job, as an admissions officer at Occidental College in Los Angeles, for a new position as an admissions officer at Wesleyan, on the other side of the country. Instead, Ralph scribbled Bertha a note on Wesleyan letterhead that was read aloud at her retirement party.

"So many people think of me as an image of my father, and it's not hard to see why," Ralph began, listing all the familiar ways in which he and Bill had grown so close. But, Ralph continued:

> I know a secret I have seldom shared with anyone. I know that the person whose life I have chosen to follow, whose works and deeds and ideals touch me every day of my life is you, Mom. Four years ago I made a choice to enter a profession that I never trained for, that I never expected, and yet one for which I felt myself unusually well-suited.
>
> I have spent those four years talking to students and counselors and parents throughout the West, the Southwest, and now the East. Helping those whose horizons are not yet wide enough to hold the vision of a future at college. Helping those who need the help that only I could give them. JUST LIKE MY MOM.
>
> I am incredibly proud of the work you have done. I am even more proud to have shared in that work.

As Ralph wrote, his younger sister, Dina, was settling into a new job as well. After graduating from UCLA Law School three years after her brother, Dina, too, had forsaken a legal career. Perhaps not surprisingly, she had become an admissions officer, joining Ralph on the staff at Occidental. In the fall of 1995, when he departed for Wesleyan, Dina left to become an associate director of admissions at Caltech. In the once-closed world of elite college admissions, the Figueroas, of all people, were quietly building a dynasty worthy of the Kennedys.

While it was Bertha Figueroa who put her youngest son on the path toward an admissions career, another woman took it upon herself to ensure that Ralph reached that destination. Ralph met Sharon Merrow on their very first day as freshmen at Stanford University in the fall of 1983, and Sharon would wind up designing nothing less than the architecture of Ralph's adult life. She would arrange Ralph's first post in admissions and help him secure the second. And in the career that Sharon would ultimately choose for herself, that of a high school college counselor, she would come to serve as an academic sommelier of sorts for Ralph and for his counterparts in the admissions offices of other top colleges. A large part of Sharon's job would be to introduce Ralph to some of the finest high school students of a particular vintage, including several who would be applying for the Class of 2004 at Wesleyan. Some of these transactions between two old friends would go smoothly. Others would be anything but, and would strain the bonds of their relationship.

Ralph had arrived on the Stanford campus on the strength of a formidable SAT score—1400 out of a possible 1600—as well as a rank in the top five of his four-hundred-member high school graduating class. In choosing the palm and stucco of Stanford over the ivy-covered brick of Harvard, Yale and Princeton, to which he had also been admitted, Ralph was following his older sister Ana, who had attended Stanford Law School. Given his parents' sparse income Ralph could afford the $10,000 in annual tuition, room and board only by cobbling together a combination of resources: scholarships, student loans and a campus job that entailed shrink-wrapping and shipping books from the warehouse of Stanford University Press. "To this day, I can still wrap gifts and pack trunks really well," he says.

At the time, Ralph thought his first day at Stanford auspicious because he had successfully auditioned as a saxophonist for the rowdy Stanford Marching Band, which was known as much for dropping its collective trousers at halftime as for its spirited rendition of rock songs like "All Right Now" by Free and "Truckin'" by the Grateful Dead. The band would consume much of Ralph's spare time for the next four years.

But a more portentous moment came hours after his audition, when Ralph and Sharon first shook hands at an ice-breaker in their dorm, which was called Adelfa, an idyllic Spanish-style building with exposed wood beams throughout and a fountain in the back. He had been assigned a double on the first floor, and she one on the second. At the mixer, the freshmen were instructed to give themselves a nickname. Inspired by his band audition earlier that day, he called himself "Raucous Ralph," even though he was normally quite soft-spoken. She identified herself as "Scared Sharon." That was comforting, Ralph thought. She had been able to say out loud how he was feeling.

With shoulder-length light brown hair, dark arched eyebrows and the freshly scrubbed, angular cheekbones of a 1940s Hollywood starlet, Sharon turned more heads than just Ralph's that first day. But that sort of attention had little effect on her, for she was a serious student who had come to Stanford to learn. She intended to become a chemistry major and had even chosen Stanford over the mild objection of her parents, who hoped she would go a little easier on herself. They had wanted her to enroll at the college that they had attended, Whitman, a more intimate liberal arts institution with less cachet and located far to the north, in Walla Walla, Washington. "I had always brought home great grades in high school," Sharon said later. "My parents would always ask, 'Are you happy?' It was like antipressure." But Sharon was convinced that Stanford would give her options in life that Whitman would not. One day, she would decide that her parents had a point, and following the example of Ralph and his mother, she would devote considerable time to making sure that her students heard her own parents' words.

Soon after they met, Sharon told Ralph that she had been raised in Pasadena, which was not far from where he had grown up, before her father's work had taken the family to San Diego, Hawaii, Washington, D.C., and back again to California. Sharon's father was a mathematician who had earned an advanced degree at Caltech and now worked as a systems analyst for the U.S. Navy. Just as Ralph had intended to follow in his father's footsteps, so, too, did Sharon, at least in pointing herself toward a career in the sciences. But it wasn't until she told Ralph that her mother was a first-grade teacher that they felt a kinship.

Before long, Sharon and Ralph were going to concerts, as well as movies, swap meets and flea markets. Along with a group of friends from the dorm, they ate all their meals together. When Sharon made her first and only appearance on a Stanford stage, in a dorm production of *Ten Little Indians*, Ralph was behind the scenes, manning the lights and arranging the props. A working partnership was born. When Sharon or any of their friends said something embarrassing, a pen and pad would mysteriously appear in Ralph's hand, so that he could transcribe the quotation for future, good-natured blackmail.

As they walked a campus that many covered by bicycle, Ralph and Sharon often talked politics. Sharon, whose father generally endorsed Ronald Reagan's quest to increase the size of the military while decreasing the federal government's social responsibilities, was amazed to learn that Ralph was a liberal who had actually been raised by liberal parents. "I often got the sense that Sharon was trying to understand how I could be a nice person, and yet think different things than what she had been told a nice person thought," Ralph said later. "I told her I had been raised to believe that the government should support social services, that people should be willing to pay higher taxes for the social good. She was going through the process of deciding for herself what she thought." Eventually, Sharon would come to adopt much of Ralph's philosophy as her own, including a conviction in the importance of making higher education as accessible as possible.

Though Ralph and Sharon exchanged occasional flirtations, the relationship never grew romantic. "It was too much of a friendship," Ralph said. "It would have spoiled it." But in the fall of their junior year, Sharon made sure that her friend would not lack for female companionship. Still living in Adelfa, Sharon and Ralph were walking down the second-floor hallway on an October afternoon as Ralph made a passing remark that struck her as out of character—something about the dorm's reputation on campus as a haven for "a bunch of cute girls." The comment hadn't been prompted by anything or anyone in particular, but Sharon decided to walk through the door he had opened for her.

"Speaking of cute," Sharon told Ralph, as they paused outside her room, "here's someone you should meet." She then introduced him to Natalie Riggs, a freshman newly arrived from Tulsa, by way of Bennett, Nebraska (population 550). Sharon had actually had her eye on Natalie for Ralph for several weeks, and had only been waiting for the right moment to put them together. Sharon had disapproved of a succession of girls whom Ralph had dated casually, because she felt they weren't all that interesting. "He had bad taste in women at first," Sharon recalled. "He was picking people only because he found them mysterious. Even then, Ralph liked to try to figure people out and then use what he knew to his advantage, though not in a bad way."

It probably didn't hurt that Natalie was a lot like Sharon, if Sharon's hair had been darker and her face partially hidden behind glasses. Not only was Natalie's mother an elementary school teacher, but her father taught, too, and had even been a school principal at one point. Like Sharon, Natalie had arrived at Stanford intent on majoring in science. She thought she wanted to be an engineer and had chosen Stanford over the Massachusetts Institute of Technology, Johns Hopkins, Williams and Rice, where she had also been accepted. Sharon hoped that Ralph would eventually find his intellect challenged by Natalie, but his initial reaction was as visceral as Sharon suspected it would be.

"I thought Sharon was right, that Natalie was a total cutie," he recalled. "She had a little drawl"—unbeknown to Ralph, Natalie had lived for four years in Oklahoma—"and I'm a sucker for accents." Natalie was initially noncommittal—"I thought he seemed nice," was the sum of her initial assessment—but before long, the two were walking the Stanford campus, just as he and Sharon had. For a long time, their friendship, too, remained strictly platonic. But that began to change soon after Natalie joined Ralph and several other friends on the exploratory expeditions of little-used buildings that he liked to mount on the Stanford campus under cover of darkness. Soon, they were undertaking those missions as a party of two.

Ralph and Natalie remained together, and Sharon stayed close to both of them, until the spring of 1987, when Ralph and Sharon graduated. Natalie, who was two years younger, would be remaining on campus while Sharon and Ralph left Palo Alto, heading in different directions, at least initially.

Ralph had always been a distracted student who preferred talking to friends in a coffee shop or practicing with the band to studying. Nonetheless, he had managed to achieve a B/B-minus average at Stanford and to cultivate an interest in constitutional theory and history. That, plus the role models of his father and two of his siblings—Ana had already graduated from Stanford Law; Bill Jr. was about to graduate from Santa Clara Law School—made legal training a logical next step. With a solid though not necessarily remarkable score on the Law School Admission Test (LSAT)—he was ranked below the top 15 percent of those who took the test that year—Ralph was admitted to two of the law schools to which he applied (USC and the University of California at Davis) but was rejected by UCLA and Stanford.

Feeling burned out, Ralph decided to take the next year off. He worked sporadically as a substitute teacher in his mother's district, near Los Angeles, and drove to Stanford every few weekends to see Natalie. The following year, he decided to reapply to law school, and this time was admitted to UCLA. On one level, the acceptance puzzled him. He couldn't think of anything that he had done differently that would have changed UCLA's decision.

Once at the university, though, Ralph began thinking about how his ethnicity might have given him an edge over white applicants. One event was pivotal. Early in his first year of law school, a group of white law students was overheard by several other classmates having a casual conversation about affirmative action. The students were quite critical of racial preferences, and their comments were soon circulated around campus by word of mouth. As Ralph recalls, they had been widely described as joking that they "should take up a collection to pay for these minority students because they help keep the grading curve down." A campuswide controversy ensued.

In the angry debate that followed, Ralph started to develop his own philosophy of affirmative action. Much of his first-year tuition at UCLA had been paid through a fellowship arranged by a campus diversity program, in which he was expected to tutor Mexican American and other students from minority backgrounds. "That confirmed for me that I had reasons for being there other than straight academic reasons," Ralph said later. "I was there in part because of the viewpoint I represented, the cultural perspective I could bring to the process."

And, he concluded, those were perfectly valid criteria for UCLA to have considered in admitting him. Other than an SAT score that ranked him among the highest-performing students in the nation in 1983, Ralph believed that his application to Stanford was otherwise undistinguished. That his race may have helped push him through the front door of Stanford and UCLA Law did not make Ralph feel as though he had gotten something he didn't deserve. What it did stir in him, however, was a commitment to give something back.

Eager to write a sequel to his father's legacy, Ralph became active in a student-run legal clinic in Santa Monica that catered to poor Mexican American clients, particularly those embroiled in landlord-tenant or child-custody disputes. Ralph felt certain he had found his life's work, but during an internship at the Writers Guild, in his third year of law school, Ralph discovered that he relished writing contracts and participating in arbitration hearings involving some of the best-known screenwriters and film companies in Los Angeles. Labor law was now his calling, and after graduating from UCLA Law in 1991, he began to seek out a small firm for which he could do such work.

By that time, Sharon Merrow was also working in Los Angeles, as a college admissions officer. As they had prepared to graduate from Stanford four years earlier, Sharon had initially applied for an opening in the Stanford admissions office, after working there as a student to help pay her tuition. She had always been curious about the selection process and, after graduating with a degree in sociology, had come to realize that she would rather be an admissions officer than a scientist. All those conversations with Ralph about advancing the social good had had an effect, and Sharon was confident that she could help a lot of teenagers by doing admissions work.

Although she didn't get the Stanford job, Sharon was interested enough in admissions that she continued to look for other such positions and ultimately landed one at Occidental College. Occidental had been founded in 1887 in Eagle Rock, in northeast Los Angeles, by a group of Princeton graduates seeking to establish a Princeton-on-the-Pacific. The school's mascot was the tiger, and its colors were orange and black, just like its cousin in New Jersey. By the time Sharon arrived in 1988, Occidental, with sixteen hundred students, ranked among the most selective institutions on the West Coast, competing for applicants with Pomona, UCLA and Whittier colleges, among others.

Three years later, when Ralph mentioned to Sharon that he was interviewing at law firms, she mentioned that one of her colleagues had announced that he would be leaving at the end of the academic year. Within moments, they would come to the same conclusion as to who should fill that job. Ralph had spent much of his free time at Occidental with Sharon and liked what he saw. He was particularly impressed that Occidental was having dramatic success in broadening the diversity of its student body. Of the four hundred entering freshmen in the fall of 1991, 16 percent were black, 7 percent were Hispanic and 16 percent were Asian. Perhaps no other American college had been as successful at recruiting minorities, while still maintaining its median SAT score at a relatively high 1200. Whoever filled the job, Sharon told Ralph, would be responsible for the Southwest, including Arizona and New Mexico. Ralph began to imagine himself as a pioneering salesman hawking higher education in and around the small, sand-swept communities that his parents and grandparents had passed through earlier that century.

Sharon warned Ralph that the starting salary was $25,000, which was fairly standard for the field, even if it was a third of what Ralph might have made starting out at a top L.A. law firm. Nonetheless, Ralph was undeterred, convinced that the range of responsibilities that he would have in the Occidental admissions office would be hard to equal in law or in any other line of work. "You travel," Sharon had said to him. "You do public speaking. You do one-on-one counseling. You plan events. You sit by yourself and read for hours and hours on end."

"And," she concluded, "there's nothing better than being on a college campus." Sharon's boss, the dean of admissions at Occidental, had also told Ralph that if he ever had aspirations of working in higher education, the admissions office was "a great way to learn about the politics of being a faculty member or administrator."

By this point, Ralph and Natalie had been married for two years, though Ralph had begun lobbying Natalie long before that. After her freshman year at Stanford, Natalie had traveled with Ralph on a vacation to Yosemite National Park, the same place where Ralph had gone on all those family vacations with dozens of teenagers from his mother's school district. This time, though, Ralph saw Yosemite in a different light. "It'd be a great place for a honeymoon, don't you think?" he asked Natalie, seeking to get a rise out of her. While they hadn't even been dating a year, they hugged and vowed to keep Yosemite in mind if they ever did decide to marry. During the summer of 1990, a year after Natalie had graduated from Stanford and taken a job as a teacher in Los Angeles, they returned to Yosemite with seventy-five close friends and family.

Now, as Ralph contemplated switching from law to admissions, Natalie encouraged him, pleased with the idea that Ralph would be carrying on the tradition of educators in both their families. After Ralph went in for a round of formal interviews—and put to rest any concerns about his lack of experience by explaining that admissions was quite literally in his blood—Occidental became as smitten with him as he was with Occidental. He decided to put his law career on hold and joined the office, as one of eight admissions counselors, in August 1992.

At Occidental, Ralph quickly discovered that a part of his personality was ill-suited to such work: He had great difficulty saying no to any applicant, particularly those applying to Occidental from some of Los Angeles's poorest neighborhoods. "There was a big risk," Ralph said, "that if we didn't take that kid, he might not land at a place as good and supportive." Ralph would have to say no, though: In his first year, Occidental had nearly 3000 applicants for only 440 seats in the freshman class.

Ralph learned early on from Sharon and his other new colleagues that few of the minority applicants to Occidental, particularly black and Hispanic applicants, had grades and standardized test scores competitive with those of white applicants. But, Ralph was instructed, he needed to examine those records in the context of an applicant's life before deciding whether to accept or reject the candidate. Occidental's philosophy, like that of countless other liberal arts colleges, was that SAT scores aren't as important in the screening of minority applicants, especially those who were the first in their families to apply to college. A body of research existed that showed that a student's verbal and mathematical aptitude, which was what the tests were supposed to measure, was heavily influenced by how much intellectual engagement he or she got after school, particularly at home.

In considering candidates, Ralph began to pay attention to students' study habits, their ties to their community, their support system and the closeness of their families—"things that society doesn't necessarily consider signs of intelligence but that are, in fact, pretty strong indicators of a kid's ability to be a successful college student." It was a philosophy of affirmative action that hardly sat well with many white applicants and their parents, who felt their rightful places were being taken by less-qualified minorities. Ralph knew that the white applicants had a point, and he hardly saw his job in terms of being a talent scout for minorities. Far from it. He viewed his responsibility to be to recruit kids with a range of life experiences and assorted strengths.

At Occidental, and especially at Wesleyan, Ralph would expend considerable mental energy trying to blaze a trail through that ethnic and racial wilderness.

By the time Ralph had begun his third year at Occidental, in the fall of 1994, Sharon had left for Cambridge to get a master's in education at Harvard. She had especially wanted to study with Howard Gardner, a psychology professor whose theory that people can demonstrate intelligence in many nontraditional ways was consistent with the philosophy of the Occidental admissions office. The dean who hired Ralph had left as well, for Caltech, and even though his sister Dina had since joined him on the admissions staff, he decided that working at Occidental wasn't as much fun as it had been and that if he was to rise in his field, he needed the imprint of an educational institution outside of California to balance his résumé. And so, like a student applying to college, Ralph began thumbing through a trade paper, *The Chronicle of Higher Education,* looking for help-wanted ads from colleges that seized his imagination.

He saw that Grinnell was looking for an admissions officer and, as luck would have it, Sharon knew the dean. After traveling to Grinnell's Iowa campus for an interview, Ralph was impressed with the staff and the students. But the prospect of being in such a remote location—as near as

Ralph could tell, the campus was completely surrounded by farmland—worried him. He also checked out a local grocery store and was disappointed to discover that the only food available in the Mexican section was called "a burrito kit." His stomach turned as he saw refried beans, seasonings and taco shells sharing one box.

Grinnell, he said to himself, *fails The Tortilla Test*.

While he hardly felt it necessary to be surrounded by a concentration of Mexican Americans, Ralph hoped that wherever he moved he could at least have access to the Mexican comfort foods that he had grown up with.

Soon after returning to Los Angeles from Iowa, he saw another ad in the *Chronicle*, this one placed by Wesleyan, which he knew to be located in the middle of Connecticut. The idea of moving to the East didn't necessarily deter him, even if it was so far from his family. As a high school student in the early 1980s, Ralph had applied to several top northeastern colleges, including Harvard and Princeton, but had never thought to apply to Wesleyan, which just wasn't as well known on the West Coast. In its ad, the university said that it was seeking an experienced admissions officer whose responsibilities would include, but not be limited to, serving as a liaison to the nation's Latino student community. The job was relatively new—only one other person had ever held it, and as it turned out, Ralph had met him on an admissions recruiting trip to a prep school in Houston a year earlier. Ralph had learned then that Wesleyan was seeking to make deeper inroads in the very communities on the West Coast and elsewhere in which Occidental had been so successful. By virtue of its size (Wesleyan's student body was nearly double that of Occidental's) and location in the Northeast, Wesleyan would be considered a step up for Ralph. The starting salary, Ralph learned from the ad, was an improvement, too: $32,000 a year. And if he could secure the job, Ralph would also have the title of assistant director of admission, several rungs above entry level.

After Ralph sent along his résumé, Barbara-Jan Wilson, then in her fifth year as dean of admissions at Wesleyan, interviewed him over the phone and was less than bowled over. "I'm high energy," she said later. "He was very low key." Still, Barbara-Jan detected enough of a spark that she offered Ralph a round-trip ticket to Connecticut for an interview. To Ralph's delight, Natalie said she would be game for the move if Wesleyan wanted him.

In the summer of 1995, Ralph flew alone to Hartford, about twenty miles north of Wesleyan's campus in Middletown, and rented a car. After checking in at a Holiday Inn west of campus, Ralph gave himself several hours to look around before meeting Barbara-Jan for dinner. Driving south on Route 3, past a knot of car dealerships and alongside several strip malls crammed with drug stores, fast-food restaurants and grocery stores, Ralph suddenly came upon the WELCOME TO MIDDLETOWN sign. He was so distracted by what he read next that he had to pull into a gas station. The sign noted that the town had been founded in 1651. "I come from L.A., where nothing is more than a hundred years old," he explained. "I tried to think about what must have been going on in 1651."

His head still in colonial times, Ralph got back on the road and eventually turned left on Washington Street and approached the western border of the Wesleyan campus, which, in lieu of a front gate, had an entrance that was more like a front porch. Though not as old as the town, Wesleyan had been founded in 1831. As Ralph made a quick right onto High Street, he stared out the driver's-side window and saw his first Wesleyan landmarks, the white Corinthian columns in front of Russell House, which, he would later learn, was older than the university, and according to Wesleyan lore had once hosted Charles Dickens. On his right were some of the most recognizable buildings on campus, a group known as College Row. These included the brownstone facade of South College, an administrative building that was constructed in 1825 and was topped by sixteen copper bells, and Memorial Chapel, which was built in 1871, its stained-glass windows commemorative of those students, faculty and alumni who had died in battle from the Civil War to World War II. During a hurricane in 1938, the chapel's spire had fallen through its multicolored slate roof. While the freshman class was concluding a meeting inside at the time, no one was injured. Though many applicants for undergraduate admission would pass these buildings and lament that they did not shine brighter, Ralph was fairly overwhelmed by their regal beauty and their obviously deep roots in Wesleyan history.

Wesleyan had been founded as something of a joint venture between the Methodist Church and Middletown's civic leaders, after several failed attempts by the town to lure its own university. In the early 1700s, Middletown had been among the sites being considered for Yale College, according to the Wesleyan archivist Suzy Taraba. A century later, the town put in a bid to become the site for Washington College, which would eventually become Trinity, but it lost out to nearby Hartford. Several of the buildings that Ralph saw on his first day had been used briefly in the late 1820s by an institution that called itself the American Literary, Scientific & Military Academy. But in 1829, the academy abruptly pulled up stakes and moved to Vermont, where it eventually became Norwich University.

Having lamented for years that Middletown produced virtually everything but college graduates—its factories churned out "spindles, combs, swords, guns, paper, cloth and machinery," said the archivist—town officials finally struck a deal in 1829 with the Methodist Church, then among the nation's largest religious denominations, to found Wesleyan University on the site of the old academy. From the very beginning, Wesleyan cultivated the iconoclasm that would become one of its trademarks. Its efforts to recruit black students in the 1960s, before virtually any other college, can be traced to its early efforts to diversify: non-Methodists were welcomed immediately, and in substantial numbers. The university also launched one of the nation's first scholarship programs, which ensured that the earliest Wesleyan students often came from backgrounds far more modest than their counterparts at Harvard and Yale. One of the scholarships even guaranteed that descendants of the original recipient would be educated at Wesleyan "in perpetuity." Occasionally, the archivist said, "heirs of the holders of these ongoing scholarships still surface, hoping for an incredible bargain on Wesleyan tuition."

True to its commitment to innovation, Wesleyan was one of the first colleges in the country to open its classrooms to both men and women, beginning in 1872, nearly a century before most other northeastern colleges. The experiment lasted for nearly four decades but was abruptly ended in 1910, when the president of the board of trustees became convinced that the presence of women had eroded Wesleyan's prestige. Women would not be welcomed back for another sixty years, until 1968. By then the university had long since severed its Methodist ties.

Ralph, who had already read enough about Wesleyan to know of its early flirtation with coeducation, was about to turn right onto Church Street, where he knew the college library could be found, when he was suddenly seized by a twinge of panic, for he realized he had forgotten a tie. He was still early for his dinner interview with the dean, Barbara-Jan, and so he drove a few blocks to Main Street in Middletown to search for a men's shop. True to form, the area looked to him like the Hollywood set of an old New England factory town, with its redbrick facades and wide sidewalks. He didn't know where to look first. Taking in the old architecture as he walked, Ralph suddenly collided with a potted tree and fell to the ground. Dazed, he heard a man cry out: "Don't worry. I saw it. It attacked you." This, Ralph thought, is not a good omen. He was having trouble finding a tie when he saw a Spanish grocery store, with a display of Mexican spices and thought, *Cool!*

Wesleyan might well pass The Tortilla Test.

Ralph, who like his father had never owned a pair of blue jeans, was not about to go to an important interview wearing a shirt open at the neck. And so he followed the directions on a billboard to a men's outlet off Interstate 91, where he picked up two ties and a camel hair blazer for eighty-nine dollars. (Ever frugal, he would still be wearing the jacket six years later.) *Things*, he remembers thinking, *are looking up in this Connecticut place.*

The dinner, at a little restaurant on Main Street called Thai Gardens, got off to a rocky start when Ralph remarked that Middletown's charm reminded him of San Antonio. Barbara-Jan wanted to say, "You must be blind," her mind flashing to any number of boarded-up storefronts that could be found just a few paces away. But she kept silent, she said later, "because I was trying to sell Middletown, too."

In stark contrast to their phone conversation, Barbara-Jan said later, she realized soon after meeting Ralph that he "absolutely knew admissions" and was "committed to the kind of admissions we do at Wes, finding bright kids from as many backgrounds as possible." Barbara-Jan told Ralph that she was looking for someone "who could walk into Greenwich and make a lot of upper-class kids excited about Wes and also walk into a tough inner-city school where a kid's never heard of Wes."

"The more we talked," she recalled later, "the more I knew he could do it."

Ralph had listed Sharon as one of his references, and, on the following morning, Barbara-Jan left her a telephone message. Barbara-Jan was astonished when Sharon appeared in person several hours later. By sheer coincidence, Sharon had picked up the message while traveling to a conference in southern New Hampshire, and she was able to stop at Wesleyan on her way.

By then Sharon had received her master's from Harvard and had taken a college counseling job at the high school level. She was working at one of the most prestigious prep schools on the West Coast, Harvard-Westlake in Los Angeles, a high-powered school for the sons and daughters of many of Hollywood's royalty. Few schools in the country boasted students with higher SAT scores, and Harvard and Yale were perennial suitors of Harvard-Westlake graduates. The elite West Coast market was one that Wesleyan had only recently begun to tap—with limited success.

Boy, do I want the Harvard-Westlake guidance counselor to feel good about Wesleyan, Barbara-Jan remembers thinking. Sharon's sudden appearance had been like a frilly ribbon fastened to the attractive package that Ralph had already presented to Wesleyan.

Ralph, with his good friend's help, had landed another job.

Two
DON'T SEND ME POEMS

Ralph Figueroa and Sharon Merrow were sitting next to each other toward the back of the auditorium of the Harvard-Westlake Upper School, where Sharon was now dean of the junior and senior classes. On the stage of the theater, with its Broadway-quality lighting and acoustics, Tony and Maria gazed longingly into each other's eyes. But Sharon wanted Ralph to notice another member of the cast of the school's production of *West Side Story*. Nudging him gently in his plush blue seat, she directed his attention to one of the dancers at the edge of the stage. She was five feet four inches tall, with mocha skin, long curly brown hair and a poise that Sharon considered remarkable for a girl just fourteen years old.

"You're going to want to know this kid," Sharon whispered in Ralph's left ear.

As Ralph and Sharon watched Julianna Bentes dance in the chorus that night in 1997, almost two years after Ralph had become an admissions officer at Wesleyan, the ninth-grader was still a student at Harvard-Westlake's middle school campus, eight miles away in Bel Air. Not until the following school year would she reach the rarefied upper school campus, a cluster of stucco-covered buildings that had been terraced into a sixteen-acre hillside that once belonged to the Hollywood Country Club. With its purple jacarandas and man-made waterfalls, the campus still looked like an exclusive resort. It was a running joke that the cars in the student parking lot, which resembled an imported car dealership, were far better than those in the faculty lot. There was even a page of the yearbook called "Wheels," which featured portraits of students' cars shot as if they were swimsuit models. Julianna was already considered such an exceptional talent—she had just choreographed and starred in her own jazz dance show—that she had received a rare invitation from the upper school to perform in its spring musical production.

Sharon's comment to Ralph that night was more of an informed hunch than anything else. Julianna had yet to test her mettle by taking the SAT's, or even the PSAT's. And she certainly hadn't taken any of the twenty-eight college-level Advanced Placement classes that Harvard-Westlake offered—more than almost any other high school in the country. But word had already reached Sharon's office at the upper school, where her primary responsibility was academic counseling, that Julianna was a gifted writer with a sharply focused mind. Though Julianna was one of the few students on scholarship at the academy, she had not shied from the spotlight. She was active in a new campus organization called Black Leadership and Culture Club, and she had already represented Harvard-Westlake at a diversity conference in Baltimore.

As Ralph watched her performance that night, he figured she was a Latina, and his assessment was partially right. Her father was Brazilian, and after being born in Los Angeles, Julianna had spent the first four years of her life in the Amazon, near where he had been raised. Her first language was Portuguese. But Julianna also considered herself black, for her father was a descendant of African slaves. Her mother, who grew up in Pasadena, was white and traced her lineage to a family that had moved to America from Holland during colonial times.

Whenever Julianna was asked to check a box identifying her race or ethnicity on some official form, she, like an increasing number of Americans, felt justified in marking more than one. In fact, she checked three. "When I check one box," Julianna explained, "I feel like I am denying part of myself." At a time when the nation's best colleges were placing a premium on admitting students of color—and were being chastised in some circles for holding minorities to watered-down standards—Julianna Bentes had the potential to compete with any student, minority or white, Sharon believed. Time would tell, of course, but Sharon wanted Ralph to write himself a note about Julianna, even if he only put it in some tickler file. Julianna wouldn't be applying to college for another two and a half years.

Just as Barbara-Jan Wilson had hoped, Sharon had been encouraging many of the students she counseled at Harvard-Westlake to consider Wesleyan. In the 1995–1996 school year, Ralph's first at Wesleyan, thirty-three Harvard-Westlake seniors had applied there. Fourteen of them had been admitted; four had decided to attend. As Ralph and Sharon sat in the auditorium in April 1997, at the end of Ralph's second year, Wesleyan had just finished processing the applications of forty-nine Harvard-Westlake students. That represented an increase of 50 percent, and it meant that a fifth of the graduating class at Harvard-Westlake had applied to Wesleyan—as many as had applied to Harvard University (which was unaffiliated with the California prep school, despite its name). Twenty-two of Harvard-Westlake's seniors had just been admitted to Wesleyan, and six would later decide to attend. With Sharon and Ralph joining forces, Wesleyan was proving that it could hold its own in the competitive West Coast market.

The relationship between Harvard-Westlake and the nation's best colleges was mutually beneficial, one reminiscent of the age-old, informal partnerships that existed between northeastern prep schools and the colleges that they served as feeders, including Harvard and Yale. Those informal arrangements still existed, of course, but more colleges were entering into them, and spreading them over greater distances, than was the case in the first half of the twentieth century. In addition, northeastern prep schools like Andover and Exeter, as well as selective public high schools like Stuyvesant in New York City, now faced stiffer competition from schools like Harvard-Westlake. Harvard-Westlake's students' average score on the SAT—nearly 1400 each year—eclipsed that of the freshman class at nearly any American college. While an average of 25 students from Harvard-Westlake usually ended up at Harvard, Yale and Princeton each year, there were plenty of other academic all-stars among the 225 who were left—many of whom were only too happy to be snatched up by the admissions officer who made the best sales pitch, academic or financial. That was the group on whom Ralph usually set his sights.

By suggesting to some of her students that they might consider Wesleyan—particularly those, like Julianna, with an interest in the arts—Sharon felt she was doing as much of a service for them as for Ralph. She, like Ralph, had come to realize that her own parents' philosophy for choosing a college was not without merit: they had long urged her to consider a less prestigious school than Stanford, one that might make her happier and still give her a good education, such as their alma mater, Whitman, in Walla Walla. At the time, Sharon didn't understand what they meant, but after encountering enough students at Stanford who had enrolled for the wrong reasons, she began to understand that the pursuit of a prestigious education in and of itself didn't necessarily guarantee satisfaction in life.

In one sense, of course, Sharon was the last person who should have been making that argument: after Stanford, she had graduated from Harvard with a master's in human development and psychology, and the imprimatur of those institutions had helped win her a job at a prep school that was regarded as one of the best in the country. To house its college counseling office, the school had attached a glorious, glass-roofed annex to its administrative building, and when Sharon met with her students there, they need only look to the ceiling to see that the sky was the limit of where their lives might take them. And yet one of the very reasons that Sharon had accepted the Harvard-Westlake job was that she welcomed the opportunity to broaden the horizons of Harvard-Westlake's students and their parents, who tended to look through her window and see only Harvard, Yale, Princeton, Stanford and Berkeley.

Though the friendship between Ralph and Sharon was exceptionally close, it wasn't unusual for admissions officers and guidance counselors to get to know one another socially. Theirs, after all, were professions that thrived on personal contact. And Sharon was hardly the only guidance counselor at a public or private school who had had experience on the university admissions side. One of her colleagues in the counseling office at Harvard-Westlake had also worked with her and Ralph at Occidental. The longer Ralph worked as an admissions officer, the more he had come to rely on a network of trusted guidance counselors throughout his regular territory, which included California, Texas, Arizona and New Mexico, as well as New Jersey, which he had been assigned so that he wouldn't always have to travel so far. Ralph viewed these people as talent scouts who could provide the names of top prospects, names he could later share with his colleagues. Some of the counselors whose judgment he valued most were employed by top-ranked schools, like Paul Schweiker at Phoenix Country Day. Ruby Solorzano worked at Garfield High in South Central Los Angeles, a public school whose students were among the nation's poorest. Though such counselors often had a vested interest in getting a student into a school like Wesleyan, Ralph knew that if a counselor pumped up an applicant's record to the point that it bore little resemblance to the actual student, then the counselor's long-term relationship with Wesleyan would be irreparably damaged.

By contrast, Ralph was less likely to attach much credence to the tips that he got from private counselors-for-hire, whom a growing number of parents were retaining to lobby admissions officers directly, sometimes for fees of thousands of dollars. Those hired guns would often say whatever it took to get a kid in, Ralph believed, and he could usually tell when a student's essay had been massaged in a private counselor's word processor. Ralph always regretted that the students who could benefit from their services the most—those at public schools, where one counselor routinely had a caseload of upward of five hundred students—were precisely those who couldn't afford such a luxury.

Because it was Sharon telling Ralph to keep an eye on Julianna, he certainly would, though he also knew that Sharon was surely whispering Julianna's name in ears other than just his.

A little more than two years later, in September 1999, Ralph returned to Harvard-Westlake for what had become his annual fall visit. He would be on the road for the next two months, more or less, drumming up interest among high school seniors to apply to Wesleyan for the Class of 2004. On many parts of his trip, Ralph would be casting a wide net, unsure of whom he'd be meeting. At Harvard-Westlake, though, he planned to spend two full days, for thanks to Sharon, he already knew the names of those students upon whom he should try to make a good impression. One of them was Julianna Bentes. Her senior year had arrived.

In the thirty months since her appearance in *West Side Story,* Julianna had managed to exceed even the highest expectations. On the PSAT, a dry run for the SAT that students usually take in tenth or eleventh grade, Julianna had missed only one question, an achievement matched by only a few hundred of the 2.3 million students who took the exam that year. And only a handful of those students with that near-perfect score had checked black or Hispanic on their test forms, let alone both. (A few weeks after Ralph's visit, Julianna would score a perfect 800 on the SAT verbal exam, and a 710 on the math. Ralph would be more impressed with the math score, because he had found that students who were so gifted verbally rarely did as well in math.)

By the beginning of senior year, Julianna's grade point average placed her near the top of her class. She had taken two college-level Advanced Placement classes as a junior—biology and United States history— and earned an A minus in each. And in the fall of her senior year, she had registered for five more Advanced Placement courses—in English literature, calculus, physics, the history of art and studio art. Just as impressive as her grades, Ralph believed, was the fact that she was challenging herself, though Sharon feared Julianna may have been pushing herself too hard. That same fall, Julianna was also taking three other intensive courses: poetry writing, advanced dance and Shakespeare. Sharon had been encouraging Julianna to drop the college-level studio art class, but she had thus far been resisting.

"She had as many elements of a great college applicant as you could have," Sharon said later. "There wasn't a weakness."

In a school where perhaps 15 percent of the students were black, Hispanic or Asian American, Julianna had emerged as a spokesperson of sorts for the minority community. One particular experience had drawn her out. In the eighth grade, a year after she had arrived at Harvard-Westlake, she was changing into her basketball uniform in a bathroom stall just before a game against a neighboring school, when she heard three girls come in.

"Who are you guys playing today?" she recalls hearing one voice ask.

"Pilgrim," someone responded.

"Oh, isn't that school mostly black?" the first voice asked.

"I don't have a problem with blacks," someone else interjected. "But I do mind Hispanics."

No one challenged the remark.

Julianna wanted to push open the stall door like Superman to confront the speaker, whose voice she couldn't identify. But she found herself too shocked to move.

"That was the first time that I felt some separation in my cultural identity," she later said.

"I knew what I was," she added, "but I didn't think I'd have to call on it to make sure people understood. I knew the next time it happened, I wouldn't be able to live with myself if I didn't speak out."

In private conversations Julianna would periodically challenge other students over comments that she considered racist. When, in eleventh grade, she selected an a cappella song to accompany a dance piece that she and a classmate were preparing, the girl had asked her if she couldn't pick "something less ethnic."

"You mean you want something that is more 'white,'" Julianna responded.

"Yeah," the girl said.

By the end of eleventh grade, Julianna explained, "I was tired of being one of the only voices that would say, 'You know you really shouldn't say that.'"

Julianna had permitted her PSAT score and basic personal information to be released by the College Board, which administered the exam, to any college that sought it out. The board had therefore added her name to a computer database that the colleges could access for about twenty-five cents an entry. Dozens of colleges paid the College Board thousands of dollars each year to buy rosters of those names—some of them arranged in descending order by score, and cross-referenced by race—from which to compile their preliminary mailing lists. Yet however the lists were arranged, the name of Julianna Bentes was always near the top. The Bentes living room was soon filled with cardboard boxes to hold the torrent of glossy college brochures that descended on them in the months that followed.

Only four decades earlier, the best colleges had been able to sit back and wait for students to come to them. But that was before the civil rights movement had helped force many of those institutions to eliminate quotas and open their doors to nonwhite applicants, and before the women's rights movement had prevailed on most male-only colleges to admit women. The resulting frenzy by colleges to draw the best applicants out of those fresh pools only intensified in the mid-1970s, as high school enrollments plunged. Suddenly, even colleges like Harvard couldn't rely only on applicants from longtime feeder high schools within their immediate geographic region. By 1999, when high school enrollments were again on the rise, the competition between colleges for the best students had grown far too intense for any institution to stand down. And so Julianna was one of thousands of American high school students being wooed to colleges both large and small in advertising campaigns worthy of a summer blockbuster. That Julianna had scored so high on the PSAT, and checked all those boxes indicating her background, had made her an especially bright blip on the radar of every highly selective college in the country.

One day, in the spring of her junior year, Julianna had reported to Sharon's office with a three-page, single-spaced list that her mother had typed: a rough draft of where she might apply later that fall. It was titled "Julianna's Infinitely Long College List," and it contained fifty-four names. All of those solicitation mailings had clearly had an impact. Harvard, Yale, Stanford and Swarthmore were at the top of page 1; Wesleyan was near the end of page 3. But Julianna cautioned Sharon not to read anything into the order, for at this point, she hadn't a clue what her top choices were.

When Sharon arrived back in her office after summer break, she was presented with a single page that had been titled "Julianna's *Somewhat Less* Infinitely Long College List." Julianna and her mother, at Sharon's urging, had managed to wrestle their choices down to sixteen, which was getting closer to the seven to ten colleges to which most Harvard-Westlake students applied. In one sense, Julianna was lucky: some private schools, particularly in the Northeast, limited the number of universities to which their seniors could apply, so that each applicant might have a greater chance to land his or her first choice. But as much as Sharon might have preferred to have seen fewer kids apply to the Ivies and instead direct their requests for acceptance to schools that might better suit their needs, Harvard-Westlake felt such decisions ultimately rested with families. The students could apply wherever they liked, putting the onus on the colleges to decide who would go where.

Like so many seventeen-year-olds, Julianna had made many of her deletions arbitrarily. She kicked Columbia off her fifty-four-college wish list, she explained, because its brochures had devoted too much space to selling New York City and not enough to touting its own programs. And yet, Barnard, Columbia's sister school, remained a contender. Harvard, Yale, Stanford and Swarthmore were still displayed at the top of her list. But solely on Sharon's recommendations, because Julianna had yet to hear Ralph's pitch, Wesleyan had made the cut, too, moving from the end of the last page to the middle of a much smaller pack.

Julianna's father, Raimundo Bentes, had been urging his only child to forget the list and consider just one college: Harvard. Like so many other immigrants who had been helping drive applications to top American colleges to record heights, and like Ralph's own father, Ray Bentes had concluded that his daughter deserved the best education that America could provide.

That was one of the reasons why Julianna was sent by her parents to Harvard-Westlake. Though the school was only five miles from the family's home in Van Nuys, it might as well have been in another state. In the course of its century-long history, Harvard-Westlake's famously connected alumni and parents—the financial titan Marvin Davis was a H-W grandparent—had built two modest-looking prep schools (one each for boys and girls, they merged in 1991) into what appeared to the untrained eye to be a small college, with an arts center and science building that had cost hundreds of thousands of dollars to erect and outfit. Julianna, by contrast, lived in a cramped, three-bedroom ranch-style home with peeling gray and white paint. It was set on a desolate street in a working-class neighborhood where, she said, "I learned to distinguish the sound of automatic gunfire."

Ray Bentes had been born in 1947 in a drought-stricken province in the badlands of interior Brazil. His life story read as if lifted from the pages of a Gabriel García Márquez novel. He was the fourteenth of his mother's children, and the last, for she died soon after his birth as a result of complications of her labor, and Ray was raised by an aunt. Much of his childhood was spent on a Ford rubber plantation in the Amazon. At thirteen he was sent to a Franciscan seminary, where he trained for the priesthood. But he stopped just short of taking his vows because "he always had a problem asking too many questions," Julianna said.

"If he had been at a Jesuit seminary," she added, "he'd probably be a priest and I wouldn't be talking to you."

After four years with the Franciscans, Ray recalls, he was indeed having "difficulty with the almost blind obedience they preached." But he also had more practical reasons for leaving. "Having grown up poor, I wanted to avail myself of some material belongings," he said. "It was also very hard to do without women."

Ray went on to attend a public college and law school in Brazil, and then won a Fulbright Scholarship to study business administration at Claremont Graduate School in Claremont, California. It was there, in 1975, that Ray met Catherine Westbrooke, who was attending nearby Pitzer, and the two soon fell in love.

Catherine had begun her higher education four years earlier at Antioch College in Yellow Springs, Ohio, a progressive institution where students went to class for a term and then worked. (On her off-terms, Catherine had sometimes driven trucks and buses.) She had transferred to Pitzer to be closer to home.

At first blush, Catherine's immediate attraction to Ray, this orphan raised in the jungle, might have seemed odd. She, after all, had grown up white and protestant in Pasadena, a breeding ground of California Republicanism not far from where Sharon Merrow had spent her early years. But Catherine's own family was not of the typical Pasadena mold, and had so many black friends that a cross had once been burned on their lawn. Catherine had always wanted to have T-shirts printed up for herself that said, "Don't presume on my whiteness."

Julianna's parents agreed that she should attend Harvard-Westlake, because they believed it was the best school in Los Angeles to cultivate her obvious intelligence. But Catherine disagreed vehemently with her husband that their daughter had to attend a "name" college. There were too many good universities that were not necessarily "prestige" schools for Julianna to consider, her mother thought. In a college questionnaire that Julianna had filled out for Sharon during her junior year, she had indicated that she was open to attending any college "where I can reconcile my need for dance and science opportunities"—she was thinking about medical school—"while maintaining a well-balanced education." Among her priorities, she wrote, was: "to be able to know and interact with my professors." She was also seeking a political climate that was "active and caring." That sounded more like her mother talking than her father.

But, ultimately, everyone in the family agreed, the decision might well come down to a far more practical concern: money. Ray's law degree hadn't been worth much in the United States, and he had wound up just getting by working as a mortgage broker with an annual income that fluctuated from $50,000 to $100,000; until Julianna was a senior, he had also sent a substantial portion of those earnings back to Brazil to support the aunt who had raised him. Catherine had worked as a case manager at a privately managed social agency, but only intermittently, having suffered from a periodically debilitating illness in recent years. Much of the $15,000 that it cost to send Julianna to Harvard-Westlake each year was provided by the school itself.

In Julianna's sophomore year, an admissions officer from Goucher, a small college in Baltimore, had visited Harvard-Westlake and sensed, like Ralph, that interest in Julianna would likely be high. And so Goucher launched a preemptive strike: It promised to set aside a dance scholarship for her that would likely pay all of her tuition. If, by the end of her senior year, that wound up being the best offer, Julianna and her mother agreed that they would likely accept it, though they knew little about the place.

Ralph would have his work cut out for him.

On the last Monday in September 1999, Ralph gave a group presentation at 8:50 A.M. to about two dozen Harvard-Westlake seniors applying to college for the Class of 2004. Julianna was not among them, for she had a class that period that she did not want to miss. Ralph's heart had sunk a little as he had noticed her absence, but he knew he would get a second chance.

The following night, Ralph returned to Harvard-Westlake to take part in a more generic workshop with representatives from other schools on the college admissions process. In the same plush auditorium where he had watched Julianna in *West Side Story,* he spoke about essay writing, and his tone was irreverent. After telling the students that he wasn't there on Wesleyan's behalf—"but don't tell my boss, she paid for my ticket"— Ralph launched into a run-through of the hard-and-fast rules on the subject that were reprinted in every how-to-get-into-college book on the market.

"Whatever you do," Ralph told the students, "don't send me poems." He then read aloud from several poems that applicants had submitted in years past and surprised his audience by announcing that those poems were among the best essays he had ever received—so good, in fact, that he had set them aside to read to his wife. *So much for that rule,* his audience thought. Lifting another maxim from the college guidebooks, he warned his listeners, "Don't use gimmicks," but, then quickly added, "they sometimes work." The point, he suggested, was that there were *no* rules, and that the students should be "true to who you are" rather than "write what you think the college wants to hear."

Julianna caught only the very end of Ralph's remarks. "He seemed very nice," she recalled later. "Very funny." She also remembered that Sharon had introduced them after she had performed in *Brigadoon* her junior year (though she wasn't aware that he had also been present at *West Side Story* two years earlier). "I knew he was a good person because he was Miss Merrow's friend," she said. And for a seventeen-year-old having trouble whittling down her college list, such an endorsement would count for a lot.

After Ralph's session, Julianna approached him to tell him something she thought he would find funny. Someone from Johns Hopkins had told her that when he tried to type the school name into his computer, the spell checker had suggested he change it to "Jan's Napkins," or something like that. Ralph laughed and told her that he might incorporate her advice—be wary of the spell checker—in future talks. And that was that; he wasn't going to give Julianna the hard sell, at least not this early in the year.

Later, Sharon told Ralph what she knew to be the truth about Julianna:

Unlike so many other top students she had sent his way, Julianna hardly seemed to be swooning over the Ivy League. No college on her list was out of the running. For now, Wesleyan's chances of landing one of the most sought-after academic recruits in the country were as good as any other college's.

That same September night, another girl in the audience had raised her hand during Ralph's presentation. She had already written a draft of her college essay, she explained, and though she liked what she had written, she was worried that it was a bit abstract. All night long, Ralph had been insisting that "there's no way to outthink this process," and his response was consistent with that theme: "If you've got something you want to write, then write it the way you want."

Becca Jannol smiled and walked away confident. *I'm sending it,* she told herself.

In her personal statement—one of the two essays that most colleges require—Becca had decided to address an incident that had occurred two years earlier, during the fall of her sophomore year. The story was so well known on the Harvard-Westlake campus that it had made Becca a polarizing figure, her actions the subject of an intense, campuswide debate. Some saw her as a hero; others, a fool. Replaying the whole affair, in a college essay no less, would surely be risky. But Becca had concluded long ago that this was what set her apart from the pack, and she wanted her prospective colleges to know that.

On a bright October morning in her sophomore year, Becca accepted a marijuana-laced brownie that a classmate had baked the night before. As she arrived at school, Becca had seen the girl standing in front of the lockers outside the auditorium before first period. A crowd had gathered around her as she held out a white paper plate partially covered with aluminum foil.

Becca, who was then fifteen, says she had never experimented with marijuana previously. But she admits she was curious, even if the brownies looked as if they had been dropped on the ground, with thick strands of green where there should have been chocolate chips. Becca would later hear that the baker had done a "really bad job."

Without thinking, Becca says, she took two quick bites of one. She was quite sure that all she ate was chocolate, and she threw the rest away.

The entire transaction had been as memorable as taking a sip of coffee, and she hurried to her first-period class, algebra II.

Two hours later, as Becca sat through a history lecture, word began circulating that the girl who baked the brownies had been vomiting in the library and had gone into convulsions. An ambulance had been summoned, and the girl was rushed to the hospital. Becca asked to be excused and sprinted to a pay phone, knowing what she had to do.

Becca reached her father at his law office in nearby Century City and told him anxiously what had happened. She didn't want him to hear the story from someone else, and she sought his approval for her plan to make things right. "I feel responsible," Becca explained, for as an elected representative to the student council, she felt she should have intervened to stop the impromptu brownie party. Henry Jannol didn't hesitate in his response: Becca should go with her gut, which was to tell school administrators what she had done. Whatever the consequences, the family would cope, and if the deans expelled her, she could always find another school. "The world's not going to end," he assured her.

Becca hung up and saw that several police cars had pulled up to the school, and on her way to the deans' offices she stopped an officer. "If a person, hypothetically, was involved in this," she blurted out, "would they be arrested?" Becca wasn't sure if the officer even knew what she was talking about, but he mumbled something like, "Probably not." Becca's nerves eased, but only slightly. Telling a stranger would be a lot easier than telling Mr. Sal.

Harry L. Salamandra, the head of the upper school, was one of those people who seemed destined to work with children. In his midforties during Becca's sophomore year, he had always looked more like a ten-year-old kid on the first day of school, with his straight brown hair parted neatly and his face ready with a relaxed smile. Mr. Sal had chosen to decorate his spacious quarters with giant collages of photos of the students he had known in his many years at Harvard-Westlake.

When Becca arrived at Mr. Sal's office, the secretary said that he was in a closed-door meeting with two other students. Becca would later hear rumors that they had implicated the dealer who supplied the key ingredient in the brownies, but that they had refused to name any of the two dozen or so students who ate them. After the other students left, Mr. Sal waved Becca in, certain she had come for some other reason. He was hoping that whatever she had on her mind could wait.

Since coming to Harvard-Westlake as a freshman, Becca had emerged as a much more conventional leader than Julianna, having been elected handily in both her bids for student council. Rather than seeking office merely to stuff her résumé, Becca had genuine ideas and worked to implement them. It was Becca who had arranged for the establishment of a local chapter of Big Brothers–Big Sisters on campus and who had persuaded the school to extend the hours of the cafeteria so that athletes could get something to eat after practice.

As Becca began to tell Mr. Sal what she had done that morning, she saw his eyes fill with tears. He was obviously disappointed in her, and she told him that she couldn't live with herself if the girl who got sick was the only one who was punished as a result of the incident. Becca also made it clear that she didn't feel it was right to "narc" on any of the other kids, and that the only person whom she was going to implicate was herself.

A stunned Mr. Sal asked if she was aware that she could be expelled for the offense, and Becca acknowledged that she was. She also affirmed her love for the school and said she hoped she could stay. Mr. Sal promised that the school's response would be swift and that he would convene a disciplinary committee that afternoon. He also informed her that he would call her parents. For now, since she herself was obviously all right, she could return to class. She had never seen him look so pained.

When Mr. Sal met with Harvard-Westlake's headmaster and several other deans that afternoon, the punishment on the table was indeed expulsion. The Harvard-Westlake handbook stated explicitly that "it is forbidden to use, sell, or possess drugs or alcohol on campus." The headmaster, according to the handbook, "may recommend dismissal for a serious violation, even on the first offense."

There was general agreement among those at the meeting that the safety of the student body, and the example that the administration set, were paramount considerations in their decision. No one wanted to be seen as condoning the consumption of marijuana at Harvard-Westlake. But Mr. Sal also felt strongly that the administration had an opportunity to send a different message.

Speaking of Becca, the only student who had come forward voluntarily, Mr. Sal told his colleagues that he had "never seen anyone that age show that level of maturity or moral fiber." At no point had she pleaded for mercy. "We'll have more clout having her at the school than dismissing her," Mr. Sal argued. "I want to expose her character to other students."

The committee ultimately decided that Becca would be suspended for only a day. (The girl who baked the brownies was later suspended for a year; the dealer was expelled.) On the day of Becca's suspension, Mr. Sal held an assembly for the tenth-graders in which he described all the shading of her behavior. "I was very impressed with the fact she was able to quickly own up to what she did and take whatever repercussions there were," Mr. Sal said. He did not identify her by name, but everyone knew whom he was praising.

Becca's friends reported back to her that the immediate reaction to Mr. Sal's brief talk was fierce: some students wondered why anyone would come forward when there was no obvious risk of being caught. That night, as she wrote in her journal, Becca seemed as confused as her classmates. *How painful could it have been to just say no, or stop?* she wrote. *The scariest part is that I thought I knew myself. I'm not who I thought I was. I should accept that I am not a leader.*

Everyone wants to know, Why Becca, why? she wrote. *I don't know.*

But others among her classmates had already discerned a silver lining for Becca in the whole affair: "I'm working my ass off to get into college," someone told a friend of Becca's, "and this girl's going to get in because she ate a pot brownie."

At Harvard-Westlake, college preparation takes almost as long as college itself. The process begins early in junior year, when students fill out extensive questionnaires regarding their preliminary thoughts about college. Then the student and his or her parents meet regularly with a counselor to flesh out a strategy and compile a list of choices, a process that is one of the value-added services included in the tuition of a Harvard-Westlake education. Each counselor is assigned to only a few dozen seniors.

As was expected, Becca began working on her college essay while she was a junior, a full year before it was due. At first, she considered telling the story of her father's mother, Urshula Jannol, who had lived in Poland during Hitler's rise to power. She had managed to avoid the concentration camps only by hiding her Jewish faith. She bought a pair of rosary beads, took the name Mary and worked as a nurse. Her survival had always been an inspiration, but Becca ultimately concluded, "Everyone's going to write about their Holocaust Gramma."

After considering a number of other alternatives, Becca became convinced that she had to tell the story of the brownie. In one of the questionnaires that is given to juniors at Harvard-Westlake, they are asked to list five words that "best describe you as a person and set you apart from your classmates." Becca took an extra seventy-six words to answer the question. "Not to stir up bad memories, but I do believe that I am one of the few people at H-W who was willing to be honest in a situation where I was completely at fault," she wrote, before adding, "I was the *only one* out of all my friends who told the truth."

At her first meeting with Sharon, who was her counselor, Becca announced the subject of her forthcoming essay. She and her parents knew that telling the brownie story was something of a risk, especially in a year in which top colleges were seeing record numbers of applicants. A single detail that raised the slightest question of impropriety in an applicant could be enough to sideline a candidacy. That was particularly true for an applicant who was white.

But from the outset, Sharon viewed the story as Becca did: a triumph. In her junior year, a year after the brownie incident, Becca had been elected president of the student body; more telling, however, is that she was also voted into a brand-new position: chair of the honor board. In the latter capacity she was now being asked to uphold the code under which she herself had been punished. "In our minds," Sharon recalled, "it was an asset."

However supportive she was of Becca's essay topic, Sharon fully recognized that her case required careful handling. In part, it was because Becca was not a student whose grades and scores would automatically make her the object of universal wooing, like Julianna. When she took the SAT's in her junior winter, Becca had scored a 630 on the verbal exam and a 590 on the math. Her combined score—1220—was below the median at many of the top twenty-five colleges in the country. Like many students who could afford to do so, she then took a test-prep course over the summer. Some educators have complained that such courses only widen the cultural and socioeconomic divide of the SAT, and in support of that argument Becca estimates that she was one of dozens of Harvard-Westlake students who paid nearly a thousand dollars that summer to an operation with the alluring name of Ivy West. When she took the SAT again in the fall, her verbal score remained the same, while her math score went up only 50 points, to 640. "You're supposed to go up 100," she said, with disappointment. "I should have asked for my money back." (Two years later, a study by a doctoral student at the University of California at Berkeley would find that students who took such courses often posted only modest gains.)

Though her transcript contained mostly A's and A minuses, Becca had her share of B's: a B plus in geometry and a B in science her freshman year; a B minus in algebra and a B in biology during her sophomore year; and a B plus in chemistry junior year. She had taken only one Advanced Placement course, in American history, before her senior year. Though that performance would probably place her in the top rank at many American public schools, one price she paid for attending an institution like Harvard-Westlake was that she would have to compete for admission against her classmates as well as with the general population.

Unlike some private schools, Harvard-Westlake did not seek to limit where its students applied to college. But the colleges themselves would often have room for only so many Harvard-Westlake graduates. And Becca, at least academically, was near the middle of the pack in her school.

In strategizing with Sharon about her college essay, Becca, true to form, wanted to reveal all of the details of the brownie incident. But Sharon encouraged restraint. "Miss Merrow taught me that you don't want to come right out and say, 'I ate a pot brownie' in your college essay," Becca recalled. Sharon was also concerned that if Becca alone told the story, it might seem as if she was making excuses for her behavior.

For that reason it was decided that Mr. Sal would write a letter to the colleges describing the facts of the situation, and that he would use those facts to make the argument that Becca should be celebrated, not shunned. Sharon in turn encouraged Becca to focus on what she had learned about herself from the experience, knowing that the relevant details would be available elsewhere in her application.

Mr. Sal's letter, which he completed early in Becca's senior year, was direct and spare. "Dear admissions officers," it began:

> Never, in thirteen years of school administration, have I met a student as courageous and principled as Rebecca Jannol. Maturity and integrity are deeply rooted in her character. This character was demonstrated following the expulsion of one of her classmates for a drug-related infraction. She voluntarily came to my office and said, "I am here to tell you that I willingly took a piece of a brownie that I knew contained marijuana. Whatever the punishment is, I deserve it."

Working on a computer in her father's study, Becca went through eight drafts of her own essay before she had a version that satisfied her, as well as her parents and Sharon. It read in part:

This morning, a group of students violated a school code, and one was caught. Alleged accomplices of the girl who broke the rules were summoned by the Head of School, and although I was involved in the wrongdoing, my presence was not requested. Pieces of the story trickled out, but there were no absolutes. Some were cloaking themselves in lies or silence while I was fighting the ultimate battle with my conscience. If I confess, does that mean I am an honest person? If I am an honest person, do I automatically have integrity? Would a person with integrity break the rules in the first place?

Although she never directly answered these questions in her essay, Becca did write that in a world where "standards and rules are written in black and white," life's truths are more likely to be found in shades of gray. She concluded that her own behavior—doing something wrong, then something right—fell into that gray area, and that she was ultimately content with how she had handled herself.

Her essay was complete. Now the only question was where to apply.

Many Harvard-Westlake parents are concerned only with how the school's counselors are going to get their child into Harvard or Yale or Princeton. But it was obvious to Sharon that Becca's parents had different priorities. When Henry Jannol had been asked on a junior-year questionnaire to "tell us more about your child that might help us to know him/her better," he had responded: "Our child should find her own road and not buy into 'tony' stereotypes. She should function well and grow at any of a number of universities." Later, in conversation, Henry observed: "At Harvard-Westlake, parents project their college fantasies onto their kids. They went to the State University of New York and UCLA"— Henry himself had gone to UCLA—"but they want their kids to go to the Ivy League. I just don't want to be a part of that."

Like those of her parents, Becca's attitudes were out of step with the Harvard-Westlake student body, and not only in her diffidence toward the Ivy League. In truth, she had felt distant from many of her classmates since the ninth grade, when she became so unhappy that she almost transferred. Though her father made a comfortable living, the Jannol's Spanish-style three-bedroom house near the Beverly Center mall—a few minutes' walk from Beverly Hills itself—was nothing like the mansions that housed many of her classmates. Many of them had never set foot in a public school, while Becca had attended public elementary and middle schools. Like the Benteses, the Jannols had drawn a line only when it came to their daughter's attending a public high school, for the choices in the Los Angeles Unified School District were limited. But the mere fact that her parents could afford the full tuition at Harvard-Westlake was hardly sufficient to make Becca feel that she was on an equal footing with her far better-heeled classmates.

On her first day at the school, she had overheard a group of ninthgraders discussing who was going to be in whose limo for the spring prom. By the fall of her senior year, while some classmates were already fantasizing about making their first million dollars, Becca had translated her alienation into action: she was determined to have a career in politics. "I know there are a lot of scumbags and dirty tricks," she wrote to Sharon on one of her Harvard-Westlake questionnaires. "But it is the idealist in me that thinks I may be able to make a difference." Becca had visited Georgetown on a trip with the track team and had thought it an ideal training ground for a budding politician. "Dorm across the street from the White House!" she had written to Sharon at one point.

Sharon was encouraging, but because relatively few Harvard-Westlake students had been accepted to Georgetown in recent years, she had no real sense of how Becca's application would fare. With the view of having some realistic backup choices, the two began working to compile a list of other colleges, which Sharon wanted to be strategically sound.

She immediately suggested keeping Duke and Stanford off Becca's list, for she knew admissions officers at both schools and felt that it would be difficult to get a full hearing of Becca's story at either institution, in part because of her standardized test scores. At Stanford, for example, the officers rarely met as a committee, which meant that the odds of someone sympathetic being able to advocate to the group on Becca's behalf were low. "There are admissions officers I know who are notoriously numbers driven," Sharon said.

Sharon believed that Becca would need a champion inside each admissions office, someone who would take the time to discern what made her unique and convey that to colleagues. Based on the experiences of prior applicants from Harvard-Westlake, she thought Becca might find such an advocate at the University of Chicago, Washington University in St. Louis, and Emory—and, in a bit of a reach, Columbia and Barnard. These were all schools that gave students' applications an especially careful and fair read, and Becca said she was willing to consider them.

Sharon's final suggestion was Wesleyan, a school that had a reputation for tolerating a range of student dissent, and therefore a good fit for someone with opinions as strong as Becca's. She also figured that once Ralph heard Becca's story, he would find it as inspiring as had the administrators at Harvard-Westlake.

Because Becca didn't know much about Wesleyan, Sharon encouraged her to attend Ralph's information session as well as his presentation on essay writing the following night. That morning session was far more personal than the ones he would present at the New Jersey schools later in the fall. Seated in a small classroom with panoramic views of the San Gabriel Mountains, Ralph discussed those Harvard-Westlake alumni who were now students at Wesleyan. One name in particular set off whispers among the girls in attendance, because they had considered the boy especially cute.

Among those who asked a question was Becca, who said she knew from friends that Wesleyan was a little "hippie dippie." She wondered whether a girl who "wears Gap clothes and likes student government" would fit in. Ralph laughed, and said: "You'll find every point of view. There is no 'in' lifestyle or 'in' group."

Yet Becca barely heard his answer, for she had immediately become self-conscious about being perceived as shallow with her mention of the Gap. In one of her questionnaires, she had described the rapport she hoped to find with an admissions officer in almost romantic terms, as if she were responding to a dating service. "I definitely want them to know that we have to mesh well for this relationship to work," she had written to Sharon. "I can't be begging to be accepted. It must be mutual." Becca had indeed liked Ralph, but now felt as if she had spilled soup in her lap on their first blind date.

The following night, she went to Ralph's presentation on essay writing and loved his premise—that the rules in the how-to books were meant to be broken. *He thumbed his nose at trying to outthink the whole process,* Becca thought. *He was antiestablishment.* It was almost as if Ralph had already read her essay about "shades of gray." Now they were clicking.

If he is coming from that place, Becca thought, *I want to go there.* Becca added Wesleyan to her list, ranking it only just below Georgetown.

As it happened, Ralph had been intrigued by both of Becca's questions and after his talk had asked Sharon about her. She described Becca as being one of the students to whom she felt closest and appraised her as an instinctive leader. Sharon recalled how she once saw Becca, who stands under five feet, insert herself between two six-foot-tall boys who were about to come to blows. "Fighting sucks!" Becca had shouted, so stunning the boys with her bravado that the tension between them immediately dissipated.

That story was intended to whet Ralph's appetite. Sharon figured she'd save the story of the brownie until he was ready to read her college application.

Nearly three weeks later, on the third Sunday in October, Ralph was back on a plane bound from Connecticut for what for him was the uncharted territory of the Southwest.

After Ralph's plane landed in Albuquerque, he walked to the Hertz counter and rented a coffee-colored Lincoln Navigator, the biggest sport utility vehicle on the lot. While the car was built for someone his size, comfort was less a priority than traction. Ralph had been told that he would need a four-wheel-drive transmission to get where he was going, even without the few inches of early snow that had fallen that morning.

His immediate destination was the Native American Preparatory School, a tiny private high school set atop a mesa at an altitude of 6500 feet in northern New Mexico. The program had been founded only four years earlier, and was so new and in so remote a location that few admissions officers even knew about it. Ralph had in fact learned about NAPS from his sister Dina, the admissions officer at Caltech.

Ralph's mission was straightforward: he was seeking to be the first admissions officer in anyone's memory to recruit a Native American teenager to Wesleyan. As far as Ralph could tell, it had been years since the school had made an active effort to bring a Native American to campus; certainly no Wesleyan student in the fall of 1999 had identified him- or herself as such. (The university had actually mounted an aggressive campaign to recruit Native Americans in the mid-1960s, but had all but abandoned those efforts by the early 1970s.) Several of Ralph's colleagues had warned him that he was wasting his time. Why would anyone want to attend a college in a place so isolated from his own culture? But Ralph countered that Wesleyan should try to broaden its definition of diversity beyond the more traditional categories of Hispanic, African American and Asian American students. Dartmouth and Stanford were among the few colleges that sought out Native American students. Why should Wesleyan not do the same?

Ralph felt not only that a Native American student could learn much from Wesleyan, but that Wesleyan could learn much from the student.

He knew, though, that achieving his goal would be as arduous as the drive that lay before him. The first hour of his journey was easy enough—all highway, as straight as a ruler. But once he exited Route 125 about a half hour north of Santa Fe, he began climbing a steep, rocky, unpaved road that seemed to never end. Finally he saw the tiny green sign for the school and made a sharp right turn into what he thought was the entrance to paradise.

Ralph's initial impression was that the air enveloping the mountaintop campus was as sweet as any he had ever breathed, heady with the scent of juniper, cedar and piñones. Everywhere grew peach, plum and pear trees, from which the students often plucked a midday snack. The campus buildings were dark tan adobe, with terra cotta floors inside and wood porches outside propped up by thick logs stripped of their bark.

Richard P. Ettinger, Jr., an heir to the Prentice Hall publishing fortune, had founded NAPS with the hope that it would one day lure someone just like Ralph. A half century earlier, Ettinger himself was a typical student at Dartmouth College in New Hampshire, a white male of some privilege. But he had never forgotten that when it had been founded in 1769 his alma mater had been established to train a very different type of student: its original mission was to educate American Indians. As the twentieth century drew to a close, Ettinger felt that that goal had taken on new urgency, for while Native Americans now represented about 1 percent of the American college population, less than half of them were succeeding in graduating from four-year colleges.

To create an intimate setting that would help prepare at least some of those students for the rigors of college, Ettinger purchased a sixteen-hundred-acre ranch, a site that had most recently been used as a retreat at which the executives of Fortune 500 companies could forge a sense of teamwork while negotiating elaborate ropes courses. In its new incarnation, it would seek to graduate as many as fifteen students a year into the country's best colleges, and ensure that they remained there for a full four years. Its efforts were not unlike what Ralph's mother had been doing for two decades with Mexican American teenagers in Los Angeles, albeit on a much smaller budget.

In the spring before Ralph's visit, fifteen members of the Native American school's first senior class had graduated and were now attending schools such as Stanford, Macalester and the University of Arizona. Seeking to follow in those footsteps, four current seniors met Ralph over a meal of spaghetti in the school's cafeteria, which, with its redbrick floor and tongue-and-groove pine ceiling, looked more like a ski lodge. Ralph gave a broad presentation similar to the one he had delivered in New Jersey, because his small audience knew almost nothing about Wesleyan. But when he got to one of the more glamorous parts of his stock spiel—the segment where he talked about Wesleyan's Hollywood connections—Ralph realized he had piqued the curiosity of a particular member of the group.

When Ralph mentioned that Jon Turteltaub, a graduate of the Wesleyan Class of '85, had directed *Instinct* with Anthony Hopkins, one of his listeners volunteered the titles of two other Turteltaub movies: the romantic comedy *While You Were Sleeping* and *Cool Runnings,* a film about the Jamaican bobsled team. When Ralph mentioned that Michael Bay, who had graduated from Wes a year later, had directed *The Rock*, the same student informed Ralph that Bay was also the director of *Bad Boys.* Like a game show host raising the stakes, Ralph next announced that Miguel Arteta was also a Wesleyan graduate, Class of '89. Ralph then paused, waiting for his listener to fill in his CV. Rising to the challenge, the same senior remarked that he knew that Arteta had spent four years raising money to make an obscure but well-received movie called *Star Maps,* about a boy pressed into prostitution by his father.

This kid is not messing around, Ralph thought. "That," Ralph said afterward, "enticed me right away."

The film buff's name was Migizi Pensoneau. With all the talk about Hollywood, Ralph thought that Migizi's own chiseled jaw was reminiscent of that of a young Val Kilmer. And Migizi's penetrating squint and his thick brown hair, which he had clipped short on the sides but left wavy on top, were vintage James Dean. He had movie-star looks, no doubt about it. But Migizi—who pronounced his name *MIH-gih-zee* yet preferred to be called "Mig"—had always been more interested in writing or directing a film than in acting in one. At the moment he met Ralph, Mig estimated he had fragments of dozens of potential scripts of his own taking up space in his head and in his computer.

Migizi, whose name meant "bald eagle," had come to NAPS a year earlier, at age seventeen. Like those of many of his classmates, his life had been in free fall. At the public high school he had attended in Bemidji, Minnesota, a small town about four hours north of Minneapolis, Mig had a C average during his freshman through junior years. One of the only A's he received—in a language class taught in his mother's native tongue—had been negated by D's in social studies, biology and geography. He also had two F's, in psychology and philosophy, as a junior. "You're not going to go where you want to go with grades like this," his mother, Renee, a professor of Native American studies at a local tribal college, Leech Lake, warned him. (Mig's parents had split up when he was young, and his biological father was often away for months at a time until Mig reached his teens.)

Mig had always assumed he would go to college, but fate seemed to be taking him in another direction. Though he didn't drink, Mig feared he was on the road to alcoholism, for he didn't have to look far to find relatives and friends whose lives had been decimated by alcohol. What was most frustrating—for Mig, as well as for his mother and his teachers— was that he was obviously bright and comprehended everything that he was taught. He just couldn't be bothered to repeat it back on a test or in an essay. "I could get a solid A if it was something I was interested in," he said. "But if I wasn't interested, I just blew it off. If I understood the material, I guess I felt I didn't have to prove it."

Mig had certainly proved that he could discipline himself, when he chose to. He had become a black belt in Tae Kwon Do, and a teacher of that Korean martial art, and had also worked hard to attain the spiritual concentration necessary to become a pipe carrier within his mother's tribe, the Ojibwa, a religious honor he earned before reaching his teens. Still, he remained bored and aimless in school.

Renee's first attempt at an intervention had come during the fall of her son's sophomore year, after he received a particularly bad round of grades. She forced him to quit his job at Burger King, the phone in his room was disconnected, he wasn't permitted to watch television and he was allowed to travel only to and from school. For a few weeks, his grades improved, but they ultimately slid back to their previous levels. "It didn't have the desired effect," Mig admitted.

One night in his junior year, Renee tried a more radical approach: she tossed him an application to NAPS. Mig's cousin Shian had already been attending the new school for a year, and "her ranting and raving about how great it was caught my mom's ears," Mig explained. "My mom knew I was better than what I was doing," he added. "She thought I was in the wrong environment for myself. I wasn't being stimulated."

In late January 1998, Mig sat down and filled out the NAPS application, having finally concluded that his mother was right: he needed help, and he had come to regret how much pain he had caused her with his indifference to his schoolwork. But as he answered the questions on the form, Mig made no attempt to conceal his sense of humor, on which he had always relied in situations that made him anxious. For example, in response to, "What subjects did you like best and why?" Mig wrote, "Math, algebra," before adding: "Learn something new every day." When he was asked which subjects had been most difficult, he wrote: "Biology. Understanding DNA took a while."

But he did grow serious in one of the essays he submitted, in which he was asked, "What would be the best thing to happen to you this year, and why?" His response: "The best thing that could happen to me is to get in to your school." He then sought to describe his existence in Bemidji:

> A lot of the natives are into drugs and alcohol. Many claim to be in gangs as well. This annoys me because it sends out a false message to other ethnic communities here. These other communities don't see natives for the beautifully, culturally rich people we are.
>
> I believe that leaving this town would signal a new beginning in my life. I feel like this school, this town and these people are holding me back from something grand. Something that I can't find here. I feel that your school will help me find whatever it is that I know I must find.

In another essay, he wrote: "As for what I see in store for myself in the future I am definitely going to college. I haven't decided which one yet, but I haven't examined my options either."

In the "parent profile" Renee was asked to prepare, she wrote that her son had "unusually high intelligence." His grades, she said, "do not always reflect this, but his life does." The recommendations that Mig's teachers submitted to NAPS also captured the erratic nature of his work. His English teacher wrote that Mig could "write powerful poems and short stories" and "has the potential to be a writer of beautiful words and ideas and characters and settings." But the teacher also lamented that Mig "is sort of a scattered person" who needed "to discipline himself more effectively." The teacher concluded: "As Mig matures he will grow into himself. I have confidence that he will choose a path that will lead to something special. He is still a man-child."

The admissions officer at NAPS, Christopher Johnson, read Mig's application and transcript and recognized all too clearly the boy staring back from the page. "I was a gifted kid whom no one paid real attention to," recalled Chris, who was raised in Michigan and is Saginaw Chippewa. "My high school didn't challenge me much. Learning wasn't really interesting to me." Christopher believed that Mig was exactly the kind of kid whom NAPS had been founded to help. Moreover, Mig's standardized test scores buttressed his mother's contention that he had untapped potential. On the independent school entrance exam, known as the ERB, he had scored in the 77th percentile for his verbal ability and the 50th percentile for mathematics achievement. Those scores, however low in national rankings, placed him near the top of the two hundred or so students who were seeking the fifteen openings in the class.

And so, it was decided that Mig would be offered admission to NAPS. The only condition, as Christopher explained to him, was that he would have to repeat his junior year, which he agreed to do without hesitation. This would truly be the fresh start he so desperately wanted. And because Renee's income was low—a single mother, she still had Mig's younger sister at home—NAPS agreed to subsidize much of the $24,000 annual tuition. In fact almost every student at NAPS received some form of financial aid. Mig would also be in good company, for not only would his cousin Shian be there, but so would her sister Sasina and another cousin, Ogema, who had been admitted along with Mig.

Soon after he arrived at NAPS in the fall of 1998, however, Mig's support system was swept out from under him. Sasina grew homesick and withdrew within months. Ogema seemed more interested in "hanging out and teasing people" than studying, Mig recalled. The boy eventually left.

Despite these distractions, Mig thrived. For the first time, he felt ready to pay back the investment that so many people had made in him. He devoured the short stories of William Faulkner and Tim O'Brien, and Louise Erdrich's novel *Love Medicine*. He pulled his GPA up to a B plus/A minus, with A's in English, geometry and Spanish. He ran for student council president and won. He submitted several op-ed articles to local newspapers, including one that called on the Washington Redskins to find a new mascot. He learned tennis well enough to earn a place on the school's team.

He took the SAT and scored a 650 on the verbal portion of the exam and a 560 on the math. His combined score of 1210, while below the average of Wesleyan and many other top colleges, was well above the national average of 1020, according to the College Board, which administers the test. More important, his scores placed him at or above all but 10 percent of the Native Americans who took the SAT's that year.

When it came time to apply to college, Mig relied heavily on the advice of teachers and counselors at NAPS. One counselor suggested Beloit in Wisconsin, because of its strong writing program. Although the visit of an admissions officer from Pitzer in California earlier in the fall had left "no lasting impression" on Mig, he figured there was no harm in applying there, as well. And then a counselor had suggested Wesleyan, because of its focus on writing and film. As luck would have it, the counselor added, an admissions officer from Wesleyan had asked to visit NAPS.

"Hey dude, nice suit!" was how Mig chose to greet Ralph on the day of his presentation. *This is rural New Mexico,* Mig thought, *can't the guy loosen up?* A crack like that would probably have ended a lot of admissions interviews before they had even begun, and no college guidebook would have advised opening so important an interview with what could have been perceived as an insult. But Mig's decision that he would simply be himself had already paid a dividend, even if he hadn't quite realized it.

Unbeknownst to him, the buttoned-down admissions officer was himself a notorious practical joker. One of the tricks Ralph liked to play on people whose cars he borrowed was to change all the preset radio stations to country music. Similarly, whenever Ralph visited the home of his younger sister Dina, whose shoe collection rivaled that of Imelda Marcos and was arranged in color-coded boxes, he would head for her closet and rearrange it, putting as many pairs of black pumps as he could find into boxes reserved for brown sandals. No wonder Ralph had felt so at home in the iconoclastic Stanford marching band, whose typical halftime formation was in the shape of a phallus. *Dude, nice suit!* Ralph thought. *That's a good one.*

But Ralph became more somber when he told Mig that he knew of no other Native American student at Wesleyan. If Mig applied and was accepted, and if he chose to matriculate, he would be a pioneer. No one else at Wesleyan would understand what it meant to be a pipe carrier, and no one would be craving the same native foods as he.

"It won't be easy," Ralph said. "But it will be a real good experience."

Ralph also explained that while Wesleyan couldn't offer him a mentor who was Native American, it could expose him to a range of diversity that rivaled that of any other American college. "You will be in an atmosphere open to cultural differences and cultural experiences," he assured him.

Mig shook Ralph's hand and promised he'd think over what Ralph had said, though he was too shy to pose the question that most concerned him: Did Ralph think he actually could get in? Had Mig asked, Ralph would have explained that he didn't know the answer. Such decisions were not up to Ralph alone. Far from it: he had eight other colleagues, and he could already foresee that with a record as checkered and complicated as Mig's, every other admissions officer at Wesleyan was going to want to weigh in on his case before arriving at a verdict.

Three
ISTANBUL (NOT CONSTANTINOPLE)

Ralph bounded through the front door of the old Dutch Colonial and padded up the carpeted stairway to the second floor. It was an unseasonably warm seventy-degree Monday in early November, and he couldn't help but smile. After six weeks on the road, his traveling for 1999 in search of the next great member of the Class of 2004 was essentially, mercifully, over. He had come home. And home, at least during his working hours over the next few months, would be Reid House, a seventy-year-old residence that Wesleyan had converted into its admissions office two years earlier. The college had renovated the four-bedroom in the northern part of campus with the hope that it would give applicants and their parents a warm first impression. The new office also had the unintended, but not unwelcome, effect of making the staff of admissions officers and assistants seem to be members of a family. Like siblings, they might be teasing one another one minute and arguing fiercely the next.

Across the hall from the dean's office, the former master bedroom, was Ralph's office, which measured just ten feet by fifteen feet and looked out on an oversized evergreen in the backyard. The space had long been used as a child's bedroom, and a visitor would be forgiven for assuming that a teenager still resided there. On one wall, a young Darth Vader looked down from a framed advertisement for *Star Wars: Episode I,* a gift from one of Ralph's brothers-in-law, who worked at a Hollywood studio. A side table adjoining the cluttered mahogany-topped desk was stacked high with CD-ROM's and compact disks, including a recording by the Stanford Marching Band.

Inside the desk, Ralph also kept hidden his "drawer of toys," among whose contents was an old earphone, which he occasionally used to create a cheap, instant costume. When the beige earphone was combined with the dark suits that he favored, he could pass for a Secret Service agent, particularly if he put on his most stern poker face. The drawer also held a kindergartner's plastic green recorder, which Ralph had been known to play like a saxophone at office parties, and a hand-held digital dictation machine, which he used solely for comedic effect, because it played back his voice at ridiculously low speeds. Another drawer was filled with snapshots of Ralph's family and friends, including several of his wife, Natalie, of course. As she had hoped, she had landed a job as a Spanish teacher at a public high school near Wesleyan. There was also a picture of a smiling Ralph and his old friend Sharon at their Stanford graduation, twelve years earlier.

But if Ralph's office was a reflection of him at his most personal and whimsical, it also displayed the parts of his life that he took most seriously. On his bookshelves, below copies of the leading college guidebooks—yes, admissions officers pay close attention to what's said about their schools—were a series of thick bound volumes. These were his old law school texts, which were not on display for nostalgia's sake. Ralph often consulted seminal cases like *Regents of the University of California* v. *Bakke* when preparing lectures in support of affirmative action in the admissions process, which he was asked to give around the country because of his legal background.

On a nearby shelf were three books with frayed green covers and yellowed pages that had helped inspire Ralph's position on the value of diversity to a college and its students. On the inside of each cover, a fifteen-year-old boy had written *"Es propiedad de Rafael Sepúlveda,"* followed by *"Pilares de Nacozari."* The boy had also scribbled a date: "1920." These were the books that Ralph's grandfather and namesake—his mother's father, Rafael Sepúlveda—had used to teach himself to become a mechanical engineer. He had done so via a correspondence course from America, while growing up in Mexico in a town called Pilares. For the elder Rafael, who had never graduated from high school, the contents of those books represented the sum of his formal education.

It was the elder Rafael, more than anyone else, who had argued most persuasively to Ralph's mother, Bertha, and then to her seven children, about the value that a top-flight university could have in the course of one's life. After his family had lost most of its land holdings in the Mexican Revolution, Rafael had moved to a small town in Arizona, where he soon found his self-taught engineering skills in great demand at a local lime mine and processing plant. From a drafting table in a tiny house that was always covered in lime dust, Rafael designed the conversion of the factory from a vertical kiln to a horizontal one, which greatly increased its capacity. He was so successful that ranchers and farmers were soon traveling from miles away to have him repair their tractors and other heavy equipment. But Bertha, and later Ralph, would recall Rafael saying that he could have put his God-given talent to far better use if he had had the benefit of an education at an institution of higher learning.

"You don't want to work with your hands," he would always tell his children and grandchildren. "You want to work with your head."

Rafael Sepúlveda died in 1995, just shy of his ninetieth birthday, during the week that Ralph interviewed for his job at Wesleyan. Once he got the position a few weeks later, Ralph, whose full name was Rafael Sepulveda Figueroa, vowed anew that a critical part of his mission in life would be to ensure that students as disadvantaged as his grandfather would have an opportunity to reach their full potential.

When Ralph returned to Middletown that November, it was at a moment of transition in the admissions calendar. While he and his colleagues had been out canvassing the country for applicants for the Class of 2004, the back office of the admissions building had begun to resemble the records room of a dentist's office. Out of sight of the public, it had already begun to fill with applications. After being opened, each application was placed in a manila folder and then coded. First, two large colored stickers, one for each of the first two letters of an applicant's last name, were affixed to the folder's spine. If an applicant was the child of an alumna or alumnus, a dark orange square was added. If an applicant had identified him- or herself as the member of a minority group, a yellow circle was added. These details were considered too important for a reader to overlook, and the coding system was designed to ensure that they were given due attention.

The deadline for seeking early admission to Wesleyan—a decision that was binding, if the applicant was accepted—was November 15. With that date now only a few days away, 356 high school seniors had applied for early decision, a total that was about 5 percent less than that of the previous year. With guidebooks like *U.S. News* keeping track of such trends, Ralph and his colleagues knew that the drop-off could be cause for some concern. But to counter that, nearly 1200 other seniors had already applied for consideration during the regular-decision period—even though that deadline was still two months off—a rise of 15 percent over the previous year's. "One thing it means," explained Greg Pyke, a veteran Wesleyan admissions officer, "is that we're going to have a lot to read this year."

The first batch of early-decision files was already in the process of being distributed to the admissions officers. As in the regular pool, each early-decision application would be read by two of them—the first selected at random, the second because his or her territory included the school from which the student was applying. A few weeks from now, in early December, the officers would convene as a committee for several days to consider most of those early-decision candidates. In each case, the majority, by a show of hands, would decide whether the student should be accepted, rejected or deferred into the regular pool.

By the end of that first week in December, even before the early-decision process was completed, the officers would also begin receiving their regular-decision reading. The piles of applications delivered to the admissions office would grow steadily after that, reaching a seasonal peak within a week or so after the January 1 deadline. As usual, there would be an office pool in which everyone would have a chance to guess the day that the mail would reach its greatest volume and the number of bins in which it would be delivered. Afterward, the officers would go into virtual seclusion for more than two months, until early March. During that period, each would read more than a thousand applications.

The officers' only interruption would be for a short, second round of early-decision considerations, in early February. Wesleyan, like Tufts University, Emory and a small but growing number of other colleges, had recently begun offering this second chance at binding early admission. It had undertaken this practice for two main reasons: so that students who had been rejected early by other colleges would consider seeking an edge at Wesleyan, and so that students who had missed the first early deadline, but who had since decided they liked Wesleyan best, might have another chance to prove their love. Like their counterparts who had applied and been accepted in December, those accepted in this special February round—two months before Wesleyan and most other colleges made the bulk of their offers—would agree to withdraw all other applications.

For the admissions officers, the main difference between the early- and regular-decision rounds was the percentage of applications that would be discussed by the committee of the whole. Fewer than a thousand students competed for early admission each year, and that was a relatively manageable number to handle as a committee. But in the main round, in which there would be nearly six thousand applicants, each application would be read by two officers and then sent on to Greg Pyke, the interim director of admissions. If the two readers were in consensus on a decision, Greg would likely endorse the choice. But if there was a split recommendation, he would probably send that application to the committee for consideration during a series of meetings in early March.

It was those committee hearings, coming just days before final decisions were due, that provided the most visible drama of the admissions process. In a form of sudden death, each applicant would be discussed by the committee for no more than five minutes, after which a vote would be called. The majority, again, would carry the day. All the decision letters would be mailed at the end of March, and then the real wooing—the attempt to get those who were accepted to choose Wesleyan over the competition—would begin.

But that was still months, and thousands of hours of reading, away. On this November morning, Ralph was to sit down with his colleagues for their first substantive meeting since August, when they had met casually at his home over bagels and coffee to begin their preparation for the coming academic year. Everyone had been away so often since then that Ralph had barely gotten to know his four new colleagues, each of whom had joined the staff over the summer. They wouldn't have long to establish a level of comfort with one another, yet they would have no choice but to do so: like members of Congress or of a local school board, each could accomplish little without the support of a majority of the others.

One newcomer, Amin Abdul-Malik, had graduated from Wesleyan three years earlier, in the Class of 1996. Amin's path to the school had been harrowing. By age thirteen, he became an orphan when his mother, Sara, had died after a long battle with cancer. Five years earlier, when Amin was eight, he had lost his father, José, under circumstances that would remain a mystery to him. His parents had been separated at the time, and he never really wanted to learn what had happened.

Like Ralph, Amin would bring a unique perspective to the admissions process. Neither of his parents had progressed past the ninth grade in his or her education. So that he might have a chance at escaping the poverty-stricken neighborhood in Spanish Harlem where he lived, an aunt had helped arrange for him to get a scholarship to boarding school. He finished high school at the elite Loomis Chaffee School in Connecticut, whose reputation was not unlike that of Harvard-Westlake. A good student, Amin would also distinguish himself by twice winning the Connecticut state wrestling championship in his weight class. As a young adult, he would still retain the thick neck, carved shoulders and sharp stare of those days.

It was Amin's wrestling coach at Loomis Chaffee, himself a Wesleyan graduate, who helped Amin get a full scholarship to his alma mater. And it was at Wesleyan that Amin, who had been born José Angel Gonzalez, Jr., was introduced to Islam by a classmate. Before he graduated, he had converted and changed his name. In the three years since leaving Wesleyan, Amin had worked as a prep school teacher, most recently at a Muslim school in Philadelphia. But he had found himself homesick for Connecticut. Amin had no idea what kind of admissions officer he would prove to be, but having survived what he had survived—in his early life, as well as a student of color at both Loomis and Wesleyan—he felt he had developed a fair idea of what constituted character, was confident that he'd know it when he saw it and was convinced that it was a crucial barometer of college success.

Two other newcomers had followed a time-honored route into the admissions office: they had applied for jobs there immediately after graduating from Wesleyan. One of those recent alums was Bozoma Arthur, twenty-two, whose father had received his Ph.D. in ethnomusicology from Wesleyan in 1977. Raised in her father's native Ghana and later in Colorado, Bozoma had majored in English and African American studies. Because she was a leader in the black students association and other groups, her ever-present smile and long braids were already a familiar sight around Reid House and on campus.

As members of minority groups, Ralph, Amin and Bozoma could easily have had jobs at Wesleyan, or at another elite college, as much as twenty-five years earlier. It would have been unlikely, however, that all three, now representing a third of the admissions staff, would have been there at the same time. But because the composition of the student bodies at the nation's top colleges had changed dramatically over that period, as the institutions' priorities shifted, the composition of their offices of admissions had changed as well.

The third new officer, also a member of the Class of 1999, was Lyllah Martin, twenty-three. A student of religion and international relations, Lyllah had also been the captain of the varsity crew team. During grueling workouts on the Connecticut River, two blocks off campus, her golden blond hair had lightened in the sun, and was unlikely to return to its normal shade anytime soon, for now she was coaching the freshman team. Lyllah had spent most of her childhood in Southern California, and both her parents were educators. Like Ralph's, her mother was a college counselor; like Bozoma's, her father was an alumnus. But unlike either, Lyllah had attended five schools in twelve years, as her parents crisscrossed the country, as well as the world, in various jobs. That experience made her certain that if an application from a similarly itinerant student reached her desk, she would be able to empathize.

Neither Bozoma nor Lyllah expected to make a career of admissions, but each figured the job would be a fun way to spend the first year out of college. What could be better, really, than helping to decide the academic fate of students only five years younger than oneself? That was power.

The last of Ralph's new colleagues, twenty-five-year-old Rod Bugarin, had worked for a Wesleyan competitor, Hampshire College in Amherst, Massachusetts, for the previous three years. Rod had been raised in Hawaii, but seeking a change of scenery on the mainland, he had forsaken tropical warmth for the deep snows of upstate New York, where he attended the University of Rochester. He graduated in 1996, with degrees in political science and public health. In transferring from Hampshire's admissions office to Wesleyan's, Rod was following a fairly typical career trajectory. As in numerous other professions, often the only way to advance in the admissions field was by being traded to, or seeking a better position with, a competitor.

The four remaining officers were Wesleyan veterans; all but one had worked at the college for at least a decade, though none was a Wesleyan alumnus. Each was married with school-age children, and like Ralph, each had worked in at least one other profession. While a few colleges, including Cornell, entrusted some admissions decisions to professors, Wesleyan had always subscribed to a more populist philosophy. Like Yale and Stanford and countless other institutions, it believed that an admissions officer's own life experiences—educational and otherwise—provided that person with the essential tools to predict how a seventeen- or eighteen-year-old high school senior would fare as a college freshman. Only in specific cases—such as those involving what appeared to be a genuine math or music prodigy—would professors be consulted.

Moreover, when considered as a whole, the various backgrounds of the Wesleyan admissions officers were judged to be a critical ingredient in creating a class that was as diverse as possible, in the broadest definition of the word. Even if each officer stared into the admissions pool and looked only for a reflection of him- or herself, as admissions officers were, in fact, sometimes wont to do, then the class that the group selected would be diverse by default. But after seven years as an admissions officer, Ralph had learned that it was virtually impossible to predict how his colleagues would vote on any given case.

It was Greg Pyke who brought the meeting to order on Ralph's first day off the road. A sometimes somber-looking man, with a full head of straight, graying hair and thick, rectangular glasses, Greg had come to Wesleyan twenty-two years earlier, and no admissions officer had worked there longer. Since early July, Greg had been the office's interim director of admission, while a university committee searched for a successor to Barbara-Jan Wilson. After a decade as dean, Barbara-Jan, the woman who had originally interviewed Ralph, had been promoted to vice president for university relations. Her chief responsibility was now raising money, ideally in million-dollar increments. Greg was said to be among the finalists for her old position, but many believed he had applied only because he thought it was expected of him. Though he was considered an unparalleled judge of a student's potential, Greg also delighted in being the office's number-cruncher, providing almost daily updates of how one year's search for a freshman class compared to another's in more than a dozen categories. It was he who compiled much of the data on which *U.S. News* relied.

Greg's most recent job, prior to coming to Wesleyan, had been even more stressful than admissions: he was a live-in administrator at a psychiatric halfway house in Middletown, just a few miles away. He had also interviewed food stamp applicants and had been an English teacher. As an admissions officer, Greg would often draw on his experiences in each of these former jobs. But for the moment, his task was to begin bringing eight very different individuals together as a team, and quickly.

The officers assembled in an olive-painted room on the first floor of the admissions building that had once been the house's dining alcove and had since been outfitted by the college with a twelve-foot-long cherry table. By March, the surface of that table would be blanketed with fast-food wrappers and the detritus of other junk food as the officers gathered under the room's elegant wall sconces almost daily, sometimes for upward of ten hours at a stretch. For now, it was relatively clean.

The main item on this day's agenda was travel. How, Greg wanted to know, had the eight officers arrayed before him—many of them glassy-eyed and leaning their chins on their hands—fared in spreading the good name of Wesleyan? The previous year may have seen a record number of applications, but for now, the cupboards were considered bare. It was a largely unspoken, but always an understood maxim, that Wesleyan would have to have an even better year this year. And sprinkled among those applicants, the admissions officers knew, should be more valedictorians, more students with high SAT scores, more science majors, more bassoonists, more infielders and more students of color, among others.

The first to raise a hand was Chris Lanser. Chris had arrived in the office a year after Ralph. He was almost forty, but he still looked like the basketball standout he had been in high school, at Fieldston, a private school in New York. His six-foot-four-inch frame was lean and muscular, and his thick brown hair was tousled over his forehead. After graduating from Haverford with a degree in philosophy, Chris had bounced around in a series of jobs. In San Francisco he had managed a Sharper Image store and also worked as a state humane officer (for the Society for the Prevention of Cruelty to Animals), where he was adept at pulling cats from car engines and once jumped into a backyard to break up a fight among three pit bulls. Like Greg, Chris had also taught high school English, in inner-city Philadelphia. No teenager applying to Wesleyan, or guidance counselor, was going to intimidate him. He was accustomed to speaking his mind.

Beginning his remarks, Chris announced to his colleagues that he had spent a productive few days in the early fall meeting high school seniors in Chicago and its suburbs, the heart of his territory. At each of two top schools, Chris reported, forty-five students had turned out to hear his presentation. "I've seen a lot of those students coming through the office here since," he said. Ralph was among those who looked impressed; he certainly hadn't received so positive a reception on that day in New Jersey.

Rod, the newcomer who had previously worked as an admissions officer at Hampshire College, was next. "Las Vegas was a complete bust," he began.

"Again," sighed Greg. For some reason, Las Vegas was one of the areas in the West where Wesleyan was perennially tapped out. But, Rod added, a subsequent trip to Southern California had been like getting a row full of cherries on a slot machine. Rod, who shared parts of the West with Ralph, because the territory was so large, said he had drawn 200 students and 20 guidance counselors to the Wesleyan booth at a college fair in San Diego. And in a subsequent tour through the Pacific Northwest, including Seattle and Portland, he had visited 23 schools and met 104 students. That was an average of only 5 students per school, but many of those schools were small and rural. Rod felt the trip had been worthwhile. If Wesleyan wanted to be geographically diverse, and it did, these were parts of the country worth mining.

Later, during a week of visits to high schools in his native Hawaii, Rod had opened his presentations with a question: "What is an Ivy League school?" He then informed the seniors in his audiences, most of whom had never left the islands, that Wesleyan could offer them all of the prestige and New England–style quaintness that they were seeking at schools whose names were more familiar. And Wesleyan's classes were likely more intimate.

On some of his outings, Rod had been accompanied by admissions officers from Wellesley, Smith, Mount Holyoke and Bryn Mawr. Ideally, he would have liked to have seen students alone, but while there was some risk that Wesleyan might lose an applicant to one of his competitors—all of them representing women's colleges—there was also a chance that a student who showed up to hear about Smith might ultimately be turned on by Wesleyan. Like other colleges, Wesleyan was increasingly receptive to participating in such ventures, even when the colleges were directly competitive. Just that morning, Greg had been mulling an offer to travel with representatives from Oberlin College in Ohio.

"More important," Rod said, continuing his report to his colleagues, "I really converted some Pomona applicants from Hawaii to Wesleyan. My big line was, 'Why do you want to go to school so close to home?'" While Pomona, in California, was just a five-hour flight from Honolulu, Wesleyan was at least ten.

Rod then told his colleagues about the most tantalizing nibble that he had gotten. A student at a private school that Rod described as "the Exeter of Hawaii" was apparently looking closely at Wesleyan, even though her father, the school's headmaster, had graduated from Williams. Several of the officers smiled at the prospect of stealing such a big catch from Williams. Rod would keep them posted.

Rod closed his report on an entirely different note. He recounted some complaints that he had gotten at several elite public and private schools on his own travels through New Jersey. At one public high school, nine seniors had sent applications to Wesleyan the previous year, and six had been accepted. From a neighboring school with a similar profile, Wesleyan had received sixteen applications but had taken only one student. Some of those it had rejected had in turn been accepted by Harvard and Yale, Rod said, and the guidance counselors were now angry at Wesleyan. "I was kind of a deer in the headlights," Rod said of his visit to the second school.

On one level, Wesleyan liked the idea that its standards might be tougher than Harvard's. Sometimes, though, Wesleyan might decide to issue a string of rejection decisions to send a wake-up call to one of its longtime feeder schools—a signal that it considered the quality of the school's applicants to be slipping. Since he was new, Rod didn't know the history of this particular school, but he did feel it was of a caliber that needed "some wounds to be healed." Otherwise, Rod feared, the school's guidance counselor might steer some future applicants away from Wesleyan. He wanted his fellow officers to keep that background in mind as they were reading, and everyone nodded in agreement.

Greg spoke next. On a visit to Georgetown Day in Washington, D.C., one of the elite prep schools in the capital, a counselor told him that at least 8 of the school's 112 seniors were likely to apply early decision to Wesleyan. "Wesleyan," the counselor had said, "is a hot place." Greg went on to describe a trip he had made overseas. Partly in the interest of diversity, Wesleyan, like many other top colleges, had begun sending some of its senior admissions officers on sales calls abroad. The rationale was straightforward: both American and international students would benefit from meeting one another at Wesleyan. Just as Ralph had stepped off the beaten path in search of Native American applicants on a mountaintop in New Mexico, Greg had managed to find a relatively untapped source in an equally unlikely place: Wales. A year earlier, he had managed to coax 2 students from a Welsh school called United World College into applying to Wesleyan and later enrolling. They had sent such good reports back to their old mates that, extraordinarily, 23 had shown up to meet Greg this year.

Greg had also traveled to Istanbul, where more than a dozen students came out to meet him on a Saturday morning. That, too, was no small accomplishment, considering that Turkey was still recovering from an earthquake that had killed thousands several months earlier. Ralph found the image of Wesleyan searching for applicants amid the rubble of Turkey to be so hauntingly indelible that he could erase it from his mind only with dark humor. For the rest of the day he would keep humming the song lyric "Is-tan-bul, not Con-stan-ti-nople," the opening bars of a 1953 novelty hit of the same name. The song, a tongue-in-cheek history lesson about the Ottoman Empire, had been rerecorded in the early 1990s by the band They Might Be Giants. Ralph knew both versions, which was not surprising given his deep and eclectic musical tastes.

One of the challenges of recruiting abroad was that Wesleyan could not afford to make the same sort of financial promises to international students as it made to American applicants. Any American citizen or permanent resident of the United States accepted to Wesleyan was guaranteed that Wesleyan would meet all of his or her financial needs, at least as the college defined those needs; similarly, no American would be rejected on the basis of his or her ability to afford its costs. But only a limited number of international students would be given that assurance, for Wesleyan would stretch its resources only so far. For that reason, it had to consider the financial means of its international applicants when deciding whether to offer them admission, and those who could not pay their own way were usually at a disadvantage. There was, of course, a side benefit to such screening: full-paying students would ease the burden on an institution struggling to keep its financial promises to many of its American acceptances.

One special program, though, paid all travel expenses, tuition and fees at Wesleyan for twenty Asian students—two each from ten countries. The program had been founded in 1995 by the Freeman family, an old-line Wesleyan family with strong ties to Asia as well. The admissions officer who drew the plum assignment of overseeing it was Terri Overton, forty-one, a native of suburban Cleveland and a graduate of Cornell. For Terri, a mother of a ten-year-old girl and an eight-year-old boy, the idea of traveling to Asia for five weeks a year on Wesleyan's behalf seemed like a perfect segue to the nearly three years she had spent in Swaziland for the Peace Corps. There, she had sometimes lived without electricity or running water while teaching science and math. Now, in her fourteenth year at Wesleyan, she was jetting across Asia to coax seventeen-year-olds to take leave of their families and travel upward of nine thousand miles to a college they had never heard of.

The Wesleyan name, Terri now assured her colleagues, was spreading across Asia. Terri told them that on a recent, two-week swing she had drawn one hundred students in Manila and one hundred more in Bangkok. "Taiwan," she said, "was not as good." But she reported meeting "the most amazing, high-powered kids" at the Jakarta International School. Terri had hit a home run at the school a year earlier, when she persuaded the valedictorian to apply to Wesleyan under the program. The student was now a freshman at Wesleyan, and others at Jakarta International were interested in applying as a result.

Terri was always a hard act to follow, and on this day, the task fell to Ralph, who decided not to say much. He told of having spent a week in Texas that had been "OK, but pretty slow overall." He also talked about the day he had spent in New Jersey but said that it had been memorable only because a prospective applicant had brought up a defunct Wesleyan advertising campaign. A few years earlier, a marketing consultant had come to the conclusion that Wesleyan should bill itself as "The Independent Ivy." For students outside the Northeast, the consultant reasoned, establishing an association of Wesleyan with the Ivy League—even if Wesleyan had no legitimate connection to the eight colleges in the Ivy League football conference—might result in more applications coming Wesleyan's way. The campaign had been a disaster. Some Wesleyan students had protested that the implied connection to the Ivies was duplicitous; others said they had selected Wesleyan specifically because it was *not* an Ivy, and wanted it to stay that way. Everyone in the admissions office had hoped that the slogan would just fade away, but it continued to dog them.

On a more hopeful note, Ralph then described his two productive weeks in Los Angeles. He didn't mention Harvard-Westlake, but he didn't have to; the veterans, at least, knew of his friendship with Sharon and that the school could always be counted on to send Wesleyan plenty of good applicants. He concluded his report with a mention of his trip to Albuquerque, Santa Fe and his first visit to Native American Prep.

Some of Ralph's colleagues had used the day's gathering as an opportunity to introduce the names of particular students who they hoped would apply to Wesleyan and be accepted that year. Like the guidance counselors at NACAC, the admissions officers figured it was never too early to start building a coalition that might later help an applicant. Ralph, however, always played his cards a little differently. The lawyer in him figured that if he signaled too early what he wanted most out of the year's deliberations, his bargaining position would be compromised. And bargaining would be inevitable in a year in which Wesleyan would surely be able to fill its freshman class several times over with stellar students.

Yet even now, Ralph had already begun to arrange some priorities in his mind, drawing from among the hundreds of good prospects for the Class of 2004 whom he had met on the road. He knew that in the coming months, he was destined to fall in love all over again, while reading the applications of an entirely different group of students, whom he would meet only on paper. He would undoubtedly make room for those applicants on his wish list, and would fight hard for many of them. But as of now, he decided that there were two students, above all others, whom he most wanted to bring to Wesleyan in the Class of 2004.

One was Julianna, the multiracial Californian with near-perfect SAT's whom he had been tracking since she danced in *West Side Story* as a ninth-grader. The other student was Migizi Pensoneau, the Native American film buff who had seemingly resuscitated his academic life by moving from Minnesota to New Mexico. Becca Jannol, who had accepted a pot brownie as a sophomore and wound up on the honor board at Harvard-Westlake, had yet to take up any residence in Ralph's consciousness. But that would change.

For those officers like Greg who were Wesleyan veterans, the absence of Barbara-Jan Wilson at the head of the boardroom table that morning was jarring. For a decade, she had not only run the office but had given it a face (freckled and welcoming, with a wide smile) and personality (fast-talking and boisterous). She was also fiercely competitive, a trait that had served her well as a scrappy infielder and pitcher on her high school soft-ball team. She had also been a spirited member of her high school cheer-leading squad, and while she tried to keep that element of her résumé under wraps, no one would have difficulty picturing her with pom-poms in her hands. As she approached fifty, Barbara-Jan seemed happiest when she was shouting herself hoarse from the stands, especially if the Wesleyan baseball team was playing on Andrus field or her beloved Yankees were playing a double-header in the Bronx. As she yelled to Derek Jeter or Paul O'Neill, sometimes offering encouragement and other times not, the fans sitting in front of her at Yankee Stadium invariably turned their heads to see who was making such a commotion. How surprised they would have been to learn that it was she who had the responsibility for deciding whether their children got into one of the finest institutions of higher education in the country.

Barbara-Jan brought that same spirit to her job as dean of admissions, during a period when the process of selective college admissions would be transformed at Wesleyan and elsewhere. In 1990, her first year as dean, forty-four hundred applicants had sought about seven hundred seats in the freshman class at Wesleyan. Ten years later, the number of applicants had mushroomed to nearly seven thousand. Over that same period, the percentage of applicants accepted by Wesleyan fell to 27 percent, down from 44. At least part of Wesleyan's newfound popularity could be attributed to the fact that more students were now applying to more colleges—some to as many as ten schools each. But part of the increase also reflected Barbara-Jan's marketing efforts. That the officers now spent so much time on the road was at least partly her doing, and the very building the officers were meeting in had been acquired at her insistence and renovated to her specifications.

Barbara-Jan's tenure had literally begun with a bang. Early on the morning of April 7, 1990, just days before she would accept the dean's job, student radicals tossed a rock and three Molotov cocktails through a window of the office of the Wesleyan president, William M. Chace. No one was injured, but the explosions touched off a small fire. The reasons for the bombing were never clear: the Wesleyan sophomore who was believed to have masterminded the crime was later shot to death in a dispute with a University of Connecticut student. But what was clear, to many professors and administrators on campus, was that this was not an auspicious time for someone to fill the vacant position of dean of admissions. "No one wanted the job," Barbara-Jan recalled.

A month before the bombing, dozens of Wesleyan students had taken over the admissions office to protest what they described as the college's insufficient support for minority students and professors. (As Ralph would tell the prospective applicants during the meeting in New Jersey, the fact that Wesleyan had a relatively large minority population didn't guarantee that everyone would feel welcome and supported there). But Barbara-Jan, who had come to work at Wesleyan nine years earlier, in 1982, as director of career planning, was undaunted. Even though she had never before so much as read someone else's college application, she was offered the job as dean of admissions. With few other real takers, Wesleyan figured it had nothing to lose.

Barbara-Jan's first priority was to find a way for the school to celebrate its often-tumultuous social climate, but also let applicants know that this would not distract them from receiving a serious education, as rich as that of Williams, Amherst or any of its other competitors. The athlete in her also wanted Wesleyan to find its footing on the playing fields, a goal that had proven elusive for much of its history.

In one respect, Wesleyan's occasional lack of interest in athletics was consistent with the maverick reputation it had enjoyed throughout its existence, including a penchant for social experimentation that could be traced back to its founding Methodists. It was not only among the first universities in the country to experiment with coeducation but was also among the first to admit Jews (beginning in earnest in the 1950s) and blacks (in the 1960s) in relatively large numbers. Wesleyan went on to send some of the first busloads of students on the Freedom Rides, and its campus formed the backdrop for some of the nation's earliest protests against the Vietnam War. In one photo of an anti-Vietnam protest—staged, as so many were, at the base of Foss Hill—the university's acting president can be seen in the middle of the fray. In the midst of a sea of T-shirts and jeans, the tweed suit he had chosen to wear belied his obvious support for his students.

The university had made national headlines in recent years for stretching the boundaries of academia, including permitting a professor to offer a course in which students wrote pornographic fiction and, in several instances, directed pornographic-style movies as a final project. The course, which was being offered for the second time and concentrated mostly on social theories about pornography, drew attention to the flexibility of the Wesleyan curriculum, which did not require students to take a core concentration of courses in disciplines outside their majors—such as the humanities or sciences—for graduation. The school also made the front page of *The New York Times* by permitting a dorm to institute a "clothing optional" policy. Never mind that few students had ever exercised the option to be naked in its halls: the point was that if one wanted to use a payphone in the buff at Wesleyan, one had the right to do so.

"Wesleyan clearly falls on the spectrum with the Berkeleys, the Oberlins, the Chicagos, the Columbias, the Vassars," Barbara-Jan said. "I always believed that if *The New York Times* wanted to write about a draft dodger, they'd call us. If they were looking for a good student athlete, they'd call Williams."

The truth about the campus, though, was more nuanced, and as she assumed her deanship in 1990, Barbara-Jan wanted the world to know that Wesleyan couldn't be pigeonholed. "At Wesleyan you could find a great student athlete," Barbara-Jan said. "And Williams had its share of draft dodgers. It's a stereotype. But guidance counselors and parents pay attention to stereotypes."

One of her first initiatives was to improve the admissions office's communications with the university's coaches. Surely, she believed, there was room in Wesleyan's definition of a meritocracy for jocks, providing they could do the work. "I didn't understand why a school would have twenty-nine sports teams, and always lose," she said. If a coach really needed a particular applicant on his team, Barbara-Jan wanted to know about it. "Academics are always going to drive the decision," she said. "But it's hard to put a football team on the field without a quarterback."

If an athletic prospect's grades were not considered good enough, Barbara-Jan would usually suggest to the coaches that the student take a postgraduate year at a prep school, and then reapply. Still, at her urging, the same standards that Wesleyan sometimes stretched to admit a student of color with low SAT scores were likewise broadened to admit a badly needed linebacker. (Wesleyan was hardly alone in this respect. In their book *The Game of Life* the scholars William G. Bowen and James L. Shulman identified Wesleyan as one of many top liberal arts colleges, including Williams and Denison, that often opened the front gate wider when an athlete was standing outside.) In the end, Barbara-Jan was convinced that the psychological value that athletes brought to campus often justified whatever bargains were struck. "I believe in winning," she said. By the late 1990s, she had achieved one of her goals: Wesleyan had beaten Williams twice on the football field in a span of four years, after having gone winless against its Division III rival for more than a decade.

At the same time that she was seeking to bring more athletes to campus, Barbara-Jan was determined to attract those budding physicists, chemists and biologists who had come to think of the school as the perfect home for a poet, but not a scientist. Again, the truth was more complex. In 1970, the university had opened an enormous, well-equipped science center across from the Ionic columns of the main library, but few applicants knew it existed. In hopes of redefining Wesleyan's image, Barbara-Jan began flagging those applicants who had taken a heavy load of science courses and who had expressed interest in a scientific career. She then deputized science professors and science majors to reach out to that group to promote Wesleyan's attractions. She told her staff that, just as a few bad grades might be overlooked for a student who played a rare instrument like the oboe, so, too, should a budding scientist be cut some slack if she had spent more time in the lab than in the gym. "Someone once asked me, 'Would you take a kid with high physics scores and nothing else?'" she recalled. "I said, 'Yes. The faculty wants them, and the faculty needs them.'"

At the same time, Barbara-Jan sought to make the general admissions process easier for all applicants. She replaced Wesleyan's customized application with the Common Application, a generic form that all but a handful of top colleges had adopted by the end of the 1990s, figuring that a student might be more likely to apply to Wesleyan if he could simply duplicate the essays he had written for most other colleges. Barbara-Jan also increased the admissions office's annual travel budget by 50 percent—by 1999, it absorbed a substantial portion of the office's nearly $2 million in expenses—so that students didn't have to come to Connecticut to get hooked on the place. By the late 1990s, that travel was paying off: Students in the freshman class hailed from forty states, and nearly thirty countries, and one out of every three who chose to enroll had met a Wesleyan admissions officer on the road.

For those prospective students who did come to visit the campus, Wesleyan provided directions from Middletown to every other top college within driving distance. Parents who sheepishly asked the admissions receptionist how to get to Rhode Island were often stunned when she produced printed cards that would take them directly to the front door of the Brown admissions office, as well as to those of Yale, Vassar, Princeton and even Williams and Amherst. The colleges' phone numbers were included on the cards, too. Since they were going to go visit those schools anyway, Barbara-Jan wagered, they might as well have fond memories of the one college that had made their trips easier.

But the single biggest obstacle to selling Wesleyan, Barbara-Jan had come to believe, was its decrepit admissions office. Since 1954, the office had been located on the third floor of North College, a converted dormitory built a half century earlier with no parking and questionable air quality. After the second grandmother in as many days fainted in the office's cramped conference room at one point in the early 1990s, Barbara-Jan ordered the room shuttered. While that solved one problem, it meant that the officers had to lead expeditions of parents and applicants on long hikes up and down the building's stairways, in search of a vacant room that was big enough to hold all of them. "It was like a rabbit warren," Barbara-Jan recalled.

The office had been adequate enough during the 1950s and early 1960s, when top colleges weren't all that competitive. In those days, a guidance counselor often worked out with an applicant where he or she would apply—such a list might contain three schools—and then the counselor might consult directly with a dean or an admissions officer to close the deal. Now colleges were competing with one another for many of the same top candidates. And Wesleyan's attic-as-admissions-office was a serious detriment—especially in comparison to the quaint, converted homes that housed the admissions offices at Williams and Amherst. If an applicant and his family traveled from Wesleyan to these schools, there was no question where they'd feel more comfortable.

Competitive as ever, Barbara-Jan, who herself had once worked at Williams as a career counselor, knew she had to move to better quarters. The only problem was that by the early 1990s, Wesleyan, unlike Williams, couldn't afford to build a new admissions office. That hadn't always been the case. From the early 1950s through the late 1960s, Wesleyan had been among the wealthiest universities in the country. In 1949, with the help of several alumni, it had purchased American Education Publications, best known as the publisher of the schoolhouse staple *My Weekly Reader*. The university's investment in the company came to generate as much as $3 million in income each year, according to an article in the university's alumni magazine. In 1965, Wesleyan sold the company for four hundred thousand shares of Xerox stock, valued at $56 million.

But like an heiress blowing through her inheritance, Wesleyan made little attempt to protect its wealth, albeit for noble reasons. It sought to keep its tuition at minimal levels and didn't ask its alumni for much money. The Wesleyan science center, in contrast to those at almost any other institution of its stature, bears the name of no major donor, simply because one wasn't needed. Yet again bucking the conventional wisdom of other liberal arts institutions, Wesleyan was spending what it had, rather than saving for future generations.

When, beginning in the mid-1980s, *U.S. News* began ranking institutions by their financial resources, Wesleyan—with an endowment of $188.7 million—was holding its own with Williams ($180 million) and Amherst ($224 million). By the mid-1990s, as those institutions grew their investments and solicited funds from their established alumni networks, Wesleyan had become so cash-poor that it was considering dropping its promise that the demonstrated financial needs of all admitted students would be met, a bedrock of its admissions philosophy. This policy existed, as well, at nearly all other top colleges. (One of the few exceptions was Brown, which was also in financial straits at the time. It did not adopt a so-called need-blind admissions policy for all American applicants until 2002. Over the prior two decades, it had taken students' financial needs into account when filling some of the last seats in the freshman class, essentially giving students of means an edge in obtaining those slots.)

Barbara-Jan felt that for Wesleyan to be competitive for top students, it would have to at least spruce up its front gate, whether it could afford to or not. (Since there was no actual gateway to the campus, the admissions office was the de facto entrance.) When the Wesleyan board appointed Douglas Bennet to succeed William Chace as president in 1995, Barbara-Jan found a kindred spirit.

Bennet had graduated from Wesleyan in 1959 and had gone on to top-level positions at the State Department, where he played a critical role in developing United States policy on United Nations' peacekeeping missions. He had also been the head of National Public Radio. Having traveled the world as a diplomat and executive, Bennet took one look at the Wesleyan admissions office, which he still remembered as North College, a dorm, and pronounced it "dingy." It hadn't changed much, he thought. A sailor who decorated his office with an extensive collection of antique compasses, Bennet made two decisions early in his tenure that would chart the course of Wesleyan admissions policy into the twenty-first century. His first commitment was that he would enhance Wesleyan's practice of need-blind admissions, however precarious the university's finances. That meant raising the money to offer students more direct scholarships so they would need fewer loans. Bennet believed that the policy was essential to recruiting from every corner of economic life, particularly a corps of students of color. As a white underclassman of some means at Wesleyan in the 1950s, Bennet felt he had received a richer education as a result of Wesleyan's long commitment to admitting low-income students as well.

Based on his high school grades, Bennet had been accepted a year early to Wesleyan, while still sixteen, and had soon overcome his youth and soft-spoken shyness to play his own small part in easing the burdens of the few blacks who then attended the university. When he learned from his black friends that no barber in Middletown would give them a haircut, Bennet drew on his experience in a local chapter of the NAACP—he had been a member since age nine, at his father's insistence—to work with state and local officials to integrate the barbershops. He later described the effort, which was ultimately successful, as a crusade, and said that his Wesleyan experience had nurtured a lifelong concern about "matters of equity and justice."

Bennet's second major admissions decision early in his tenure was that he would raise a new admissions building before any other on campus. He agreed with Barbara-Jan that Wesleyan could not improve its student body without replacing the building that would be the first stop for most prospective applicants to view the campus. Other departments, however antiquated their classrooms, would have to wait in line. Likewise, Bennet wanted to have his students before he had modern spaces in which to house and educate them.

With Bennet's help, a large house with a barn-style roof on the edge of campus was designated as the new quarters, and Stewart M. Reid, a wealthy alumnus from the Class of 1972 who had made some of his money in the oil and gas business, was persuaded to contribute a considerable chunk of the $2.7 million refurbishment cost. Part of the money was used to renovate the house and to add an addition where a soaring meeting space would be housed.

When the yellow-painted building opened in the fall of 1997, Barbara-Jan finally had her cottage. Rather than being greeted in what appeared to be a Medicaid office, prospective applicants to Wesleyan now met the admissions staff in a wood-paneled room with a fireplace and thirty-foot windows. Out one side, the students could see the football and baseball fields; out another were the soccer grounds. "What could be better?" Barbara-Jan asked.

A campus that had had no front door suddenly had a veranda that opened onto its most eclectic and historic features. Immediately across Wyllys Avenue was Foss Hill, the campus's idyllic center, the one to which Wesleyan had given a digital spit-and-polish in the posters Ralph had passed around in New Jersey. Not only had the hill's giant oak and hemlock trees stood guard over Wesleyan's anti-Vietnam protests, but they had also hosted the Grateful Dead, who once played there. So had more than a few uninhibited couples in the 1960s, who liked to make love on the hill, even without the cover of darkness. Now students were more likely to climb to the top of Foss Hill, with its distant view of the Connecticut River, to pound African drums or to slide down it on sleds.

Also visible from the new admissions building was the marble rostrum of Denison Terrace, where Martin Luther King, Jr., gave the baccalaureate address in 1964. King, who was friendly with one of the school's professors, was a frequent visitor. Behind the terrace loomed Olin Library, with its granite steps, Palladian windows and red leather doors. Its initial architect was Henry Bacon, who designed the Lincoln Memorial, and he had been followed by the firm of McKim, Mead & White, which designed the original Madison Square Garden. The nineteenth-century brownstone buildings known as College Row, which Ralph had driven past on his first day, were just around the corner.

Wesleyan might no longer be exceptionally wealthy, Barbara-Jan thought, but at least brokers like Ralph now had a beautiful office from which they could show prospective students the college's most impressive real estate.

While hundreds of potential applicants got a glimpse of Ralph Figueroa during his road trip in the fall of 1999, thousands more saw him perform on his home court, the glass-walled meeting room inside the new admissions office. Wesleyan offered information sessions virtually every morning and afternoon—Thanksgiving Day and Christmas week were the only real exceptions—and each of those sessions was led by an admissions officer. Ralph, like everyone else, took his turn when he was not traveling.

In contrast to his presentations at individual schools, Ralph could assume in his sessions at Wesleyan that the students and their families had at least heard of the place. Indeed, if those students had made the effort to come all the way to Wesleyan—driving or flying hundreds of miles in most instances—then they were likely to apply. And every year, more and more of them made that trip.

By the fall of 1999, after only two years, the new admissions office had already become too small. A carpenter had been dispatched to install more shelves in the mail room, to accommodate the increase in applications. And the public meeting space, despite enough maroon sofas and tan easy chairs to seat at least fifty people, was overflowing at almost every session. Even some parents who showed up on time were forced to stand at the back of the room, while their children were relegated to sitting cross-legged on the floor.

Even in such a cramped setting, Ralph could really relax at these gatherings. Wesleyan was now selling a product in great demand, and he had been in admissions long enough to know that people gravitated toward something that would be a challenge to acquire. His only real job at such sessions was to sit back and field questions.

At a presentation of Ralph's that fall, one boy had made a point of arriving early enough to get a coveted front-row seat. Jordan Goldman had been chauffeured to Wesleyan by his mother and her parents, but he asked if they wouldn't mind taking a seat at the back, so that he wouldn't be distracted. That was fine with them for they knew the moment belonged to Jordan, a seventeen-year-old senior from a public high school in Staten Island whose dreams were far bigger than his five-foot-seven-inch frame, on which he carried only 130 pounds. Like so many of the kids in the room that afternoon, he was on a college tour. He had seen nine other schools in eight days, and Wesleyan would be the last.

With his brown hair cropped close to his scalp and then brushed to attention with a heavy application of gel, Jordan exuded confidence as Ralph walked into the room and positioned himself in front of the fireplace, just a few feet away. Ralph began by hitting his usual selling points but then devoted the bulk of his fifteen-minute introduction to describing how he analyzed an application. This was a topic that Jordan hadn't heard discussed at many of the other colleges he had visited, and he edged toward the front of his chair so as not to miss a word.

"The first thing we look at is your transcript," Ralph said. "We're looking first for the rigor of your curriculum. We're looking to see five courses each year. We're looking for four years of a single foreign language. Only then are we going to look at your performance." He told his listeners that he usually attempted to gauge an applicant's writing ability by reading the essays, before turning to the recommendations of teachers and counselors. As for tests like the SAT, Ralph said: "They're an important evaluation tool. But they can only be used in conjunction with everything else in the file." That was how he had been trained at Occidental, and it was consistent with the Wesleyan philosophy.

Then, raising an issue he knew was on everyone's mind, Ralph said a few words about extracurricular activities. He explained that as he considered a list of outside interests, he sought evidence that an applicant was a leader in several core activities, rather than someone who simply ordered every item on a menu but barely touched his meal. At this point, Ralph interrupted himself to anticipate a question before it was even raised. He said he knew that applicants liked to send along supplemental materials that illustrated special talents—slides of paintings or videotapes of musical performances—and yes, he acknowledged, Wesleyan was happy to receive such materials. He said he'd even be willing to send them to Wesleyan's art and music professors for evaluation, which the admissions officers would then consider as part of the application.

But, his voice growing grave, Ralph cautioned that there was one exception to this policy. "Don't send me extra writing," he advised. "We don't have time to read it."

As soon as those words left Ralph's mouth, Jordan Goldman sank visibly in his chair. His mother, who knew exactly what Jordan was thinking, craned her neck for a glimpse of his face, which had gone pale. If there was one arrow in his quiver that was going to hit the bull's eye at a top college, Jordan believed, it was his writing portfolio. The hundreds of pages of short stories he had written in his spare time over the years—including one, in particular, that was told in the voice of a woman married to an inattentive husband—made the strongest argument for his admission. He had planned to submit a half dozen of these stories with each college application, and he was confident that the colleges would be so impressed with the talent of this would-be Hemingway that they would overlook his weaknesses.

Jordan knew that his class rank—teetering on the precipice of dropping out of the top 10 percent—was barely at the level that the top colleges expected. And while his combined SAT score (1460) placed him just above the median of schools like Wesleyan, his performance on the SAT II exams—which were intended to assess achievement, as opposed to aptitude, in subjects like English literature and mathematics—had been only average. Jordan had read enough guidebooks to recognize that those scores might be acceptable for a minority applicant who could bring a unique cultural perspective to a place like Wesleyan. But colleges weren't exactly beating down the door for white, Jewish boys who couldn't otherwise distinguish themselves from the pack.

When Ralph announced that supplemental writings wouldn't be read, Jordan felt as Roger Clemens might have if he were informed by his manager that he wouldn't be able to throw his fastball against the Red Sox: he couldn't possibly win without it. When Ralph finished his hour-long remarks, Jordan sprang from his chair and was among the first in line to seek a private word.

"My writing portfolio is really important to me," Jordan announced. "I think it's the only way I can get into your school." Wasn't there some way, Jordan asked, that Ralph could make an exception?

Ralph, his mind already on the fifteen hundred applications that he was about to begin reading, was firm. It was hard enough finding time to read just the applicants' responses to the two essay questions that Wesleyan required. A good writer, Ralph assured him, would be able to shine through in that limited space. Jordan shouldn't worry.

But Jordan was having none of it. He wanted to be a writer, he said, and he wanted his collected works to be considered. "If you send them in early enough," Ralph finally allowed, "there's a possibility someone will read them." But as Ralph said a brusque good-bye to Jordan, each knew that it wasn't going to happen.

As he went to find his mother and grandparents at the back of the room, Jordan was in a panic. But it wasn't really Wesleyan or Ralph he was worried about, for more than anything else, Jordan wanted to go to an Ivy League college. As he sat in the audience at Wesleyan that day, he knew that Brown was likely to be his first choice, and the University of Pennsylvania not far behind. He was confident that, largely on the basis of his writing, he'd be accepted to both of them. He had come to Wesleyan looking for a backup.

But, he suddenly worried, what if the admissions officers at Brown and Penn wouldn't read his stories, either? Then he might be in real trouble.

Like so many students whose applications clog the inboxes at the Ivies, Jordan was looking for a prominent name to attach to his own. Attending an Ivy, Jordan believed, would be his ticket off of Staten Island—a sixty-square-mile tract of mostly middle-class homes that, at least judging by its location, neither Manhattan nor New Jersey seemed to want.

Jordan longed for the day when he would affix an Ivy League sticker to the back window of his mother's one-year-old Toyota Camry. He could almost hear what people would say to themselves as he drove by: "*That's* where he's going to college? Oh, *good school!*" And then, Jordan was certain, anyone who saw that sticker would have to conclude: "Smart kid!" Jordan didn't know what they'd be likely to think if they saw the name "Wesleyan" on his mother's car. They'd probably confuse it with Wellesley.

For the first seventeen years of his life, Jordan had often been as isolated and lonely as Staten Island itself. His parents had divorced when he was two, and his father eventually moved to Florida to start another family. Jordan was raised by his mother, a schoolteacher, and his stepfather, a floor-covering salesman, whom she married when Jordan turned nine. They lived in a two-bedroom house sheathed in aluminum siding that was smaller than many apartments. Jordan had no siblings. It was a life that left a lot of time for daydreaming, and for eager anticipation of the celebrity that the future might bring.

There had in fact been plenty of time to fantasize during the two months of his sophomore year that Jordan had spent out of school. That year, a hole had been discovered in his heart. The flaw, a genetic one, was considered fatal if not corrected. It took two operations to mend it.

The pale blue walls of the bedroom where Jordan spent so much time looked more suitable for a Manhattan Chinese restaurant than the incubator of an aspiring author. They held pictures of Jordan with the actor Samuel L. Jackson on the set of the film *Shaft*; Jordan with Patrick Stewart of *Star Trek: The Next Generation;* Jordan with Hollywood producer Scott Rudin. There was even one shot of Jordan with Al Gore. Linked to each photo was a unique story, but all shared a common denominator: a teenager who had managed to talk his way into meeting some of his heroes without the benefit of any professional or personal connections. Jordan was charming, and he was sincere, but he was also relentless, as Ralph discovered in their brief encounter that fall afternoon.

Jordan had also persuaded Richard Price—the author of the bestselling novel *Clockers* and the writer of the Oscar-nominated screenplay for the film *The Color of Money*—to give him private writing lessons. Price had become so impressed with Jordan that he had modeled a character in his novel *Freedomland* on his new young friend. Price even wrote an appraisal of Jordan's writing, which he sent to each of the colleges to which Jordan was applying. It was the kind of blurb for which any author would have killed to have on the back of his first novel:

> He leans toward a kind of urban hard guy persona with an exquisitely observed noir-ish atmosphere and dialogue which is close to pitch perfect. Yet, as fitting his age, he is an experimenter, keeping to short stories, attempting different voices, different points of view. He also knows to quit when he has lost his thread. He is a self-educator; he reads novels in order to learn how to write.

Jordan had gotten to know Price through mutual friends: the family of Devin Cutugno, a bright, effervescent boy who was a year younger than Jordan and who was confined to a wheelchair by cerebral palsy. Jordan's mom knew Devin's mom, Donna, who ran an organization that tracked down missing children. Someone had directed Price to Donna as he researched his novel *Freedomland*, which concerned the disappearance of a four-year-old white New Jersey boy and the racial turmoil that ensues, but in the course of that research he stumbled upon the relationship between Jordan and Devin. In *Freedomland* Price had created characters based on both boys and made them brothers, because he knew how badly they wished they were brothers in real life. As he contemplated how he might help Jordan into college, Price also wanted the schools to know the role that Jordan had played in Devin's life:

> Over the years, Jordan has become more than Devin's helper— they are best friends. Jordan is his interpreter to the world and his de facto big brother. Jordan humbles me; I could never do his job, or if I could, I doubt I would possess his radiance, his sheer joy in being Devin's "guide."

With a portfolio of short stories that had the imprimatur of someone like Richard Price, Jordan had long figured that he was a shoo-in at just about any college. And for most of his young life, he had assumed that college would be Princeton. His home in Staten Island was only about ten minutes' drive from the Verrazano Narrows Bridge, and from there it was only about an hour to Princeton. From the time he turned four, he would go to Princeton twice a year with his mother, Melanie, a special-education teacher and administrator in the New York City public schools. They'd have lunch and then stroll the upscale shops in Palmer Square and on Nassau Street. "Work hard, and this is where you could go," said Melanie, who herself had attended Rutgers, a state university about twenty miles away. Jordan would always respond, "I want to go to Princeton."

During his junior year of high school, when he began looking at colleges in earnest, he learned that Princeton had a number of core requirements, including one in the sciences. Jordan didn't like the idea of being told what to do, or that he might have to take classes that he had no interest in—and with other students who didn't want to take those classes either. When he also began to hear sentiments like, "God couldn't get in to Princeton," he resolved to set his sights on an Ivy where the gate might not be as high. After traveling to Philadelphia with an uncle, Jordan decided that Penn was it. "I was all about Penn," Jordan recalled. "I didn't even look into the academics. I just thought, 'I can have a lot of fun here and it's got a great rep.'"

By the middle of junior year, it was time for him to share his thoughts with a guidance counselor. Jordan attended Tottenville High School, one of the biggest high schools in the state, a big box of gray cement that housed nearly four thousand students and graduated three-quarters of its students in four years. About 7 percent dropped out, a low figure for a New York City public school, but it was surely no Harvard-Westlake. Unlike Sharon Merrow, who was responsible for fewer than fifty juniors and seniors each year, Jordan's counselor at Tottenville was juggling the files of hundreds. While Harvard-Westlake students filled out pages and pages of questionnaires, and then met with their counselors for hours of discussions, Tottenville students' first glimpse of their counselors usually came in a fifteen-minute session that each junior was granted. They would often see little of them afterward.

Jordan arrived at that initial counseling session with an arrogant attitude and armed with a PSAT score high enough (top 2 percent) to qualify him as a semifinalist for a National Merit Scholarship, just like Julianna Bentes. He had also been admitted as a freshman to Tottenville's gifted program, which accepted only 120 students a year. Surely that would be impressive to an Ivy, Jordan reasoned. But his counselor was determined to bring him down to earth. "If you apply to the Ivies," Jordan was warned, "it's always a reach." When a deflated Jordan announced he was interested in creative writing, the counselor proposed a list of private liberal arts colleges that had good writing programs and that might be more realistic for Jordan, given that he barely had an A-minus average at a school where dozens of others earned straight A's. The schools that the counselor suggested included Sarah Lawrence, Vassar and Bard in New York; Brandeis and Emerson in Massachusetts; and Colby in Maine. "At this point," Jordan recalled, "I was put off. I go in expecting to hear, 'Kid, you're going to get into an Ivy.' I walked out with a list of schools I hadn't heard of. I thought the reason I hadn't heard of them was because they weren't good schools."

But instead of tossing out the list, he headed for the Waldenbooks at a nearby mall. Sitting on the floor, he began cross-checking the counselor's recommendations in each of a half-dozen guidebooks, like a movie maven who wanted to read all the different ways that a particular film had been reviewed. He looked up Bard on page 68 in the *The Best 311 Colleges,* published by Princeton Review, and read:

> A sophomore tells us that, true to its motto, "Bard College is, I swear to God, a place to think. I'm learning more than I ever have in my whole life and finally gaining some understanding about why the world is the way it is." The "highly self-motivated" students in this "rich academic environment" receive substantial individual attention from "extremely supportive" and "incredible" professors. Small classes are the norm, and "at Bard, teaching assistants are regarded much like incest: just plain wrong."

The Insider's Guide to the Colleges, another popular college guide, edited by the staff of the *Yale Daily News,* reported:

> The Bard experience can be said to exist in inverse proportion to the ordinary college experience: artists constitute a majority of the population, rather than a minority, frats don't exist, and "mainstream" is a dirty word. Famed for its quirkiness, Bard provides its students with the opportunity to indulge in sheer difference.

That paragraph appealed to Jordan. *This is a godsend,* he said to himself. *I didn't know this existed.* He also thought about the huge size of his high school. He had been president of the student body but had found that leading thousands of teenagers was so unwieldy a process that he had been unable to accomplish much. Bard, in bucolic Annandale-on-Hudson in upstate New York, had only 1159 students—nearly 3000 fewer than Tottenville. For the third time in as many months, Jordan had fallen in love with another college.

But love can be fickle. Later that same day, he read about Sarah Lawrence, in Westchester County, New York, and thought that it sounded like "a better version of Bard," until he learned that it was only 25 percent male. "I like hanging around with guys," he would say later. "When guys are in the minority, the atmosphere of the school changes." The biggest activity at Sarah Lawrence, Jordan surmised, "is teatime."

But only moments after dismissing Sarah Lawrence, he found himself intrigued by another former women's college that also had more women (60 percent) than men (40 percent): Vassar. As he read about Vassar in the guidebooks that day, Jordan remembered having seen a brochure in the mail that had shown its campus in all its Hudson River splendor. The brochure had also made a point of emphasizing "how competitive Vassar is"—or at least that's how Jordan remembered it—and he liked to think of himself as competitive. He also recalled the brochure's indicating that the school was actively recruiting males. *It's a competitive world,* Jordan thought to himself. *If this is one of the top schools, and being a guy can help you out, you do what you gotta do.*

Jordan left the bookstore that afternoon more confused than ever about where he wanted to go to college, and why. But the counselor had succeeded in getting him to entertain an idea that had been foreign to him: maybe there was life beyond the Ivy League. That concept was like a new shirt that Jordan would try on and then take off, again and again, over the next year.

As he embarked on his college search, Jordan heard two competing voices whispering in his ear. One belonged to his father, who thought the counselor was right—Jordan should look beyond the Ivies. But Bill Goldman believed his son would do better to focus on state schools. "Education is education," he told him. "You work hard and you'll get the same out of any school, regardless of the name. Plus, going to a state school will be cheaper." Once Jordan had graduated, he could work his way up to the level of those who went to prestigious colleges, just as his dad had. Having dropped out of Queens College before graduating, Bill had gone on to start an employment agency. Jordan didn't have too clear an idea of what his father did, but he did know that he drove a BMW and lived in an eight-bedroom house near Fort Lauderdale.

But in his other ear, Jordan heard the voice of his uncle Jay, his mother's brother. Like Melanie, Jay had gone to Rutgers. He had contemplated transferring to Amherst in his sophomore year, but ultimately chose not to because his family couldn't afford it. He had become a successful venture capitalist, but only through sheer pluck, and had always wondered whether graduating from a top-shelf college might have eased his path. "I think he felt that coming from Rutgers, there was a bit of prejudice against him," Jordan said. "Maybe not prejudice, but that he had to show these people who he was." Jay, whom Jordan respected as a role model, had a firm sense of how the world worked: the old-boy network was alive and well; connections still got you jobs, and the bonds between people who had graduated from the same colleges, years apart, remained strong. That would hold true, he was certain, even for an aspiring writer. Jay advised his nephew that he could afford to broaden his search beyond the Ivy League—but not by much. "When I said Vassar, Sarah Lawrence and Bard, my uncle said, 'Go higher,'" Jordan recalled. "He felt Amherst, Williams, Wesleyan, Swarthmore, Haverford, Middlebury—that's where I should apply."

As the summer between his junior and senior years approached, Jordan would often parrot his dad's philosophy, announcing to whoever would listen, "I don't care about the status of the school I go to, as long as there's good conversation and people I can learn from, and as long as I'm happy." But he soon realized he was deluding himself. "I craved the validation," he recalled. "The best and the brightest are going to these Ivy"— he caught himself—"I mean *good* colleges. You want to be amongst the best and the brightest."

Jordan reasoned that if a college had an international reputation for excellence, the best professors would be attracted there, and good students would inevitably follow. But he had another reason for pursuing a "name" college. Sixty-eight students were ranked above him in his high school class—almost two classrooms full of kids who, at least on paper, were considered smarter than he. The top twenty would even be feted at a dinner during senior year. Jordan already knew in his junior year that he wouldn't be invited. A 93 average just wouldn't cut it. He felt certain that many of the members of the top twenty looked down on him, and he could almost hear them snickering when he made a point in English class, particularly when he played devil's advocate—disagreeing, for example, with a teacher's analysis of *Tess of the d'Urbervilles,* the novel they were then reading. "I had no doubt I was every bit as good as they were," Jordan said. "But I couldn't prove it." Unless, that is, he could get into a school whose reputation no one would question.

Intent on finding his new "name," Jordan and Melanie hit the road for a series of college visits in the late summer and early fall of 1999. Their itinerary had been cobbled together from the disparate recommendations of his uncle, his father and his guidance counselor.

Their first stop was Amherst, the school in western Massachusetts that his uncle had longed to attend. Jordan's first impression was good: the town of Amherst itself seemed New England–postcard perfect. And he

liked the idea that despite its size—about sixteen hundred undergraduates—
Amherst drew on the resources of four other neighboring colleges.

But anyone who's ever seen a college in a two-hour drive-by visit
knows that the smallest of details, however trivial, can take on outsized
importance. Jordan, for example, soured on Amherst when an admissions
officer told him that the college discouraged interviews, because of the additional staff that would be required. *Don't they even want to get to know
me?* Jordan wondered. He also grew frustrated with the student tour
guide, who would not answer the most basic questions about what his
own SAT scores had been or where else he had applied, when Jordan had
simply wanted to get a sense of the profile of the typical Amherst student.

By the time the visit ended, Jordan decided that he'd probably still
apply to Amherst—he did respect his uncle's opinion—but he wasn't
"jumping off the bridge enthusiastic."

Days later, as the Goldmans pulled into Providence en route to the
Brown University campus, he would have no such reservations. Seeing
Brown firsthand would only serve to confirm what he had already decided
in advance: this was a school that had been built for him. He had read in
the guidebooks that there were no required courses, and even though he
had gotten A's in subjects like math and chemistry, he was intent on fo-
cusing on the humanities. "Brown's innovative," Jordan told Melanie as
they approached the campus. "It's got a name that just oozes prestige.
You say 'Brown' to someone, and they just say, 'Wow!'"

Brown would have no trouble passing The Bumper Sticker Test.

With the enthusiasm of a tour guide, Jordan told his mother that the
student body of six thousand was "not too big, not too small." Brown
also had a creative writing major. As the sun beat down on the campus, he
wondered if he had ever seen any place as beautiful. College Street, which
connected Providence to the campus, was lined with brick-and-wooden
clapboard homes that had been built in the eighteenth century and street-
lights that had once been powered by gas. On the campus itself were a
Greek-style temple that housed a chapel and classrooms; dormitories built
of red sandstone; and a main green swarming with students and dogs. "I
know that shouldn't play a factor," Jordan said of the campus's physical
allure, "but it does."

A few days later, Jordan drove with Melanie and her parents to Bard,
about 120 miles north of New York City. But the magic conveyed by the
guidebooks just wasn't there, particularly after Brown. "The campus was

ugly," Jordan said afterward. "It was very spread out. It was kind of falling apart in some places. The grass was brown. The kids, a lot of them had crazy dreadlock hair. They'd dye their hair purple. They'd have twenty-three rings on each finger." Uncle Jay had been right about Bard, he decided. Vassar, twenty-four miles farther south, in Poughkeepsie, didn't fare much better. Jordan found the Tudor buildings and the "trees everywhere" appealing, but he "hated" the information session. Among his concerns was that he would have to take two years of foreign lan guage, despite having already taken Latin, French, and Spanish in high school.

Melanie had allotted one final day for the college fact-finding trip and in preparation had printed out two sets of directions from Poughkeepsie to Connecticut. One route would take them to New Haven, to see Yale; the other would lead them to Middletown, and Wesleyan. There wasn't enough time to visit both.

As they headed east on Interstate 84, Jordan had yet to decide which school would be their destination. Sitting in the backseat as his grandfather drove, he decided to let Edward B. Fiske make the call. Opening a two-year-old copy of *The Fiske Guide to Colleges* that his mother had borrowed from a friend, he first turned to the entry for Yale. The SAT range for most of those the school accepted was 620 to 710 verbal, and 680 to 760 math, heartening Jordan, whose scores fell solidly in the middle. But then he read that "students are required to take three classes of their choosing in each of four broad areas: language and literature; humanities (other than literature); social sciences; and natural sciences and math."

Wesleyan, in contrast, encouraged its students to take classes outside their majors, but did not require them. Jordan also read:

> Wesleyan students are marked by an unusual commitment to debate, from political to cultural to intellectual. "Any and every issue is important here. Students are constantly organizing and rallying. This is a very active political and social place," volunteers a senior. Consistent in their praise of the school's academic philosophy of independent study, Wesleyan students take their work very seriously.

Jordan decided he didn't need to read any further. Wesleyan had a "name" that would satisfy his uncle—it was Jay, along with a friend of Melanie's, who had suggested they visit Wesleyan—and the school was flexible enough to allow a student to do what he wanted to pursue his education. Jordan directed his driver to bypass New Haven for Middletown.

He had had nothing but good feelings about Wesleyan until he was sent reeling by Ralph's refusal to consider his short stories. That colored the rest of the visit, preoccupying Jordan as he toured the campus—in the rain, no less.

But afterward, as he curled up in the backseat of the car on the drive home, Jordan started to regain his composure. His thoughts first turned to Brown. The admissions officers there had indicated their willingness to read his short stories, and Jordan would take them at their word. Brown was his first choice, and he decided that he would apply early, with full confidence that he would be accepted.

Despite Ralph's intransigence, Jordan had to admit to himself that he had enjoyed the rest of his visit to Wesleyan. He agreed with his mother that the view from the top of Foss Hill to the Connecticut River was spectacular. He also had to agree with his grandmother that the admissions staff couldn't have been more courteous, plying her with bottles of water bearing a special Wesleyan label. And unlike at Amherst, the tour guide had happily divulged his SAT scores and the names of the other schools to which he had applied, with candor that Jordan appreciated.

But all these considerations about whether to apply to Wesleyan or Amherst or Vassar would likely be moot, Jordan thought. There was no need to sort out his backups now, for in all likelihood he'd be heading to Providence in a year, a proud member of the Brown Class of 2004. With his college tour now officially over, Jordan Goldman fell soundly and peacefully asleep.

Four
CONSIDERED WITHOUT PREJUDICE

On the first Tuesday of December, eight admissions officers were seated around the long cherry table, considering the case of a seventeen-year-old senior from a private school in northern California. She had more A's than B's, but she hadn't taken the toughest math and science courses that her school offered. Her combined SAT score of 1290—630 verbal, 660 math—was impressive, but it was about 50 points below the median of those other seniors from around the country who had applied thus far for the Wesleyan Class of 2004. While that was clearly a liability, of more concern was the fact that she appeared to be the kind of teenager who would become involved in a lot of extracurricular activities only to drop them soon after. She had worked with AIDS patients, repaired local hiking trails and volunteered as a government intern—each for no longer than a year.

But the girl could sing.

A Wesleyan music professor had reviewed a tape she had sent along with her application and rated it a 9—the highest score possible.

"Ralph," someone asked, "how many 9's are we going to see for vocal?"

"My sense," answered Ralph, who was responsible for tracking those applicants who specialized in the arts, "is that as a vocalist, a 9 is going to be pretty rare."

Like a judge addressing a jury, Greg Pyke sought to frame the case before the committee.

"The academic stuff seems marginally OK," he said. "The question is, does a high rating in music, which takes a lot of time to develop, offset what is obviously a thin academic record?"

Yes, answered Ralph, who had been the second reader of the girl's application. He assured the committee that for this applicant, singing "isn't just a hobby."

Rod Bugarin, who had read the girl's application before Ralph, disagreed. "This is a candidate who might sing all day long and not get involved in anything else."

"Just singing?" someone else in the room said, as if standing up from the gallery. "That's not a problem. That kind of talent could affect so many different areas—theater, ensembles. The fact that she's focused on one thing, I like that."

"OK," Greg announced. "She's had her moment in court."

Clearing his throat, Greg asked his colleagues a one-word question: "Admit?"

Four admissions officers, including Ralph, raised their hands.

"Defer?" Greg asked.

Three other hands were raised.

"Reject?"

One last hand went up.

It took five votes to be admitted to Wesleyan, and this candidate had come up one short. But it also took five votes to be rejected. The committee was not yet ready to make a decision, and the girl's case would be tabled for several months. The committee would wait to see the other applicants to Wesleyan that year, to better assess how this candidate measured up. Within a week, she would receive a letter informing her that the college she had identified as her first choice had neither accepted nor rejected her. Wesleyan, she would be told, needed more time. And in the interim, she was of course free to apply to college elsewhere.

So it went on the first day of deliberations on many of the 356 teenagers who had sought early acceptance into the Wesleyan Class of 2004. Each had agreed to be considered under a binding set of rules—if accepted to Wesleyan in December 1999, two weeks before regular applications were even due, they would promise to withdraw all other applications and attend Wesleyan.

For the applicants, early decision represented a chance to short-circuit the anxiety of the college admissions process six months before the end of their senior year. While they couldn't stop attending classes if accepted—Wesleyan would still check their final senior grades—they could certainly sleep better. Each year, as it became harder to get into a top college, more seniors were seeking to go the early route. Some set their sights on schools like Wesleyan, which, like Stanford, Yale and most other elite colleges, compelled those who were accepted early to enroll. (Though the university would take no legal action against someone who got cold feet and sought to withdraw, it would inform several dozen of its competitors that the student had been accepted.) That put a lot of pressure on a seventeen-year-old, and there was growing concern among both guidance counselors and parents that so many students were making premature decisions that they might regret later. (For those who wanted more flexibility, a handful of other colleges, like Harvard and MIT, permitted those students who were accepted early to still put in applications elsewhere.)

Wesleyan had been offering students the early-acceptance option since the 1960s. For the admissions officers, there was little to lose, for it gave them the opportunity to get an advance look at some of the best students who would be applying to college that year. Those who applied early were often a self-selecting group—their test scores, for example, were usually higher than those in the regular pool. Not only could the university start building a top-flight class early by locking in some of its top choices, but it could also get a head start building its case before those pesky editors at *U.S. News.* Among the statistics that *U.S. News* measured was "yield," the percentage of applicants accepted by a college who then agreed to attend. Since anyone who got into Wesleyan early had committed to enroll, accepting students by this plan was a surefire way to improve the college's yield. Little wonder that under the deanship of Barbara-Jan Wilson, who was so sensitive to how Wesleyan measured up to other colleges, the percentage of the freshman class accepted early rose to more than 40 percent, up from 25 percent just a few years earlier. At the beginning of the new century, the chances of getting into Wesleyan, and into other colleges, early were far better than they were in the main round.

But in admitting so many students early, Wesleyan was also taking a risk. The more seats in the class that it locked up in December, the fewer seats would be available to students who applied in the main round. And the students in the main round, like those applying early, were getting better every year. The more applicants Wesleyan rejected in April, the more impressed the editors at *U.S. News* would be. But at what price?

For the admissions officers at Wesleyan in the fall of 1999—a third of whom had never participated in an admissions decision here or elsewhere—the two days of early-decision hearings were a lot like spring training for a major league baseball team. Here was their chance to take the field, but with the stakes relatively low. (Indeed, the hearings had proceeded even though one of the new officers, Bozoma Arthur, was away overseas, at the funeral of a friend.)

The most wrenching decision for any admissions officer is always whether to reject someone, and that was rarely an issue at this point in time: an applicant had to be considered unsalvageable to be rejected early. The toughest calls, like that involving the singer from California, were put off to another day, when the profile of the entire applicant pool became clear.

Rookie and veteran admissions officers alike valued these hearings mostly as an annual opportunity to pit the institution's various priorities against one another, and see which prevailed. Did a 9 in singing cancel out an applicant's failure to take calculus? What was being the child of an alumnus worth? How much stock should be put in a teacher's recommendation?

The hearings were also a chance to start keeping score. Before the committee had even cast a vote, Greg, as acting dean, had already admitted 105 of the 356 students who had applied early to the Class of 2004. Their applications had been read by at least two other admissions officers, and the case for acceptance had been considered so clear-cut that Greg merely rubber-stamped it. There was no need to consult the committee. Nearly a month before regular applications were even due, 1 out of 7 seats in the following year's freshman class had already been reserved.

Greg had come to the meeting armed with two full pages of statistics about the new class so far. The median SAT score of those admitted was 1370—690 verbal, 680 math—identical to that for the previous year's class. That was good; Wesleyan didn't want to lose any ground. Of those accepted so far, 85 percent ranked in the top 10 percent of their high school class. That figure was running about 15 percentage points higher than the previous year's. And that, too, was a number to which the guidebooks—and alumni—paid attention. While Wesleyan was already receiving applications from some of the highest-performing teenagers in the country, the only statistic that Greg asked the admissions officers to pay some heed to was one of gender. Sixty percent of those who had applied early were women. There was no particular reason why, as far as anyone could tell, but the administration hoped that the class would eventually be split evenly. Greg told the officers not to concern themselves too greatly with the early disparity, which would surely work itself out in the main round.

The three newcomers in attendance that morning—Rod Bugarin, Amin Abdul-Malik and Lyllah Martin—could take heart from the fact that there was someone at the table even greener than they were, at least when it came to knowing things as basic as where the rest rooms were. Just moments before they took their first vote, the staff members were introduced to a forty-six-year-old woman with short-cropped, reddish hair, a warm smile and fashionably tiny wire-rimmed glasses. Her name was Nancy Hargrave Meislahn, and she was their new dean.

For the previous two decades, Nancy had worked as an admissions officer at Cornell, most recently as its director of undergraduate admissions. At Cornell, an Ivy League institution that had more undergraduates than Wesleyan, Nancy had been the second-in-command in the admissions organization. At Wesleyan, she would report directly to the president, who had selected her. She told her new staff that she wouldn't be casting any votes on her first day but said that in the main round, she and Greg would divide the work of resolving each student's case, after it had been considered by at least two officers. That meant that just a few weeks after leaving Cornell, her alma mater, Nancy would be making the final decision on whether several thousand students would be accepted or rejected at Wesleyan. No one in the room was especially alarmed, though, because leaving one admissions office for another in midseason was a lot like being traded from one professional basketball team to another: the faces might be different, but most of the diagrams in the playbook were the same.

Though Cornell relied heavily on professors—as well as lay admissions officers—to give its applications a read, the criteria for consideration at Wesleyan and Cornell were essentially the same, as they were at any other top college. Nancy immediately felt at home in her new job, and if Greg Pyke felt any disappointment at being passed over for the position, he didn't show it. If anything, as he sat at the head of the table in an open-necked white oxford and argyle vest, he looked relieved.

After the officers went around the table and introduced themselves to their new boss, Nancy turned to Greg, who was sitting to her immediate right, and said: "I'm really intrigued to get down to business." And so they did. Over the course of two days, the admissions officers were told, they would consider 97 of the 356 students who had applied early. The 105 students whom Greg had already admitted were off the table as were 135 others whom he had decided, based on the comments of two readers, to defer until another round of early-decision committee hearings, which would be held in February. An additional 19 students had either been rejected or been informed that their applications were incomplete. The remaining 97—almost a third of those who applied early—were considered enough of a toss-up to be sent to the committee for a ruling.

There is wide variation among colleges over how much to rely on committees to make admissions decisions. Some schools, like Dartmouth or Stanford, make few decisions in the committee of the whole, because they fear that cliques among the admissions officers could cloud the respective merits of the actual students. Harvard, by contrast, makes almost all of its decisions by consulting at least a subcommittee of the whole, having long believed that such decisions were too important to be entrusted to two or three people. In the fall of 1999, Wesleyan, like most colleges, fell somewhere in the middle—convening the committee in only those cases where it felt that the collective expertise of the staff would be a benefit. Wesleyan was committed to giving every applicant a chance to shine. And sometimes, what initially appeared cloudy to two or three people became clearer in the presence of others.

Because there was not enough time for all the officers to review an application before the committee met, Greg began each case with a summary. He first directed the officers to scan the candidate's entry in the docket, a bound, confidential document that contained basic information on everyone who had applied to Wesleyan thus far. Each officer had been given a copy and each was instructed not to remove that copy from the admissions office, for the data it contained, about both individual students and the applicant pool as a whole, was considered far too sensitive for Wesleyan to risk its falling into the wrong hands. At this early date, the docket was sixty-eight pages long. By April, it would grow to well over a thousand pages. In the interest of fairness, the docket was organized alphabetically, first by state, and then by high school. The applicants from each high school were then listed alphabetically.

Under the name of each student were four or five lines of abbreviations and numbers. Those lines comprised the barest statistical rendering of a high school senior, almost like a police sketch of a suspect. But when viewed as a whole, these data suggested something much greater: a strong hint of what Wesleyan considered important in an applicant. Prominently listed in the upper-right corner, for example, were the applicant's best scores on the verbal and math sections of the main SAT exam, known as the SAT I, as well as on three SAT II exams of the applicant's choosing. The main SAT exam was designed to measure problem-solving skills and vocabulary, while the latter sought to assess students' achievement in subjects like writing and mathematics. When taken together, Wesleyan believed, those scores provided an indication of a student's potential and what he or she had accomplished academically. No one looking at the docket entry could miss seeing an applicant's standardized test scores, though how those numbers were interpreted varied greatly, depending on the applicant and the admissions officer.

Below the test scores, an applicant's class rank was noted, if available, as well as the size of his or her high school graduating class. Beneath that was the student's race or ethnicity (if the student had checked a box). The entry also noted whether a student had been a captain of a varsity sport (coded as "CAPT") or editor in chief of his newspaper, literary magazine or yearbook (coded as "EDIT"). These were applicants who were considered obvious leaders. There was also a notation of whether the applicant had taken four years of the same foreign language ("LANG") and a year of calculus ("MTHM"), as well as a full sequence of biology, physics and chemistry ("SCIE"). An admissions officer coming to the file cold would consider an absence of any of these codes to be a red flag, absent mitigating circumstances.

On the left-hand side of each entry, under the student's name, were the initials of the two officers who had read the file. Next to each of the officers' initials were three numbers that he or she had assigned—an academic rating, a personal rating and an overall rating, which was supposed to encompass the previous two. This was the part of the process where the admissions officers sought to impose a bit of scientific rigor on themselves. Each rating was on a scale of 1 to 9. An overall rating of 9 from two officers virtually guaranteed admission, but almost no applicant received 9's. An overall rating of 8 was also considered likely for admission, particularly in the early-decision round. But those applicants who had been awarded 6's and 7's were considered on the bubble, and most of them went before the committee; anything lower, and admission was unlikely. Almost every other college had a similar ranking system, varying only in the scale—some rated students 1 to 5, others 1 to 7—and in the categories assessed.

The officers at Wesleyan, like those at other colleges, were provided with customized guidelines on how to assign those numbers. An 8 or 9 in the personal category, according to the cheat sheet that the officers consulted, was described as someone who was sure to "have significant impact on campus in leadership roles." A 7 or 6, by contrast, would be assigned to someone who was "likely to be a leader in some areas, contributor to many." In addition to taking into account extracurricular involvement—which also got its own separate rating—the personal rating was intended to reflect such factors as whether an applicant had triumphed over extreme hardship.

Like the personal rating, the academic rating was a rough average of numbers assigned in several component categories. One number that was factored into the overall academic rating was intended to act as a summary of the student's standardized test scores: for example, it usually took a combined score of at least 1400 on the SAT for an applicant to get an 8 or better in the overall academic category, and any applicant with less than an 8 in the academic category would likely be sent before the committee for debate. But also folded into that overall academic rating were such amorphous categories as "intellectual curiosity." This, too, was judged on a scale of 1 to 9. Someone who had demonstrated a "sophisticated grasp of world events and technical information," as well as a "passionate interest in numerous disciplines" would likely receive an 8 or 9. Someone who had shown merely "strong interest and activity" in "research, independent projects, competitions, etc." would probably draw a 6 or 7.

For all the appearance of scientific rigor, such ratings were obviously and unabashedly subjective. Often, one officer might assign a rating of 8, where another would see a 6. As a result, the admissions officers were instructed to take the ratings with a grain of salt, and to consider them as only one of the many factors that they were to include in mixing a class. These numbers were intended to serve as guidelines as they made their decisions, not cutoffs.

Like fortune-tellers, the admissions officers were engaged in a task that was, in fact, anything but scientific. They were attempting to predict nothing less than how a high school senior might fare at an institution as academically rigorous as Wesleyan, to say nothing of his or her potential in the world at large. The officers were also trying to foretell what the same applicant might contribute to Wesleyan and, after graduating, to a much larger community. Those answers rarely lay in numbers.

And so, before any applicant was discussed, Greg wanted the officers to have more information than the statistics printed on the docket. After they had finished scanning the docket entry, he would read aloud to them from the extensive notes that had been scribbled on the file by each of the two admissions officers who had read it. In their notes, for example, the readers logged every year-end grade in every major subject that the student had taken in the first three years of high school, a list that was then shared with the committee, in rapid-fire succession. To Wesleyan, grades mattered. For an outsider, it would take a while to crack what sounded like a secret wartime code. For example, the officers would hear Greg say something like: "2B, 2A, followed by 3B, 1A, then 3B, 2A and, at the quarter, 3B, 2A." That meant the student had gotten two B's and two A's in the freshman year, followed by various combinations of A's and B's in the two years thereafter, leading up to the first quarter of the senior year. If there had been any C's or D's, Greg would have mentioned the particular courses. Earlier Greg would have recited two other sets of numbers, such as: "4–4–4–3 and 0–0–1–3." The first set signified the number of courses that the student took in each of four years of high school in the so-called solid, or major, subjects: English, math, science, social studies or foreign language. A "4–4–4–3" signified that a particular student had taken four "solids" every year until senior year, when he took three. (The Wesleyan officers preferred to see five every year, and any number below that would detract.) The second set of numbers signified how many courses in each of those years had been an honors or Advanced Placement course. Greg would then read off the actual Advanced Placement course titles that the student had taken. Again, the message was clear: grades mattered, but so did the quality of the courses in which they were earned. Straight A's in light courses would be considered a liability, but B's in Advanced Placement courses, particularly in math and the sciences, were probably OK. Greg would usually dispense this information so quickly that one of the officers would invariably ask to have him read back the transcript.

But the assessments weren't conducted entirely in code. In their notes, for example, the admissions officers also wrote a précis in which they sought to distill the main points of a student's essay and indicate whether they considered it exceptional. The officers' notes also summarized the recommendations of the student's teachers and guidance counselor (yes, what a teacher writes about an applicant is sometimes bracingly frank, and those impressions do count) as well as the impressions of the Wesleyan senior or alumnus who may have interviewed the student, on campus or off. An interview wasn't considered critical, and the admissions officers often didn't have the time to conduct them themselves.

In the end, every piece of information that was gathered was taken into account, and only after the committee had been presented all of the relevant material would the discussion be opened to the floor. For the admissions officers, the excruciating challenge was attempting to synthesize this data in just a few minutes, and then determine the final balance of strengths and weaknesses.

Sometimes, the committee did its job with amazing alacrity.

One of the earliest applicants under consideration was quickly dubbed "Kinko Boy" by one of the committee members. Often, dark humor was the only way to cut through the stress of passing judgment on so many promising young lives, and this was a case that cried out for some levity. Nothing about the applicant stood out. He was ranked in the middle of his class at a public high school in California, with scores on the main SAT exam that were ordinarily low for Wesleyan—in the low 1300s. But in his essay, he had written of "an obsession with melding photocopying and art." Hence, the nickname. Not surprisingly, the essay had struck a chord with Chris Lanser, the admissions committee member who had been both a state humane officer and a high school teacher, who had described it as "bizarre, fast-paced and good." Rod Bugarin, the newcomer from Hawaii, who had read the piece next, seemed less impressed and decided it was "quirky." There was also some confusion between the readers over whether the applicant worked at Kinko's, or just hung out there until three in the morning. In the end, it was moot.

When the vote was called, two hands went up supporting admission, none were raised for deferral, and six supported rejection. Kinko Boy would be among the few banished from Wesleyan's front gate so early in the process.

After lunch on the first day, the committee was briefed on the application of a senior at a public school who had straight B's with the exception of a single C. The applicant's score on the math portion of the SAT was in the high 600's—barely above the median in the Class of 2004 so far. But the verbal score—in the mid 600's—was below the median. The student had played on several sports teams but there was no indication in the file that Wesleyan's coaches had shown any interest. That was the sort of information that Barbara-Jan, the former dean, had sought to ensure that the committee would know at this point. If it wasn't included, the coaches probably didn't have the applicant on their radar, perhaps because the student was no longer interested in playing at a competitive level. As Greg read from the docket, the applicant's chances for early admission appeared to be fading.

But then Greg noted that the student was a child of a Wesleyan graduate, who had also been a university employee. A sibling had attended as well. "With the B's and no C's this year," Greg said, "he's pretty clearly an admit." The officers did not even raise their hands to vote, so inevitable was the outcome. Their preference was recorded as unanimous.

The officers knew that Wesleyan, like other colleges, was expected to be a bit more generous with the children of its older alumni, whom it referred to as "legacies." The same went for the siblings of its younger alumni and the children of others who had served the college with distinction. This applicant could be counted in all three categories. In the previous year's class, the acceptance rate among those with at least one "Wesleyan relative" was 45 percent, as compared to an acceptance rate of only 27 percent for the class as a whole. At least statistically, a legacy was nearly twice as likely to be admitted as someone with no prior connection to Wesleyan. Indeed, "Wesleyan relatives" made up 11 percent of the previous year's class. An institution like Wesleyan sometimes regarded such decisions as unofficial payback for past donations to the alumni fund or as a marker for future contributions. Barbara-Jan had always believed that the practice had another benefit: Wesleyan had been so diverse for so long that tapping its alumni body almost inevitably guaranteed the continuing diversity of the class. That might sound like a rationalization, but like lawyers and journalists, admissions officers were very good at tailoring evidence to fit a particular argument.

Consider what happened when the committee, after admitting the child of the Wesleyan graduate, took up its next case: a student at the same public school. This applicant's combined SAT score, also in the 1300's, was only 20 points lower than that of her connected classmate. But this applicant had the better grades: as many A's as B's on her transcript. As a result, this candidate had a higher grade point average than the legacy student—and was also taking Advanced Placement courses in biology and physics.

Wesleyan usually went to great lengths to ensure that it was consistent in how it treated the applicants from the same school. That was one of the reasons the docket was organized by high school. In that context alone, this candidate seemed to be a certain acceptance. Like her connected classmate, she had received an academic rating of 7 from the first admissions officer who read her file and a 6 from the second. (Both 7 and 6 were defined on the officers' cheat sheets as "excellent academic record in demanding curriculum.") But the committee could be hard to read, particularly so early in the process.

Terri Overton, the admissions officer who had come to Wesleyan via the Peace Corps, had been one of the committee members who had read the file and had written of the candidate's extracurricular activities, "Only horseback riding"—in which the candidate had won awards—"distinguishes." In most cases, an admissions officer would like to see a candidate stand out in at least two extracurricular activities, ideally two very different activities. Moreover, Terri had written: "All rec's mention how shy she used to be—still came across that way in interview." That observation was read aloud to the committee and probably didn't help the candidate's chances, for Wesleyan was generally acknowledged to be a community of extroverts. (The shyness had probably pulled down the candidate's "personal" rating, which Terri had scored as just a 5; in contrast, she had awarded the more connected classmate a 7.)

The committee members grew even more concerned when Rod, who also read the file, told them that he feared that the candidate's "grades were slipping." While she had an average on the border between A and A minus, she had earned only one A as a junior, compared to three as a freshman.

"Vote your conscience," Greg instructed the committee, as he cut off the discussion.

As in the case of the singer from California, the committee voted to defer a decision on the shy girl until the next round of early decision, in February. (At that time, she would be rejected.)

In this instance, the committee was passing over one applicant after accepting a classmate from the same school, even though the accepted student had poorer grades. That would appear to be unfair, a judgment with which the university's president, Douglas Bennet, wouldn't necessarily disagree. But he had a ready retort to such observations: "It's a mistake to hold out that total fairness is the only objective." Instead, admissions was a process in which the objective criteria were always changing, depending on the particular candidate and the institution's specific need at that moment. In these two cases, the committee's stated goal of being consistent within the same high school was outweighed, at least in part, by other concerns: the sliding grades and limited extracurricular interests of one applicant, and the risk of alienating the family of another. Such calculations would become even more complicated when the objective of diversity was introduced into the mix. But that would come later in the process, after trade-offs like these—which came relatively easily—had been made and after the class had taken better shape.

Nonetheless, when diversity or an alumni connection wasn't a factor, the committee actually appeared to be following certain basic parameters. It turned out that Jordan Goldman—the Staten Island striver who was applying early to Brown, not Wesleyan—was right to be concerned about a relatively low class rank. An applicant's standing in his class was discussed a great deal in the early-decision round at Wesleyan, as it was at other colleges. How one scored relative to the rest of the field in high school was regarded as one indicator of how one might perform relative to the field at Wesleyan.

For example, a candidate for Wesleyan's Class of 2004 from a public high school in an affluent Connecticut community had received noteworthy praise from her English teacher, who wrote: "Reading Emerson and Thoreau genuinely thrilled her." That sounded good when juxtaposed with a combined SAT score over 1400 and an A-minus average. But apparently A's at this school were relatively easy to come by, because the candidate was ranked below 25 percent of her class. She also had one C, and one of the officers asked what course it had been in. The readers couldn't remember for certain, but one said: "I think it was math." It was hard to tell from the officers' expressions whether they considered the low grade excusable, but in the end, it didn't matter. "She has a strong program," someone remarked, meaning the candidate had taken a lot of hard courses. "But I think if we start letting in kids in the top 25 percent, what are we telling them?"

Only one hand was raised to admit. Seven voted to defer her to another round.

But just when it appeared that the committee, like a court, was setting down a series of rulings that drew a bright line under a class rank in the top 10 percent, the criteria changed, if only temporarily. The candidate in question, a student from Illinois, had as many B's as he had A's, and his performance had cost him: 16 percent of his class—more than a hundred students in a class of more than seven hundred—had a higher grade point average than he did. "The issue here is rank," someone asserted, but Chris, who had read the application, was convinced another factor should take precedence. "He loves physics," Chris said, quoting from a teacher's recommendation. This was one of those cases Barbara-Jan had instructed her officers to be ever watchful for—the rare applicant who would please the science faculty.

The vote was unanimous, in favor.

In this case, a love of physics and obvious aptitude—the applicant had near-perfect scores on the math portion of the main SAT and on the SAT II physics test—had trumped all else. Here was a candidate who would also help boost the median SAT score of the class, so *U.S. News* might be impressed in the bargain.

The uneven pattern of decisions like these underscored why admissions officers put so little stock in those guidebooks that promised hapless students and their parents a virtually guaranteed formula to getting into the "top college of your choice." Every applicant to Wesleyan was considered by at least three admissions officers, if not the full committee, and all the materials that Wesleyan requested—grades, essays, teacher recommendations—would be read. That much was assured. But there were few other certainties about how the process would play out. Admissions was messy work, done by humans, not machines. Anyone could program a computer to analyze the various facets of thousands of applicants and from them assemble a class. (That's what some of the largest state universities did, usually by necessity.) But computers didn't have intuition. "As with everything in life," President Bennet commented, "gut sense is essential."

During the two days of early-decision hearings on the Class of 2004, almost all of the admissions officers were battling lingering colds that they had picked up on the road. At one point, Terri ordered Ralph, "Get a tissue!" so obvious was his suffering. She sounded like a big sister—one who happened to be seven years older, though nearly a foot shorter, than he. When Ralph ignored her, Terri went and procured a wad of toilet paper for him. During a break, Ralph readily admitted that it was hard to get excited about a candidate when your sinuses were blocked. But the process was what it was: If a candidate got a fairer shake when the committee was healthier—or got a fuller read at the beginning of a long day, than the end—so be it. The clock was ticking, and there was a lot to be accomplished.

California, the biggest piece of his territory, was discussed on the first day of early-decision hearings, as it always was, coming at the beginning of the alphabet. And that meant his friend Sharon's school, Harvard-Westlake, took its turn high in the batting order. Julianna Bentes hadn't applied to Wesleyan early, nor had Becca Jannol. That didn't mean much, Ralph knew. He had yet to give Becca much thought, having met her only in a large group several months earlier, and as for Julianna, he'd cross his fingers that she'd apply to Wesleyan in the main round. But there were three other students from Harvard Westlake under discussion that day. Because the school was part of his territory, he had been designated as the second reader of each file. When Greg announced, "Now begins the saga of Harvard-Westlake"—an obvious rib at Ralph's well-known connection to the school, and its annual bumper crop of good applicants—Ralph sat up a bit straighter.

The first applicant, a boy with a combined 1460 on the SAT, got an early boost when Greg read aloud what Chris, the first reader, had written in his notes: "He's a great guy with vision and energy who will add." That was a quality the officers were always looking for—someone who would "add" something to Wesleyan. At seventeen, the boy had already invented a device that would help ophthalmologists measure the dilation of a pupil. His essay, as summarized by Chris, was about "his growing conflict with his dad over higher education, resisting his father's push to Ivy League." The father, according to the son's essay, referred to Wesleyan as "second tier," and several of the officers smiled at the candidate's defiance. If the son got into Wesleyan early, he would have to go; that would show the father.

Ralph had acknowledged in his notes, which were also read to the committee, that the boy's course load was light. He hadn't taken physics, which seemed an odd omission if he was inventing sophisticated medical devices. But he had taken five Advanced Placement courses, one of which was in environmental science. "I still have trouble trying to figure out what to make of environmental science," Greg said. That kind of remark, however casually tossed off, was sometimes all that was required to jettison a candidate to the deferral pile. But just then, Ralph introduced a fresh piece of evidence from the applicant's portfolio: the boy played guitar in a Simon-and-Garfunkel-style duo that was good enough to have already been booked at a popular Los Angeles club called the Roxy. Chris, who had grown up on Bleecker Street in Greenwich Village in New York City, underscored Ralph's comment by adding: "He's pretty cool." Chris had, of course, only met the applicant on paper.

At this point, Greg interrupted to summarize the case: "He's a musician. He's an inventor. He's got a couple of C's in the freshman year." What was the committee's pleasure?

After Greg called the vote, six hands were raised to admit. Two hands rose to defer.

"He's in the class," Greg announced.

Ralph allowed his poker face to break into a small smile. The Class of 2004 at Wesleyan would include at least one graduate of Harvard-Westlake. Not only was Wesleyan glad to have him, but, Ralph knew, Sharon would be pleased, too.

The next case, as it turned out, was the other half of the duo from Harvard-Westlake: the young woman who was the singer in the act, as well as its songwriter. Unlike her partner, this applicant had sent along a tape of her singing to be reviewed by a Wesleyan music professor. He described her as having a "smooth, pleasant, blues-club voice." He had rated her an 8, a near-perfect score. Again, Chris had read her file and had relayed a teacher's description of her as a "gifted and original thinker," as well as "a sensitive and imaginative interpreter of literature." Unlike her partner, she had no C's. And she had earned more A's than B's. Things were looking good.

But like her partner, she, too, had skipped physics, and her combined SAT score, 1310, was a full 150 points below her partner's. Ralph again sensed a deferral in the air. "You can't break up the act," Ralph implored, with a grin, as if Sonny had just been admitted to Wesleyan and the committee was now weighing the case of Cher. When the vote was called, only Ralph voted to admit. Six others voted to defer; one voted to reject.

However painful the suspense might be for the applicant and her partner, the committee didn't feel the need to make a decision on her now. It would take up her case again in February. While she certainly had the option to withdraw her application to Wesleyan and apply elsewhere, the committee felt confident that she had more incentive than most others to stay in the pool. She and her partner had cared enough about keeping their act together that they had apparently coordinated their college applications. Wesleyan had the upper hand.

Late on the following afternoon, the proceedings were concluded, and the committee was adjourned. In two days, the admissions committee had added 46 more students to the Class of 2004, raising the total to 151. Three weeks before regular applications were due, there were only about 550 seats left to be claimed. Over the course of the two days, the median verbal and math SAT scores of the new class had remained at 680 and 685 respectively. The combined score of 1365 was still running about even with that of the previous year's group, which meant that there was some room in the new class to accept some students with SAT scores substantially below the median, without jeopardizing the overall number reported to *U.S. News*, among other watchdogs. As it embarked on the main round, therefore, the committee now had some leeway to take risks, particularly with students of color, who, at least historically, tended to apply mostly in the main round and present scores lower than those of the applicant pool as a whole. More often than not, their families were still so unfamiliar with the college admissions game that they did not have a clear first choice of where to apply in November, and the applicants didn't know what many savvier white applicants did: that the odds of getting into a particular college were higher in the early-decision round than the main round. At this point, there would also continue to be a premium put on boys. So far, the new class was still about 60 percent girls.

The committee had also sent 35 applicants to the pile of applications it would consider again, during the second round of binding early decision, in early February. Those applicants, along with the 135 others whom Greg had decided unilaterally to defer, would be given the option to move themselves to the main round, so that they wouldn't be bound by Wesleyan's decision if accepted. While some would choose that alternative, most would roll the dice and seek to be admitted in February, taking their chances in a far smaller field. In the main round, in which the students were, of course, not bound by Wesleyan's decision, more than 6000 applications would be considered.

As the hearings broke up, the admissions officers knew that with the exception of those two days of hearings in early February, they wouldn't be seeing much of one another over the next three months. In early March, after most of the cases had been decided, they'd reconvene for more than a week as a committee to consider the four hundred or so applications that remained unresolved. The stakes, and emotions, would be a lot higher in that last round of meetings, as the number of available spots in the class dwindled to just a few. But before then, everyone had a lot of reading to do.

* * *

As Ralph and his colleagues at Wesleyan were closing out their early-decision deliberations during that first week of December, so were the admissions officers at Brown.

Jordan Goldman had mailed off his application to Brown in early October—more than a month before the early-action deadline. And ever since, he had been racing home from school to try to beat the mail carrier serving his Staten Island neighborhood. He felt sure he knew what Brown's response would be.

Ralph may have been reluctant to read the short stories that Jordan considered to be the ace in an otherwise mixed hand, but the admissions officers at Brown had expressed genuine interest in his writing when Jordan met them on campus. Accordingly, he had attached a twenty-nine-page single-spaced addendum to his Brown application. It was thicker than the application itself—so thick that Jordan had added a table of contents as a cover page. These, he believed, were four of his best short stories.

One piece, "Runaway Train," concerned a six-year-old boy staring at a Thomas the Tank Engine doll in a toy store window, not realizing that he has become separated from his mother and father. Any parent of a young child would want to race ahead to the ending, and Jordan was banking that there were a few of them among the admissions officers at Brown. After staving off an abduction, the boy is ultimately reunited with his family.

Another story, "Five O'Clock Shadow," was even darker. It told of a man slowly dying in the midst of a ten-day blackout, the clock at his bedside stuck hopelessly on 10:46 and his fingernails growing "as brittle as those thin Ritz crackers he ate when he was still a boy." A third story, "Fertile Grounds," began on an entirely different note:

> I can hear him calling me, but it doesn't matter—I won't go to him until I'm finished. After all, the flowers are helpless. They have no one but me, and if I were to just walk away—if I were to leave them like that, they could *die*. And who would help them if not me? My husband Jim? Surely not. More likely he would leave them to their own means, fragile things, allow them to wither away in the cold until they were nothing more than fodder for any passing crow or hawk or vulture that might fly overhead and take a fancy to them. Surely Jim would let that happen, in his mind-numbing selfishness. After all, nothing matters to him but

his goddamn income taxes and stocks and paychecks and that little whore *Sandra* from work who calls the house five times a day
just to breathe heavily into the mouthpiece, and the arrogant little
bitch thinks she has me fooled when she hangs up as soon as she
realizes it's me that picked up the phone and not *him*.

These were the cadences of a writer whose voice was far more mature
than that of a seventeen-year-old boy, Jordan was sure of that. But the admissions officers at Brown didn't have to take his word for it. Preceding
his packet of stories was the letter of endorsement from Richard Price, as
well as one from Scott Rudin. Jordan had met Rudin, the producer of the
Mel Gibson movie *Ransom* and the remake of the film *Shaft,* through
Price, who had written the films' screenplays. In his letter to the admissions committee, Rudin began by invoking Price: "Richard told me, on
numerous occasions, about 'this boy on Staten Island' whose work excited him greatly. He told me, too, about who Jordan is, and of the traits
in him that are so admirable. Now, I have seen first-hand Jordan's intelligence, his compassion, his wit, and his openness—all qualities vital to the
arsenal of a writer, and all of which he possesses."

As he awaited word from Brown in the late fall of 1999, Jordan became more and more convinced that these testimonials and the quality of
his stories—when combined with an SAT score of 1460—would allay any
admissions officer's concerns about him. Was a class rank of 69 out of
741, and a bit of softness in the sciences, really a problem when two of the
most respected names in Hollywood were willing to vouch for you?

On December 17, a Friday morning, Jordan had completed his
classes by 11:30, thanks to a light senior year schedule. He figured the
mail would already be there when he got home, but on this day, the regular carrier was ill. It was midafternoon before the mail arrived, and Jordan
saw immediately that a letter from Brown was in the stack.

"From the first line of the letter," Jordan recalled, "you could tell the
answer." But he wanted to read every word:

Dear Jordan:

After a careful evaluation of your credentials, the Board of Admission has voted to postpone a final decision on your application.
During the winter months, we will review all previously submitted

materials as well as any additional credentials you may wish to send to us.

By no means should you interpret this deferral as a denial of admission. The majority of Early Action applicants are neither accepted nor rejected, but deferred; and your application remains under very active consideration. We sympathize with the disappointment that you must feel, but you should not be discouraged. This decision means that the Board wishes to have additional time in order to ensure a complete comparison of your application with those of our regular applicant pool. You should know that in the past few years, the admit rate has been nearly the same for early action deferrals as for regular decision applicants.

You should see to it that your school sends to us the Mid-Year School Report by mid-February at the latest and that the College Board reports to us the scores of any senior year test you have taken.

Let me repeat—you will be considered without prejudice in the spring evaluations of the regular applicant group, and you will be notified in April of the Board's final decision. Please do not hesitate to write to me if you have any questions or if I may be of assistance to you.

Sincerely,

Michael Goldberger
Director of Admission

Melanie watched her son's eyes fill with tears as he read the letter silently to himself, all too aware that he would interpret the deferral as a profound setback, rather than as something inconclusive. She had largely stayed out of the family debate over Jordan's future. As summer had given way to fall, Jordan had abandoned the position of his father (attending a "name" college was overrated) for that of his uncle, Jay ("name" schools could make life's road easier).

As he awaited word from Brown, he had narrowed Jay's definition of a "name" school considerably, so that now, only an Ivy would do. Without the imprint of an Ivy League institution, Jordan wondered whether his career as a writer might be over before it started. "It's a matter of your whole future in an envelope," he had told friends and family at the time.

Jordan cried again when, upon arriving at school the following Monday, he learned that one of the top five students at Tottenville High had been admitted to Brown early. "With full scholarship," Jordan said later, making no effort to hide his envy. "She was one of those nose-to-the-books people." He became even more enraged when he heard that the girl had informed Brown that she'd be waiting until spring to let the university know whether she'd enroll. *She* was deferring *them*. Unlike Wesleyan's, Brown's early action was not binding. The girl was going to see where else she got in before making her decision. *That's my spot she's taking up*, Jordan thought, *and by the time she decides what she wants, it may be too late for me.*

Jordan's cocksureness had put him in a bind. It was now the third week of December, and he had not filled out an application to a college other than Brown. Most of those other applications were due by January 1, including those for Johns Hopkins, Vassar and Wesleyan; Amherst's was due by December 31. Each of those schools accepted the common application, which would cut Jordan's workload, but as Brown had its own form he wouldn't be able to simply copy what he had already prepared. Moreover, Sarah Lawrence and the University of Pennsylvania, like Brown, had their own customized applications. While Sarah Lawrence's wasn't due until February 1, the deadline at Penn was the first of January.

As the first deadline approached, Melanie began telling friends that she felt as if she was living with a schizophrenic. "I didn't know who'd wake up in the morning," she said. "There was the confident Jordan. There was the Jordan who needs his mother. There was the Jordan who wanted no part of his parents." He continually assured Melanie and his stepfather, Craig, "I'm handling it. I'm handling it." When he wasn't in school, he shuttered himself in his room, but Melanie and Craig soon realized that he didn't seem to be doing anything other than fretting and staring at all the photos of himself with his celebrity acquaintances. Melanie had edited a few drafts of her son's essays for Brown but had otherwise left him alone. Now she realized she would have to take over the mechanics of the application process.

Having been knocked off his heels by Brown's letter, a frightened Jordan had concluded that Wesleyan and Vassar and Hopkins could no longer be counted on as his safety schools. Now, he worried, he'd be lucky to get into any of them. And if Brown didn't see him as worth committing to early, what were his prospects in the main round at Amherst, the dream school of his uncle Jay? Jordan decided to expand his list to include New York and Boston Universities, as well as Emerson in Boston and George Washington in the nation's capital. These were colleges where an aspiring writer could thrive, according to the guidebooks, but where the bar of admission was unmistakably lower. They might not have names that would satisfy his uncle, but Jordan was genuinely worried that he might not be going to college at all if he wasn't more realistic about his prospects.

Melanie began drawing up detailed to-do lists for him to execute, as the living room in the family's small home soon became piled with stacks of manila envelopes and white sheets of paper filled with the story of her son's life. Jordan's no-give timetable was made even tighter by his insistence that he go ahead with his plans to visit his father in Florida over the winter holidays. After several all-nighters, he had finished almost everything he needed to do before his January 1 due date. But as he flew to Fort Lauderdale, he was still working on his essay for Penn, which he wound up e-mailing to his mother once he arrived.

But as the new year approached, Jordan's spirits began to lift, as he learned to take some comfort in the fact that no other college had yet passed judgment on him. And even Brown had yet to reject him. Maybe Mr. Goldberger, the director of admissions at Brown, was sincere when he wrote that Jordan would be "considered without prejudice" in the main round. He decided that it was premature to start imagining the sticker from a college other than Brown on the back window of his mother's car. For now, Jordan committed to catching up on all his lost sleep and enjoying the remainder of his senior year.

Three thousand miles west of Staten Island, at a small but much more affluent home near Beverly Hills, Becca Jannol was standing guard in front of her family's mailbox that same December day, awaiting word from Georgetown.

Becca had never met Jordan, of course, but she knew the type: there were enough students at Harvard-Westlake who bought into the idea that Ivy League admission was the sole determinant of success in life. Becca's own brother, who had applied to college two years earlier, had been rejected by many of his top choices and had been left with little option but to go to the University of California at Berkeley or Los Angeles. Becca had been deeply affected by how hard her brother and parents had taken that news, however bright it might seem to an outsider, and she had vowed that she would not be as narrow in her perspective—as had her parents.

Nonetheless, Becca figured she had nothing to lose by applying to one college early, and so decided on Georgetown, her primary choice. Sharon Merrow couldn't quite predict Becca's chances there, for few students from Harvard-Westlake had been accepted early to the school during Sharon's tenure. Becca's grades—more A's than B's—and SAT's (a combined 1270) were probably in the ballpark to at least get her a serious consideration at Georgetown, and the Harvard-Westlake name wouldn't hurt. But Sharon had no idea how the straightforward letter that the head of the upper school had written about Becca's fall and redemption would play at a college affiliated with the Catholic Church. Nor was she sure how Georgetown would receive Becca's personal statement, in which she reflected obliquely on the consequences of doing something wrong, followed by something right. Becca would use that essay as the response to the first question in the Georgetown application: "The admissions committee would like to know more about you in your own words. Please submit a brief essay, either autobiographical or creative, which you feel best describes you."

Georgetown, which did not use the common application, also asked applicants in a second essay to "relate your interest in studying at Georgetown to your future goals." Becca's answer began:

> I am a young American woman, and I want to be a politician. I spend more time watching C-SPAN than *Dawson's Creek,* more time musing about the lives of former leaders than the lives of current movie stars, and more time reading *Foreign Affairs* than *Seventeen.*
>
> I am also the most pitiful member of my school's cross-country team. I have clutched this sought-after title for four consecutive years, and I will leave a style of running as a legacy when I graduate. It is called "The Jannol Shuffle," and it consists of barely lifting your feet off the ground for three gruesome miles. For the complete effect, you must contort your face into an expression of agony so that if someone were to freeze the image in a photograph, it would appear as if you were setting a world record.
>
> Some people may see me as shuffling through my life, preparing for a burst of speed at an appropriate moment. Just the same, my generation is allegedly spearheading a crusade into the future;

preparing for a sprint. We have been labeled the leaders of tomorrow, the children of the millennium, and other exhausted epithets since we can remember. But I disavow that we are the future—*I refuse to be the future.* I am not tomorrow or next week or ten years from now, nor will I wake up one morning and realize that the future is upon me and that it is time to start doing something. I have been steadily shuffling along for four years now.

After describing her political accomplishments—starting a Big Brother/ Big Sister program on campus, advising a state legislator on youth issues—Becca concluded: "There is no soapbox waiting to be occupied tomorrow. I don't want to have opinions next week, and express them ten years from now. I have an idealism that accompanies youth, and I believe that one person has the capacity to affect many in a single moment."

But in her attempt to persuade her first-choice college to take an early chance on her, Becca was no more successful than Jordan had been, and her application was deferred.

For Becca, like Jordan, the deferral came as something of a wake-up call. She did not respond by closeting herself in her room for a week in depression, for a college acceptance just wasn't that critical to her self-esteem. But she did realize that she had to spend a little less time listening to her classmates' assurances that the student body president at Harvard-Westlake could write her own ticket to any college she liked. Sharon had tried to warn Becca and the school's other students that no single accomplishment guaranteed anything—nor, for that matter, did multiple accomplishments. Too many students were applying to college from too many other places. Now Becca realized that Sharon was probably right and that she needed to be a bit more strategic in her choices.

Having met Ralph in person, Becca felt confident that her application would get a full and fair reading at Wesleyan, and she was eager to submit an application there. Though she was still in the running at Georgetown, Wesleyan might even emerge as her first choice. She would also apply to the other colleges that she and Sharon and her parents had discussed: the University of Chicago, Washington University in St. Louis and Emory in Atlanta. And she'd reach a bit by seeking admission to Columbia and Barnard. As at Georgetown, she felt she had nothing to lose. Her family wasn't wealthy, but they could swing an extra hundred dollars or so in application fees.

At Sharon's suggestion, she also decided late in the year to add Cornell to her list, though she wasn't particularly swayed by the fact that it was an Ivy. Instead, Cornell was one other college where Sharon felt she knew the admissions staff well enough to predict that it might appreciate how Becca had conducted herself at Harvard-Westlake. Now all Becca could do was wait, and hope.

Like any dictum, Sharon's Law—that there was no magical combination of attributes that assured an applicant acceptance to any college—was bound to have an exception. With her mixed racial background, her perfect SAT verbal score, her near-perfect grade point average, her commitment to dance and her leadership on racial issues, Julianna Bentes appeared destined to prove Sharon wrong. But even Julianna would be rejected at least once in this competitive marketplace, and that rejection would come early.

Harvard-Westlake was one of just a few dozen schools outside of North Carolina that was invited each year to nominate a student for a prestigious Morehead Scholarship. Early in her senior year, the administrators at Harvard-Westlake decided that Julianna would be the school's choice. For a high school senior, winning a Morehead was like winning a Rhodes Scholarship: all four years of college at the University of North Carolina at Chapel Hill would be paid in full, as would four summers that could be spent anywhere in the world. Like the Rhodes committee, the administrators of the Morehead program evaluated nominees on the basis of their academic performance, physical vigor, leadership skills and integrity. The year Julianna applied, 770 seniors from within North Carolina—and only 75 from outside the state—sought a total of 60 scholarships.

In early October, Julianna received word that she had been passed over.

Had she gotten the Morehead, Julianna surely would have gone to Chapel Hill. With her father's income as a mortgage consultant irregular and her mother, Catherine, out of work for prolonged periods as a result of illnesses that had plagued her since childhood, she could have put her family at ease with a free ride. Now they would have to take their chances in the main round. The only question was where she would apply.

Julianna and Catherine had succeeded in whittling their list from fifty-four to sixteen, which was still too many. As December approached,

Julianna managed to lop off three more names. Without the cushion of the Morehead, she saw no reason to apply to the University of North Carolina, and she decided against Tulane and the College of William and Mary because she presumed she could get a better education elsewhere. That left thirteen, but they decided not to make the list any smaller. Their goal was to get Julianna the best education possible for the least amount of money. If it cost more than five hundred dollars in application fees to do so, so be it. The expense would be justified by the range of choices they'd likely have as a result.

Throughout the fall, Julianna had continued to refuse to rank her selections: every college would be on equal footing. On an erasable memo board on the door of the tiny room that Catherine had converted into a cluttered study, Julianna divided her choices into only two categories, along purely practical lines. One listed schools that accepted the Common Application; the other, schools that did not. Among those that accepted the common form, Julianna had included: Harvard (which was her father's preference), Goucher (the liberal arts college outside Baltimore that was floating the prospect of a full dance scholarship), Kenyon, Swarthmore, Washington University in St. Louis, and Wesleyan. Those that had their own customized applications were Yale, Stanford, the University of Chicago, two of the University of California campuses (Berkeley and San Diego), the University of Michigan and the University of Texas at Austin.

Filling out those applications would be a time-consuming process, and as deadlines neared, Julianna, who tended to be a procrastinator under even the best of circumstances, would come to learn which post offices in Los Angeles were open the latest. "If anything," she recalled, "I was too laid back."

Ralph had learned from Sharon that Julianna was Harvard-Westlake's Morehead nominee, and after returning to Middletown from California in September, he had wondered whether she had been selected. If she had, Wesleyan would have surely lost any claim on her. But Ralph decided not to prod Sharon about the girl, for he didn't want to jeopardize his chances. It was always better to say too little than too much. Ralph would only find out about Julianna's loss of the Morehead indirectly, when, to his elation, her application arrived at Wesleyan in early January.

But while Ralph may have been the first potential suitor whom Sharon introduced to Julianna, he was not the only one. At a college fair in the Harvard-Westlake gymnasium one night during the spring of her junior year, Julianna had met André Phillips, an admissions officer who was staffing the booth for the University of Chicago. Like Ralph, André had grown up as a member of a minority group (he was black), in a big city (Chicago's impoverished west side) and in a family that impressed upon him the critical importance of education as the ticket to a better and more rewarding life. Unlike Ralph's, neither of André's parents had gone to college. After graduating from Loyola University in Chicago in 1980, André had initially sought to help those in circumstances similar to his family's, as a community organizer who arranged for poor people in his old neighborhood to get the low-income loans and technical assistance to rent and eventually buy their own homes. But he had been persuaded by a close friend in the admissions field, then working at Chicago, that he would be good at such work and should give it a try, particularly as a recruiter of black and Hispanic talent. André, who was now in his early forties, had worked at Chicago ever since, expanding his portfolio to plot recruitment strategy and serve as a liaison to the athletic department.

As Julianna and her mother shook hands with André in the spring of 1999, Julianna wasted little time on pleasantries. While most students had filled out a form requesting an application and then moved on to the next booth, she had a question for André, and she put it to him bluntly: "I've heard a lot about the University of Chicago. I've heard it's unique, but not what makes it unique. What can you tell me?"

André took a half hour to answer the question, and the Benteses proved to be a rapt audience. At the heart of his answer was how the great books were integral to the Chicago curriculum and had been for some time. If she was accepted at Chicago, and chose to attend, Julianna might read Plato's *Republic* in several different courses—in a social science class, a humanities class, a civilization class—and read it in a different context each time. "This is participatory education," André explained. "Faculty and students truly engage each other, not just on the subject matter but on how one might begin to figure out how to make a difference with one's life."

Julianna asked several follow-up questions that made clear to André that she was intrigued. As the two women walked away, Catherine Bentes turned to her daughter and said, "That sold me." Julianna was also smitten, with André as well as his pitch. But Catherine knew that if her daughter's academic excellence was as rare as everyone had led the family to believe, there would be no shortage of suitors seeking to woo her. And Catherine, at least, was going to make them work to win her.

Once the Benteses were out of range, André picked up the application request that Julianna had left behind, and added a note to himself on it, drawing two asterisks, rating his encounter with her as if he had just watched her performance in a movie. On André's scale, two stars were the highest grade, and he couldn't remember the last time he had awarded them to a potential applicant whom he had only just met. At this point, he knew nothing about her, other than the impression she had made. That she appeared to be black or Hispanic, he said later, did not even register, particularly since she was light-skinned and her mother was obviously white. "She just struck me as the kind of intellectually curious person for whom this approach to learning would not be intimidating," he said. At the conclusion of the evening, he made his way across the gym to find Sharon, so that he might learn more about Julianna Bentes.

On a Monday toward the end of December, as the final deadline for receiving applications approached, Ralph was walking through the back room of the admissions office when he spied a thick envelope with a logo that caught his eye. The envelope, slit open and sitting atop a cart, was from NAPS, the Native American Preparatory School, in Rowe, New Mexico. In the two months since he had visited there, he had heard nothing from either the counselors or the students he had met.

As it happened, Ralph had inadvertently intercepted this envelope before it had been emptied and filed. Reaching inside, he pulled out two applications. One was from Migizi, the boy from Minnesota who had been so impressive with his broad knowledge of film and his own story of perseverance. The other was from a classmate. Ralph had gone out to New Mexico on a somewhat quixotic mission to find one Native American willing to apply to Wesleyan. Now he had found two.

"Cool! Cool! I got two," he sang, as he did a small jig in the records room. "I got two from NAPS!" Several secretaries looked over at him suspiciously; none had the slightest idea what he was raving about.

Ralph had been stern in warning Mig that it would be a challenge to be a trailblazer at Wesleyan, while at the same time assuring him that it would be worth the effort. With his application, Mig had signaled that he was willing to take the risk. On the eve of sending in his application, Mig had told a counselor: "If Ralph is one of the top admissions officers at this place, I'm going to love it."

Mig said he wasn't daunted by the prospect of being around so many non-Native kids. Among the Native Americans at his old public high school in Minnesota, he was one of the few who counted whites among his close friends and was part of an even smaller group who were willing to walk down a school corridor with a white person. On his application to NAPS, Mig had written: "I get along with people from all walks of life. I can fit in with about any group of people pretty easily and enjoy cultural diversity." Though Wesleyan was far from Minnesota and even farther from New Mexico, he relished the idea of living in Middletown, Connecticut, which he imagined as being "one of the quaint little towns" of New England.

Mig had decided to take his counselors' and teachers' advice and apply to six other colleges: Pitzer (whose representative had also visited NAPS), Colorado College (his mother's first choice, because it was close to home), Beloit (for creative writing), Bard (the progressive college on the Hudson River that had initially caught Jordan Goldman's eye, as well), Oberlin and Grinnell.

But Wesleyan was his first choice, and his only remaining question was now out of his hands: Could he get in? He was not optimistic, fearing that, as Wesleyan pondered his case, "the past would factor into it." For all his A's and B's at NAPS, those C's, D's and F's from his old high school would still be on his transcript. He and Ralph hadn't talked about his grades at all.

After they met, Ralph had concluded that Mig was mature enough to handle the social and cultural pressures of being a Native American at Wesleyan. He knew that the boy had much to add to the campus. That was the easy part. But now that Mig had actually applied, Ralph would have to consider whether he in fact merited admission and whether he had proven that he could do the work at Wesleyan. Ralph would spend much time in quiet contemplation weighing such questions. But whatever his personal feelings for Mig, Ralph's answers would hinge, in large part, on whether he thought he could convince his colleagues that Mig was worth the obvious academic risk. And that was by no means a sure thing.

Five
READ FASTER, SAY NO

Although a half inch of snow had fallen before dawn on the first Thursday in February, the slick roads posed no threat to Ralph Figueroa's commute that morning. After pouring Diet Pepsi into a sixteen-ounce plastic cup, Ralph stepped from the kitchen into the den of the fifty-year-old, redbrick three-bedroom Cape that he and Natalie had purchased a year earlier. It was the first home they had owned. Ralph moved briskly past all the distractions that might slow his journey: the olive-and-white striped couch, the upright piano decorated with family photos and the television stacked high with videotapes like *The Truman Show* and *The Usual Suspects*. Finally, he reached his destination: the adjacent enclosed porch.

The heat on the porch was turned off, which was the way Ralph liked it, for he would need to stay alert. The Diet Pepsi would help, and he would refill his cup throughout the day. But he was careful to avoid the Pepsi that had caffeine, which made him jittery, and chose instead to keep himself awake by shivering. It was certainly cold enough on the porch to wear a ski jacket, but Ralph was dressed only in sneakers, crisp tan chinos, a white T-shirt and a light-green V-neck sweater. Although Ralph wouldn't be seeing any colleagues or students that morning, he was one of those people who couldn't imagine not being freshly shaved.

For the last five weeks, the porch had been Ralph's office, and it would remain so for the next five. Eschewing even the most basic comfort, he had selected a folding blue metal party chair in which to sit. As a

desk, he had commandeered a simple plastic-topped card table with re-
tractable legs. Surrounding the table, in neat piles, were stacks of manila
folders that rose knee high. This was his quarry.

On this bright winter morning, Ralph was midway through a grueling reading season. As expected, applications for the Class of 2004 at
Wesleyan had broken the record set only a year earlier: a total of 6862 applicants had sought admission to the incoming freshman class, which represented an increase of 460 applicants, or 7 percent, over the previous
year. The winner of the contest to guess the greatest amount of mail that
would arrive in a single day was Lisa LaBreque, a student who worked in
the office. She had correctly predicted that 31 bins full of mail would arrive on January 4. Each bin held at least 30 applications, for a one-day
total of more than 900. (To get a sense of how much paper that represented, consider that it took one person an entire day to empty and sort
the contents of only one bin.)

Wesleyan's admissions office wasn't the only one that was buried in
mail that winter. Several dozen other colleges had received record numbers of applications in early January of 2000, including Harvard and
Columbia, where applications were up 3 percent over the previous year;
Middlebury, which was up 6 percent; and the Massachusetts Institute of
Technology, which was up a remarkable 16 percent. Ralph, like his colleagues at those other institutions, had devoted a considerable amount of
time to soliciting those applications. Now, though, someone had to read
them all.

The first of the two readers of every Wesleyan application was chosen
at random and was almost always an admissions officer, though occasionally a senior or former admissions officer would be recruited, just to give
the staff a break. The second reader was always the admissions officer who
was responsible for the state from which the application had been received. At this point in the year, Ralph was still reading files that had been
routed to him at random. All told, he would read close to fifteen hundred
applications that winter, devoting at least twenty minutes to each, and
sometimes more than an hour. On average, he would spend upward of
twelve hours a day, six days a week, just reading, thinking and recording
his impressions. If he was diligent, and the choices were fairly straightforward, he could process as many as thirty applications in a day. But more
often than not, he became bogged down.

The meetings of the committee might provide the most compelling
theater of the admissions process, but the fate of most applicants to top

American colleges was written, at least in draft form, in isolated moments like these. The toughest calls were usually made when an admissions officer had to decide, for example, whether a student's race and socioeconomic background should be taken into account in assessing a poor performance in school or on a test. Such calculations required intense concentration. After reading each file, Ralph would have to circle one of four choices on a ballot attached to the applicant's file as his preliminary vote on the student. "Admit" meant he felt unequivocally that the applicant should be accepted. If he had some reservations, but still believed the applicant should be admitted, he could choose "admit minus." "Deny" indicated that he was convinced that the applicant should be rejected. Finally, there was "deny plus," which meant that Ralph was fairly convinced that rejection was the proper course, though he did not consider the applicant without merit.

Wesleyan had received so many applications that Ralph knew that, on average, he had to say no to three candidates for each one he accepted, while knowing full well that most were capable of doing the work at Wesleyan and would likely thrive there. Watching her husband fall behind in his reading as he struggled to reject so many good students, Natalie, the realist in the family, would continually try to urge Ralph forward with the following mantra: "Read faster, say no." Even when she was away at work, he could hear her voice inside his head. If only it were easier to follow her advice.

For the two and a half months from early January to mid-March, when the committee convened for the last time, Ralph was a virtual hermit. He spoke to almost no one and ventured out only to get a quick bite of lunch or to pick up more files. Occasionally, he would take a rare break to play saxophone in the Middletown Symphonic Band, which was considerably more buttoned-down than the Stanford Marching Band. On Sundays, he played hand bells at his church, South Congregational, an affiliate of the United Church of Christ. No one who knew him, or who knew someone else engaged in the same line of work, would have been surprised to learn that he had taken down the Christmas decorations on February 2. Ralph, at least, had the advantage of being able to read uninterrupted. For those colleagues like Terri Overton or Chris Lanser, who had school-age children, reading that began in the morning had often to be suspended in the midafternoon, and picked up again only after the children had gone to bed.

That Ralph and Natalie had yet to start a family didn't necessarily make their lives any easier than those of Ralph's colleagues. Ralph was traveling for more than a month each fall. And in the winter, their friends had long since learned not to bother asking them to go out as a couple. By the end of February, Natalie's serenity would start to wear thin. "I get a little short-tempered," she acknowledged, "because I'm doing all the cooking and all the cleaning and all the shopping." But she never wavered in her support of Ralph, for she knew his family's story and how much it meant to him to be carrying on his mother's legacy of shepherding students into college.

For the Figueroas, there was one silver lining within the dark clouds of the reading season. Ralph's favorite section of each application was the essay. Ever since he had worked at Occidental, he had set aside the best-written and most heartfelt among them to photocopy for his personal file. This was the file that he would consult whenever he spoke at schools like Harvard-Westlake about all the different ways that students had succeeded in capturing his attention through their writing. Ralph would also read them aloud to Natalie as they sat in rocking chairs in the living room, a fire in the fireplace, between ten and eleven each night. Sometimes, they would cry together at the depth of feeling some of those pieces expressed. But it was always a long day's journey to reach that night.

On this February morning, Ralph got started just after nine A.M., as he always did. Almost immediately, he came across an essay that he knew he wanted to share with Natalie. An applicant from upstate New York had answered the first essay question—a query about the high school activity that had meant the most to her—by describing how she had come to love the clarinet. But, she wrote, she had taken up the clarinet only after being disqualified on the instrument that was her first love. "I was flatly told that I could not play the saxophone because my fingers were too short," she explained. "Imagine that, my dreams shot down because of a biological trait completely out of my control!" As he read, Ralph paused for a moment to consider how lucky he had been to have fingers long enough to play the sax. But it was the student's answer to the general essay question—in which she was asked to write up to five hundred words on the subject of her choice—that caught Ralph's eye:

> In fifth grade, my handmade rocket maintained a strictly terrestrial existence. In sixth grade I inadvertently murdered my prenatal baby chick. I was not what you would call a science-oriented child. But life has its twists and hairpin turns.

Four years ago I was chosen to take Regents Biology early, as an eighth grader. That year, I came to see biology as a totally new realm of limitless corners to explore. I was enthralled by genetics and cloning, xylem and phloem, neurons and synapses, mitosis and meiosis, photosynthesis and respiration . . . you name it. While other girls shirked from the task of dissecting a fetal pig, I dug right in. And now I find science worming its way into my future aspirations. Science research currently tops the list.

Ralph believed that the applicant's humility was genuine and could tell that her essay was true to her transcript and résumé. She had not only gone on to take the hardest science courses available to her, including an offering at a local college, but had assisted a cancer researcher at a laboratory near her home the previous summer.

This was an easy call. Ralph circled "ADMIT" on the workcard, the form that served as the official record attached to each applicant's file. But after casting his preliminary vote, he did something he almost never did, and placed an X through the section on the card that would ordinarily be filled out by the second reader. He wanted this file to go directly to Nancy and Greg for an expedited verdict. Why waste someone else's time on an applicant who was so obviously qualified, particularly this season? If Nancy or Greg disagreed with his assessment, they could always reassign it to another reader. Before sending the packet on, Ralph separated the essay and put it in the file that he would photocopy.

A few applications later, Ralph came across an essay from a student that would also leave an impression, though probably not the one that the applicant had intended. The applicant had chosen to tell the saga of his extended family, and the pride he felt "in being a part of something unique." The piece continued:

How did this pride come about? It came from those trips to my grandmother's house where we made the pasta fresh. Yeah, you heard me right, fresh. Not out of a box. We as a family also consider it a sin to put Ragu on our table. It's impossible to completely describe the atmosphere of my grandmother's house. The feel of linoleum floors under my feet and some type of Italian cooking teasing my nostrils and causing my mouth to salivate are just a start.

The indescribable aspect is the history that resonates through that house. For instance, the stories of how my Uncle Mike cut off his index finger with a bit saw and had to have my grandfather drive him to the hospital. It was stories like this that not only made me a good listener, but an entertaining storyteller.

The applicant went on to describe his attitude toward women. "The first rule," he wrote, "is if you're wise to your mother, it's a slap upside the head. If you're wise to your grandmother, it's a slap upside your head." The essay continued for another hundred words, but by this point, Ralph had pretty much decided how he would vote. This, he concluded, was not the work of the next head writer of *The Sopranos*. Perhaps on another day, or even an hour later, he might have found the essay as funny as he had Migizi Pensoneau's opening remark to him in New Mexico. But timing was everything. At this moment, Ralph's response was clinically dispassionate: "A very disorganized description of various aspects of his family," he wrote on the workcard, and also noted that the essay needed "major editing." Those impressions would accompany the student's file through the remainder of its journey through the admissions office.

Ralph had also seen that despite a respectable SAT score of 1300, this student had taken no honors or Advanced Placement courses. He knew that this particular high school had plenty of honors and AP offerings, which the school itself had said in the description that it had enclosed with the student's transcript. Also soiling this applicant's record were several C's and a D.

This, too, was an easy call, and Ralph circled his choice: "DENY." Unless someone disagreed with him—and made an argument persuasive enough to reroute this applicant to the committee—the student would not be admitted to Wesleyan.

These were not the only cases that day that Ralph considered relatively cut and dry. But as he worked from morning until deep into the night, two other applicants in particular would occupy his thoughts, even after he had set their folders aside. In these two instances, Ralph would second-guess himself as he struggled to make a recommendation, his ambivalence evident in the crossings-out he would leave behind on their workcards.

One applicant was Tiffany Wang, an Asian American woman from the affluent community of Palo Alto, about twenty-five miles south of San Francisco. Tiffany's scores on the PSAT—the dry run in the junior year before the SAT—had been high enough to earn her a coveted designation as a National Merit Semifinalist, just as Julianna Bentes of Harvard-Westlake had been. Fewer than 2 percent of the students who took the PSAT would reach that pinnacle, which some colleges or corporations rewarded with a merit scholarship of as much as $10,000 annually. Tiffany's SAT showing had demonstrated that her earlier performance was not a fluke. She had a combined score of 1470—750 on the verbal portion of the exam and a 720 on the math—well above the median score of 1360 of the full applicant pool at Wesleyan. The verbal score in particular was no mean feat, considering that Tiffany had indicated on her application that her parents, both natives of Taiwan, spoke primarily Chinese at home. She had learned English as a second language. After spending nearly an hour deliberating her case, Ralph would wish that the rest of her accomplishments had been as impressive.

Ralph spent nearly as much time that day pondering another applicant whose primary language had likewise not been English. Agueda Ramirez—who indicated on her application that she preferred to be called "Aggie"—wrote that Spanish was the main language spoken in her family's apartment in Washington Heights, in the northern part of Manhattan in New York City. Neither of her parents, who were natives of the Dominican Republic, had graduated from high school, though Aggie herself had managed to get a scholarship to what appeared to be a fancy girls' boarding school outside of Baltimore called Oldfields.

Ralph didn't know the school, but he could tell that, at least academically, Aggie's four-year stay there had been a rocky one, especially in recent months. At the midpoint in her senior year, she had earned C's in physics, international politics and a course she should have aced: Advanced Placement Spanish. She also had a D in English literature, another Advanced Placement course, and her only midyear B was in ceramics. That performance was consistent with an SAT score that had not broken 1100. Her best score on the verbal portion of the exam was 550, while her best score on the math was 540. Still, as with Tiffany, Ralph agonized over what to do about Aggie, for there was a lot to be said for the rest of her application, most notably that a fish swimming so far from her home waters had succeeded in being elected president of the student body her senior year.

Tiffany and Aggie were not pitted directly against each other; how Ralph decided one case would not necessarily affect the other. He could have recommended admitting, or denying, both. But his ultimate reaction to each would be strikingly different, and how he decided to vote would reveal much about his perspective on merit, as well as the various perspectives of his colleagues at Wesleyan and elsewhere.

In addition to her excellent SAT scores, Tiffany had impressed Ralph with her essay. Given several choices of what to write, she had underlined the question that directed her to "evaluate a significant experience, achievement or risk that you have taken and its impact on you." She had begun her response as follows:

> It's not abnormal to keep the bedroom door closed when doing homework or reading—many people do it in the hopes of avoiding nosy parents or pesky younger siblings. I close my door, however, not to obtain privacy but to keep the *guai*, or keeper of bad luck, from casting his destructive spells. My doorway faces the stairs, after all, and who knows what kind of evil resides there. Leaving the door open while trying to do work would definitely be inviting in that evil.
>
> To say that my parents are superstitious would be an understatement; they believe that our entire lives can be influenced by the air that flows through the house, or as the Chinese call it, Feng Shui.

Tiffany wrote that the concept of Feng Shui had always baffled her, especially after her family moved from Taiwan to California in the mid-1990s. When her father proceeded to have a bad year in business and her sister broke her left ankle playing basketball, the family enlisted the services of a well-known *laoshi,* or geomancer, who diagnosed the problem: the family's new home in Palo Alto faced a courtyard and busy street, where, he concluded, "all the bad spirits were gathered." When Tiffany challenged such beliefs, she was branded *butinghwa,* or disobedient.

But as she grew into her late teens, she recounted, a funny thing happened: she began to see why her parents saw the world the way that they did. She wrote:

> Growing up in a society where everyone believed the fantastical (or the truth, depending on one's point of view), they hardly had any say in the matter. I realized that perhaps that explained my

stubborn resistance to their beliefs—that I didn't want to be subjected to the same pressures to believe that they had. It wasn't as if my parents were forcing me to believe anything I didn't want to. In fact, was I being downright selfish by not letting *them* carry out the traditions that they had honored since childhood? I suddenly became aware of how inconsiderate and unreasonable I must have seemed.

The change in Tiffany's mindset was evident to her parents when she enthusiastically agreed to move to a house that the *laoshi* had located. She concluded:

No doubt they had been ready to fight another battle of words. To my surprise, however, while I had been taking a step into their lives, they had evidently done the same with mine. The house we were moving to was only about two blocks down the road—I wouldn't have to change schools or even my daily route of getting there. It was apparent that we had unwittingly come to a compromise—and both sides had come out satisfied. I was genuinely glad that my parents had found a house in which they could be comfortable and with the fact that they had considered what I felt instead of just viewing me as the *butinghwa* daughter.

So we moved into our new house, which I have to admit, I became fond of immediately. It was capacious but cozy, and with it came a backyard with gigantic trees that offered shade, and a hammock that offered respite. I didn't overlook the touches added by feng shui, of course—how our front door did not face the same direction as our garage, and how all the bedposts had to be placed as far away from the door as possible, among other things. I ended up with the bedroom next to the staircase, which alarmed my dad at first, but finally he just advised me to close the door when I was using the desk. So that's what I've been doing for about four years now, and though I would never admit to anyone, if I was ever in another room facing a staircase, I'd probably close the door too . . . just in case.

Although Ralph didn't set Tiffany's essay aside for Natalie, or for his "greatest hits file," he was sufficiently impressed to write on the workcard attached to her file: "Nicely done—learning to compromise w/parents over cultural ideas—well written." As the first reader, Ralph was responsible for boiling down everything in the file, so that his colleagues, who would likely be pressed for time, would get the gist. With this he was sending a signal to Greg or Nancy, or to the committee, when it considered Tiffany's case, like the blurb on the billboard for a Broadway show. Everyone would recognize it as high praise, coming from Ralph. On the workcard, he also added a one-line summary of the evaluation that Tiffany's guidance counselor had written: "Independent spirit and original thinker. Conscientious, thoughtful, involved."

Still, much of the rest of Tiffany's application threatened to undermine whatever distinction she had achieved with her high test scores and obvious skills as a writer. One of Tiffany's teachers had echoed the counselor's description of her as "conscientious" but had then remarked:

> There were times, I must admit, that I thought Tiffany might have taken a stronger interest in mastering the material in our course. When I saw that Tiffany was a National Merit Semifinalist, I was a bit surprised. While clearly bright and competent, I had seen in Tiffany neither an exceptional skill for testing nor a particular affinity for the subject.

In his one-line summary of the teacher's evaluation, Ralph included the phrase: "Surprised she's NMSF." That criticism wouldn't help, nor would Ralph's observation, lifted from the counselor's evaluation, that Tiffany had taken a "very demanding" program of courses at her school—but not "the most demanding." On its face, the description seemed unfair: Tiffany had taken six Advanced Placement, college-level courses—more than most other Wesleyan applicants. But Gunn High School, in the heart of Silicon Valley, had an especially rigorous curriculum. How else to explain that twenty-two other members of Tiffany's graduating class— a full 6 percent—were National Merit Semifinalists? Most schools were lucky to have one or two. Whether fairly or not, Tiffany would be competing with her classmates who had applied to Wesleyan.

Ralph was more concerned about the counselor's evaluation of Tiffany's program—that it could have been harder—than he was about her actual grades. But those, too, gave pause, for while she had more A's than B's, she had also received C's in science and algebra as a freshman, and in an Advanced Placement statistics course as a junior.

Ralph's ambivalence about Tiffany was reflected, finally, in the ratings he assigned to her. On the workcard, he was responsible for rating a candidate on a scale of 1 to 9 in three academic categories—academic achievement, intellectual curiosity, commitment—as well as two nonacademic categories: personal and extracurricular. Little wonder he often felt like an Olympic judge, displaying his numbered cards as if Tiffany had just attempted a triple axel.

Under "academic achievement," Ralph wrote down a 5. The cheat sheet that he and his colleagues consulted defined such an applicant as carrying only a "solid academic" load—as opposed to "an excellent academic record in demanding curriculum" (a 6 or 7), or "flawless academic record in most demanding curriculum" (an 8 or 9). Though these numbers were intended only as guidelines, the other admissions officers at Wesleyan would be expecting to see at least a 7 in this category to consider any candidate seriously for admission—unless there was a mitigating circumstance.

But Tiffany rebounded by getting a 7 from Ralph in the important category of "intellectual curiosity," for he believed she had met the criterion of showing "strong interest" in research and independent projects, according to the definition on the cheat sheet. And she drew a pair of 7's for academic commitment, which denoted she "goes well beyond required assignments," and in the extracurricular category, where Ralph had noted that she had spent four years doing community service and four years playing basketball and running track. (There was no indication, however, that she wanted to be evaluated by Wesleyan's coaches.) She had also spent two years picking up drunken revelers on Saturday nights (as part of a safe-rides program organized by her church) and two years working for a human rights club she had founded. That met the criteria for a 7, Ralph thought ("leadership in several clubs or organizations") but not an 8 or 9 ("talents, accomplishments have unusual depth and passion"). In the "personal" category, Ralph rated Tiffany a 6, meaning she was "likely to be a leader in some areas" but not necessarily a "memorable personal presence" (the criteria for an 8 or 9).

In an attempt to come to some conclusion on a candidate, the officers were expected to condense their academic ratings into a single number. This didn't have to be a straight average of the rankings in the component categories, but was more a back-of-the-envelope calculation of a student's performance in high school as measured against his or her ability. This was also the one rating where, for the first time, Ralph could factor in

Tiffany's high SAT scores. After spending considerable time staring out the window, he wrote down a 6. Considering her SAT performance, he concluded, she clearly had the ability to have taken tougher courses and to have performed with more distinction. She simply wasn't meeting her potential. Again, the committee would generally expect to see an overall academic rating of at least 7 to consider her for admission.

Ralph was also expected to summarize all of his impressions of Tiffany outside the classroom into one rating. If there were any extraordinary personal circumstances that she had overcome—or that had kept her back—this was the number that was supposed to reflect them. Here, Ralph assigned her a 7, which implied, finally, that Tiffany seemed more impressive as a person than she did as a student.

Now came the hardest part: a one-line description encompassing all the reader's thoughts on the applicant and a comprehensive vote. "Very mixed performance, up and down," he wrote first, knowing it wasn't an auspicious introduction to Tiffany. He also knew, however, that despite her performance, Wesleyan considered Tiffany a "priority" applicant in two categories.

First, she was from California, and Wesleyan was always trying to expand its geographic range. The prior year's class had, as always, been heavily dominated (67 percent) by students from the Northeast and mid-Atlantic states. The more the class reflected the diversity of the nation, Wesleyan believed, the richer the experience for all its students. Ralph agreed with this reasoning and wrote "Geo" on his summary line, for geography. In the parlance of the admissions trade, Tiffany's home state would give her "a push."

She also had the advantage of being Asian American. Besides seeking to be geographically representative of the United States as a whole, Wesleyan, like so many colleges, also wanted to reflect the ethnic and racial composition of the country. Wesleyan considered this balance crucial to the education of minority students and nonminority students as well; each, ideally, would learn from the other. But sometimes, to forge that balance, the standards to which a white applicant was held were eased for a nonwhite applicant. (Among the exceptions to the practice was the University of California, which, in the mid-1990s, had been the first public institution to bar its admissions officers from considering race as a factor in admissions.) Ralph concurred with Wesleyan's policy, in principle, particularly when he was considering a black or Hispanic applicant. But having grown up in California, where he knew many second- and third-generation Asian Americans who were living quite comfortably, he wasn't always vigilant in adhering to the philosophy of Wesleyan, which, like some other eastern colleges, usually considered Asian American applicants a minority.

Merely checking the Asian American box on an application—and yes, the admissions office almost always took an applicant at his or her word—was supposed to give a candidate an advantage, however slight, at Wesleyan and most other eastern and midwestern colleges. Thirty-five percent of the applicants to the prior year's class at Wesleyan who had identified themselves as Asian American had been admitted, compared to 29 percent of the applicant pool as a whole. Though Wesleyan had no established ceiling on the number of minority students it admitted, it did have a floor: Ralph and his colleagues were expected to admit at least as many Asian American applicants—as well as black and Hispanic applicants—as they had the year before. Any falling-off would be duly noted in the college guidebooks, which might in turn discourage future minority applications. Moreover, some of Wesleyan's Asian American alumni were quite vocal about bringing any perceived slight to the attention of the university president himself.

With all this in mind, Ralph wrote the abbreviation "DIV"—for "diversity"—in his summary of Tiffany, as a signal that he had noted her ethnicity. But as he prepared to cast his preliminary vote, he couldn't get past the issue of the girl's potential. Unlike so many minority applicants, Tiffany had grown up with many advantages. Her parents were both college graduates, and her father was apparently a successful businessman. She attended one of the better public high schools in the country, and while her high SAT scores at least suggested that she was exceptionally bright, her performance in school—the rigor of her curriculum, her grades—suggested she was dogging it. She seemed distracted.

Tiffany would likely make an important cultural contribution to Wesleyan. Surely her classmates would learn, as Ralph had, from her experiences with things like feng shui. And that was part of what affirmative action was intended to accomplish. But Ralph believed Tiffany's potential contribution to the incoming class was far outweighed by the level of her schoolwork thus far. "Very strong scores, but hasn't performed well," he wrote, in conclusion.

Ralph felt fairly sure that Tiffany did not merit a place in the incoming class, given the strength of the applicant pool; there would undoubtedly be other, better-qualified Asian American applicants. And so, he circled "DENY PLUS" on the workcard. A student given this designation was defined, on his cheat sheet, as "capable, but not compelling without significant push." That, in a phrase, was Tiffany.

If another reader disagreed with that assessment and thought the girl deserved a better fate, then Greg or Nancy could overrule Ralph, or they could bring Tiffany's case before the committee of the whole. But if it were up to Ralph, she would be turned away. As a final note, he scribbled "v. confusing" next to his decision. He then set Tiffany's file aside and took a rare break, a quick trip to the bathroom, after which he would take up the case of Aggie Ramirez, whom he would find equally perplexing.

Ralph had been privy to only a few details of Tiffany Wang's young life, all of them provided by her and her teachers in her application. She hadn't traveled to the Wesleyan campus for an interview, and he hadn't visited her high school in northern California. But he hadn't needed to meet Tiffany to conclude that in some critical respects, she was slacking off. Had they met, Tiffany would have told Ralph that his analysis was correct. She certainly liked to have fun and she liked to hang out. But she had at least one other extracurricular activity that she hadn't mentioned in her college application. Had she done so, Ralph, at least, might have rated her more favorably.

Tiffany's family, as they were described in her essay, had seemed to provide an ideal incubator for achievement, at least early on. Her parents, both born and raised in Taiwan, forbade their three daughters not only from watching television during the week but also from dating. Nothing was to distract the girls from their work—especially Tiffany, whom her father considered the most gifted. Bryn Mawr was good enough for her older sister, Katherine, who enrolled there two years before Tiffany applied to college. But to Herbert Wang, who had moved to the United States to study engineering at Columbia University, his middle daughter was destined for greater things, and it was he who pushed her to apply to Yale, for example. But while so many children rose to the challenge of such rules and expectations, so many others, including Tiffany, only chafed or wilted in the face of them.

Her own rebellion began during her freshman year of high school. One night after midnight, with her parents and sisters asleep, she slipped out of the family's town house to rendezvous with friends. Intoxicated by how easy her escape had been, she increased the frequency of her nocturnal excursions from once a month to two or three times a week. Her friends decided to make her departures easier by buying her a rope ladder, one that she could hide in her room. In her college essay she mentioned how the trees in her backyard provided her "solace." But they also provided her cover, and neither she nor her friends were ever caught, she said. Before long, she had multiple piercings atop her left ear, another in her belly button, and a butterfly tattooed on her hip.

Sometimes, Tiffany and her friends would gather in a parking lot or a park to sip orange juice and vodka, but mostly, she said, they just talked. What they didn't do much, together or apart, was study. "Every year, I'd say to myself, I'm going to do really well," Tiffany recalled. And sometimes she would make a genuine effort, raising her average from a B minus late in her freshman year to an A minus for her entire sophomore year, for example. But by the end of junior year, a critical time for any college applicant, she was hovering at a B minus again. She was regularly skipping classes, and her absences were taking their toll. Echoing concerns that Ralph would later express, Herbert Wang would lament that she was squandering her gifts. She knew he was right. Maybe it was all the pressure that she felt her father was putting on her; maybe it was all coming from inside of her—she was as puzzled as everyone else as to why she wasn't doing better.

Her activities suffered as well. During her freshman and sophomore years at Gunn, Tiffany, who was almost five-nine, played forward on the girls' junior varsity basketball team. She scored, on average, a respectable eight points a game and enjoyed playing. But during her junior year, she stopped going to the team's three-hour daily practices, even after an ankle injury she sustained early in the season had fully healed. She no longer cared about basketball, and her only passion, it seemed, was the Human Rights and Cultural Awareness Club, which she and several friends founded her sophomore year.

Tiffany had listed the club on her college application but without a description. That would turn out to be a misstep, though she could not have possibly known it at the time. As a result of her omission, Ralph had not known what to make of the club and had paid it little heed. In fact, Tiffany herself had had trouble deciding how much stock to put in the club's work. In an interview after her senior year, she acknowledged that she had founded the club, at least in part, as a "way to pad my résumé." One of her cousins had started a human rights club at her high school, and she had told Tiffany that it had boosted her application—helping her, she believed, get into Harvard. Gunn already had a Beatlemania club and a Yo Yo Club, so why not a human rights group? But as it turned out, the club actually became a serious enterprise, even if the term "human rights" didn't quite capture its mission.

During the hour or so a week that they met, Tiffany and the fourteen other members did work that was actually hard to classify: they wrote letters of encouragement and support to inmates on death row. It was Tiffany who had gotten the idea, after stumbling upon a website that asked for volunteers to write to convicted killers. The organizers of the site wanted the inmates to know that no matter how heinous their crimes, someone still cared about them. At the time, Tiffany was a fourteen-year-old eighth-grader, and the site stipulated that any correspondent had to be over eighteen. But she was too curious and sent postcards to four of the listed inmates, which the organizers passed along to them. Tiffany had written something along the lines of: "Don't give up hope"; she said she opposed the death penalty and believed that "everyone deserves a second chance," even those "who killed someone," going on to explain that her "soft heart" had been borne of her faith. Though her parents were not religious, she and her sisters had attended a Protestant school in Taiwan and had ultimately found Christ on their own. Though only in elementary school, they had soon begun attending church, a practice they had continued in California. The lessons she learned about forgiveness had resonated with her.

To Tiffany's surprise, three of the inmates responded, their letters forwarded to her by the site organizers. Before long, she was corresponding directly with one of them. He said he was in his fifties and then told her seemingly everything about himself, from the name of his former cat to the most recent meal he ate. He didn't reveal exactly what he had done to wind up on death row in Texas, and Tiffany didn't want to know the details. But he did say that he regretted his actions "twenty-four hours a day, every day of his life" and had been largely abandoned by his family. "From what I know of him," Tiffany said later, "he's not a bad person now. Maybe he's changed."

Tiffany began writing to her inmate once a month, and he wrote back three letters for each one that he received. Often he played the role of teacher, writing about his impressions of *Ulysses,* for example, in sentences so cogent and thoughtful that they read like Cliffs Notes, Tiffany recalled. He was obviously intelligent. Her mother, though, was deeply unnerved by her daughter's correspondent and urged her to cut him off. But Tiffany never feared for her safety. "He's on death row," she reminded her. "He's an old man." Tiffany encouraged her friends to engage in similar correspondence, and a club was born.

But they didn't just send letters to the inmates. By now Tiffany was "determined to do something to protest this horrible system that offered no second chance." She joined a statewide organization opposed to the death penalty and began writing to senators and congressmen. She even contemplated a career in politics. All the while, she never stopped corresponding with her new friend. When she mentioned to him that she was having difficulty finding a topic for a fifteen-page psychology project junior year, he suggested several ideas, one of which she ultimately chose. The topic was narcissism, and her paper received an A.

As she struggled through the college admissions process, her inmate offered only encouragement. "He was like, 'You can get into any of those schools,'" she remembered him saying, as she told him about her applications to Yale, Bryn Mawr, Wellesley and Wesleyan, among others, each recommended to her by friends or family. "I don't think I told him my SAT's. I think he just assumed I was smart."

Tiffany had flirted with the idea of writing about the convict in her college essays and had even composed a draft that began with the declaration that "a person shunned by people around the nation" had become a "hero to me." But she decided that discussing her experiences and the evolution of her position on the death penalty would be "too personal," and instead chose to focus on her parents and how she had come to respect their beliefs and traditions. That was safer ground, Tiffany thought.

While she was probably right on that count—a lot of people would have found it difficult to summon sympathy for convicted killers—her correspondence was not only unique but revealed a great deal about who she was and what she cared about. And as Ralph made clear in his chats at Harvard-Westlake, the odds were good that at least one person on an admissions committee somewhere would share an applicant's view of the world.

In Tiffany's case, by sheer luck of the draw, that person would have been Ralph Figueroa, who, as it turned out, was opposed to the death penalty. Lots of people at Wesleyan were, of course, but unlike many of them, he had actually acted on his beliefs. While at UCLA Law, he had taken a criminal law course with a former United States Attorney who had described his own fierce opposition to putting anyone to death. Ralph couldn't believe that a prosecutor would take such a position and was so influenced by what he learned in the course that he applied for a summer fellowship at the Southern Poverty Law Center, specifically to work with those lawyers at the advocacy group trying to spare the lives of death row inmates. Although he hadn't gotten the job, an activist was born.

When told by an outsider, long after the selection of the Class of 2004 was completed, about Tiffany's strong opposition to the death penalty and the campaign she had undertaken, Ralph was visibly moved. "I probably wouldn't have changed my mind on her," he said. "But who knows? It would have definitely struck a chord." Because Tiffany Wang had decided not to mention in her application the work that was her passion, neither she nor Ralph would ever know for certain.

As he had for Tiffany, Ralph had picked up Aggie Ramirez's folder from the random pile that had been set aside for him as a first reader. Like Tiffany, Aggie had described herself as a child of immigrants. In a section of the application that was optional, she had checked the box next to "HISPANIC, LATINO" and had typed "Dominican Rep" in the space allocated for "COUNTRY."

Unfortunately, Tiffany and Aggie also shared a propensity for erratic grades.

Prior to her senior year, Aggie had actually done admirably. She received an A minus in sophomore English, which was an honors course, and in a junior-year anatomy lab. And she had a B plus in math during each of her first three years at Oldfields, including in algebra as a freshman and sophomore, and in precalculus as a junior. Most of her other grades were either B or B minus.

But her final year had begun disastrously, and her guidance counselor had sent along a letter contending that Aggie's midyear senior grades—those C's in physics, international politics and Advanced Placement Spanish, and that D in Advanced Placement English literature—did not reflect how much better she had performed during the second half of the fall semester, versus the first. In fact, she had actually pulled her grades *up* to reach those C's and that D.

On the workcard, Ralph paraphrased what the counselor had written—"Note from GC saying 2nd Quarter grade in English was 80, Spanish was 84; so 1st Q was what brought her down."—followed by his own one-word editorial response: "Hmm." He hadn't read far enough into the file yet to decide whether he was willing to accept this analysis.

The counselor went on to suggest that it was Aggie's overcommitment to extracurricular activities during senior fall that had caused her crash, and it was obvious to Ralph that the girl was doing a lot—probably too much. In each of her first three years, Aggie had sung soprano in two vocal groups, played goalie on the junior varsity field hockey team and volunteered as a Big Sister. During her senior fall she not only undertook all those activities, but became a dorm proctor and was elected president of the student council.

Setting aside her grades for the moment, Ralph was impressed that Aggie had succeeded in becoming a leader at Oldfields, however much it may have detracted from her schoolwork. In the description of itself that the school had enclosed in Aggie's file, it noted that the student body at Oldfields was 88 percent white. With an annual tuition of nearly $30,000, the school drew many of the forty-five girls it admitted each year from well-mined pockets of wealthy families in Georgia, North Carolina and Texas, as well as from around the world. Among its distinguished alumnae was Wallis Warfield, a Baltimorean who graduated from Oldfields in the early 1900s and who, as a divorcée two decades later, began a romantic relationship with King Edward VIII of England that forced him to abdicate. Founded at the end of the Civil War in a clapboard farmhouse that still served as the main administration building at the beginning of the twenty-first century, Oldfields occupied only a small corner of a two-hundred-acre forest dense with elm and oak, azalea and forsythia. Surrounded by rolling "old fields" on the Maryland–Pennsylvania border—the center of the world for enthusiasts of the equestrian sport of steeplechase—the school offered its students a unique perk: for an additional $10,000 a year, they could bring their horses with them from home and board them at the school. One of out of every three girls at Oldfields took the school up on its offer and brought along her mount. Aggie, whose education was almost entirely subsidized by the school, was not among them.

Oldfields had long committed itself to educating young women with a range of educational abilities—some went on to Harvard, others to community college. But because of its remote location it had to work harder than many boarding schools to diversify its ranks, which it considered part of its mission. Aggie had been recommended to Oldfields by a

New York–based organization called Prep for Prep, which, for two decades, had been sending poor minority students from New York City to prep schools throughout the metropolitan New York region and beyond.

While Aggie was not the first student sent by Prep for Prep to Oldfields, she was the first to be chosen to serve as president. By all accounts, she had won over her classmates by her obvious and infectious exuberance. Picking up early on her classmates' musical choices, Aggie, whose own taste generally ran to hip-hop, began memorizing the lyrics to songs by the country stars Garth Brooks, the Dixie Chicks and Shania Twain. She surprised even herself by genuinely starting to love these artists, whom her friends at home had never heard of. At a school where the girls were divided up each year into green and white teams for an annual academic and athletic competition that was similar to a color war, it was Aggie who usually coaxed her classmates into painting their faces and singing ridiculous cheers at the top of their lungs. Whenever the school mounted a musical production, whether *Damn Yankees* or *Anything Goes,* Aggie, who stood not much taller than five feet and was a bit heavyset, could nonetheless be counted on to land one of the leads.

That was the easy part of fitting in. What was harder for Aggie, who was dark-skinned and often presumed to be African American, was that several of her classmates had seen fit to decorate their rooms with Confederate flags. "It makes me more sad than anything," she commented. "But I don't think it offends me. The explanation I was given by kids who have them is that it's their way of showing their Southern pride. I know they're not racists, even if they do need to be more sensitive." Aggie would say later, with her own pride obvious: "Some of those kids with flags became my good friends."

During her senior year, she encountered one of the few instances of overt racism that she would experience at Oldfields. On a cork bulletin board inside a dormitory, someone had posted a note that said something like: "Latinos leave, get out of here all of you." As one of the few young women of Hispanic background at the school at the time, Aggie knew that the note was intended at least partly for her. But instead of just letting the remark pass, Aggie convened a campuswide forum in the school auditorium, a cavernous, 150-year-old white building crossed by old wood beams. (It was formally known as the David Niven Theater; the actor's granddaughter was an Oldfields student and her family had been instrumental in the building's recent renovation.) Aggie usually led the campus through its regular morning meeting there, but she used this opportunity to address the issue of racism square on. "This is very hurtful," she told her schoolmates. "I think it's important that you remember that the person you chose to lead you is also a Latina." Most of the students were too stunned to speak. Though the note writer was never caught, Aggie said that she never struck again.

Aggie had chosen to leave many of these details out of her college application, simply because there wasn't the space. But as he sat reading it on his porch, Ralph was certain that he had been able to fill in enough of the outlines to get a good picture of who Aggie was. For as the main topic of her essay, Aggie had reflected on someone whom she, too, had never met: Gary Simons, the founder of Prep for Prep, the organization that had brought her to Oldfields:

> I wanted an education so that I could become rich and famous, and so that I could get away from Washington Heights, my neighborhood. My thirst for wealth stemmed from my family's low socio-economic background. I would always dream of living and owning a house with a basement, a backyard, and a swimming pool. I always thought that would be so much better than the old, small, stuffy, broken down apartment that my family lived in, but never owned.
>
> My longing for fame was brought on by my frustration with the youth of my neighborhood. I was saddened and angered by the girls my age, who were having multiple babies, by multiple men, without having the resources to care for these kids, and the young men who neglected their kids and dropped out of school to sell drugs. My anger did not allow me to befriend any of the kids in my neighborhood, and as a result I did not have many friends. I felt that fame gained through education would eventually end my loneliness.
>
> The society of New York's Washington Heights depressed me. Here I was living in a place largely populated by immigrants from the Dominican Republic. These people, like my parents, came in search of a better life, for themselves and their children, yet they seemed to be getting nowhere fast. The government often discriminated against them and to make things worse, their kids got involved with the wrong crowds, causing their immigration to be in vain. I was determined not to let that happen to me, and the only way was through education.

But as she went on to explain, she came to recognize that her initial motives for seeking an education had been "shallow," an understanding that came to her only after becoming involved in Prep for Prep. She concluded:

> Through the leadership training that I have received, I have come to realize that I can use my education to obtain leadership positions that will help to end a lot of the misery that originally drove me to crave an education. Whether I obtain wealth and fame by educating myself is irrelevant now.

On Aggie's workcard, Ralph wrote of her essay: "Well organized, strong voice. Basic, but clear and competent." What he was thinking, however, was much more personal. Aggie, at least in her essay, reminded Ralph of a lot of the Mexican Americans girls he had met growing up in California, the kids whom his mother had to practically kick in the rear to get them to apply to college, because they were getting no guidance at home.

It should be noted here that in gazing into the admissions pool, and being excited to see a familiar reflection staring back, Ralph was hardly alone. For example, Nancy Meislahn, the new dean, sometimes had a soft spot for applicants who had attended small rural high schools, who had taken all the tough courses at those schools and who had then graduated at the top of their classes. Nancy, who had grown up in the tiny upstate New York community of Wayland in Steuben County, would have fit that description perfectly. Terri Overton, the veteran admissions officer who came to Wesleyan via the Peace Corps, was often attracted to Midwesterners who had solid grades but who weren't savvy enough to rack up a list of extracurricular activities as long as a rap sheet, just because they thought the colleges were watching. Terri herself had not had the benefit of sophisticated advice about how to apply to college and had ended up as a freshman at Cornell only by following the example of a schoolmate who was a few years older. She was also a former cheerleader, and it had been a long-running joke in the office that she was sometimes willing to cut some slack to any cheerleader who was applying to Wesleyan.

That isn't to imply that the Wesleyan admissions officers pulled only students like themselves into Wesleyan. But like their counterparts at other schools, they inevitably had their pet interests and causes. And in the end, the diversity of interests and backgrounds of the committee members helped ensure the diversity of the incoming class. Who else but Ralph would keep a keen eye out for the rare applicant who listed handbells as a musical interest?

Mindful of his colleagues who would be reading her file next, Ralph cut Aggie a small break on the next line of his evaluation of her. The girl had written a single paragraph as an addendum to her application, which was, technically, the sort of extraneous material that Ralph was free to overlook. But in this case he was inclined to let her have her say. She wrote that she was "aware that Wesleyan really looks at a student's transcript" and acknowledged that "my past semester grades would be classified as unbecoming of a Wesleyan student." She explained that she had "felt it necessary to join almost all the activities offered at Oldfields" but had cut back after her grades suffered. Ralph decided to paraphrase Aggie's appeal, on the workcard, as follows: "Explanation of poor grades—She says joining too many E.C.'s, not learning to prioritize." Ralph didn't know how this defense would play, but he wanted Aggie to be able to make her own case to the committee, if it came to that.

Returning to the main application, he also noted on the workcard that Aggie's counselor had written of her: "When prepared, she does well." It was almost a backhanded compliment, a line that raised as many questions as it answered, but Ralph's job here was to summarize. He also included a quotation from Aggie's counselor that she was "a work in progress." Again, that could be interpreted as praise or criticism, depending on the reader.

Now it was time for Ralph to rate Aggie. As in the case of Tiffany, it would not be an easy task.

In academic achievement, the first category, Ralph wrote down a 4, which indicated that a candidate had "fair to good recommendations" and "some weaknesses apparent in application." It also meant that Aggie, who had taken only two Advanced Placement courses, had come nowhere near to taking full advantage of what her school offered. Ralph also assigned her a 4 for academic commitment, meaning she was "inconsistent or uneven in some areas." He gave her a 5 for intellectual curiosity, though, because several teachers had described Aggie as conscientious, which was precisely what the category was designed to measure.

Those ratings, which were low, would be available to the next reader, as well as to Nancy or Greg. But if Aggie's case went before the committee, Ralph's other colleagues would be informed only of his overall academic rating, which represented a rough average of those other numbers, along with a general sense of whether the applicant's SAT score was high or low. He began to contemplate that critical number.

When calculating that overall academic rating, Ralph was supposed to be as objective as possible. This was not the place to cut Aggie some slack because she did not have the cultural or economic advantages of other applicants. He could factor such life circumstances into the personal rating, which would come next, and it would be up to future readers to weigh the academic performance in light of the personal circumstances. For the moment, what was relevant for the purpose of this rating was that Aggie's combined SAT score of 1090—a 550 verbal, 540 math—was more than 200 points below the median of those students applying to Wesleyan for the incoming class. Ralph stared out the window for what seemed like an eternity. Turning back to the card table, he knew what he had to write: putting his green ballpoint pen to paper, he marked Aggie's overall academic rating as a 3. This would likely decide her fate. She would almost surely be rejected with a number that low. Few who applied to Wesleyan that year would receive a lower rating.

The personal rating came much more easily, given all of Aggie's extracurricular activities and the fact that she had been elected president of the student body. For the first time, he was permitted to award her points for having overcome a tough background. Ralph quickly scribbled an 8, a near-perfect score. Nonetheless, it was unlikely to save her, so low was her academic rating.

But as he weighed his vote, and what he would write in that final line to summarize Aggie, Ralph started to second-guess himself, as he worried about that 3. While he truly believed that the girl's academic performance thus far merited no more than a 3, he decided to cut her another break. Bearing down heavily with his pen, Ralph began to write over the number 3 until he had turned it into a 4.

A moment later, he explained why he had revised his assessment. "She's definitely a 3, and I know I said I try to be objective with that number. But I couldn't do it. I was thinking about what I'd argue before the committee. I can hear a dean saying, 'I can't support a 3.' But a 4, that could make a little stronger base to make an argument." Had Aggie been white or even Asian American, Ralph had to concede, she'd have gotten a 3 from him. As a Hispanic, she was still supposed to get a 3. He was ambivalent about what he had done, but he also knew his wouldn't be the last word. At least two other people would consider Aggie's file. They were welcome to rate her differently.

Now, though, it was time for Ralph to register a preliminary vote. If his final summary had been a baseball box score, Aggie would appear to be winning one inning, only to be losing the next, with the outcome of the game not known until the last inning. "Impressive leader, person," Ralph scribbled on the line set aside for his final evaluation. That was a good start. "But," he added, again quoting her guidance counselor, "still 'a work in progress' on academics." Early in her bid for admission to Wesleyan University, Aggie Ramirez was falling behind.

But Ralph next wrote the words, "clear priority," which was like hitting a bases-clearing double. This was a euphemism for Aggie's having a desirable ethnic background, and it would be worth a lot.

Of the nearly seven thousand applicants for the Class of 2004, only about 5 percent were Hispanic, according to Greg Pyke's most recent figures. Yet, if the previous year's class was any guide, roughly 50 percent of this year's Hispanic applicants would be admitted to Wesleyan. (In contrast, those who applied who were white would have an acceptance rate of only about 30 percent.) That, in part, was how diversity was achieved, at Wesleyan and so many other colleges. Part of the description of the job Ralph had accepted at Wesleyan stipulated that he was to be on the alert for qualified Hispanic applicants. By writing "clear priority" on the file of Aggie Ramirez, Ralph Figueroa was doing his job.

He next noted on his summary line the abbreviation "NCP"—"non-college parents." This would instantly be understood by his colleagues as a partial explanation for Aggie's low SAT scores and perhaps even her low academic rating. From everything he had read about her, Ralph assumed that Aggie hadn't gotten the sort of academic enrichment at home that an applicant like Tiffany Wang had. That Aggie had had the benefit of attending Oldfields for the previous two years would not have been enough time for her to make up that deficit, as Ralph saw it; the damage had been done early.

Scholars might be divided over to what degree the SAT measured factors other than aptitude or intelligence, but the position of the Wesleyan admissions committee was fairly clear: it expected students of means, whose parents were educated and usually white, to score higher on the SAT than students whose parents were neither educated nor affluent. From that perspective, Aggie's 1090 should not really be considered 380 points below Tiffany Wang's 1470. More than a few white parents would consider that analysis unfair. But the previous fall, Ralph had read Nicholas Lemann's book *The Big Test,* which had only served to confirm what he had always suspected: that the SAT was being used in ways for which it had never been intended. Lemann had written that it was originally developed more than a half century earlier as a determinant of merit scholarships at Harvard, not a yardstick against which every college in the country would measure their applicants. If the SAT played a role in college admissions—and Ralph felt that it most certainly should—the scores ought only be considered in the context of a student's life.

Returning to Aggie's workcard, Ralph next wrote the word "leadership." Any applicant who had been president of the student body got a bit of a push at Wesleyan, as at other colleges. But Ralph felt Aggie's leadership potential was especially striking. She had written in her essay that she eventually intended to return to Washington Heights, which he thought was laudable. "You are talking about communities where there is no encouragement—there is active discouragement—of daughters going to college," Ralph remarked later. With a good education, Aggie could influence a lot of kids who needed a role model like her.

Ralph ended his summary of Aggie with a question: "Take risk?" His colleagues would have their own opportunity to reach a conclusion, but Ralph knew what his response was. Again putting his green-tipped ballpoint to the workcard, Ralph circled "ADMIT MINUS" by which he was acknowledging Aggie's flaws but also signaling that hers was a "strong, admissible profile," according to the definition on the office cheat sheet. He was willing to bet that Aggie would perform at Wesleyan as she had during her first three years at Oldfields, not her fourth. His early preference was to admit her.

Next to his vote on Aggie, Ralph scribbled "discuss," his signal that he was hoping he could push Aggie's case into the committee of the whole, where he was looking forward to defending her. But before he would get the chance, Greg Pyke would have his say, for it was he who was responsible for reading all the files of students applying from Maryland schools, including Oldfields. Ralph wondered if Greg would see Aggie as he had. He also wondered whether anyone would see fit to revive the candidacy of Tiffany Wang.

*   *   *

Over the course of the day Ralph would read a total of twenty-three applications, though his goal was thirty. He rarely reached that target, for the choices were too hard. Aggie's had not been the only case that day for which Ralph had written down a rating, or even circled a vote, only to cross it out moments later and write something else. "I think it's knowing it's a record number of applications, and not knowing where the line is going to be," he said, explaining his equivocating. "I find myself second-guessing myself a lot."

Ralph had been interrupted by only a few phone calls that day. One had been from his sister Ana, who was writing a freelance article for *People en Español* on a topic near to Ralph's heart: *General Hospital,* the soap opera that he had watched on and off since his senior year in high school. Ralph often taped the show and watched it in the evening, though rarely during reading season. Talking about Luke and Laura with Ana had been a welcome respite.

Another call he had taken was on a more serious matter. It was from Greg Pyke, who functioned not only as the office statistician but also as an occasional prod to slow readers. Greg informed Ralph that midway through the reading season, the committee members, each working diligently at home, had given a first read to nearly four hundred more files than they had by the same date the previous year. That was no small accomplishment, considering that the number of readers had not increased, though the number of applications had. Unfortunately, Greg reported, the officers were falling behind in getting to those applications that they were supposed to consider as second readers. At the pace Ralph was working, he calculated, he would have to read seven days a week for six straight weeks, from now until the committee hearings began in mid-March, to catch up.

Ralph was also struggling with part of Natalie's advice: "Say no." Wesleyan intended to offer admission to about eighteen hundred of the sixty-eight hundred students who applied, or 26 percent. If past numbers held, about seven hundred of those eighteen hundred would say yes to Wesleyan, with the remainder of the Class of 2004 drawn from the waiting list, if necessary. On this day alone, Ralph had voted, however tentatively, to admit ten of the twenty-three applicants whose files he had read, or about 43 percent. If he were keeping to the average acceptance rate, he probably should have recommended admitting only six. He would have to be a little tougher tomorrow, and probably the day after that, but how? So many applicants presented good cases for admission.

On this day, in addition to the budding cancer researcher from up-state New York, Ralph had recommended admitting a young Korean American woman from Westchester County, New York. Her SAT scores were near perfect, and she had competed in a national chemistry competition. Like Tiffany Wang, she was a National Merit semifinalist; unlike Tiffany, she had received almost all A's in the toughest classes her school offered. Ralph also liked the editor of the French magazine of a private school in New York, as well as a boy who volunteered as an ambulance attendant. The boy wrote that he had once saved a man's life by giving him CPR during a treacherous ride to the hospital, a story that a teacher had alluded to as well in her recommendation. The applicant's academic credentials were impeccable—he was taking a crushing load of sciences each year—but Ralph had circled "ADMIT MINUS" on his workcard, rather than "ADMIT," only because he wanted to see if Wesleyan had gotten even better applicants from the boy's school.

Among the other candidates whom Ralph had recommended taking a pass on were a girl who had devoted her entire essay to her doll collection ("way too much information about Barbie," he had scribbled) and another girl who was ranked near the middle of the pack of her prep school. He had been a bit alarmed by the report of the Wesleyan senior who interviewed her during a campus visit, which mentioned that the applicant had "disturbed him" by making allusions to "being mean to people and wishing to start over in college." Nothing else in her application suggested she was worth the trouble, Ralph thought.

As the night approached nine, he figured it was a good time to take a dinner break, if only for a few minutes. As he and Natalie sat at a small wooden table in the kitchen, talking more about her day than his, he told her that he had an essay that he wanted to read to her later—the one about the would-be scientist accidentally killing her prenatal baby chick. After quickly downing a hamburger that Natalie had brought him from Burger King and drinking yet another Diet Pepsi, he went back to work. It was past ten before he put down his pen for the night; thirteen hours after he had first picked it up. Indeed, he had written so much for so long that he had gone through three pens—a green ballpoint, then a purple and finally a blue.

At that point, without getting up from the card table on the porch, Ralph picked up a cordless phone and dialed the number of a young niece in California. He wanted to wish her a happy birthday and to offer her a free plane ticket to the East. He was definitely missing his family back home, and the girl said she'd consider it.

Then, at the time that he would have ordinarily read to Natalie, he decided that the essay about the chick could wait. He needed to get to bed. If the last few nights were any indication, he'd soon be dreaming about reading files and filling out workcards. Just before he went upstairs, he reflected on the applicants whose cases he had considered that day. "They're out there somewhere," he said. "They don't even realize we're agonizing about them and spending time really worried about their lives and what's going to happen to them."

If he awoke during the night with worries about those applicants he had rejected, Ralph said, he would ease his conscience with a soothing thought that had helped him through other such moments: "They're going to end up in good places. They're going to have good lives. I don't have the ability to bring them all to Wesleyan."

Six
THUNDERCATS AND X-MEN

The next admissions officer to consider the complicated case of Aggie Ramirez was Greg Pyke. In a sense, Aggie was fortunate: Greg was a believer in affirmative action as a cornerstone in the foundation of a liberal education. He, like many of his colleagues in the Wesleyan admissions office and at other private colleges, considered the Supreme Court's 1978 decision in *Regents of the University of California* v. *Bakke,* which applied directly to public universities, to be a guidepost as well. In the *Bakke* case, in which the court split 5–4, Justice Lewis Powell wrote that admissions officers were permitted under the Constitution to consider race and ethnicity "a plus," if they liked, as they weighed the many other facets of a college applicant—provided they didn't establish a separate admissions process for minority applicants, which is what the University of California Medical School at Davis had done. "The race of an applicant," Justice Powell wrote, "may tip the balance in his favor just as geographic origin or a life spent on a farm may tip the balance in other candidates' cases." That was precisely how admissions had been practiced at Harvard in the mid-1970s, which Justice Powell cited as a model, and it was certainly how admissions was being practiced two decades later at Wesleyan.

But as Ralph, Greg and their colleagues on other private campuses were reading applications in the winter of 2000, hewing close to the direction of Justice Powell, the public university systems in California, Florida and Texas were heading in a different direction. In 1996 California voters followed the lead of the regents of the state university system and ordered their public colleges to eliminate racial preferences as they considered whom to admit. In Texas that same year, the U.S. Court of Appeals ruled in the so-called *Hopwood* case that the University of Texas Law School could not establish targets for the percentages of black and Latino students it hoped to admit. In Florida, the governor had done away with such preferences by executive order. At the University of Michigan, white applicants rejected by the undergraduate and law school admissions offices had responded with lawsuits, just as Alan Bakke had in California when he was rejected from medical school two decades earlier. The Michigan cases were just then advancing through the federal court system.

While the policies of these individual states had no bearing on Wesleyan, a private institution in Connecticut, its admissions officers could hardly afford to ignore their implications: the legal and intellectual arguments that underpinned their daily work were under fierce attack. While both Greg and Ralph continued to support affirmative action as they labored to assemble the Class of 2004, the degree to which they and the other admissions officers at Wesleyan, and elsewhere, were committed to it fell along a spectrum. The national debate might be waged on the extremes, but at a place like Wesleyan, the distinctions were far more subtle. And it was cases like those of Aggie Ramirez that drew out those differences.

Like Ralph, Greg Pyke, who was fifty-three, had read a seminal 1998 defense of affirmative action titled *The Shape of the River,* written by William Bowen, the former president of Princeton, and Derek Bok, the former president of Harvard. Drawing on years of admissions statistics that were supplied by Wesleyan and many other colleges, Bowen and Bok concluded that the nearly four-decade-old effort to integrate top American colleges had succeeded in producing a cadre of black doctors and lawyers and business people, as well as the broader foundation for a black middle and upper class. Contrary to conventional wisdom, they found that the graduation rates of black students at Wesleyan and other universities were only a few percentage points below those of whites. Blacks, the only minority group that *The Shape of the River* had studied, were holding their own.

Bowen and Bok also argued that while black students had surely benefited from access to such institutions, their white classmates had also benefited from having minorities on campus. From personal experience, Greg knew this to be true. His own upbringing had been a sheltered one.

He was raised in Gary, Indiana, the third son of a high school dropout who rose from a blue-collar job on the mill floor at U.S. Steel to a white-collar post as a manager in the production planning office. Greg had attended Catholic schools through the end of high school, and because of where he lived, those schools were all white. Not until he was an undergraduate in college, at Oberlin in Ohio in the mid-1960s, had he been exposed to anyone who looked or sounded different from him. By the time he enrolled in Oberlin in the fall of 1964, there were blacks and Jews in the freshman class. "I still remember the first time someone on my hall said they were going home and would bring back bagels," Greg recalled. "Everyone was putting in orders. I didn't know what they were talking about."

Greg learned a more visceral lesson in diversity when the Oberlin town police outfitted themselves from head to toe in riot gear after the Detroit riots in 1967. Around that time he was covering a civil rights demonstration on campus as a photographer for the student newspaper when the police decided to break it up with canisters of tear gas. He was overcome by the fumes, as well, and soon decided that he sympathized with the protesters. "I certainly became more liberal in my social values than the rest of my family," Greg recalled. "It made it hard to go home."

After graduating in 1968 with a degree in English, he took a job as a seventh-grade English teacher in the Oberlin public schools. Presiding over a class with a substantial percentage of black students, Greg watched as his adolescent charges played out their own version of the tensions that they were watching on television each night. "I had a mini–Black Power movement in my class," he recalled. "I tried to get them all to talk to each other, and put their ideas into words. It made me see the extent to which privilege and race were joined. Most of the privileged in my class were white. Most of those who weren't white, weren't privileged."

He resolved that someday he would work to right that balance. After bouncing around between several odd jobs, he relocated to Connecticut, where his then-wife had enrolled at Wesleyan in pursuit of a master's degree. In 1977, while working as a live-in administrator at a halfway house in Middletown, Greg saw a help-wanted ad placed by the university, which was looking for an admissions officer. The job had instant appeal. "If your life experience makes you value education, which mine does, then you care about who's getting access to education," Greg explained. "And if you've had a really good undergraduate education, it's quite attractive to attach yourself to an undergraduate institution that matches your values."

In the mid-1960s, Wesleyan had been in the vanguard of American colleges seeking to tear down barriers of admission to minority students, barriers that had been erected more than a century earlier. Until 1965, Wesleyan, like many other liberal arts colleges, had admitted only two or three black students into each class, at most. The majority of those students had attended prep schools like Philips Exeter Academy or one of the nation's top public schools, according to an exhaustive, unflinching examination of Wesleyan's racial history that was published in the college's alumni magazine in the fall of 1999.* But as the civil rights struggle raged around the Wesleyan campus, and sometimes spilled onto it, the pressure to open the school's gates to minorities became unavoidable.

In 1964 Wesleyan hired a new dean of admissions, John C. Hoy, who had graduated from the school in the Class of 1955. He had gone on to work in the admissions office at Swarthmore where, as dean, he created one of the first minority-recruitment programs in the country. By the mid-1960s, he was invited to do the same at his alma mater. In a precursor of the recruiting trips that the admissions officers would mount three decades later, Hoy and his colleagues began fanning out into urban school systems across the country, searching for the best minority applicants.

Hoy explained the college's new, broader admissions philosophy to a reporter from the Wesleyan student daily newspaper, the *Argus,* in December 1964:

> It is too early to guess how diverse the new class might be, but we are looking for an enormous range of candidates. We are looking for socio-economic differences and personal value difference. We are looking for the able young man, the versatile, the adventuresome. We are looking for the independent young man who stands the best chance of accomplishing something in his lifetime, as opposed to the dabbler.

This definition of admissions policy, which represented a radical shift at the time, would still guide the officers thirty years later. They, like Hoy, saw themselves not merely as talent scouts, but as social engineers, building a community in which the definition of diversity was broad enough to

---

*Much of the account that follows was drawn from that article.

include oboists and second basemen. That was hardly a controversial goal. But in that same interview in 1964, Hoy also added: "In regards to the distribution of races in the incoming class, we seem to be tending toward a reverse prejudice in the matter of Negro applicants. We can't ignore this fact." (It would take another five years before Wesleyan would stop overlooking women and begin recruiting and admitting them, too.)

In the spring of 1965, under Hoy's leadership, Wesleyan admitted 27 minority students to the incoming Class of 1969. Fourteen of them—13 blacks and 1 Puerto Rican—went on to enroll, representing nearly 4 percent of a class of about 380, a virtually unprecedented number at an elite northeastern college. (The previous year, 3 black students had been accepted, and 2 had enrolled.) The following year, 33 black students matriculated at Wesleyan. By the fall of 1999, nearly 10 percent of students in the Wesleyan Class of 2003 were black, and another 7 percent were Hispanic. These percentages were the envy of many of Wesleyan's competitors, including Williams, where the proportion of black students in the Class of 2003 was 6 percent, and Amherst, where it was 6.5 percent.

Yet until Doug Bennet arrived as president in 1995, Wesleyan continued to lose a higher percentage of its students—minority, as well as white—after the freshman year than many competitors. Some of them transferred to other institutions; others dropped out. In 1995, fifty-seven students left Wesleyan during or immediately after the freshman year, a loss of 8 percent of the class. By 1999, that figure had fallen to 5 percent, a loss of about thirty-six freshmen—an improvement, but still high. Greg knew that at least some of those students left because they had found the workload too arduous, and even President Bennet would have conceded that Wesleyan was often not doing enough to support its students once they arrived there.

Greg was also aware that some of those same students had shown signs of struggle in high school, too. Wesleyan, a tough place academically, wasn't for everyone, and it was concerns like these that passed through his mind as he picked up the application of Aggie Ramirez and spread its contents across the walnut-stained table in his kitchen. Like Ralph, Greg relished reading at home, particularly in the kitchen, which was in the southwest corner of his sixty-year-old house and lit by the morning sun. After his wife had left for her job—like Natalie, she was a teacher—and their two children had departed for high school, Greg would clear the breakfast dishes, brew a pot of coffee and get down to the business at hand.

He noted from the initials on the outside of Aggie's file that Ralph had read her application first, twenty-five days earlier, but he was careful to lay a piece of paper over Ralph's ratings and final vote. He would read Ralph's notes but wanted to compile his own numbers.

Greg was not reading Aggie's file as the final arbiter of her fate; that was a role that he would play on several thousand other applications, as Nancy worked to find her footing as dean. In this case, he was merely the second reader. Like Ralph, he would be making a recommendation. If he and Ralph ended up being in agreement, Nancy would likely endorse their choice. If they disagreed, Nancy would have to make a decision on her own or consult the committee.

Greg looked first at the transcript, and it wasn't just those three senior-year C's and that D that irritated him. It was that Aggie had dropped math that year as well, perhaps to squeeze in all those extracurricular activities. Aggie had gotten good grades in math the previous three years, so there was no valid reason for her to avoid the subject. "I wouldn't expect to see her taking calculus," Greg said later. "But maybe a statistics course." Wesleyan liked its applicants to challenge themselves academically, and Aggie could have been working harder.

As he made his way to her SAT scores, he wasn't inclined to hold her modest performance against her. "These were decent scores for someone with no college in the family, and who spoke Spanish at home," Greg explained, agreeing with Ralph's analysis. But as he weighed his evaluation, Aggie's senior-year grades and course selection kept tipping the scale. As he did before he made so many decisions, Greg paused and looked out the kitchen window, across the driveway to his frosted-over garden. He even thought for a moment about what he might plant in the spring. Then he turned back to the single sheet of paper in front of him, locating the space provided for the second reader on Aggie's workcard, and wrote out Aggie's first-quarter averages in enormous block print. If this went to committee, he wanted to make sure that no one missed those scores. He wrote "60, 73, 74, 77" under the abbreviations "EN" (English), "SP" (Spanish), "PH" (physics) and "POL" (politics). On the next line, he wrote the second-quarter grades—an impressive 80 in English and an 84 in Spanish—along with question marks in physics and political science. The school had not supplied second-quarter grades in those particular subjects, but Greg inferred that they were largely unchanged from the first quarter. He then wrote Aggie's final averages for the first semester, or first two quarters, of her senior year: "68, 77, 71, 75." Anyone could see that she had brought her grades up in English (by 8 points) and Spanish (by 4), but the final result in all four classes remained disturbingly low.

Before Greg could ponder how Wesleyan might change Aggie's life—or how she might change Wesleyan—he felt it was his obligation to consider whether she could do the work. "The first reason to admit," he said, "always needs to be that you think the student can succeed here. Otherwise, you'd not only be hurting the kid, you'd be hurting the institution." A decisive clue as to how Aggie might perform at Wesleyan lay in determining how well her school prepared its students for college. Though Oldfields was located in his territory, Greg wasn't especially familiar with it, and couldn't recall ever having visited it. No one other than Aggie from its forty-five-member senior class had applied for the Class of 2004 at Wesleyan. Indeed, Wesleyan had received only three applications from Oldfields in the previous five years, and none of those applicants had been admitted.

In an attempt to gauge the quality of Oldfields's graduates, Greg turned to the list that the school had supplied of where its students had been accepted in the previous three years. He underlined Brown, Cornell and Pomona on the list, but drew arrows where Amherst, Dartmouth, Harvard, Princeton, Wesleyan and Williams would have been, had any of the school's graduates been admitted there. "How good is this school?" he wrote on Aggie's workcard, "Very few to HSC's"—"highly selective colleges." The track record of Aggie's predecessors would count against her.

Greg moved on to the ratings. Being careful to keep Ralph's numbers hidden, he filled in his own with relative ease. When he exposed Ralph's choices, he would see that they were almost identical. Though Ralph had worried he had been too generous in giving Aggie the overall academic rating of 4—the category he had initially scored as a 3—Greg had come to the same conclusion with little hesitation.

Greg was not supposed to consider Ralph's final recommendation in making his own, but he was permitted to read Ralph's raw notes. He saw that Ralph had appeared to be laying out a strong case for Aggie as someone who would be a leader at Wesleyan—and, someday, within the neighborhood where she had been raised. It was a classic argument for affirmative action. But just because Wesleyan—and Greg himself—placed a premium on bringing Hispanic students to Wesleyan, didn't mean that every Hispanic applicant would be admitted. *She's not succeeding in this program, and there's nothing to predict she'd succeed here,* Greg thought. He circled his choice: "DENY PLUS."

Nancy would have a decision to make.

A day after Greg read Aggie's file, his colleague Rod Bugarin picked up the other case that had vexed Ralph on that snowy day three weeks earlier: the application of Tiffany Wang.

Rod had drawn the file next because her high school, Gunn, in Palo Alto, was within his jurisdiction. Indeed, he knew it well, having visited it earlier in the fall, his first at Wesleyan, as well as during the last of the three years that he worked at Hampshire College in western Massachusetts. Gunn was not far from Stanford but hardly looked it. Set on a commercial block near a cemetery and a Veterans Affairs office, its campus was basically a series of low-rise brown buildings with shingle roofs extending back some distance from a green lawn. On its outskirts were a number of portable trailers that had been painted to appear as if they were part of the main building. But what Gunn lacked in style it more than made up for in academic excellence. A number of its parents were executives in the software industry, and the school sent plenty of students to HSC's. Whether Tiffany Wang had been well prepared to do the work at Wesleyan would not be an issue.

Just as Ralph's responsibilities included keeping alert for talented Hispanic students, Rod was charged with the same duty for any applicants of note who checked the box "ASIAN AMERICAN" or "NATIVE HAWAIIAN, PACIFIC ISLANDER." His own background qualified him, at least in part, for this subspecialty of his job. His parents, neither of whom had graduated from high school, were born in the Philippines. He himself had been raised in Honolulu, in a neighborhood not far from Pearl Harbor that he described as "the ghetto of Hawaii." It was an area populated mostly by Chinese and Vietnamese immigrants, who often lived several families to the same house. Until the age of sixteen, Rod, whose father worked as a construction worker, slept on a floor.

Rod had always been driven, and remembers looking at a college guidebook as early as age seven, when he was in the second grade, and deciding then that he would apply to the University of North Carolina. His reasoning was simple: that was where his mother had moved after she and his father had gotten divorced. (At the time, he was living with his father.) Troubled by a fatal shooting and several recent stabbings at his high school in downtown Honolulu, he decided on his own to transfer to a more affluent, suburban public school eight miles away. Despite being one of the most impoverished students enrolled there, he was outranked by only 2 of his 425 classmates when he graduated in 1992.

Rod's class rank and extracurricular activities—he was active on the tennis team and the school newspaper—would probably have made him a formidable applicant to any college, regardless of his background. But he knew that his parents' limited education and his family's economic struggles had also helped explain the gap between his score on the math portion of the SAT (a formidable 750) and an underwhelming verbal score (550). Moreover, the colleges that accepted him—Reed in Oregon, Franklin & Marshall in Pennsylvania and the University of Rochester—didn't get many applicants from Hawaii. If his candidacy had gotten a boost from his hometown or ethnicity, so be it, Rod thought. Other students had advantages that he did not.

After Rochester flew him out for a visit to coax him into accepting its offer, Rod decided to enroll there. He wanted an adventure far from home—the extreme difference in temperature from Hawaii didn't bother him—and he liked the premedical and medical programs at the school, for at that point he thought he was going to be a doctor. But he soon discovered that he enjoyed his work-study job in the Rochester admissions office more than the organic chemistry courses that were required of a premed. He had even gotten to live out every college student's fantasy by managing to unearth a record of how his application had been reviewed at Rochester. "I was shocked at how well I was rated," Rod said. By the time he graduated, he decided to look for an admissions job. And after three years working at Hampshire, where 2010 students sought 1200 offers for the Class of 2003, Rod moved to Wesleyan, where the level of competition was much stiffer.

Mindful of all the opposing forces at play—the need for him to say no to a higher percentage of applicants, but not necessarily more Asian American applicants—Rod began to consider the case of Tiffany Wang. Like Ralph and Greg, he did his reading at home, a rented condominium that overlooked one of the largest bodies of water in Connecticut, Lake Pocotopaug, in a wooded area about ten miles west of the Wesleyan campus. But Rod's habits were more nocturnal, and he went through his files from late evening until dawn, which was the only time he could concentrate. "There's nothing to watch on TV, no banks are open and the gym is closed," he said. After a night of reading, Rod would usually sleep until noon, have lunch, drive to the admissions office to drop off the files he had read the previous night, pick up a new stack, work out for two hours in the Wesleyan gym and then begin the whole ritual again—but only after "Must-See TV" programs like *Friends* and *E.R.* had ended. Rod worked at a simple white table that he had purchased from Target and decorated with assorted family photos. He read only in his bedroom and had the freedom to do so because his partner, Jeff, whom he had met a year earlier, lived in Providence. For now, they had agreed to commute to see each other on weekends.

As he scanned the file of Tiffany Wang late on a February night, one of the first sections that Rod examined was under the heading of extracurricular activities. He was always looking for the impact that an applicant had made in high school, and he found concrete evidence on Tiffany's résumé. In addition to running track and playing basketball for four years, Tiffany was vice president of the Asian Pride Club and a cofounder of the Human Rights Club. Tiffany indicated that she spent only an hour a week on the activities for the latter but provided no description of what the club was. No matter; Rod was willing to give her a lift because she had started her own student group, a detail to which Ralph had scarcely paid attention.

Rod had already noted the courses that Tiffany had chosen to take, which, to him, were almost more important than her grades themselves. He knew that the total of six Advanced Placement, college-level courses she had had in her junior and senior years would be considered a heavy course load almost anywhere else, but at Gunn, it was only average. (The school offered about fifteen AP's.) Rod was particularly concerned that Tiffany had not taken any Advanced Placement English courses, which Wesleyan considered a virtual prerequisite for students at good high schools. He marked the fact that the recommendations of her teachers and counselor were only lukewarm, and noted her middle-range class rank and her high SAT scores. Like Ralph, Rod found her test performance impressive for a girl who had grown up speaking English as a second language.

On Tiffany's workcard, he wrote: "Great tester with initiative and leadership." With that promising beginning, Tiffany appeared to be getting a better hearing from Rod than she had with Ralph. But then he added, "rank and program"—meaning grades and course selection—"hurt."

Now Rod had a decision to make.

In the six months that he had been at Wesleyan, he had emerged as a vocal critic of how Wesleyan sometimes treated Asian American applicants. At times, he complained that his colleagues were not as forgiving as he thought they should have been when they considered the academic shortcomings of such students, and he stated, "I have seen the bar set unfairly high for Asian kids applying to Wesleyan." Although Rod wished the other officers would be more willing to give a less-than-stellar Asian American applicant the benefit of the doubt, he quickly concluded the case of Tiffany Wang "was not one of those instances."

For Rod, Tiffany's economic circumstances and her parents' education were more relevant factors than her ethnicity. Her parents had graduated from college and they lived in an affluent area. Her SAT's may well have been among the highest that Wesleyan would see that year, but that only underscored the fact that she wasn't living up to her potential. In the end, Rod's ratings of Tiffany would turn out to be almost identical to Ralph's: both gave her a slight edge personally, but not academically. But where Ralph had circled "DENY PLUS," Rod had chosen "ADMIT MINUS."

In fact, both officers were ultimately in agreement. Rod had scribbled the initials "WL"—"or waiting list"—next to his recommendation, suggesting that Greg or Nancy defer a decision to admit or reject Tiffany until after May 1. By then, Wesleyan would know which of those students whom it had accepted were planning to enroll. Rod had read the applications of all six students who had applied to Wesleyan from Tiffany's high school and had recommended accepting several who were ranked higher than she. He wanted to see if any of them chose to come to Wesleyan before deciding Tiffany's fate. If she was admitted elsewhere in the interim, and decided to go, that was a risk Rod was willing to take.

After Ralph had advised Jordan Goldman not to submit his portfolio of short stories, Jordan comforted himself with the thought that the odds were good that someone other than Ralph would read his file. After all, Ralph had said in his group information session that there were nine other admissions officers at Wesleyan. Jordan could just imagine one of Ralph's colleagues picking up one of Jordan's stories and becoming engrossed; the alternate image—that of Ralph tossing his short stories into the trash—was too much for Jordan to contemplate, particularly as he reeled from his early deferral from Brown.

But odds are a funny thing. A week and a half after agonizing over the cases of Tiffany Wang and Aggie Ramirez, Ralph reached over to the pile of applications that he had been assigned at random and pulled out the submission of Jordan Michael Goldman of Staten Island. Opening the folder, Ralph saw that the computer had printed the code "cv"—indicating that Jordan had made a campus visit—at the bottom of the workcard. Occasionally, that might have jogged his memory that not only had he met Jordan, but Jordan had fairly begged him to consider his work. But the fact was, Ralph had met hundreds of kids at group information sessions that fall, and Jordan was hardly the first to raise the issue of submitting supplemental materials. As near as Ralph could tell, Jordan was a perfect stranger to him. And according to the file, he would be the first person at Wesleyan to read his application.

Over the course of the next few minutes, Ralph would note that Jordan had checked the box for Caucasian, that he was interested in English and creative writing and that his SAT's were strong—750 verbal, 710 math, for a combined 1460. Ralph also read that Jordan's parents had both attended college and that his mother had a master's degree. With a profile like that, Ralph would be expecting a lot.

He noticed that Jordan was ranked 69 in a class of 741. That fell within the top 10 percent, and Ralph scribbled Jordan's standing on the workcard. While Jordan may have been preoccupied about being ranked below the top 20 kids in his class, admissions officers at most of the elite colleges didn't usually set the bar that high. The top 10 percent was the unofficial threshold, and Jordan—unlike Tiffany Wang, who ranked only in the top 30 percent—had met it.

Ralph noted that Jordan's grades were almost all A's and A minuses, and that he had taken four Advanced Placement courses—American history, European history, political science and English. While that was two fewer than Tiffany Wang, Jordan's counselor had rated his program among the most demanding in the sprawling public school that he attended. Wesleyan liked to see its applicants "max out" what their high schools offered, and Jordan appeared to be doing so. That Tottenville High in Staten Island did not have as many Advanced Placement courses as Gunn in Palo Alto may have helped Jordan, at least in terms of applying to college.

Jordan had also taken four years of foreign language (Spanish) and calculus as a senior. He was hitting every mark that Wesleyan expected.

Jordan had entered all of his extracurricular activities on the form provided: junior class president, business editor of the school newspaper, volunteer in a homeless shelter, among many others. But Ralph grew a bit irritated when he saw that much of this information had been repeated on a typed, five-page résumé. *I'm getting tired of seeing résumés,* Ralph thought, and without even looking at it, returned it to Jordan's folder and picked up the first of his essays.

In response to the question about the extracurricular activity that had the most meaning for him, Jordan had written:

> I first met Devin Cutugno the summer that I turned seven. For me, being seven was all about plastic Thundercats' lunch boxes and X-Men action figures and day-glow fluorescent clothing that seemed to exist only so the wearer could loudly proclaim to everyone within a ten mile radius—"Here I am!"

Ralph paused after finishing that opening paragraph; it was the reference to X-Men that stopped him. As luck would have it, he loved the X-Men comic books. At Stanford, a friend of his had written a major research paper on the ragtag bunch of superheroes and how they existed as a mirror of teenage angst. The friend had collected virtually every X-Men comic ever published, and Ralph had read many of them.

Just two sentences into his essay and Jordan had made a good impression, but a shared love of comic books would get an applicant only so far with Ralph, who was eager to see where Jordan was going with this idea:

> That summer Mom sent me to Sports Camp at a nearby school. She told me that it was "about time I learned what a football was," and so, with a plastic Thundercats' lunch box in hand and a brand spankin' new pair of Keds Athletic Footwear on my feet, I was shipped off to camp.
>
> At the very same school a boy named Devin was going to a Special Education summer program. The way our schedules worked out, Devin and I ate lunch at the same time everyday. And it's funny, the way people remember things; for the life of me I can't tell you how many days into camp it was, or what I ate for lunch that day—but I can still remember exactly what I was

wearing the first time I spoke to Devin Cutugno. My day-glow orange T-shirt was being sported in full effect, complementing a pair of cut-off blue jeans and a formerly new pair of Keds that was, by now, so fully encrusted with dirt that the Keds logo was reduced to K——S. I remember this because, as I sat down to eat my lunch that particular day, I noticed some other kid halfway across the cafeteria whose day-glow orange T-shirt just screamed, "Look at me, too!!" So I decided to walk over to that kid with all the unabashed courage of my full seven years, unsure if I was planning on hugging him for sharing in my fashion sense or demanding that he take the shirt off right way, but moving toward him nonetheless.

I took about eight steps before I realized the boy was in a wheelchair.

By ten steps I saw that there were X-Men action figures on his wheelchair tray.

Eighteen steps and I saw that our shirts were, in fact, exactly alike.

I remember everyone else in the cafeteria looking at me strangely that day, but I didn't much care. I had decided I was overjoyed by our common interest in clothing. I asked the boy his name and why he was in a wheelchair, and, more importantly, if I could play toys with him. He told me that his name was Devin Cutugno, and he couldn't walk because he had cerebral palsy, and then he began to attack me with his favorite X-Men figure. Within mere minutes we were immersed in an X-Men battle of epic proportions. Since Devin cannot speak clearly, we used a series of clicks and head movements to communicate. We soon invented our own secret language.

And that was that. Every day afterwards Devin and I would bring in toys to play with one another, and when everyone else went to the school yard to climb on the monkey bars and then swings, I wheeled Devin around and we played our own games. We raced together and planned on taking over the world with evil cybernetic robots that we would build ourselves. His wheelchair quickly became a spaceship and Devin hunted me down, since I was the last surviving member of that terrible race of *"hideous legged ones."* Together we flew through the playground galaxy, and when our spaceship landed safely amongst the rest of the children in the cafeteria, I learned how to feed him. At the time I never thought much about what Devin couldn't do, because we were having too much fun with what he *could* do.

Ralph went on to read how the two boys had become best friends, "eagerly awaiting the newest issue of *Sports Illustrated*'s swimsuit calendar," "debating Euclidean Geometry," and now talking about college. That Devin's dreams had not been impeded by his inability even to go to the bathroom unassisted prompted Jordan to come to the following conclusion: "Anything can be overcome with the proper amount of effort and resolve."

Ralph put his pen down and just shook his head. A year later, he would still be able to tell the story of Devin and Jordan without having the essay in front of him. "It touched me that a kid could be so unselfconsciously good and have it be so natural," Ralph recalled. As he read Jordan's essay, he had remembered a news report he had seen on television a few nights earlier. A boy attending a local elementary school had lost his hair to chemotherapy treatments, and all the boys in his class had shaved their heads in solidarity. The story featured footage of them all rolling around on the grass together, a bunch of cueballs. *That was something Jordan would do,* Ralph thought.

Ralph set the essay aside for Natalie to read later and began to contemplate summarizing Jordan's words on his workcard. How could he do justice to what he had just read? He decided not to even try, and instead, simply wrote: "Very touching essay about friendship with boy in wheelchair since age 7 (when they met). Nicely done."

Jordan had also been asked on his application to write a second essay, on a topic of his choice, and Ralph decided to read it quickly. What more did he need to know? Not surprisingly, the second piece was a bit of a letdown. Jordan had sought, like so many applicants, to convey his uniqueness. But his references to being "an oil painting that has yet to receive its finishing touches," or his Seinfeld-esque realization that "it is counterproductive to put laundry detergent in the dishwasher" only made Ralph yawn. And when he got around to Jordan's conclusion—describing himself as a dreamer, with a "dream of attending Wesleyan University"—he found himself dreaming, too, and wishing that Jordan's second essay had been less contrived. But no matter. "I forgave him," Ralph said later, "because the first one was so good."

Ralph next noticed that Jordan had enclosed a thick portfolio, which began with a series of testimonials and then, according to the table of contents, included four short stories. Ralph hated when kids bent the rules like this. With a recommendation from one guidance counselor and two teachers, each applicant had more than enough references. Moreover, he believed that any truly good writer should be able to shine in the space provided. Jordan's first essay was testament to that.

Ralph was about to put the packet back in the folder, unread, and make his recommendation when he noticed that it included a letter that Devin's parents had written on Jordan's behalf. He decided to break his rule about not considering extra materials, simply because he was curious. Was Jordan for real? The letter went on for two pages, but one passage near the bottom stood out:

> Jordan has spent a great deal of time with our family, and he has often traveled with us as a companion for Devin. Jordan has aided our son in all facets of his life, and the grace in which he has carried, fed, dressed and toileted our son is far beyond his years. He has always been there as a role model for our son, and his ability to make Devin laugh is endless.
>
> When Jordan was diagnosed with a heart ailment in June 1997, Devin was distraught. It was somewhat ironic, because Devin had always been the one with medical problems throughout the years, and the fact that Jordan could be ill was inconceivable to our son. Once again, however, we witnessed the incredible strength of their friendship, and now Devin had the opportunity to be strong for Jordan. . . . After two attempts, Jordan's heart surgery was finally successful in April 1998, and we don't know who was more relieved—Jordan or our son. I don't know what Devin would have done if something ever happened to this wonderful friend.

Ralph, who had seen a reference to Jordan's heart surgery in a teacher's recommendation, didn't need to read any further. He turned to the ratings and quickly moved down the list, giving Jordan all 8's, with two exceptions. When Ralph came to the rating for Jordan's extracurricular activities, he thought again of the long list the boy had presented. Other than being elected junior class president, he hadn't distinguished himself with his activities. Ralph gave him a 6. "It could have been a 7," Ralph admitted later, "but I was trying to temper my enthusiasm." But when it came to Jordan's personal rating, Ralph didn't hold back, and awarded him a perfect 9. Of the nearly fifteen hundred applications that Ralph would read that year, he would assign only about twenty-five perfect scores. Jordan had gotten one of them.

I want this kid, Ralph thought to himself.

Ralph quickly scribbled his final evaluation: "Strong student and compelling person, too. Very gifted writer." Almost as an anticlimax, he circled his recommendation: "ADMIT." As he had with that nascent cancer researcher, he decided it would be a waste of time for someone else to read Jordan's application. He had worked at Wesleyan long enough to know that Jordan was an obvious admit and drew an *X* through the line for the second reader.

On March 2, two weeks after Ralph read Jordan's file, Nancy Meislahn picked up his workcard inside the dean's office in the Wesleyan admissions building. The card, like several thousand others stacked on a circular table nearby, had been separated from the rest of the application, to make it easier for her to read. While her colleagues struggled to read thirty applications in a day, Nancy had to make hundreds of decisions during that same time period. Scanning Ralph's summary of Jordan's case, she saw that this would be an easy call. Under the line set aside for "ACTION," Nancy circled an *A,* for admission.

Jordan Goldman would be offered admission to the Class of 2004 at Wesleyan University. But would he accept?

Before closing Jordan's file and sending it on to Nancy, Ralph had written "HP" on the front of the workcard and the folder, identifying him as a "hot prospect." After going to the dean, Jordan's folder—along with several hundred others that spring—would be rerouted to a windowless office in the basement of the admissions office. There, a recent Wesleyan graduate had been assigned a newly designated task: to reach out early to those applicants whom the school wanted most.

Wesleyan and other top colleges long ago made a handshake agreement that they would not tell an applicant from the regular pool that he or she had been admitted before the end of March. That way, all of the colleges would be competing on an even playing field. But there were more subtle ways to let an applicant know he was wanted—a friendly e-mail message, a note from a professor—and Ralph wanted Jordan to be on that priority list. Wesleyan, like other colleges, had been sending coy notes like these for nearly a decade. Now, with the advent of e-mail and a heightened sense of competition, that effort was getting more organized and sophisticated.

Asked later why he thought he had been admitted to Wesleyan, Jordan had a ready answer: that letter of recommendation from the author and screenwriter Richard Price. When told that Ralph had barely noticed the letter—indeed, he had breezed right past it without reading it—Jordan was incredulous. Not only did Ralph decline to read short stories, Jordan was told, but he didn't read celebrity endorsements, either. It was the studied opinion of Ralph and other admissions officers that Hollywood types, as well as senators and chief executive officers, who wrote on behalf of applicants rarely knew them, let alone their families. If Ralph had had the time to examine it carefully, he would have seen that this particular letter was an exception: the famous Richard Price and the less-than-famous Jordan Goldman *were* good friends, however improbably.

In the end, it didn't matter: Jordan had gotten into Wesleyan on his own, with a little boost from the only friend he had needed: Devin.

One of the perks of working at a rarefied prep school was that simply by picking up the phone the college counselors at Harvard-Westlake in Los Angeles—like their counterparts at Choate or Exeter—could arrange an audience with an admissions officer at Harvard, Yale or any other top college, even in the middle of the busy reading season. These were, in fact clandestine meetings, their existence unknown to most parents and students, to say nothing of those schools that didn't have such pull. The informal conversations were usually conducted over the phone, but sometimes in person.

So it was that in February, Sharon Merrow and her colleagues at Harvard-Westlake flew east on a pilgrimage. It was a journey that she, as well as the admissions officers at the nation's top colleges, would find mutually beneficial. For Harvard-Westlake, and other elite high schools, these sessions represented one last opportunity to discuss the candidacy of a particular applicant. The colleges, meanwhile, could ask specific questions about that student or, more important, get a sense of how that student might be leaning, in terms of where he or she might go if accepted. Even without the relationship between Ralph and Sharon, this was a meeting to which Wesleyan would have agreed. With *U.S. News* having put such an emphasis on "yield"—the percentage of students accepted at a college who then actually enrolled—some colleges had, in fact, begun rejecting top applicants, not wishing to waste an acceptance on someone who appeared unlikely to attend.

Wesleyan wasn't usually so severe. But as the reading season gave way to the final round of decisions, the admissions office wanted to get a sense of where Wesleyan stood at the top high schools in the country. No matter how good a school was, Wesleyan would set aside only so many spots for its students. The definition of diversity at Wesleyan, as elsewhere, dictated that the freshman class represent as broad a range of schools as possible. But if a top applicant appeared to be unlikely to choose Wesleyan even before the formal decisions were out—remember, Wesleyan wasn't the only college signaling its decisions to students before the formal letters were mailed—then the committee might be inclined to admit one more student from that particular school than it would have otherwise.

In the winter of 2000, Sharon and three colleagues from Harvard-Westlake were scheduled to visit with Ralph at Wesleyan during the third week in February. Their timing was good. Ralph, who was the second reader on all the Harvard-Westlake applications, liked to consider all candidates from the same school on a single day. This year, twenty-four Harvard-Westlake students had applied to Wesleyan—not as many as in past years, but still more than the total number of applicants from nearly every other high school in the country, with the exception of a few other powerhouses like Stuyvesant in New York. As the end of the reading season neared, Ralph could tell by the rate he was reading that he wouldn't be getting to the Harvard-Westlake files until early March. Talking to Sharon in advance would provide him with some of the background essential to make his choices.

As it happened, the Harvard-Westlake group was delayed in their travel and wound up having to talk to Ralph by phone, on a Saturday morning. He had taken the call at his desk in the admissions office, so that he could print out a list of Harvard-Westlake applicants from his computer. As he sat at his desk, Sharon and three other counselors took turns passing around the phone. They mentioned to Ralph that they were in a room at the Sheraton Towers hotel in midtown Manhattan, and though Sharon was always unwilling to disclose her full itinerary to Ralph—in this case, business trumped friendship—he deduced that they had made a stop in New York to visit the admissions office at Columbia University. Sharon had tried to lure Ralph to New York—only a two-hour drive south of Middletown—with the offer of a good dinner on Saturday night. But Ralph had declined the invitation, preferring to get a good night's sleep in preparation for his Sunday morning performance of a movement from Holst's *Jupiter Suite* on the handbells at church, for which he would need to be alert. Sharon already knew that nothing came between Ralph and his handbells.

At the outset of their phone conversation, the Harvard-Westlake counselors indicated they wanted to run through the applicants' names alphabetically, which meant Julianna Bentes was near the top of the list. In this case, Ralph would be the one asking the questions.

"Is there any chance she's going to be interested?" Ralph asked.

Without disclosing that Julianna had applied to twelve other colleges, Sharon diplomatically told Ralph only that she would be casting a wide net. That didn't bode well, Ralph thought, but Sharon assured him: "Julianna's going to be fair. She isn't ruling anybody out."

If almost any other counselor had given him such assurance, Ralph would have read between the lines and concluded: *I'm backup*. But this was Sharon talking, and after sixteen years of friendship she had no reason to be coy with him. If he was out of the running, she'd have every reason to tell him so. *Maybe I've got a shot*, Ralph thought.

Sharon had given Ralph one other cause for encouragement: Julianna was still concerned about the crossed signals that had caused her to miss an interview with a Wesleyan alumnus. Earlier in the winter, Catherine Bentes had arranged an alumni interview for Julianna with a local judge who had graduated from Wesleyan in the 1960s and whose name had been given to the family by the school admissions office. When Julianna showed up for her interview, she waited at least a half hour while court was in session. After the courtroom had emptied, she went in and approached the bench.

"Your interview was yesterday, and you missed it," Julianna says she was told, abruptly. The judge said he was now late for another appointment and was then going on vacation. She would have to reschedule.

Julianna and Catherine were certain that they had gotten the date for so important an appointment correct, but the judge would not be swayed. Shaken, Julianna had tried to reach Sharon from a payphone at the courthouse but, unable to do so, worried that her chances of being accepted at Wesleyan had been irreparably damaged. The next day at school, Julianna made her daily trip to the college counselors' office. The sight of Julianna coming through the door raised no eyebrows: she spent so much time with Sharon and her colleagues that they would take it upon themselves to find her a prom date. But once Julianna told Sharon the story, she immediately got Ralph and the girl together on the phone. In a brief conversation, Julianna told Ralph that she felt terrible about the miscommunication. Ralph apologized just as profusely and told her not to worry. If she couldn't arrange an alumni interview, Wesleyan would not hold it against her.

Soon afterward, the judge called Julianna on his own to reschedule their appointment. When they finally did meet, she felt that the conversation went well. The judge turned out to be an impressive spokesman for Wesleyan, describing all that the school had done to prepare him for his adult life. The only strike against him, Julianna decided, was that he said he had once worked in the Nixon administration.

Ralph finally got a chance to read Julianna's application, and all the others from Harvard-Westlake, a few days later. As he opened Julianna's file, he thought to himself: *I've heard so much about you, now let's meet you*.

For all of the pregame buildup, Julianna did not disappoint.

Just as Jordan Goldman had, Julianna Bentes jumped every hurdle that Wesleyan set in her path, and then some. Ralph was aware that Julianna was a student of color but didn't know her background. Now he saw that she had checked "MULTIRACIAL" on her application, and then written in "Brazilian-American (Latina, African, North European)." *Cool!* Ralph said to himself out loud. That was some combination; Julianna was definitely a "priority" applicant. Moreover, she indicated that she had learned English as a second language, since she had grown up speaking Portuguese. All of these elements would ordinarily help an applicant. But Julianna needed no assistance.

Julianna's SAT's were among the best Ralph had seen all year—a perfect 800 verbal, and a 710 in math, for a total of 1510. She had taken two Advanced Placement courses her junior year—biology and American history—and five her senior year—studio art, English literature, calculus, physics and the history of art. Other than a B plus in calculus, all of her grades in those courses were A's or A minuses. Indeed, there was only one other B on her transcript, in precalculus. *Way cool!* Ralph said. On the part of the school report that identified Julianna's course load as "most rigorous," Ralph recognized Sharon's handwriting.

Ralph guessed that Julianna was one of the top applicants to Wesleyan from Harvard-Westlake, if not *the* top applicant, but she had also said she was interested in becoming a science major. Few applicants to

Wesleyan, particularly women, expressed such intentions so early. With its reputation in the arts, Wesleyan was more likely to attract fledgling poets. *Minority woman in science,* Ralph thought. *Way, way cool!*

Ralph had known firsthand about Julianna's intense participation in dance. But he learned from her application that she had also led the black culture club, attended local and national diversity conferences and served for four years on the admissions committee at Harvard-Westlake. At some point as he read her application, he would later recall, he turned around in his chair as if to tell someone sitting nearby that the admissions officer's equivalent of Tom Cruise or Julia Roberts had landed on his desk. But, of course, he was reading at home, and there was no one else in the room to tell. He would remember thinking: *How many kids are there in the whole country who are like this?*

Even before he read Julianna's essays, Ralph knew she would be admitted to Wesleyan, but he was still curious to see what she had written. As the subject of her main essay, she had chosen Los Angeles, and Hollywood in particular. It was her hometown, as it was Ralph's. Julianna wrote first about how important it was to look below the "glitter and cartoons" of the entertainment industry, to find "dreams unfulfilled." As someone who had grown up black and Latina in a relatively poor neighborhood, Julianna saw Hollywood as a metaphor for what ailed the city that she loved. She also believed that the city's future prospects for success were, like hers, unknown. In her conclusion, Julianna wrote:

> As much as I admire the moxie and determination of the actors who work at Starbucks or Jerry's Famous Deli, I also have seen many like them come and go, and many who stayed much longer than they meant to. From the glow on their faces as they speak of performances, I have seen the importance of dreaming; from their chill when they find that the winds of reality blow cold, I have learned the value of practicality. I have big dreams, but I also have contingency plans. In *I Know Why the Caged Bird Sings,* Maya Angelou's mother advised her to "hope for the best, be prepared for the worst, and you'll be ready for everything in between." While she wasn't the first mother to say that—or the last—the advice is sound. Maybe they should post it here along with the city limits. But life lessons are often best learned through life, and advice or no, dreams die hard. Sometimes though, im-

possible dreams do come true. That is what's best for me about growing up in a city on the border between wonderland and reality, where the stage lights and electrical tape meet.

Ralph liked Julianna's tone. However gently, she appeared to be tweaking the more privileged classmates who surrounded her at Harvard-Westlake.

As the second reader of Julianna's file, Ralph wasn't responsible for laying out the case for her. Amin, who had drawn her application first, had already done that. Ralph was pleased to see that Amin, the wrestler who had graduated from Wesleyan in 1996 and was new to the admissions office, had "gotten" Julianna. It would have been hard not to. But the girl appeared to have struck a chord with him: like Julianna, Amin had escaped a bad neighborhood, in his case East Harlem, and had gone to an elite private high school, on scholarship. Amin had written of Julianna: "Real contributor to community. Lots of Diversity. Fine person and outstanding student."

In filling out his ratings, Ralph tried to contain his enthusiasm, to the extent that was possible. He gave Julianna perfect 9's in two categories—academic achievement and commitment; 8's for intellectual curiosity and for how she came across as a person; and a 7 in extracurricular activities. Before circling "ADMIT," Ralph wrote: "Superior in every way. Top of the pool by far—great program, performance."

Ralph had waited almost three years to write those words.

As with Jordan Goldman, Nancy's call on Julianna was an easy one. Only a day after Ralph's ink dried, she picked up Julianna's workcard in the dean's office, saw what Amin and Ralph had written, and immediately circled *A,* for admit.

Before relinquishing the workcard to Nancy, Ralph had noticed that Amin was already one step ahead of him in strategizing to get Julianna to come to Wesleyan, having designated her as an "HP" (hot prospect). But Ralph wanted her to get more than just a friendly e-mail message from Wesleyan, and so he added the words "Fly her out" on the front of her folder. Once the acceptance letters were in the mail, Wesleyan would contact its top minority candidates and invite them to campus for a visit, all expenses paid.

This was a gesture that would be made to few other Wesleyan applicants, even if they were impoverished. Such was life, as the school saw it. If a white applicant spurned Wesleyan, there was usually someone of equal talent and ability to take his place. That was not the case with Julianna. Ralph wanted the office staff to make sure that Julianna got one of those tickets. So that everyone's competitive juices were flowing, he also wrote, "Already being flown out by 3 schools." He didn't know which, but he knew from Sharon's conference call that Julianna was being pursued.

Ralph also wrote the abbreviation "Univ. Scholar" on Julianna's workcard. Wesleyan had started its University Scholars program a year earlier. If Julianna qualified for financial aid—and such decisions were not up to Ralph, or his other colleagues in admissions—then she'd be eligible for consideration for the special program, which was lucrative. Only 10 students were to be designated as university scholars each year. They not only got a cash award of at least $12,000, but also a special mentorship arrangement with a faculty member. This was a program reserved for serious students who were likely to do important work at Wesleyan. Ralph wanted to make sure that the committee considering those coveted scholarships was aware of Julianna.

While Julianna may have been worried about how her initially botched alumni interview would affect her candidacy at Wesleyan, Ralph knew the truth: Wesleyan was the one with egg on its face, not her. The way that the judge had first treated her—whether she was a day late or not—constituted a public relations gaffe, and Sharon had told Ralph as much. At the least, Ralph should have let the judge know in advance how badly Wesleyan wanted this candidate. Ralph had not only neglected to do so, but didn't even think to call the judge after Julianna had called him to complain how she had been treated by him. By then, he was deep into the reading season. Now as he intensified his courtship of Julianna Bentes, Ralph couldn't afford for Wesleyan to make another mistake.

Seven
NOTHING TO DO
WITH THE DOPE

A few minutes before nine on a Wednesday in early March, Ralph walked out of his office and down the main staircase of the Wesleyan admissions building, visibly anxious. Within minutes, he and his nine colleagues were scheduled to convene as a committee for the final round of hearings on the Class of 2004. As he made his way to the morning meeting, Ralph was wondering how the committee would rule on a half dozen of his most prized candidates, all of whom remained in limbo. He was most worried about one applicant in particular: Becca Jannol. He had been strategizing for days about how he would present Becca's case to his colleagues that morning. He knew that his remarks, and the debate that followed, would likely determine whether Becca was offered admission to Wesleyan.

Ralph had first learned of Becca's involvement with the pot brownie in a conference call, the same one that Sharon, Becca's college counselor, had placed to his desk from her Manhattan hotel two weeks earlier. As Sharon and her colleagues moved briskly down the list of the twenty-four students who had applied to Wesleyan, assessing the prospects of each, Sharon had paused at Becca's name. "You have to know about this incident," she said, and then told Ralph how Becca had been the only student who accepted one of the brownies and then came forward. Another counselor, who was sitting in the hotel room with Sharon, interrupted to remind her that

Becca had gone on to be president of the student body and the chair of the honor board. The spin was as carefully choreographed as in a presidential campaign, but Ralph needed no convincing: he had already concluded that Becca had demonstrated exceptional character. And she had certainly left her mark at Harvard-Westlake, which was not easy to do.

Ralph hadn't yet read Becca's application when he spoke to Sharon, but if the suspension was discussed in her file—and Sharon assured him it was—then he knew that her case would almost certainly go before the committee, as did that of any student with a disciplinary record, no matter how innocuous and easily explained. In building a community, the admissions officers wanted to be sure that they weren't admitting someone who was already a certified miscreant. Becca's academic performance—mostly A's in tough courses at a top school—would likely help her, though her SAT's (a combined 1270) would not. Because she was white and her parents were educated, the bar would be set high for her. Wesleyan would have expected her to have scored closer to 1400, putting her in the 98th percentile nationally. As it stood, she was in the 87th percentile. Having worked in admissions at Occidental, Sharon knew how admissions officers' minds worked. But she also believed that Becca's story was so remarkable that it would trump any perception of deficiency.

Ralph would only promise Sharon that he was "going to push" for Becca but wouldn't presume to speak for his colleagues. She signed off by saying: "She's interested and would love Wesleyan. You could get her." *That would be nice,* Ralph thought. He remembered meeting Becca at Harvard-Westlake, at the presentation he had given on college essays, and he remembered having liked her. Now he really liked her. And more than anything, he trusted Sharon's judgment.

When he finally got the chance to read Becca's application, on the same day he read Julianna's, he noticed that she had written two names—his and Sharon's—when she had been asked to "list any persons who encouraged your interest in Wesleyan." Ralph smiled. "They do get brownie points for putting me down," he said later, with no trace of irony. "It boosts my ego."

Several weeks later, as he gathered his thoughts before that crucial committee meeting, he knew he wouldn't have much time to make Becca's case. The admissions committee had only five days to consider about four hundred applicants, each of whom had been deemed an especially tough call. Two readers, along with Nancy or Greg, had evaluated all of these applicants but had been unable to reach consensus. As if playing in a

Super Bowl with the score tied at the end of regulation play, this group of candidates would now be competing in overtime.

Nancy would allot the committee no more than five minutes to discuss each; then, as it had during the early-decision hearings, the committee would vote. But unlike in previous rounds, deferral was no longer an option. The committee couldn't afford to procrastinate, for the letters of decision, from Wesleyan and its competitors, would be mailed to students at the end of the month. In each case, the committee had only three choices: accept, reject or relegate to the waiting list. The letters of acceptance and rejection were definitive, of course. But at this point, Wesleyan had no idea whether an assignment to the waiting list was, effectively, a rejection, for it would not know until May, nearly two months from now, how many applicants it could accept off that list. The number of slots remaining in the class then would be determined by the number of applicants who received an initial letter of acceptance from Wesleyan, and then wrote back to say they wanted to attend. And how many of them accepted that offer would hinge, in part, on how many of them had been accepted at Wesleyan's competitors, including Brown, Dartmouth, Amherst and Williams. For now, Ralph and his colleagues would be fighting to get the candidates whom they cared most about, candidates like Becca, a clear-cut acceptance. The waiting list was too much of a crap shoot.

The admissions officers had all dressed down that morning, looking as if they were about to cram as a group for a battery of final exams. In expectation of sitting for upward of seven hours that first day, Ralph wore baggy black jeans and a comfortable red sweatshirt emblazoned with the logo of Stanford, his alma mater. He had shaved, but he didn't appear to have slept very much. Like his colleagues, he had stepped up his pace in recent days, reading almost around the clock. To Ralph's immediate right, Chris Lanser, the lanky former athlete and high school English teacher, was wearing a faded T-shirt that he had picked up at the Women's Final Four college basketball championship. Near the head of the table, Greg Pyke looked even more sleep-deprived than Ralph. His usually immaculate graying hair was barely combed, and his T-shirt, a souvenir from an annual gathering of New England admissions officers, appeared better-suited for a workout.

Before the meeting had even begun, the shiny boardroom table was strewn with cups of coffee, bottles of water, oranges and green-and-white cupcakes (Saint Patrick's Day was around the corner). There were also several boxes of energy-boosting, sugary cereals, which the officers passed around like cartons of popcorn. Other than the opportunity for a quick lunch, Nancy informed her nine colleagues, there would be only two fifteen-minute breaks between nine A.M. and five P.M.

"Think about your personal fluid intake," she advised. And she wasn't joking. Anyone who ducked out in the middle of a presentation would not be permitted to vote on that candidate. Halfway through the first day, Nancy herself would become so fatigued that she would ask her new colleagues to relieve her of the responsibility of summarizing each case aloud and tallying the vote. "I'm spent," she pleaded, but others were even more exhausted. Toward the end of that same day, one of Ralph's colleagues would fall asleep for several minutes during the discussion of a candidate. He awakened just in time to cast his vote though, mercifully, he broke no tie.

The last few weeks of the admissions season were always frenzied, but because this had been a record year for applications to Wesleyan, the level of disorganization had risen in direct proportion. As the officers gathered at nine, their dockets—each containing a statistical snapshot of every applicant for the class—were still being photocopied; the machines were having trouble bearing the load. A stack of paper that had been the equivalent of a short story in November had since ballooned to an epic 1198 pages, as thick as a New York City phonebook. While the officers waited for their documents, Greg gave them an update.

Of the nearly seven thousand applicants for the next freshman class, fourteen hundred—or 20 percent of the entire pool—had been admitted thus far. Nearly three hundred of those applicants had been accepted during the two rounds of early-decision hearings, in November and February. Their selection was binding, and they were considered part of the class. The other eleven hundred applicants had been accepted in the main round, their selection certified by Nancy or Greg before the committee would ever have its say. Those applicants would be under no obligation to accept Wesleyan's invitation to the class. As the committee hearings began, Greg had calculated that there was probably room to admit four hundred more candidates in the main round, for a total of eighteen hundred acceptances overall.

Because only about one of every four applicants accepted by Wesleyan in the main round was expected to say yes, the university always extended more acceptances than it could possibly accommodate. But if things went as in years past, by the time all the dust settled the freshman class would end up having about seven hundred members as of May 1. The remainder of the class, about fifteen students, would then be drawn from the hundreds of applicants relegated to the waiting list. Some years, more than fifty were taken off that list; in other years, so many applicants said yes from the main round that there was no room to take anyone else.

Thus the competition among the admissions officers to secure the remaining four hundred offers of acceptance, the only sure way into the Class of 2004, would be stiff. And it wasn't just the applicants who had already been earmarked for consideration by the committee who had a shot. Greg told the committee that, despite the late date, nearly twenty-five hundred other applicants still remained to be considered by him or Nancy. About half of those applications had been read by only one admissions officer and were still awaiting a second read; many hadn't yet been considered by anyone. Because the five, day-long meetings of the committee would be staggered over the next two weeks, those remaining cases would be resolved in between the hearings, with some sent to the committee in the interim. All told, Wesleyan would only be able to admit about one out of every six applicants who remained in the pool. As tough as it was to be admitted to Wesleyan in January, it would be even tougher in March. And sometimes, only chance had dictated when in the calendar an application had been considered.

As they awaited the arrival of their dockets, Greg reminded his colleagues what it was they were looking for. One of the first issues he raised was the SAT, and on that point he had some good news: thus far, the median SAT score of those invited to join the incoming class—a combined score of 1430—was running 60 points above the previous year's. "We have some room in the score profile," Greg told his colleagues, by which he meant that Wesleyan could take some risks in considering the applicants who remained. A handful of prospects with low SAT scores who otherwise met Wesleyan's varied criteria for admission could be welcomed into the class without doing damage to Wesleyan's standing. *That would help Becca Jannol,* Ralph thought.

Greg also told the group that the new class thus far exceeded the previous year's in its concentration of minority students; at this point, the new class was 11 percent black (compared to 9 percent in the class of 2003), 8 percent Hispanic (compared to 7 percent) and 12 percent Asian American (compared to 10 percent). Again, the alumni and the guidebooks would take note, and they would be impressed. But no one at the table should let down his or her guard. Those percentages, Greg advised, should not drop as the class was rounded out. Still, Ralph knew that this, too, boded well for Becca, who was white: the push to admit minority applicants into the class would be no more intense than it had been thus far. Now the only trend running against Becca was gender: men represented only 44 percent of the new class, and the goal was 50. Even so, there were still plenty of seats left for women.

Having received its charge, the panel was now ready to take its seats in the jury box. From the outset, the tentativeness that had marked the deliberations in early December was replaced by a bold, almost fearless decisiveness. One of the first cases to come before the committee was the application of a high school senior from northern California whose file had a special message attached. The president of another university had written to Doug Bennet, the president of Wesleyan, saying that the candidate was a family friend and that Wesleyan was her first choice. President Bennet had passed the letter on to the admissions office. The applicant's SAT's were strong (a combined 1400) and her grades, at a private school, were good. She had taken four years of a foreign language and the holy trinity of science: biology, chemistry and physics. What made this even more impressive, the committee was told, was that her father had not attended college.

In many admissions offices, a letter from the president would have effectively ended the discussion at this point. But Doug Bennet didn't like to strong-arm the committee, for he respected the integrity of the process too much. As a result, the committee felt it could speak freely, and it was in that spirit that Terri Overton expressed a concern about the applicant: "Her senior program is not that great." There was only one Advanced Placement course on the applicant's transcript, in English, and despite her 730 on the math portion of the SAT, the applicant was only taking precalculus. The implication was a by-now familiar one: she wasn't challenging herself. It was time to vote. The committee's sentiment was unanimous: the candidate was rejected. If that put the Wesleyan president in a tough spot with his counterpart, so be it; that was his problem. On to the next case.

Soon after, the committee considered a woman who had played three varsity sports and been the captain of the lacrosse team. "She's not the captain of the SAT team," someone at the table observed dryly of a combined score that was below 1200. Moreover, there appeared to be no family circumstances that could mitigate those low results. Nonetheless, this applicant, too, had a guardian angel: one of the most respected professors at Wesleyan had written to the committee to vouch for her. "What's the connection?" someone at the table asked. Bozoma Arthur, the rookie admissions officer and recent Wesleyan alumna who had read the file, responded: "She's a friend of the family, something like that."

As the committee prepared to vote, Greg said, "If we don't take her, its going to be easy to explain why." The committee then had its say: while two officers voted to put her on the waiting list, eight others voted to reject her. She was out.

But for all its newfound brusqueness, the committee also revealed it still had a softer side. A lot of the applicants who had ended up in these sessions shared stories about how the circumstances of their lives—sometimes an act of God, other times a mistake by their own hand—had impacted on their performance in school. And the committee members, like the audience at a taping of *Oprah,* were often visibly moved. This was precisely how Ralph had planned to play the committee with Becca: on its heartstrings.

In one case that came up not long before Becca's, a boy from California had written about the deaths of his father and two family friends in a car accident. His father had been driving at the time and had become distracted; compounding the horror was the fact that the boy had been in the car, as well. His case had likely reached the committee because his SAT's were in the 1200s. Though the accident had occurred midway through his high school career, the committee was told, the applicant's grades had never wavered: four A's and a B each year. "It's more than just a sympathy case," someone at the table said. "It's really just a case of extraordinary resiliency."

As Nancy had been reading the applicant's story from the notes that had been provided her, the eyes of Amin had filled with tears. The rookie admissions officer had lost both of his own parents by the time he was thirteen, and he would later acknowledge that the applicant's description of his violent loss had resonated deeply. But merely surviving a tragedy was never enough to earn his vote, Amin said. "There's a lot who write about loss," he observed. "Some use it as an excuse. Others use it as an opportunity to grow." This case, Amin was sure, was an example of the latter.

When Nancy called the vote, Amin was one of eight officers who voted to admit.

A little later, Amin would find himself moved again. Chris, who had taken over Nancy's job of reading to the committee, told everyone about an applicant from Winter Park, Florida. She played soccer, built houses for Habitat for Humanity and was taking Advanced Placement courses in English, calculus and physics. She had a mix of A's and B's, with straight A's her junior year. And her SAT's were a combined 1360. A 1400 would have been better, but these scores put her in the ballpark. Nonetheless, as the number of seats in the class dwindled, she would need something distinguishing to push her in. Picking up on an element that Chris had described in her essay, Amin spoke first.

"She had five A's in her junior year," Amin said, "during cancer treatment."

"She was still doing soccer while being treated," Terri interjected.

"She was the captain," Chris observed.

"What about the chemotherapy?" Ralph asked.

"She lost all her hair," said Bozoma, who had read the application. "She stayed in the hospital for weeks."

"She's apologized to the committee for not having a third SAT-II score," Chris said, referring to those College Board exams that assess achievement in particular subjects. "But damn it," Chris added, "she has Hodgkin's disease!"

With that, Chris rapped his hands on the long wooden table to call the vote. Three arms were raised to recommend the waiting list. Seven others were raised to admit. She was in.

It was Chris, acting as chair for Nancy, who also had drawn the responsibility of introducing Becca Jannol to the committee. As Chris said her name, Ralph had a silent hope: that the committee's mood of leniency—demonstrated so often in the cases of students with wrenching excuses for low grades or scores—would extend to someone who had shown remarkable growth from a youthful mistake.

Chris began by reading aloud from the notes of the first reader, Cliff Thornton, who had worked in the office for more than a decade. Cliff's opening line immediately put Ralph on the defensive, however unintentionally: "Solid recovery from suspension in 10th." These words would form the committee's first impression of Becca, and Ralph wished Cliff had begun on a different note. Though the line suggested that he had been impressed with Becca, his reference to "recovery" immediately raised the question of what she had recovered *from*. Had he been the first reader, Ralph would have noted Becca's leadership first, but the damage was done. This part of the presentation was out of Ralph's hands.

Cliff had gone on to report, "Maturity and influence noted by all"—
that was OK, Ralph thought—but then added: "Scores undercut." There
was no denying that, and the committee could see in the docket that
Becca's best scores on the SAT had been a 630 verbal, 640 math. Chris,
still reading from Cliff's notes, then got into the meat of the file.

"Student government president, prefect, honor board chair," he announced. Finally, Ralph thought, a reference to Becca's status as a leader
at Harvard-Westlake. Cliff went on to summarize Becca's essay, the one
she had asked Ralph about at the essay-writing session he had conducted
at Harvard-Westlake all those months ago. "Shades of gray," Cliff wrote,
picking up on Becca's theme of doing something bad followed by something good. "Confessed to violating honor code soph. year." Because
Becca had thus far chosen not to disclose the reason for her honor code violation in her application, Cliff's notes had said nothing about it as well.
For the committee, the mystery surrounding Becca's "recovery" deep-
ened. But after noting Becca's three Advanced Placement courses—
English, environmental science and government—and her grades (more
A's than B's), Cliff finally reached the letter from Mr. Sal, her dean. He
summarized the letter as follows: "True leader, concerned about bettering
the lives of others . . . *accepted a brownie laced with pot*—suspended."

Well, Ralph thought, *it's out there now.* Chris then read Cliff's recommendation: deny plus. That was disappointing, Ralph had thought, but
would not be surprising to the committee, given the tone of Cliff's
notes.

As the second reader, Ralph's written comments were to be kept
brief; he would be given ample opportunity to speak in committee. "Program not great," he had noted, conceding that Becca could have taken
more of the harder courses—like physics and calculus—that Harvard-
Westlake offered. But then Ralph had started building a case in his notes
for overlooking Becca's course selection: "Performance good, and strong
leadership." He concluded with an abbreviation: "PQ +"—a signal to his
colleagues that he considered Becca's "personal qualities" a valuable asset
for Wesleyan. His recommendation: "admit minus."

If Ralph had been a bit muted in his written comments, it was because he knew that his colleagues were not above punishing one of their
own for "liking a candidate too much." The officers all knew about his
close friendship with Sharon, and though each of them probably had at
least one good friend who was a guidance counselor at a top American

high school, Ralph could see them rolling their eyes whenever Harvard-Westlake came up in the docket. "How much are they paying you?" they would invariably ask him. Privately, they would acknowledge that Ralph was a consummate professional and that his relationship with Sharon had not only brought top students to Wesleyan each year but also provided the college with unparalleled insight into the senior class at one of the nation's premier prep schools. Still, the needling wouldn't help Ralph with the delicate task at hand. Chris had now finished reading from Becca's workcard. The floor was Ralph's. He would try to play it cool.

He began by addressing the brownie head on, because he knew it was the topic on everyone's mind. After noting that the student who distributed the brownies had been suspended for a year, Ralph said that Becca had drawn just a day's suspension. "She was the only one who came forward to say she accepted a brownie," Ralph told the committee. "It's a positive."

One admissions officer was immediately skeptical. "She may have turned *herself* in," he said. "But she didn't turn in the brownie."

The implication was obvious: perhaps Becca had eagerly consumed it. Maybe she had a drug problem. Never mind that nothing in her file indicated that was the case.

At this point, Terri Overton raised what she saw as a more pertinent weakness: "She's not a great student."

Terri, who had been a straight-A student herself, was often the admissions officer who reeled in her colleagues when they talked more about an applicant's personal qualities than grades. But in this case, her suggestion that Becca was "not a great student" was debatable. Though there were some B's on Becca's transcript—a B plus in geometry freshman year, a B plus in chemistry junior year—she had more A's, in subjects such as Advanced Placement American history, trigonometry, English and Spanish. All this at one of the toughest schools in the country.

Ralph could have challenged her, but because he wasn't usually confrontational, he decided instead to return to territory that was uncontested. "She's a leader," he said, reminding the committee yet again that Becca had used the incident as the foundation to ascend to great heights within her school community.

Now, Chris informed the committee, it was time to vote. Ralph took a deep breath as Chris asked that fateful, one-word question: "Admit?"

Ralph raised his hand. As he looked around the table, he saw that he was alone.

"Wait list?" Chris asked.

Again, no hands were raised.

"Deny?"

Nine hands went up.

The committee had voted to reject Becca Jannol's application to Wesleyan, without even giving her a chance on the waiting list. Ralph may have tried to underplay his interest in the case, but everyone could tell how much he believed in her. His tight frown made it clear that this had been a bitter defeat. Nonetheless, one of his colleagues couldn't resist a parting shot.

"I want to assure you, Ralph," the person said. "It had nothing to do with the dope."

During a break, Ralph confided that that last line had wounded him deeply, as he believed, "It was probably mean." He said he had felt as if he was suddenly on a playground. "It's what you get when you play with these kids," he said. "Sometimes you get spit on." For one of the first times all year, at least inside the admissions office, his generally sunny disposition had been replaced by something else entirely. Ralph was angry.

The line about "the dope" lingered in his mind for days. In one sense, his colleague was suggesting, however much in jest, that Becca's smattering of B's were the grades of someone stupid—a dope. That wasn't fair, Ralph thought: Becca had shown, unquestionably, that she could handle the work at Wesleyan. But Ralph believed the line, dripping with sarcasm, had another meaning that was much more relevant: Becca's admitted *consumption* of dope had indeed knocked out whatever chance she had of earning admission to Wesleyan, or even earning a spot on the waiting list.

For all their willingness to take in students who had overcome personal obstacles like illness or poverty, the admissions officers at Wesleyan often recoiled at the slightest indication of drug use in an applicant's file. This was often a knee-jerk reaction, one that rarely took into account the extent of a student's involvement. It wasn't that the committee members were holding themselves forth as "never having inhaled"; instead, Ralph explained, their thinking went something like this: "There's a lot of kids here who take drugs, anyway. Why accept one we *know* has that involvement?" No one stated that philosophy quite so bluntly in discussing

Becca, but Ralph had heard versions of it repeated in countless committee hearings over the years.

Indeed, not long after turning back Becca's bid, the committee took up the case of a boy who had been in a rehabilitation program for alcoholism at a very young age—his freshman and sophomore years of high school. Yet the boy had gone on to earn straight A's in his junior and senior years, and his file contained numerous testimonials to his hard-won, enduring sobriety. "I certainly think people can redeem themselves," one of the admissions officers said. "But given the selection this year, I don't think it's a risk we need to take." The applicant, like Becca, was rejected.

Ralph had found his colleagues' attitude on drugs and alcohol to be at odds with their general position on a related issue. Student health officials at Wesleyan had asked the admissions office on several occasions to avoid admitting an applicant with "any kind of mental or emotional problem," Ralph said. The health officials' rationale, he explained, was that "enough kids are going to get depressed here, anyway, so why make the doctors' job harder?" The admissions officers' reaction to that informal directive was emphatic: they resented the health service's position and rejected it. "And yet," Ralph lamented, "this office has the same philosophy about drug issues."

Ralph knew that Becca's case was complicated. But she certainly didn't deserve to be dismissed so unequivocally, her comeback in high school barely considered. As he regrouped, he wondered how he was going to break the news to Sharon.

After the committee broke up around five P.M. that afternoon, Greg and Nancy retreated to the dean's office. Surrounding them were stacks of workcards, hundreds of them, each representing an applicant whose case had been considered by at least two other readers but whose fate Nancy or Greg had yet to decide. It was going to be a long night.

Given the time pressure, Nancy and Greg wanted to make sure that the applicants they considered first were those who were most likely to be admitted. Thus, the piles were arranged to reflect the recommendations of the two previous readers. If one reader had recommended deny, and another deny plus, that card went in a group that was not likely to be read until the end. The likelihood that either of them would find reason to admit those applicants was considered slim. On the other hand, they had made it a priority to work through those applications in which one officer had recommended admit and another admit minus, for these candidates still had a shot.

As Nancy and Greg reached for the admit/admit minus pile on the afternoon after the committee rejected Becca, the workcard on the very top belonged to another of Ralph's prized recruits: Migizi Pensoneau.

As it turned out, Nancy had been the first admissions officer to read the file, only two days earlier. Though much of her time was taken up endorsing, or mediating, the choices of her colleagues, she had also been assessing a number of applications at random, both to give her colleagues a break and to get a general feel for this year's pool. Ralph had read the file next, because New Mexico was part of his territory. In this case, Greg alone would be charged with deciding the next step for Mig.

In considering Mig's application, Greg saw that Nancy began her report by highlighting Mig's most glaring weakness: the mostly C's and D's that he earned at his old high school. But she had also noted that he had gotten mostly A's at his new school, having repeated his junior year. After documenting his extracurricular activities—the four years of Tae Kwon Do, his work with the student council and the drama club—she came to Mig's first essay, in which he was asked to describe his most meaningful activity. His choice was a sixty-hour-a-week construction job, which Mig had taken during the summer after his first year at the Native American Prep School. As he wrote:

> I made eight dollars and fifty cents an hour. I got tan. I got buff. My pocket got fat. I'd work with my shirt off and girls would whistle. They'd stop and I'd get their numbers. I got a raise right away. Nine bucks an hour. I didn't think I had earned it, so, to compensate, I worked harder and harder everyday. The tan turned to sunburn.

Mig had always relished being irreverent in formal situations, and because he had believed that his sense of humor clicked with Ralph's, at least in their meeting at Mig's school, he had decided to write his response to Wesleyan's first question—"That Essay *Thingy*," as he had titled it—with Ralph in mind. He had never stopped to consider that someone else might read his words, not least the new dean of admissions. Nancy's response was direct. "Immature language," she wrote on the workcard, "i.e., 'I'd work w/my shirt off and girls would whistle!'"

Greg, still reviewing Nancy's notes, saw that she had next turned to the second essay, in which Mig had been asked to write about a subject of his choice. This time, he titled his piece: "My Future Depends on This Essay." *Here we go again,* Nancy thought, but the writing quickly grew serious. Mig had decided to write about his biological father, who lived elsewhere and who called only a few times a year, at least when Mig was in elementary school. Mig wrote to the committee that he had half imagined that his father was the "President of Uruguay," but he knew from his mother that the man was battling demons. He said he wanted Wesleyan to know about an overnight visit that he and his father had made to Mig's grandfather's home when Mig was ten. He wrote:

> I remember seeing my grandpa sitting in his rocking chair. That's how I'll always remember him: smiling at me with a few teeth, and picking me up. He sat my ten-year-old ass on his lap and said to me (I swear this is the first thing he said): "Have you ever seen *Spartacus?*"
>
> "What?"
>
> "Have you ever seen *Spartacus?*"
>
> "No."
>
> "This is the widescreen version. You should watch it."
>
> "When was it made?"
>
> "Before you were born."
>
> "Sounds boring." (Ten-year-old logic.) He laughed and replied with a smile, "You'll like it. Try to watch it." So I did. It's the first time I really remember taking in a movie. I watched it for the first time, as if it were the last. The whole time, Grandpa and my dad explained things to me. "They were slaves then, Migizi. . . . . .Poems were called songs then, son. . . . . Crucifixion was the way people were punished by the rulers of the time. . . . ." So I watched the movie in all its epic splendor: vibrant colors, beautiful scenery, wonderful direction, good story. It's still one of my favorite movies.

Mig reported that he had left his grandfather's home elated, but his good feelings would not last, for when he and his father returned to their hotel room, his father "showered, shaved and left for the night." He had a date, and Mig, at age ten, was left alone with the television. A few years later, Mig's grandfather died. Mig concluded his essay:

When my granpa passed on, my dad lost something in himself. At the same time, however, he gained something. He calls more. He keeps in touch. He sends me news of the weird from the Star Tribune, and Uruguayan money (just kidding.) And! We always watch movies together.

Again, Nancy's response was unequivocal: "*V. interesting!* Anecdotal-style-relationship w/father—a bit cynical, but clever." She was clearly starting to like this guy, and Mig gained even more ground when she came to the evaluations of his current teachers. They described the "dismal learning environment" at the boy's old school and then observed how he had found his "voice" and "natural ability" at the Native American Preparatory School. On the line in which she was asked to summarize Mig, Nancy wrote: "Intriguing! NAPS has done wonders for him! Solid scores"—he had a 650 verbal, 560 math, for a combined 1210 on the SAT—"and promising perf. at NAPS + +."

Still, she had two nagging questions about Mig: she wrote that she wasn't sure that Wesleyan "would be a good place" for him, and she wanted to see his midyear grades, just to confirm he had not reverted to prior form. And so Nancy circled "ADMIT MINUS"—admit, but with reservations—as her recommendation, and wrote the word "committee" next to her vote. She wanted her colleagues to make the call on this one.

Greg, functioning as Nancy's backup in this case, would be the one to decide whether Mig indeed went before the committee. As he continued the review of the summary of his file, Greg saw that Ralph's evaluation had been more emphatic. He knew how hard Ralph had been trying to recruit a Native American to Wesleyan, for the first time in recent memory, and Ralph's brief notes indicated how strongly he felt that Mig was the guy. "A real intriguing young man," Ralph wrote. "Absolutely devoted to film. Determined and capable. Not great academic case but incredible person." He had closed with another of those code words that would be instantly recognizable to his colleagues—"Would add," Ralph wrote, meaning Mig would add much to Wesleyan—before circling his choice: "ADMIT."

But after taking one look at those C's and D's from Mig's first high school, Greg was certain that Nancy was right: this one should go before the committee.

Nearly two weeks later, during the last of the committee's five all-day hearings, Mig's case came to the floor. As he had been on the day that Becca was considered, Ralph was a bundle of nerves. Though he knew that Becca's experience with the brownie might work against her in the committee, she had the advantage of attending a proven prep school, and she had never earned a C, let alone a D. Mig represented a far greater risk for Wesleyan, and not just because there was no one else at the university who shared his background.

Nancy, who had regained her stamina and returned to serving as the chair, first read her notes aloud to the committee, and then Ralph's. Before the discussion even began, Ralph wanted to answer one of Nancy's questions immediately. It seemed that Mig's grades during the fall of senior year had dipped from his junior year level, but only slightly. Reading from a piece of yellow legal paper covered in green ink, Ralph told the committee that he had received C's in honors precalculus and physics, but a B in Spanish and A's in English and civics. Mig was still far ahead of where he had been in Minnesota, Ralph said.

Ralph knew what the next question from the floor would be. Before considering Mig's case, the committee had also debated the application of one of his fourteen classmates at NAPS, a far better student who had four A's and a B in his senior year, and an impressive 700 on the verbal portion of the SAT. The committee had wasted little time in voting to take him. Now, they wondered, why should they put themselves on a limb to take Mig, who appeared so inferior to his classmate, at least on paper?

"There's no doubt about it," Ralph said, confirming that Mig's classmate was "a stronger student," and he went on: "there's some risk here with Mig. But Mig's someone who has had a background harsher than anything we typically see." After talking about how Mig had lost friends and relatives to alcoholism, and been surrounded by so much hopelessness in his high school, Ralph said: "In surviving this far, he's come farther than most of our students will, in terms of personal strength—in terms of literally being alive."

Now Greg had a question for Ralph: "How likely is it these kids are going to come?" He was genuinely curious, but he also wanted to know whether Wesleyan, if it accepted both boys, would be throwing away two acceptances. A few weeks earlier, Ralph replied, he had spoken with the school's guidance counselor in an off-the-record chat not unlike his conversations with Sharon about Becca and Julianna. The counselor hinted that Mig's classmate would have several choices, but said that Mig "really wants to come" and was eager to be a part of the vaunted Wesleyan film program.

Someone else asked Ralph about how Mig had reacted to the prospect of perhaps being the sole Native American on campus?

"I was very straightforward with him," Ralph told his colleagues. "I told Mig that Wesleyan could be a supportive place but that he would be part of a beginning effort. Just the fact that he went to NAPS shows that he's willing to do something different, to make a change for the better."

Ralph sensed that his colleagues weren't buying his arguments, for there was immediately discussion of taking the classmate, and not Mig. Wesleyan was always reluctant to admit someone with C's and D's, not only because of the risk that he might flunk out but also because of the message it might send to his school, and others, about the grades that Wesleyan considered acceptable.

And what about NAPS itself? The school had only been in business for four years and had just graduated its first class the year before. Several committee members wondered how much value to attach to Mig's A's and B's there, just as at Aggie's boarding school in Baltimore. There was no way to know for certain.

One officer rose to Ralph's defense, at least partially. He confirmed Ralph's characterization of the lives of some Native Americans in the Midwest as grim, describing it as "third-world stuff." Ralph was grateful for the support, but could see from his colleagues' expressions that they felt they had talked enough.

"Ready to vote?" Nancy asked.

They nodded that they were

"Admit?" she asked.

Just as when Becca's nomination was on the floor, Ralph lifted his hand high. This time, as he looked around, he saw that six others had joined him.

"Wait list?"

There were no hands.

"Deny?"

Two hands.

By a vote of 7 to 2—with one officer absent—Migizi Pensoneau would be offered admission to the Class of 2004 at Wesleyan University.

Nearly two weeks after what he considered his biggest defeat of this admissions season, Ralph had posted an important victory. Becca may have been the better student and had the more impressive test scores, but Ralph knew that such comparisons were rarely so simple. In the end, the committee had deemed Mig's redemption more admirable than Becca's. And while Wesleyan had no shortage of applications from upper-middle-class Jewish women applying from the West Coast, it had received precious little interest from less-affluent Native Americans. Mig's timing was good: Wesleyan had decided that in building a diverse community, it really needed a Native American. The committee agreed with Ralph: Mig "would add."

At the conclusion of the committee hearings, Ralph retreated to his office, the old teenager's bedroom now filled with law books and gadgets, to call several dozen guidance counselors. These were courtesy calls, to counselors at schools of all sizes and pedigrees. Like his colleagues, he would offer to inform the counselor of Wesleyan's decision regarding a particular student—provided the counselor promised not to discuss the decision with the applicant until after the mail had arrived. When the news was good, Wesleyan hoped that the counselor would appreciate the advance notice and perhaps say complimentary things about Wesleyan to the student if he was choosing between Wesleyan and a competitor. When the news was bad, Wesleyan wanted an opportunity to explain its decision, confident that a little advance notice would help ease the pain, both the student's and the counselor's.

The call to Mig's guidance counselor was a gratifying one. Ralph confided that Mig's classmate had fairly breezed into the class, and that with a little push, Mig was in, too. The counselor was elated, and Ralph said that once they received their letters, he'd be willing to arrange a trip for Mig and his classmate to visit Wesleyan.

Soon afterward he picked up the phone to call Sharon. This one was going to be tougher. He began the conversation by raising a far more innocuous matter, yet another trip that Harvard-Westlake was planning to the East Coast. At the end of the month, Sharon would be leading a group of thirty juniors to nearly a dozen top schools, including Wesleyan. Her students wouldn't be applying to college for at least another eight months, but it was never too early to start preparing for next year. Other schools and families surely were.

After Sharon and Ralph had picked a date for him to meet her newest crop of potential applicants, the talk turned to how Harvard-Westlake had fared in this year's decisions, including the committee hearings. She already knew that two applicants, including the guitarist in that critically acclaimed duo, had been accepted by Wesleyan in the first round of early decision hearings. She had also been informed that after being deferred in November, his partner, the female singer, had been admitted in the second round of early hearings, in February. Wesleyan hadn't broken up the band after all.

In the main round, Ralph now related to Sharon, an additional seven applicants had been accepted, for a grand total of ten, out of twenty-four. He gave her the names of those students, along with the names of four others who would be invited to join the waiting list. He could tell she was pleased, though she wouldn't be for long.

"Sharon," Ralph finally said, "I've got some bad news about Becca. I couldn't make it happen."

Ralph heard Sharon say, "Uh-oh."

"The committee shot me down," he explained. "They were just focused on the brownie."

"Why is everyone so focused on that?" Sharon asked, almost to herself. "Why do they miss the point?"

From the tone of her remark, Ralph suspected that this was not the first phone call that she had fielded from an admissions officer bearing bad tidings about Becca. But he opted not to ask, and decided not to tell her how lopsided the vote had been. She was probably angry enough.

What a waste, Sharon thought to herself, as she sat in an office with a glass ceiling that made it look more like a greenhouse than a guidance center, three thousand miles from Connecticut. Since applying to Wesleyan, Becca had begun making a movie as an independent study project at school. Sharon was on the committee monitoring Becca's progress and had been impressed with the early footage she had viewed. With its strong emphasis on film, Wesleyan was now an even better fit for Becca than it had been in the fall.

"Is it done?" Sharon asked Ralph. "Was the door left open?"

"It was pretty clear," Ralph responded.

At this point, Sharon had a decision to make: she could let it go, or she could ask Ralph to intercede one last time. Quickly scanning her list of applicants, she noted that several of the Harvard-Westlake students whom Wesleyan had accepted had lower grade point averages than Becca. She began to consider how Wesleyan's rejection of Becca would play at Harvard-Westlake.

Students and parents at Harvard-Westlake analyzed the colleges' decisions each spring as assiduously as if they were baseball boxscores. After all the decisions were in, Sharon would help compile a thick, gray-covered volume documenting each decision on a Harvard-Westlake applicant at each college that year. The guidance counselors would first type a college's name at the top of a page and then list the grade point average, standardized test scores and number of Advanced Placement courses of each individual applicant from Harvard-Westlake. At the end of each student's entry would be the college's decision. The book was intended to guide students the following year, so that their choices of where to apply would be realistic. (Though no names were included on these lists, the kids and parents often figured out who each applicant was.)

Sharon decided she wasn't going to let Ralph, or Wesleyan, off the hook.

"This isn't going to make a lot of sense in our community," Sharon told Ralph. "Becca is by far our most high-profile applicant. Even more so than Julianna." While Julianna Bentes was an academic all-star with a formidable racial background, Becca was a far more prominent presence on campus.

"Denying Becca," she added, "might send a strange message."

The implication was obvious: if Wesleyan rejected the president of the student body at Harvard-Westlake, parents and students, to say nothing of their counselors, might be reluctant to consider Wesleyan in the future. Sharon told Ralph that Becca was a "puller," a code word indicating that Becca's friends and admirers in younger classes might try to follow her wherever she went to college. By the same token, they might also ignore a college that had rejected her.

Then, drawing on their sixteen years of friendship in a way that she never really had in the past, Sharon changed her tone entirely.

"Go back in there and fight," Sharon told Ralph. "Talk to Nancy. Beg her. We'll do anything."

The receiver in Sharon's ear went momentarily silent.

"I'll try," Ralph eventually responded. "But they don't want to overturn committee decisions. It's not something they do all that often. No guarantees."

After they had hung up, Sharon wondered, perhaps for the first time in their professional relationship, whether she had pushed Ralph too hard. No, she decided, she was proud of the argument she had mustered.

"I probably wouldn't have pushed so hard if it wasn't Ralph," she acknowledged later. "I felt I could express my utter disappointment to him. I knew he wasn't going to judge me as a counselor if I didn't accept this."

Still, Sharon was a realist, and admitted, "I didn't expect anything."

The following day, Ralph poked his head out of his office periodically to peer across the hall, where he could see Nancy sitting at her desk. He was waiting for that rare moment when the dean wasn't on the phone or reading files or talking to someone. When he finally saw an opening, he gathered his ammunition and stepped quickly into the old master bedroom.

In addition to Becca's workcard, Ralph was carrying the cards of two other applicants, both from a school in Texas. They were among six applicants from the same school, all of whom had been rejected, and he wanted to appeal their cases, as well. He had also brought along the workcard of an applicant from another school who had already been accepted to Wesleyan, but he was willing to make a deal: he would rescind that candidate's acceptance in exchange for a more favorable ruling from Nancy on Becca or one of the Texas students. Ralph had remembered Nancy's predecessor, Barbara-Jan, saying, "You want someone in, then gimme two I can take out." In the few months that Nancy had been at Wesleyan, Ralph had never heard her express a similar sentiment, but he decided it couldn't hurt to offer to make a trade. Because Becca was the "toughest sell," Ralph had put her card at the bottom of his short pile.

After presenting his Texas argument, Ralph began to make good on his promise to Sharon. "I know we don't as policy overturn committee decisions," Ralph told Nancy, as she sat at her desk and he stood across from her. "And I know that the committee was not thrilled by the brownie incident. But I really do think that denying Becca Jannol was a mistake. It's a mistake we shouldn't make, given that she has such extreme leadership capability and is so tremendously respected at the school. It would be a mistake not to at least hold on to her.

"I've met this girl," he added. "I've talked a lot about her to Sharon."

Though Ralph would have avoided reminding any other colleague of his close friendship with Sharon in this case, for fear of its backfiring, he didn't hesitate to do so with Nancy. He didn't even need to use Sharon's last name, for the two women had met several years earlier, when they had been assigned to be roommates at a private gathering of about one hundred admissions officers and guidance counselors. In their free time, Sharon and Nancy had discovered that they were both avid readers, and they became fast friends, staying in touch afterward.

But Ralph knew that Nancy's friendship with Sharon would ultimately count for very little in this case. "I'm really hesitant, really reluctant, to overturn the committee," Nancy finally said. "I don't know if I should be doing this." She agreed only to keep Becca's workcard and told Ralph she would need a few days to sleep on his request.

As it turned out, each of the other veteran admissions officers had also gone in to see Nancy to appeal a case or two, in response to an invitation she had extended. Ralph and his senior colleagues were far more familiar with the schools in their territories than she was, Nancy had told them, and if Wesleyan had made a decision that was inconsistent, or unfair, she wanted to know about it. She wouldn't necessarily do anything in response, but she would hear them out.

In Becca's case, Nancy remembered being impressed that the girl had "turned herself in and taken responsibility" for her actions. Becca did have integrity, but Terri Overton had made a valid point about her academic record. Now Ralph was offering a competing argument, one that had not been introduced in the hearings: Wesleyan was about to rankle one of its most important feeder schools. An appeal from a guidance counselor at a lesser high school might never have reached Nancy's desk, but sometimes, the admissions world was no different than politics or business: clout, or the perception of clout, counted for a lot.

On March 23, a week before Wesleyan would mail letters to each of its applicants, Nancy made her decision. Placing Becca's workcard on her desk, she noticed that during the committee hearings, it was she, as the chair, who had recorded the committee's vote by circling the letter *R,* for "rejection," on the top line. Now she placed her pen on the line beneath that decision and circled *W,* for "waiting list." Before Becca Jannol had even been notified of her rejection, Wesleyan was withdrawing it and moving her to the waiting list. At the least that gesture would help both Sharon and Ralph save face within the Harvard-Westlake community, and it would buy both sides some time.

"Great," Sharon had told Ralph, when he called with the news. "The door's open." Any tension that had risen between the old friends dissipated.

At a brief meeting a day or two later, Nancy announced to the admissions staff that she was setting aside the committee's vote in Becca's case, as well as moving the two applicants from Texas to the waiting list. In the end, Ralph had not had to trade anything in return, for Nancy had politely declined his offer to undo the admission of the other applicant in his satchel, as his sacrificial lamb. Her colleagues, all of them distracted by assorted last-minute issues, registered no reaction to the mention of Becca's name. Whatever passion they had had about her case during the hearings had long since subsided.

Besides, Ralph's colleagues knew that Becca wasn't going to come off the waiting list. They, like Ralph, figured he had exhausted all of his goodwill with Nancy just to get her reinstated.

If Becca Jannol accepted Wesleyan's offer of a spot on the waiting list, then she would likely have plenty of company. After the committee finished its work and Nancy had heard all the last-minute appeals, the number of students being invited to join the waiting list climbed to thirteen hundred—nearly one out of every five of the students who applied for the class. By contrast, thirty-three hundred others, or nearly half of those who applied, had been rejected outright. An additional five hundred had already withdrawn their applications before Wesleyan made a final determination after being accepted in the early rounds at other schools.

If past years were any indication, about half of those offered a spot on the waiting list would turn it down immediately, taking their chances at other colleges. Those who accepted a spot would decide they had little to lose: they could still field an offer from another institution in the interim. Wesleyan wouldn't begin looking at the list until after May 1, when decisions were due from those applicants who had already been offered a seat in the Class of 2004.

A few colleges had made a concerted effort in recent years to trim their waiting lists, believing it was unfair to hold out hope to so many students when the odds were overwhelming that they would never get in. But like many others, Wesleyan had always taken a more self-interested approach, viewing the waiting list in the same way that a basketball coach views the players on his bench. If things didn't work out with the team that the coach had decided to put on the floor at the beginning of the season, then he could always dip into his reserves. The more reserves, the better, at least from the coach's point of view.

On the waiting list, as on the bench, each of those reserves had unique strengths. If the admissions officers at Wesleyan were seen as social engineers, then the waiting list contained the raw materials to fill any remaining gaps in the community they were creating. For example, if too many valedictorians or class presidents or students with high SAT scores turned down Wesleyan's offer of acceptance—all statistics that the guidebooks liked to tally—then the university could always go to the waiting list to try to find a comparable replacement.

"You want to address any imbalances and fill in any sort of absent talents," Greg explained. "If you get six linebackers but no quarterback, it'd be nice to go into the wait list and get a quarterback. Same thing if you've got lots of violinists, but no oboists."

The same was true of any perceived racial imbalances in the class. If too many students of color turned Wesleyan down, the waiting list offered the college a way to keep its percentages of minority students constant from the previous year. "Those numbers are markers," Greg said, "because people outside the university are going to refer to them as an indication of whether you've been more or less successful than last year in arriving at a racially diverse student body."

Becca was hardly the only applicant who crossed Ralph's path in the spring of 2000 who ended up relegated to Wesleyan's stable of reserves. When the letters went out at the end of March, Tiffany Wang and Aggie Ramirez would be invited to join the waiting list as well. In both instances, Nancy had made the final decision herself.

Nancy deliberated both cases on March 19, the day before the last committee hearing. Each workcard had reached her desk three weeks earlier, but both applications had languished as Nancy and Greg considered other applicants, particularly those who had been rated higher by their readers, which took priority.

The case of Tiffany Wang was an easy call for Nancy. She saw from the workcard that Ralph had serious reservations and had recommended deny plus. She also noted that while Rod had circled "ADMIT MINUS," he had written "WL" for waiting list. The two weren't all that far apart—Ralph could have recommended an unequivocal deny, but chose not to—and it was too late in the process for Nancy to agonize. If Tiffany agreed to take her chances on the waiting list, then Nancy and Greg might be willing to reconsider her in May. Only then would Wesleyan know whether her perceived assets—her high SAT scores, her racial background, her mastering of English as a second language—were in demand. If Tiffany was unwilling to take that chance—in past years, some applicants had come off the waiting list as late as August, as students' plans changed—then Wesleyan was willing to let her go elsewhere.

Ordinarily, Aggie Ramirez might have presented a good case for the committee to debate. Nancy saw from the workcard that, like Migizi Pensoneau, she had some C's and D's on her transcript, blemishes Ralph was willing to overlook. Aggie's parents had not attended college, and yet Aggie had gotten herself into an all-girls boarding school near Baltimore, on scholarship; like Becca Jannol, she, too, was president of the student body. While Ralph had circled "ADMIT MINUS," suggesting that Aggie was a risk he was willing to take, Greg had circled "DENY PLUS" and had taken pains to make sure that Nancy noted all those shaky grades in the first half of the senior year, from a low of 68 (in English) to a high of only 77 (in Spanish, Aggie's first language).

As Nancy weighed Aggie's case, she knew that Wesleyan had almost no acceptances left to offer, at least not until after the letters went out and the more than eighteen hundred students who were already accepted made their decisions. To make it through the gate now, Aggie would have to be exceptional. Nancy's first thought was that Greg was right to be concerned with Aggie's grades. Then again, Ralph had seen a lot to admire. Nancy agreed with Ralph that Wesleyan had nothing to gain by rejecting Aggie outright, for she had much to offer. In the space on the workcard indicating which decision letter Aggie should receive, Nancy wrote: "WL."

Ralph would learn about the fate of Aggie and Tiffany from the computer terminal on his desk, for Nancy had made these decisions too late in the process for them to be included in the printed docket made available to the committee earlier in the month. Like his colleagues, he would monitor Nancy's last-minute decisions by tapping into the admissions office database, which was updated throughout the day.

Even though he had believed that Aggie Ramirez merited a place in the class, and that Tiffany Wang didn't, Ralph decided not to challenge the relegation of either to the waiting list, for he could understand Nancy's thinking in each case. And in each case, he had been the first reader, not the second. Because the second reader always had responsibility for the applicant's school, the first reader was expected to defer to the judgment of the second in almost every circumstance, unless the committee was convened. Ralph's only disappointment was that neither Greg nor Nancy had responded to a comment he had written on Aggie's workcard at the time he had read her file: "Discuss." At the least, he had wanted to talk to one of them personally about Aggie. Ralph felt certain that Greg would have taken a look at Ralph's ringing endorsement of Aggie and asked him: "What were you thinking?" But Greg had said nothing. At best, Ralph had hoped that the entire committee would have an opportunity to discuss Aggie.

Ralph understood that Greg and Nancy had simply run out of time, but he also knew that he himself could have taken more initiative. He was the one officer charged with monitoring the cases of Latino applicants. But he had become so bogged down in other matters, including the protracted cases of Becca and Mig, that he had not checked up on Aggie until it was too late.

It was not the last time that the collective sight of so many applications would distract Ralph's gaze from someone he had once considered a priority.

Eight
THINGS SEEM TO HAVE GONE WELL

Two armed guards patrolled the perimeter outside the doorway with their weapons loaded and drawn. One brandished what appeared to be a pistol; the other, an Uzi. When the intruder approached, he came under immediate and heavy fire. He was hit but somehow managed to get past the door and inside the room. Ignoring the tarantula and lizard that stood like guard dogs in his path, he grabbed the confidential documents and slipped out the door. Under fire again, he sprinted across the granite floor and up two flights of stairs to safety.

It could have been a scene from a James Bond movie, but this heist occurred in the basement of the Wesleyan admissions office. The obviously urbane agent involved in this caper was none other than Rod Bugarin, who struck just two days before Wesleyan was scheduled to mail out its responses to the nearly seven thousand applicants seeking seats in the Class of 2004. After eight arduous months, the committee's work was finally done, and all its verdicts complete. Nonetheless, because Rod still wanted Nancy to consider overruling two of the committee's decisions, he retrieved the corresponding letters, which were already in their envelopes.

To obtain those precious documents, Rod had dodged the spray of two water pistols fired by office assistants and had risked being bitten by a spider and sharp-toothed reptile, though each was only made of rubber. The toys were on loan from the young son of the office manager, Judy

Goodale, who had also been responsible for inflating the six-foot-high Godzilla that stood sentry outside the room at the corner of the carpeted basement where the letters were stored. During her two decades running the back office of the admissions operation, Judy had always found that a serious warning delivered with a little humor could help cool the inevitable tensions that arose in the final hours of the admissions process. And Rod was definitely making things tense, for at the least, a stunt like his could cause the office to make a clerical mistake. Now that the letters were "locked down," Judy wished that the admissions officers would just leave them alone. But every year, there were always one or two officers who couldn't let go.

Over the previous three days, Judy and her team of eleven assistants had engaged in the painstaking but critical task of ensuring that the decision in each letter matched the corresponding decision on each workcard. Only once in the twenty years that Judy had overseen the process had the office sent a student a decision in error. A few years earlier, a warm letter of acceptance had been mailed to an applicant whom the committee had decided to reject. A secretary had made the mistake by entering data into a student's record that actually belonged to a vastly more qualified applicant with the same last name. The problem was not detected until after the erroneous letter had gone out. When informed by phone that the committee believed that he could not handle the rigors of Wesleyan, the applicant was defiant: he insisted on holding the university to its letter of acceptance. Wesleyan felt it had little choice but to permit him to enroll, but he later left before graduating.

To guard against repeating such an error—particularly as the number of applications grew each year but the staff did not—Judy had installed an elaborate security system. First she split the women on her staff into pairs and had them divide the piles of letters and the corresponding workcards. Then, like technicians who just had received a presidential order to detonate a nuclear warhead, the women engaged in a complicated process of verification. Her voice a clear monotone, one woman would read aloud from the workcard, stating the applicant's name and address, followed by the committee's decision. In an even tone, her partner would then respond by reading the same information aloud, this time from the actual letter. As they spoke, five other pairs of women at adjoining rectangular tables quietly went through the same routine. By Wednesday, March 29, a week after the conclusion of committee hearings, all the letters regarding the Class of 2004 had been checked and stuffed into envelopes. Judy's only remaining task was to keep the letters safe and untouched, until the mail carrier came to get them on Friday afternoon.

As it turned out, Rod's last-minute attempt would be in vain. He had hoped to alter the fate of an applicant whom the committee had deferred from the early-decision round into the main pool, only to reject him in the end. Rod still thought that the candidate merited admission and, taking a page from Ralph's play book, was now offering to make a trade: he would rescind the acceptance of another applicant from his territory as an exchange. But Nancy would hear no more appeals. "We don't do things like this, Rod," she told him, gently. Time had run out. Rod would have to put the letters back, carefully.

Inside the dimly lit basement, the letters had been organized on three separate tables. To the far right were the rejections. These envelopes were the thinnest, and had been arrayed vertically in six long rows, as regular as the tombstones in a military cemetery. There were more envelopes on that table than on any other: over three thousand of them, destined to arrive at the homes of almost one of every two students who had applied for the Class of 2004. The rejection letters, which began by addressing each applicant by his or her first name, continued:

> I am sorry to bring you what may be disappointing news; the admission committee at Wesleyan is unable to offer you admission to the Class of 2004. This was a particularly difficult decision, and I want to assure you that the admission committee read your application, your essay and your recommendations with care. We thought long and hard about the decision and regret that you are one of the people to whom we have to deny admission.

Nancy, who had written the letter, went on to state that "competition for a place in this year's freshman class was even greater than in the past" and that it was "extremely difficult to choose a class of 700 from 6850 qualified and interesting students." She closed with what she had hoped was on an upbeat note—"You obviously have the ability and the character to do well in college"—but she knew that for most of the recipients of that letter, no words of encouragement could take away the sting.

The middle table contained more than twelve hundred envelopes that were slightly thicker. These were the offers to join the waiting list. "I realize this news may be a disappointment if Wesleyan is one of your top college choices," Nancy wrote to each applicant, and went on to say that the

school would not know for a month how many students it might be able
to take off the waiting list. But she urged each applicant to "choose to
keep the option of attending Wesleyan viable by returning the enclosed
postcard." In some years, she wrote, as many as seventy applicants had
come off the waiting list.

About a foot away, on the far left table, were the acceptance letters.
These were addressed to 1854 recipients—about a quarter of those who
had applied—including the 300 who already knew that they had been admitted in the early rounds. While the rejection and waiting list letters had
been folded into standard, four-by-nine-inch envelopes, the acceptances
were inserted, unfolded, into bright red folders that measured ten by thirteen inches. The contents had been assembled with all the care of a wedding invitation.

In contrast to the other letters, which were printed at a copy shop off
campus and signed by a machine, each of the acceptance letters had been
printed in the admissions office, too important to be delegated elsewhere.
Nancy had taken the acceptance letters home, and while her husband, a
former head crew coach at Cornell, watched the NCAA college basketball
tournament on television, she opened a bottle of Merlot and set about
signing each letter personally. Using an ergonomically cushioned Cross
pen that was painted as blue as a sports car, she wrote her name in round,
swooping strokes and then appended a brief message at the bottom of
each letter. About a third of the students received an exhortation: "Come
to Wes!" Another third were told: "Great news!" Those in the final group
got a simple "Yes!" Nancy made no effort to determine who got which
message; she simply thought that an extra gesture might help distinguish
her from her counterparts at other colleges, which couldn't hurt in so
competitive a year. But adding even those brief messages was time-
consuming: the entire task of signing each had taken more than ten hours
spread across two days.

When she was done, Nancy reviewed each letter, discovering that in
several instances she had spelled her own last name wrong, so weary had
she become. Those letters would have to be reprinted on Monday. In one
case, she even found that she had written "MILK" as her personal message when her mind had drifted to her grocery list.

Once signed and edited, each acceptance letter was placed into its
Wesleyan-red folder (not quite crimson, but not maroon, either) along
with several other items intended to lure the applicant into enrolling.
There was an invitation to visit the campus in mid-April, for a long week-

end that had been christened WesFest; a personal note from a senior interviewer, if the applicant had been interviewed on campus; a sealed envelope containing a specific offer of financial aid, provided the applicant was one of the 40 percent who were deemed qualified; and a transparent sticker bearing the Wesleyan logo that was intended to be affixed to the back window of the applicant's car.

As the letters were being checked, signed and stuffed in those final days, Ralph closeted himself in his second-floor office, mostly finishing his calls to guidance counselors. Unlike Rod, he now felt at peace with the decisions that had been made. Moreover, he feared that if he so much as poked his head into the basement, he might cause something to go wrong. He still remembered how embarrassed he had been after he had left a student's application to Occidental inside a Fuddruckers Restaurant in Phoenix, nearly a decade earlier. It had never been found, and he had to call the student and ask her, sheepishly, to resubmit it.

It wasn't just the basement that Ralph was avoiding, but the main floor of the admissions office. While Judy and her staff were putting the finishing touches on the letters to the Class of 2004, the juniors contemplating applying for the Class of 2005—and even some sophomores thinking about the Class of 2006—were already streaming through the front door of the old house. The last week of March, spring break at many high schools, had become a popular time to get an eight-month head start on the process of applying to college. Every day that week, Wesleyan had scheduled four tours and two information sessions to accommodate hundreds of teenagers and their families. The task of greeting them was mostly left to the Wesleyan seniors. The last thing Ralph and his colleagues wanted to do was to start thinking about next year's class.

On Friday, March 31, just before noon, Judy ascended the stairs to Nancy's office. As she had with previous deans, Judy looked Nancy straight in the eye, her stern expression framed by golden blond hair that fell to her waist. She addressed Nancy as if Nancy were a commanding officer in the army. "Are you ready to release these letters to Wesleyan Station?" she inquired. Like her predecessors, Nancy had come to have immense confidence in Judy and was unable to imagine how the office had ever run without her, so carefully and thoroughly did Judy approach her task. If anyone knew if the letters were ready, it was Judy; nonetheless, Nancy realized that Judy didn't want to be the one responsible for turning the letters over to the postal service. And so, Nancy rose to her feet and told her charge: "I have faith in the process. You're good to go."

Less than an hour later, Judy sent a mass voice mail to everyone in the office: "They're gone." Everyone knew what she meant. As he had for each of the last fifteen years, Mark Melmer had driven up to the admissions office in a gray van with a handcart. The bins that Mark had filled with applications in the fall and winter were now the same ones that he pressed into duty to carry out Wesleyan's responses in the spring.

A few hours later, Nancy invited her admissions officers to join her at a dimly lit pub called Eli Cannon's on Main Street in Middletown. The setting was a welcome change from the admissions office. The pub had big barber chairs with leather seats in the waiting area, hundreds of bottles of hot sauces from all over the world on the walls (their flashy labels served as decorations) and antique wheelbarrows suspended from the ceiling. Nancy wanted her colleagues to have some fun, and she wanted to say thanks for having helped her through such a difficult first year on the job. Everyone but Amin, who did not drink alcohol because of his religion, accepted her invitation. Even Ralph came out of hiding. And for perhaps the only time all year, Ralph had a drink, one of those light honey brews. "Here's to us," Nancy said, panning the faces crammed into the oak booth. "We need to take a moment to celebrate what we've done."

But as his colleagues drank and nibbled on nachos, Ralph didn't feel much like celebrating. It wasn't just that he was exhausted; it was that yet another nerve-wracking part of the process was about to begin: the agonizing month of waiting to learn who would accept Wesleyan's offer. For the admissions officers—and the applicants whom they coveted most—the roles that each had played over the last eight months were about to reverse. In phone calls and in conversations with visitors to the Wesleyan campus, Ralph would now be the one who was the supplicant, trying to mount the best argument he could for the school. And now, the decision-making power would rest with the applicants, particularly those who had received multiple offers. While his colleagues unwound, Ralph's mind raced. He was thinking about two applicants in particular: Julianna Bentes and Migizi Pensoneau.

The thick white envelope from Wesleyan arrived at Julianna Bentes's home in Van Nuys, California, during the middle of the first week of April. It did not lack for company, for within the span of just a few days,

Julianna learned that she had been accepted to all thirteen colleges to which she had applied. Ralph's competition, as expected, would be formidable. In addition to Wesleyan, those laying out the welcome mat were Stanford; the University of California campuses in Berkeley and San Diego; the University of Texas at Austin, Washington University in St. Louis; the University of Chicago; the University of Michigan; Kenyon; Goucher; Swarthmore; Yale; and Harvard.

Sharon Merrow figured that anyone else at Harvard-Westlake would have been ecstatic to have such a range of choices. For so many of Sharon's students, and their parents, every decision that they made during their time at Harvard-Westlake seemed calculated to gain admission to the Ivies, or to Stanford or Berkeley. But Julianna, like Becca and like Sharon's own parents, had always been different, and seemed to pursue her classes and activities for the sheer joy of the experience. True to form, Julianna was almost subdued in her response to all of this attention. "She was sort of hoping that the colleges would make the decision for her," Sharon said. "She knew, in the end, that she'd have to make the decision." But, Juliana conceded, she had no idea how she would.

She had sought admission in a year in which most colleges had received record numbers of applications. But, as Sharon and Ralph recognized early on, few applicants presented a college with the package that Julianna did. As a result, each college went well beyond its simple letter of acceptance in its attempt to woo her. Goucher in Maryland, which had dangled the possibility of a dance scholarship as early as her sophomore year of high school, was now sending her a free plane ticket to visit. So was Kenyon in Ohio.

Admissions officers at Harvard, Yale and Stanford were more subtle: while they didn't send her airfare, each made specific references, in phone conversations or in e-mails, to the content of her essays. "We hope to welcome you to a 'new wonderland,'" someone at Stanford had scribbled at the bottom of her acceptance letter, picking up on the theme of Julianna's story about Los Angeles as a maker and breaker of dreams. (The new dean at Wesleyan, it seemed, wasn't the only one who went beyond merely affixing her signature.) Julianna was amazed that her application had been read so closely at so many places.

A history professor at Stanford had also written to Julianna, inviting her to sit in on one of his classes and even dangling the possibility of having "the first daughter give you a pep talk." This was a secret weapon that only Stanford could wield: Chelsea Clinton, then a junior, was one of the professor's students. Though Stanford had gone to great lengths to protect Chelsea's privacy—the college had leaned on the student daily newspaper to refrain from covering her comings and goings—it was apparently not above using her as a closer on one of its more important deals that year.

Amid all of this courting, Wesleyan stood out for its near silence. Throughout the spring, Julianna had not received a single e-mail message from Ralph. That had been intentional; his style was never to push. Still, Sharon knew that he had wanted to have Wesleyan send Julianna a free ticket to visit the campus. Yet none was ever offered. Ralph had been careful to write "Fly her out" on the outside of Julianna's file, but he had been too overwhelmed during the endgame of the admissions season to verify if anyone in the office had received his note. When informed later that she had been Ralph's number one priority that season, Julianna would express surprise, stating, "I wasn't as aware of it from him as I was from the other schools."

Julianna's criteria for making a decision amid all the attention being paid her were fairly simple: she wanted to attend a school with a strong academic environment that would challenge her activist notions yet still not consume all of her family's income. But because most of her suitors were offering financial aid of roughly similar magnitude—about $9,000 to $11,000 in scholarships and loans, to reduce tuition and fees of about $36,000 a year—Julianna wouldn't have to make her initial decisions based solely on money. At least at this early stage, her mother told her, she could go with her gut and not necessarily sell herself to the highest bidder.

Thus, after visiting one of her more generous suitors, Goucher, in early 2000, Julianna crossed the school off her list, largely because she was concerned it still had the feel of the all-girls school it had once been. (Julianna counted thirty women and "one guy" in the dorm in which she stayed.) She likewise eliminated Kenyon from contention after visiting its campus in mid-April, for despite having been greeted with hugs by the admissions officers, she ultimately found the campus too remote. She felt so cut off from civilization that she convinced herself that the enormous bags of what appeared to be cooking salt that she spied in a rural gas station were for people "who didn't get into town very often." (Having lived her entire life in either Los Angeles or Brazil, she had never seen salt that was used to melt ice on roads.)

On the way back from that trip, which was paid for by Kenyon, Julianna had scheduled an overnight layover in Chicago so that she could visit the University of Chicago. André Phillips was the admissions officer who had charmed Julianna and her mother during a visit to Harvard-Westlake a year earlier, and the "two stars" he had scribbled on her information card that night had proven prophetic. As it did every year, a faculty committee was convened at Chicago at the end of the admissions process to rate the school's sixty-eight hundred applicants, for the purpose of awarding nearly three dozen merit scholarships, regardless of family income. Of those, the most generous was intended to fully cover the university's $32,000 tuition and other fees, and was reserved for the one candidate considered at the very top of that year's pool—the student Chicago considered "the most interesting and most desirable." Several days after she received her letter of acceptance, Julianna was informed she had won that prize. The offer stood out as the most lucrative that she would receive.

When she visited Chicago soon afterward, Julianna was immediately struck by how engaged everyone seemed. Her campus tour guide had been particularly impressive, for after the tour, as Julianna and Catherine waited for an hour for a taxi that didn't come, the student stayed at their side, amusing them with his renditions of old Monty Python sketches. But Julianna soon decided that André hadn't conveyed how bleary-eyed the students looked. "Everyone I met just sat and ate and studied," Julianna remarked, and with the exception of her tour guide, "no one talked." One student told her: "You're the most social person here." Even worse, though the calendar said mid-April, it started to snow. The prize money was tempting, Julianna had to admit, but in the end decided it wasn't worth being unhappy, which she was quite sure she would be at Chicago.

And so, she informed the university that she was turning down its very generous offer. Because she hadn't been able to bring herself to tell André, he found out indirectly when a dean called him with instructions to get in touch with the applicant who had been the committee's second choice for the scholarship. In the twenty-five years that Chicago had been offering the award, almost no one had refused it. Nearly two years later, André, ordinarily a good-natured man, would still sound regretful. "I've been doing this for a long time," he said. "I can probably count on two hands the number of times I've felt sure that this was without doubt the right undergraduate place for the kid, and this was the kid who was right for the place. Julianna was warm, interesting and bright. She was in that camp."

After she returned to Los Angles from Chicago, Julianna counted only five colleges that remained on her list of possibilities: Harvard, Yale, Stanford, Swarthmore and Wesleyan. Faced with those choices, Sharon thought, most students would probably have eliminated Wesleyan and Swarthmore and selected from among the two Ivies and Stanford. But Julianna insisted on visiting all five of her finalists in a seven-day blitz. Sharon was elated, not only for Ralph, but because Julianna's was the sort of open-minded thinking that Sharon had hoped to foster at Harvard-Westlake. The Benteses agreed to pay for the plane and train tickets on her journey, which would total more than $1,000 for Julianna and Catherine.

On Tuesday, April 18, at seven A.M., they began their journey, flying out of Los Angeles International Airport, changing planes in Nashville, and disembarking in Hartford, Connecticut, about a half hour north of Middletown. Wesleyan had been dealt an early advantage: it would be given the opportunity to make a final impression on Julianna before any of the remaining contenders.

Before she had even set foot on campus, that impression was a good one. She liked Ralph, of course. She had read that the professors at Wesleyan were especially intelligent and interesting, and that their classes were small. And she was intrigued that so many students were vocal in their support of various political causes. Wesleyan was very much in the hunt, Julianna decided. The visit would be critical.

Because of the time change, the women arrived at Wesleyan after dinner, its patchwork architecture cloaked in darkness. Julianna would have to wait until morning to take a look around, but it was still early enough to get a sense of the campus's atmosphere. After she met up with the sophomore who had been assigned by the admissions office as her host, the young woman immediately extended an invitation: Would Julianna like to accompany her to a club meeting? Julianna said she was game. Her host didn't say what the club was, and she didn't ask, though she figured she'd be treated to some passionate discussion on a controversial issue. Julianna had no idea how right she would be.

When they arrived at the meeting, which was held in a drab conference room somewhere on campus, they were joined by about ten other women, as well as two men. Julianna still hadn't figured out why they had assembled. After the session was called to order, one of the young women opened a bag to share several items that she had recently collected in New York City, on what she described as a field expedition. Julianna craned forward, and her seventeen-year-old eyes soon widened. Spread out onto the table were a number of sex toys, including several vibrators of various dimensions. There were also instructional videos that promised to teach the viewer how to make love like a pro.

For that evening, Julianna Bentes was an honorary member of The Cunt Club at Wesleyan University.

The group's primary objective, as near as she could tell, was to empower women in sexual situations, either involving men or other women. "They wanted to reclaim that word"—Julianna had trouble saying it without blushing—"as their own." In a mission statement that it had filed with the college, the club listed various goals, including its desire for "every woman to know how to pleasure herself and teach her lover to pleasure her," and for everyone, woman or man, to express outrage at any violation of a woman's body, whether in instances of rape or of more systematic mutilation, as was practiced in some African countries.

Many colleges would surely be loath to recognize such an organization formally, at least by its given name. But Wesleyan, with its reputation for extending the boundaries of student expression, was not like most other schools when it came to issues of sexuality. The college listed the club on the website of its student activities office, which meant it had been designated by the student government as an official Wesleyan organization. As a result, the student government gave it a few hundred dollars every year, just as it might Wesleyan Students for Campaign Finance Reform or the Wesleyan Animal Rights Network.

Julianna had read that Wesleyan could be a bit out there, yet the *Fiske Guide* had failed to mention anything about a club dedicated to the celebration and protection of the female anatomy. Mercifully, the session that Julianna attended was all discussion, much of it intellectual and historical, and actually fairly tame. Julianna considered herself openminded, but she was relieved that no one turned on those vibrators.

The experience had caught Julianna off-guard. How could it not have? Still, she hardly considered the club's existence to be a deal-breaker, for she had been raised to be far more tolerant than that. In fact, she was more unnerved by what happened on the following morning. As she toured Wesleyan's campus, she passed several women from the meeting, some of them more than once. Though they appeared to look straight at her and her host, not one said hello. Wesleyan began to seem as unfriendly as Chicago. Julianna had always planned to leave Wesleyan before lunch, and she saw little reason to extend her stay. As Catherine sat idling outside in the rental car, Julianna had only one last stop that she wanted to make on campus.

She found Ralph standing in a hallway on the second floor of the admissions office. The only reason she had sought him out, Julianna told him, was that she wanted to thank him for his interest in her throughout the year. (She still had no idea he had been tracking her since she was in ninth grade.) Ralph thought her gesture endearing; it was as if she had just had a fine meal at his home and was acknowledging his hospitality. Julianna also thanked Ralph for Wesleyan's financial aid offer, which, while well short of a free ride, was as generous as almost any other school's. She did so even though she knew from Sharon that Ralph, as an admissions officer, had little to do with the money that students received, but she figured she had to thank someone at Wesleyan, so why not Ralph?

Ralph could tell that Julianna was rushed, and the whole conversation lasted just a few minutes. As she disappeared down the stairs, he wondered whether she had conveyed anything to him about Wesleyan's chances of getting her. He decided that she had not. But here it was, April 19, less than two weeks before her decision was due, and she had at least made time to visit. "I'm glad she got here," Ralph said afterward. "Things seem to have gone well."

For her part, Julianna was relieved that Ralph had not asked how she had spent the previous evening; she didn't know how she would have responded. As she embarked on the half-hour drive to New Haven, Julianna wondered whether Yale's version of rolling out the red carpet would be similar to Wesleyan's.

Jordan Goldman's body may have been present at Tottenville High School on the first Tuesday in April, but his mind was several hundred miles away from Staten Island. As his teachers droned on about the relationships between the executive and judiciary branches of the government, he doodled aimlessly on a piece of notebook paper, writing the same word over and over: *BROWN*. At one point, a friend snatched the paper and passed it around the Advanced Placement government class. When it landed back on Jordan's desk, he saw that more than a dozen classmates had written, "Good luck!" This was wishful thinking, for Jordan had not heard a word from Providence since December, when Brown deferred his candidacy into the regular admissions pool. But he suspected that a final decision letter from his dream school would be waiting for him when he got home that afternoon.

As it happened, Jordan would receive three letters that day. One was from Brown. The others were from the University of Pennsylvania and Wesleyan. Jordan slit open the envelope from Brown first, but its thinness had already betrayed its contents. He had been rejected, and didn't even wait to get to the bottom of the letter before tearing it into pieces. The news was no better from the University of Pennsylvania. Jordan ripped up that rejection, too. The thick packet from Wesleyan was obviously an acceptance—Jordan saw that there was even a sticker for his mother's car window inside—but he barely paid it any heed. His dream of attending an Ivy League college had ended; so, for that matter, had the only other scenario that would have permitted him to save face with his peers, at least as he saw it. A day earlier, he had learned that he had been rejected by Amherst. This was the school that his uncle Jay, the venture capitalist, had wanted to attend as a transfer student in his sophomore year, two decades earlier. Jay had had to turn down Amherst for financial reasons. In the absence of an acceptance from Brown, Jordan had relished the prospect of completing his uncle's unfinished business. Now he wouldn't get the chance.

Just as he had when he got the word from Amherst, Jordan called his mother at the school where she worked. He told her about Brown and Penn, and that he had now been rejected by his top three choices. If he mentioned Wesleyan's acceptance, it was only as an aside. Melanie tried to console him with the suggestion that he was a victim of a numbers game. While she didn't know the specifics, her instincts were on target. Brown, for example, had received nearly seventeen thousand applications, more than double the number of Wesleyan (and a staggering two thousand more than only a year earlier), for a freshman class of fewer than two thousand. Penn had received nearly nineteen thousand applications, for a class only slighter bigger than Brown's. Amherst had only fifty-three hundred applications, but for fewer than five hundred seats.

Jordan was obviously in shock, but Melanie could tell from his voice that this time he was going to be all right. He wasn't crying, and he wasn't talking about locking himself in his room as he had after being deferred by Brown in December. "I don't know what I'm going to do," he told his mom. "But I'm dealing with the reality of the situation. I'll figure something out."

After being deferred by Brown in the fall, Jordan had worried that he would not be admitted anywhere in the spring. But those fears had been unfounded. In addition to Wesleyan, he had been accepted by every other college to which he had applied: Johns Hopkins, Vassar, Sarah Lawrence, Boston University, Emerson and New York University. And each had made clear that it wanted him, badly. There may have been no shortage of white males applying to selective American colleges for the Class of 2004, but Jordan's SAT scores ranked him in the top 2 percent of his graduating class nationally. And anyone could tell from his essays that he was a talented writer.

Jordan had received his first acceptance letter the previous week, from NYU. The university's Tisch School of the Arts—whose graduates included the director Ang Lee (Class of 1984) and the entertainer Billy Crystal (Class of 1970)—had offered him a $15,000 scholarship based on his academic promise. Moreover, the school had promised him several complimentary round-trip tickets to Europe during his four years as a student there, should he accept, which he was welcome to use to get to and from the university's study-abroad programs, which lasted from six weeks to six months. Because Jordan's father's income was high he would not have qualified for this much financial aid based on need. But unlike the Ivies, NYU rewarded talent as well as need, just as the University of Chicago had in Julianna's case. And it wasn't alone in trying to buy Jordan's acceptance. Boston University offered him a $12,350 merit scholarship; Emerson, a merit scholarship of $9,500; and Vassar, a $5,000 scholarship. And while Sarah Lawrence's offer of direct aid was relatively paltry—$2,500—Jordan smiled when he read what the dean of admissions had scribbled at the bottom of his acceptance letter: "Your essay about Devin was moving and beautiful. Thank you, Jordan."

Jordan, in turn, made a note to tell his friend that his story of perseverance had moved at least one admissions officer.

Neither Johns Hopkins nor Wesleyan offered students scholarships based solely on merit. Like the Ivies, the two institutions reserved almost all of their direct scholarships for students with financial needs that were far more pronounced than Jordan's. Hopkins had not even extended him an offer of a loan; Wesleyan offered him loans of $5,000. Yet both colleges were clearly wooing him. Hopkins had sent his acceptance letter by priority mail, and the sense of urgency had really impressed him. It had then followed up the letter with phone calls and e-mails from professors and students touting the university's writing programs.

Wesleyan, too, had begun its campaign to win Jordan early, with a letter it mailed to him in mid-March, about two weeks before he received his letter of acceptance. "Although we are still in the process of reading applications," the writer stated, "one of the deans has passed along your name as someone I should contact." The writer identified himself as a recent Wesleyan graduate now working as an assistant in the admissions office. (Jordan would have been shocked to learn that the "someone" who recommended that he be contacted was Ralph, who had been so discouraging about his short stories in the fall.) Jordan found the letter curious: it was mostly an ode to Wesleyan that made no reference to whether he had been accepted or rejected. But in a carefully worded end-run, it had concluded: "FYI, all admitted students will be invited to Wesleyan for Wes-Fest, April 13–15, so mark your calendar." Why, Jordan thought, would he be instructed to mark his calendar if he had been rejected? Still, the early notice from Wesleyan had arrived at a time when he had eyes only for Brown. Jordan had put the letter in a drawer as soon as he received it.

While many students would have killed to have such a range of choices, Jordan was little moved. "I'm going to have to weigh the cons, which is a really pessimistic view, and go to the one with the least cons," he said at the time. (In retrospect, he would acknowledge: "This was a ridiculous view.") Like so many of his contemporaries, he paid close attention to the rankings in *U.S. News* though he often rearranged the editors' choice a bit to suit his own hierarchy of the academic universe. The most recent issue of *U.S. News* said that Hopkins (number 7 on the list of national universities), Wesleyan (number 10 on the liberal arts list), Vassar (number 17 among liberal arts schools) and NYU (number 34 among the nationals), were not in the same tier as Amherst (number 2 in liberal arts). Although Hopkins was rated in a tie with Penn, and Brown (number 14) was actually ranked lower, Jordan nonetheless weighted Brown and Penn higher because Hopkins was not in the Ivy League. Jordan's only solace was that his father, mother and stepfather had absolved him of having to make his decision based on money. He could attend the school that he thought was most likely to make him happy, and if need be, his family would help pay his way.

As a first step toward playing the hand he was dealt, Jordan planned a final round of college visits. As in Julianna's case, Wesleyan would be his first stop. Though Julianna had declined its invitation to the big recruiting weekend that it called WesFest—she had not been able to fly to campus until several days afterward—Jordan decided to attend. His two-day visit to Wesleyan also began on an inauspicious note: soon after he greeted Jordan, the student who had been assigned as his host informed him that he had a major term paper due at the end of the weekend. Jordan would be mostly on his own. *Brown wouldn't have let that happen,* Jordan thought.

But things only got better from there. Jordan requested a meeting on short notice with a creative writing professor, and she cleared her schedule to grant him a half hour. She was definitely aware that Richard Price was a critically regarded author and screenwriter, and she expressed confidence that his protégé could nurture his talent at Wesleyan. Jordan felt encouraged. But a short while later, the only emotion he was feeling was panic. During lunch in Wesleyan's main cafeteria—a space built in the 1960s that was shaped like a circular spaceship—Jordan looked up from his cheeseburger and side of Spanish rice and saw Ralph Figueroa walking over with a tray. Ralph asked if the seat next to Jordan was taken; it wasn't.

When Jordan introduced himself, Ralph did not recognize his name. Jordan would have no way of knowing, of course, but his essay about Devin was among the most touching and memorable that Ralph had read all year. But Ralph had read nearly fifteen hundred applications; it was hard to keep track of everyone. He had long since forgotten that the boy with the friend in the wheelchair was named Jordan. All Jordan could tell was that Ralph didn't seem to remember his face from their confrontation in the fall. He could barely contain his curiosity over whether his short stories had ever gotten read at Wesleyan, but he decided not to broach the topic and risk reminding Ralph that they had met earlier. Still, his impression of Ralph was now much more positive: he appreciated that Ralph had sensed his obvious loneliness and attempted to fill the void.

Jordan also liked what he saw as he and hundreds of other prospective freshmen in attendance—Wesleyan called them "pre-frosh"—moved about the Wesleyan campus. It wasn't just the eclectic nature of the architecture— the stone-cold concrete of the arts center, the warmth of the red leather doors of the library—but that everywhere he turned, he saw signs of protest. One group of students had hung posters to let the pre-frosh know that the alcohol-free weekend they were experiencing was not representative of Wesleyan on any other weekend. Other protesters had used pastel-colored chalk to mark up the sidewalks between buildings with washable graffiti. Jordan had never seen anything like it. Much of the oversized writing was intended to herald the presence of the most vocal members of Wesleyan's gay community. One message, in bright yellow, read: "Wesleyan ♥ Queer Prefrosh." Other messages paired phallic symbols with words that were hardly complimentary of President Bennet. Jordan was amazed, and impressed, that the administration had permitted such dissent during what was arguably Wesleyan's most important weekend of the year.

Besides the absence of his student host, Jordan had only two regrets about his visit. One was that he had wound up liking so many of the pre-frosh whom he met, nearly all of whom had reported to him that they had been accepted at either Brown or Yale or Williams or Amherst. He certainly wouldn't be going to college with any of them, Jordan assumed, because each would choose one of those other schools over Wesleyan. He, in turn, had told no one of his rejections. When anyone asked where else he was looking, he would only say, "A lot of places," as he was too embarrassed to give the names.

Jordan's only other disappointment was that he had arrived too late to get a seat at the Wesleyan Cinema on the first night of the open house, to hear the weekend's keynote speaker. He had thought that Wesleyan's choice was inspired: John Waters, the director and writer of such offbeat films as *Hairspray, Cry Baby* and *Serial Mom.*

For all the good feelings he had experienced at Wesleyan, Jordan was no closer to making a decision when he left on Saturday than when he had arrived two days earlier. After a quick trip home, he planned to hit the road again, this time bound for Vassar in Poughkeepsie. "My view of Wesleyan," he said at the time, "is that no one at my high school knows what it is. And they don't know Vassar, either." For Jordan Goldman, this presented a problem.

As Jordan was waiting on line to hear John Waters speak on that Thursday night in mid-April, so was Migizi Pensoneau. It was the last place Mig had expected to be. Two weeks earlier, as he was anxiously awaiting Wesleyan's decision letter, he had convinced himself that it would contain bad news. Those C's and D's from his high school in Minnesota had surely been his undoing, even if he had started his life over at the Native American Preparatory School. When the thick packet from Wesleyan finally arrived, he hugged the counselor who hand-delivered it to him.

Mig had desperately wanted to attend WesFest, but when his mother could not afford the fare his counselor took Ralph up on his offer to have Wesleyan send Mig a free plane ticket, to help him make his decision. Mig had also been accepted at Pitzer, Beloit College in Wisconsin, Colorado College and Bard in upstate New York, all schools that his counselor had recommended; he had only two rejections, from Grinnell in Iowa and Oberlin. Ralph was eager to land one of his most prized recruits and glad to have Mig on campus for WesFest. Wesleyan would also be flying out several dozen other minority applicants that weekend, having found that the tickets were a good investment, one that usually helped maintain its high concentration of minority students. (A white applicant with financial needs who was savvy enough to request a ticket might receive one as well, but Wesleyan, like other colleges, made little attempt to advertise this.)

Standing outside the gray walls of the Wesleyan Cinema, Mig felt as if he were at a Hollywood premiere. In front of him, two Wesleyan students were playing the game "Six Degrees of Kevin Bacon," trying to figure out how to link Bacon's career to that of the actor Lou Diamond Phillips. As the girls were taking a circuitous route through five films to do so, Mig, the film projector in his head whirring, apologized for eavesdropping but just had to interrupt. In the most modest voice he could muster, he told the two young women that Bacon had starred in the film *Flatliners* with Kiefer Sutherland, who had then appeared with Lou Diamond Phillips in *Young Guns*. Impressed, the two women tried to stump Mig by asking him to connect Kevin Bacon to Winona Ryder. But before he could do so, they were all ushered into the theater. While Jordan idled in vain behind them, Mig and his new friends had scored 3 of the 260 coveted seats for John Waters's talk.

Mig took his seat in the middle of the theater and began scanning the room. As his eyes reached the top of the aisle, he saw Ralph, who was dressed in a suit, just as he had been at NAPS, and carrying a walkie-talkie. With dozens of events scheduled over three days, WesFest required military-style coordination among the admissions officers. Mig and Ralph had not spoken at all since their initial meeting in the fall; each had liked the other so much that neither had wanted to jinx the transaction.

But now that the transaction had been successfully completed, Mig leaped out of his seat and sprinted up the aisle to pump Ralph's hand in gratitude. He could tell that Ralph was distracted; the John Waters event had proven so popular that even one of the interns who helped organize it had not gotten a seat. Ralph, who was trying to get the intern admitted to the theater, only had time to ask Mig one question: "How are you liking it?"

Mig responded simply: "I'm liking it." Both smiled, and then Mig slipped away.

Just as it had with Martin Scorsese, Clint Eastwood and the family of the late director Frank Capra, Wesleyan had persuaded John Waters to entrust his papers and an array of props to the university's growing cinematic archives. The archives were tended by Jeanine Basinger, a film historian who seemingly knew everyone in the business.

Waters began his talk by explaining why he had deposited his most prized possessions in Middletown, Connecticut. Wesleyan, he readily acknowledged, was a long way from Baltimore, where he was born and where he had set many of his films. But as he explained to the audience, as quoted in the next day's *Wesleyan Argus,* "When I realized that Divine's fake tits would rest in peace next to Dirty Harry's police badge, I knew this was the place." He went on like that for more than a half hour, and when he was done, the audience, Mig included, gave him a standing ovation.

Mig, who had written in his college essay about women whistling at him on a construction site, concluded that it wasn't just Ralph who shared his sense of humor, but the entire college. If Wesleyan had tapped John Waters to be its emissary to its prospective freshmen, then Mig was sure he wanted in. That early impression was only confirmed over the next few days as he spent hours walking the campus, past Foss Hill, around the circumference of Van Vleck Observatory, even inside the student mailroom. Everywhere he went, Mig beamed. Never mind that Wesleyan was a bit sprawling, with no obvious center or unifying architectural style. "It's like in the movies," he told his student guide. "I've never seen a campus like this." He also enjoyed the way that his prospective classmates greeted him. "After everyone found out I was Native American, they treated me like I was some kind of exotic," he recalled. "Everyone was like, '*Ohhh!*'" Migizi Pensoneau was a celebrity.

After a taxi hired by Wesleyan dropped him at the airport on Sunday morning, he asked the driver for his business card, certain that he would need it in the fall. He already knew that a classmate at NAPS had been accepted at Wesleyan but had decided to attend Stanford. No matter, Mig thought; he would go it alone. He was hardly concerned that no one back home had ever heard of Wesleyan and actually liked the idea that he'd be perceived as going off to someplace mysterious. Now all he had to do was tell his mother.

Mig readily acknowledged that his mother, Renee, was the heroine of his story. It was she who had pushed him so hard to make a fresh start at NAPS. And she had already gotten an early payoff on that investment: in December, while Mig was visiting for Christmas, a letter had arrived from

Pitzer informing him that he had been accepted early. Since Pitzer's acceptance was not binding, he had until April to decide, but it hadn't been too early to celebrate his first college admission, and the family had proceeded to laugh and dance around their one-story home in northern Minnesota. Mig's had been an incredible comeback; after causing Renee so much pain with his grades, he was proud to be able to give her such joy.

Mig had never been especially enamored with Pitzer and had applied only because a representative from the California school had visited NAPS. Of his remaining choices, he didn't know much about Bard or Beloit, other than that his counselor told him that either would be good for an aspiring screenwriter. His mother wanted him to go to Colorado College, which was less than eight hundred miles southwest of her home in Bemidji, Minnesota; she had missed him while he was in New Mexico.

After WesFest, Mig called Renee to tell her that he had chosen Wesleyan, instead. While the East Coast was far from home, at least her financial worries would be minimal. Mig had been awarded a $24,890 annual scholarship, which, when combined with a $1,750 federal grant, $3,500 in loans and a $1,600 work-study job, meant that his mother's contribution to Mig's $35,000-a-year education would be a modest $3,600. Mig realized that would still be a stretch for her as a single parent with a part-time job, but Renee put any of his remaining concerns to rest. "We'll raise it somehow," she assured him. She could tell how much he wanted to go.

It had never occurred to Mig that he should tell Ralph, too.

Since the second week of April, Ralph had been checking his computer several times a day to see which applicants had sent in the $250 deposit to reserve a seat in the freshman class. Those deposits could be postmarked no later than May 1, but would trickle in throughout that first week. On May 4, Ralph logged on, punched in Mig's name and saw the code "MS"—"matriculating student"—flash on his screen. "All right!" Ralph said out loud.

Ralph had pulled off something that none of his colleagues had thought he could: he had recruited his first Native American student to Wesleyan. Mig's experience at Wesleyan would likely have a profound effect on him, as well as on his classmates. He would face enormous academic and social hurdles, but, Ralph believed, this was no time to dwell on the risks both he and Mig had taken. At this particular moment, Ralph was only thinking about how great it was going to be to sit down with Mig at the campus dining hall to talk about movies.

Nine
420-ED

Tiffany Wang of Palo Alto, California, was hardly the first seventeen-year-old who failed to seize the extraordinary opportunities that were presented to her in high school. In a less competitive time, almost any college would have forgiven her indulgences and taken a chance on her. A decade earlier, she probably would have coasted into schools like Wesleyan, Duke or Wellesley, which were three of her top choices, on the strength of her potential and in response to the demand for applicants of Asian descent—at least at colleges off the West Coast. But as Wesleyan and its immediate competitors selected the Class of 2004, they were blessed with too many other applicants with similar profiles who had worked harder than Tiffany and accomplished more, both inside the classroom and out. Like Wesleyan, Duke offered her a spot only on the waiting list. Wellesley, along with Yale and Penn, rejected her outright.

"Just title the chapter on me 'Lazy!'" Tiffany said in an interview after receiving her letter from Wesleyan. "I definitely could have done better in high school." Tiffany would still have attractive choices: UCLA, NYU, Colby (in Waterville, Maine) and Bryn Mawr were all eager to have her. But by the standards of an immigrant father who thought few schools were prestigious enough to educate his middle daughter—"He didn't even think Brown was very good," she recalled—those options were a disappointment. "I wish I had studied more," Tiffany said after her senior year. "I wish I had taken school more seriously."

Nonetheless, considering her designation as a National Merit Finalist, Tiffany was surprised when the best that Wesleyan could muster was an offer for the waiting list. When a friend of her sister's suggested she apply to the school, Tiffany had sought out *The Best 311 Colleges* and had noted that her SAT scores were 100 points above the Wesleyan median. She had no idea that Wesleyan and other elite colleges routinely turned down a lot of applicants with high SAT scores, even higher than hers. That same spring, Harvard would reject one of every four students who applied with a perfect SAT score of 800/800. ("Dialing toll-free," in the admissions lexicon.) Feeling put off by Wesleyan, Tiffany didn't even respond to its letter about the waiting list. Instead, she decided to choose among the schools that had already accepted her.

She had been thinking lately that she wanted to be on the East Coast, for a change of scenery, so that worked against UCLA. And though her sister was at Bryn Mawr, Tiffany had found it too small. Her concern about a small campus—along with her dread of the three connecting flights it would take to get to Maine from Northern California—had also worked against Colby, which she was reluctant even to visit. But she did want to see NYU, and so flew to the East Coast in mid-April.

Tiffany stayed with relatives in New Jersey, and after an aunt dropped her off in lower Manhattan, she decided almost immediately that she didn't like what she saw of NYU. For all her desire to be in a city, the school didn't seem like a college at all. Tiffany knew she didn't want to be in the country, but she was seeking at least a little bit of a campus atmosphere. She noted that Washington Square Park, the closest to a center that NYU had, was filled with lots of people who obviously weren't students, and the dormitories looked to her like faceless New York City apartment buildings. "The people never talk to each other in their dorms," a friend had warned her before she visited. "They're always in and out. They keep their doors closed." Having risked life and limb in high school to climb out the window of her house to be with her friends, Tiffany figured that she would need to embark on similar adventures to have a social life at NYU.

She had visited friends several times at UCLA, and now that she had seen NYU, Los Angeles was starting to look better. It was not only prettier and sunnier, but also cheaper: only about $11,500 a year, compared to about $35,000 a year at NYU. The only scholarship she had received at NYU would be worth $2,000, what she was entitled to as a National Merit Finalist. On either campus, she could pursue her political interests, as well as prepare for the career she was now contemplating: criminal law.

She might well find herself keeping someone off Death Row someday, she thought.

But as was the case with so many of her peers, Tiffany ultimately made her decision based on two small details, along with a little help from a friend. Though she had done her best at times to avoid going to class in high school, she surprised even herself by realizing that she relished the prospect of sitting in the spacious lecture halls that she had seen at NYU. She wasn't even necessarily impressed by the professors whose lectures she had ducked into on her tour, but for some reason, responded to the theater-style seats, the spot lighting and the projectors. Going to class at NYU would be like going to the movies—it seemed like fun—and she hadn't seen anything similar at UCLA. Also, while the dorms at NYU initially came off as foreboding, there was one perk that Tiffany was eager to take advantage of: she would likely have a private bathroom. Nearly every undergraduate did, she was told. If she attended NYU, as opposed to UCLA or almost any other college for that matter, she would not have to wait on line for the shower.

It was her death row pen pal, though, writing from his cell in a Texas prison, who sealed the deal. "He thought NYU was a really good college," she said, though he was careful not to influence her. Tiffany had no idea what knowledge he had of NYU, but she did know he had received a master's degree at some point in his life from a university in the South. And so she decided: NYU it was. Even her father, who had attended rival Columbia, said in the end that he was pleased with her choice and that he would "mortgage the house" if that's what it took to send her to NYU. Tiffany was relieved.

She sent in her deposit long before the May 1 deadline. A few weeks later, after she failed to respond to Wesleyan's initial invitation to join the waiting list—and after she ignored a follow-up e-mail message—her application was stamped "WAITLIST CLOSEOUT." But Wesleyan would hardly suffer, for it still it had more potential customers than it could possibly accommodate.

Aggie Ramirez had applied to Wesleyan on the advice of several young alumni who worked at Prep for Prep, the organization that had shepherded her journey from a hardscrabble neighborhood in Upper Manhattan to Oldfields. The people at Prep had spoken so affectionately about the intimate classroom environment at Wesleyan that Aggie was eager to attend.

The decision letter from Wesleyan was among the first that Aggie received, and its offer of only a place on the waiting list saddened her. But she was also a realist, and had always suspected that her C's and D's during her senior year might weigh down the rest of her record, which was mostly A's and B's. She was also well aware that her SAT's—550 verbal, 540 math—were much lower than what Wesleyan usually expected. She had considered Wesleyan a reach and had not even visited the campus. While the school was inviting her to join the waiting list, she gave herself little chance of coming off it, and so would set her sights elsewhere, having no idea how strong an impression she had made there, at least on one admissions officer.

Aggie knew that applying to Connecticut College had been a stretch, too, and it had been more definitive in its response than Wesleyan: it had rejected her outright. But she was pleased with her remaining choices, having received acceptance letters from Goucher, which was near Old-fields; Lake Forest, thirty miles outside Chicago; Wheaton, in southeastern Massachusetts; and Muhlenberg, in Allentown, Pennsylvania. None had the name recognition of a Wesleyan; still, Aggie knew that each rejected plenty of applicants. The disappointment that she felt at being rebuffed by Wesleyan and Connecticut College was soon replaced by swelling pride: She would be the first in her family to go away to college. Merely by applying to those schools, she had broken new ground.

Aggie's parents had moved to the United States from the Dominican Republic as adults, in the early 1970s. Neither had progressed past high school, with the exception of a few community college courses. Her father worked at a photocopying shop. Her mother, whose English remained limited, worked as a classroom aide for disabled children at a public school. Aggie knew that her parents had to work hard just to keep her and her two younger brothers cared for, and was confident that no matter which college she chose, she would receive a good education, one that offered her—and perhaps her family—the prospect of a better life.

Just as Jordan Goldman was being pursued by Wesleyan and NYU after being turned down by Brown, so was Aggie Ramirez being wooed by schools that were only too happy to have an applicant of her caliber. It was almost like a professional sports draft: colleges like Harvard and Yale and Brown and Stanford usually got to make their picks first, and then every other college fell into some kind of order afterward. Muhlenberg, in particular, was relieved that Aggie had not been snapped up by another college before it got the chance to make a play for her.

Melissa Falk, who had been an admissions officer at Muhlenberg for eight years, had read her application at around the time that Ralph had, in February. Like Ralph, Melissa had been gripped by the trajectory of Aggie's life, culminating in her improbable election to the presidency of the student council. She thought Aggie had to be a natural leader, and had been able to persuade her colleagues at Muhlenberg that despite Aggie's rough grades senior fall, she was worth the academic risk.

Muhlenberg was a 151-year-old collection of regal Tudor- and Gothic-style buildings that sat high on a hill overlooking the dormant factories and partially shuttered downtown of Allentown, whose plight had been memorialized in the 1980s in a Billy Joel song. In the eight years since her graduation, Melissa had risen from campus tour guide to one of the senior people in the eight-person admissions office. She was twenty-nine. When Melissa came across Aggie's application while sitting at her kitchen table on a winter night, her inner social worker sprang to attention. *I have to meet her,* Melissa thought to herself. But while Melissa was sure that Muhlenberg would be good for Aggie, she was even more sure that Aggie would be good for Muhlenberg.

Melissa sensed from reading Aggie's application that she was mostly self-made, which was an all too accurate assessment. Aggie's efforts to remake herself had begun early. Embarrassed by a score below the 20th percentile on a citywide reading test in the third grade, Aggie had forced herself to spend the following summer learning to read a book of Greek myths. While the book had been simplified for an elementary-school audience, Aggie still found it a challenge, and the experience had been transforming. "I became an intellectual," she recalled. "I just wanted to know stuff for the sake of knowing it." The following spring, she took her next city reading test and scored above the 90th percentile.

A year after that, as a fifth-grader, Aggie decided to take another test. This one was voluntary—an entrance exam for one of the best public middle schools in New York City, Mott Hall. She was desperate to avoid attending her neighborhood middle school, which was frequently riven by violence. Successful in that effort, she set her sights even higher, on Prep for Prep. After being rejected by the program as a seventh-grader, she was accepted in eighth grade. The tutoring that she received in the program after school and on weekends eventually led to her admission to Oldfields. "I really wanted to go to private school," Aggie recalled. "I had this image that if I went to private school, I wouldn't get swallowed up. I wouldn't be one of those girls who just hung out on the street corner near my house after school, if they even went to school." Aggie had wasted little time in seeking to influence others. Her younger brother followed her into Prep for Prep, and during her senior year at Oldfields, had applied, successfully, to Philips Exeter.

It didn't hurt that Aggie's application landed at Muhlenberg at a time when the college was working diligently to diversify its two-thousand-member student body, which was drawn mostly from the suburbs north of New York City, New Jersey and Pennsylvania. The freshman class that was admitted the year before Aggie applied was 2.5 percent black and 3.5 percent Hispanic. Wesleyan, by comparison, had a freshman class that was 9 percent black and 7 percent Hispanic. And while Wesleyan had managed to maintain a median SAT score of 1370 that year, Muhlenberg's was 200 points lower, at 1168.

Thus, at Muhlenberg, Aggie's SAT scores—a combined 1090—were not really a detriment. Indeed, in 1996, Muhlenberg became one of a small but growing number of mostly liberal arts colleges that had stopped requiring students to sit for the main SAT exam. The college not only considered the test biased in favor of students of means, but also disapproved of the way that it had come to dominate the high school careers of so many. Surely, making the SAT optional worked to Muhlenberg's advantage as well: having been unable to draw applicants who tested as consistently well as Wesleyan's, it could now put an asterisk next to its median SAT score in those college guidebooks. Its policy was now this: Those applicants (like Aggie) who wished to submit their scores and have them considered were welcome to do so; those who chose not to would not be penalized. Nor would Muhlenberg.

While Aggie's scores would likely be a plus, Melissa knew that her C's and that D senior year were problematic, to say the least. She had read the letter that Aggie's college counselor had enclosed, suggesting that the girl's myriad activities had contributed to her bad grades, and that after she had cut back, they had already started to rise. And just as she had at Wesleyan, Aggie had added a letter of her own, on plain white paper with no heading. "I am aware that Muhlenberg really looks at a student's transcript," she wrote. "My past semester grades would be classified as unbecoming of a Muhlenberg student, however they are not an accurate reflection of my ability." After underscoring that her self-imposed overload of extracurricular interests was partly to blame, she explained that she had learned a valuable lesson: "Prioritizing is crucial." Ralph had noted a similar letter that he received (identical but for the substitution of Wesleyan for Muhlenberg) only in passing. But Melissa felt it gave her some ammunition when bringing Aggie's application to her dean. "There was not an ounce of self-pity in that letter," Melissa recalled. "She was able to convey that the results in front of us were not what she would have hoped for herself." Melissa thought that the letter showed maturity.

Considering Aggie's A's and B's prior to her senior year at Oldfields, Melissa was willing to gamble that the student could handle the work at Muhlenberg. It was a risk, she knew, but one worth taking because "there was such a big person here." After discussing the case with Melissa, her dean, who would make the ultimate call, was inclined to agree. But he wanted to meet Aggie before signing off officially.

Melissa had first contacted Aggie's guidance counselor in March, to let Oldfields know that Muhlenberg was seriously considering her. If Aggie was eventually accepted, the counselor was told, money would not be an issue: her family would be responsible for paying only $4,000 a year. The remainder of the school's $25,000 tuition and fees would be covered by scholarships—all of them based on need—as well as Aggie's work-study job. Melissa encouraged the counselor to urge Aggie to take the two-hour bus ride from New York City to Allentown during her upcoming spring break, to check the school out. To Melissa's delight, Aggie readily agreed.

As she stepped off the bus in downtown Allentown, Aggie was surprised to find Melissa waiting, having expected a student to pick her up. At five feet four inches, Melissa was only slightly taller than Aggie, and the two were wearing nearly identical blue pea coats. *This was not the typical admissions officer,* Aggie thought. Melissa had also arranged for Aggie to be hosted on campus by a freshman from New York City whose family had been born in Puerto Rico. Melissa was aware that the young woman had also participated in Prep for Prep, but had no idea that Aggie knew the young woman well.

When she met up with her old friend, Aggie was blunt. "What's it like for you here?" she asked. "I came here because the white girls were nice to me," her friend replied. Aggie, whose skin was as dark as her friend's, liked the answer and was savvy enough to know that her background may have given her an edge in the admissions process. "Some people overcome obstacles in their lives," Aggie remarked later. "The admissions officers have to look at those people differently."

Aggie's host clinched the deal for Muhlenberg when she took her to a rehearsal of *West Side Story*. Aggie, having enjoyed her work on musicals at Oldfields, dreamed of becoming an actress someday. Yet she had always felt self-conscious about her body: her small five-foot-two-inch frame carried 160 pounds. But when she looked up at the stage in the theater at Muhlenberg, she felt as if she was staring into a huge mirror, and she liked what she saw.

"The dancers were all my size," she recalled. "And they were all *good*! There was a girl who had bigger boobs than me, and she was wearing her tight-fitting jazzy pants and her spaghetti-strapped tank top. When she did her leaps, you could see her navel. She was moving with such grace."

Later that same day, as Melissa introduced her around the admissions office, Aggie was stunned that everyone seemed to know who she was, including the dean, greeting her, "Oh, *you're* Aggie." Melissa, who had ranked Aggie among her top priorities that year, had been on a campaign for weeks. In lobbying her colleagues, Melissa had repeatedly used a code word to describe Aggie that would have been instantly understood in many other admissions offices: She called Aggie a "water walker." And while the term usually applied to those applicants with the highest grade point average, Melissa wanted to convey that Aggie was "going to make a difference" at Muhlenberg. "You get the opportunity once in a lifetime to bring someone like her to campus," Melissa told anyone who would listen. Even with Melissa's buildup, Aggie had not disappointed: after she departed campus, Melissa got the green light to make her an offer. The acceptance letter arrived at Oldfields before the end of March.

Aggie didn't need to overthink her decision; she felt wanted at Muhlenberg and she felt comfortable. The guidebooks made it clear that though the school didn't have the name recognition of Wesleyan, it would still give her an outstanding education. And her father assured her that even if he had to take out a loan, he would make up the difference in her tuition. Aggie sent off all her paperwork to Muhlenberg, accepting the offer to attend. And then, as a courtesy, she dropped a quick note to Wesleyan, thanking the admissions office for its consideration.

After receiving Aggie's letter, someone in the back office at Wesleyan stamped her application "WAITLIST WITHDRAW" and then wrote in the name "Muhlenberg" next to the space set aside for the college that Aggie had decided to attend. Whenever possible, Wesleyan liked to keep track of where its applicants ended up, even those applicants whom it had passed over.

* * *

Becca Jannol slipped through the open door of the college counseling annex at the Harvard-Westlake School in Los Angeles, the office flooded with so much sun and light, and sat down hard on the khaki couch inside. Before Sharon could even ask how she was doing, Becca pulled her knees close to her chest and began to sob. It was the second Monday in April, the students' first day back after spring break. When she calmed down, Becca told Sharon that she had been in Israel for a week on vacation and had returned to a stack of college letters. She already knew before she had left for the Middle East that she had been rejected by Georgetown, where she had hoped to start a political career. Now Becca had learned that Duke had rejected her, too, as had an honors program at George Washington University, also in Washington. Wesleyan had placed her on the waiting list, as had Cornell and Columbia. Other than Emory University in Atlanta, which had accepted her, Becca's only other choices were three campuses of the University of California: Santa Barbara, San Diego and Santa Cruz.

Prior to mailing out her applications, Becca had vowed that she wouldn't get caught up in the frenzy of attending a college with a prestigious name. But as time passed she had now become entranced by the idea of attending a college that ranked near the top of the guidebooks' rankings. "Everyone sort of measures you by where you're going, where your parents went, how smart you really are," said Becca, whose father graduated from UCLA (relatively cool, as Becca saw it) and whose mother graduated from a teaching college in New Jersey (definitely not cool). "I tried not to get caught up in it," she said. "But I totally did. I was as guilty as everyone else." As she cried on Sharon's couch, Becca worried aloud that her classmates were unlikely to consider Emory or the UC campuses as worthy of the president of their student body.

Sharon first attempted to piece together for Becca what had happened, telling her that she had spoken to several admissions officers in recent days, including Ralph, and that each made clear that the brownie incident had been difficult for several of their colleagues to accept. But Sharon, like Becca, refused to second-guess the decision to play the incident as prominently as they had. It had become a source of pride for Becca to have been the lone student who turned herself in to school administrators, and then become chair of the honor board. That was who she was, and she knew from the outset that the strategy of stressing that fact had been risky. But Sharon assured Becca, now as then, that without her account of her redemption, the outcome would have likely been no better.

Becca was a white, upper-middle-class applicant whose grade point average (3.71) and SAT's (a combined 1270) placed her only in the middle of the pack at her own school. And the elite colleges would judge her against her classmates. She was one of twenty-four from Harvard-Westlake who had applied to Wesleyan, and one of thirty-five who applied to Cornell. Although from the vantage point of Eastern colleges, Harvard-Westlake was the Andover or Exeter of the West Coast, diversity—in the broadest definition of the word—dictated that there was only going to be room for so many Harvard-Westlake students at each of those colleges.

Becca's only regret now was that she had not worked more aggressively to parlay her four years on the Harvard-Westlake track team into a greater asset. Her best time in the 100-meter dash, 12.9 seconds, was probably fast enough for her to contend for a spot on the team at a Division III school like Wesleyan or even an Ivy League college like Cornell. But the truth was, she was not sure that she wanted to run anymore. She worried that if she got in to a college on the strength of athletics, knowing already that she was ambivalent about competing, she would be gaining her admission under false pretenses.

As Sharon sat next to Becca on her couch, the counselor felt as if she were consoling a daughter. She had such feelings for a lot of her students, but she particularly believed in Becca. "If they spent a month with you and rejected you," Sharon told Becca, "then you could feel bad about yourself. They're only rejecting a bunch of pieces of paper, not you." Then Sharon decided to regroup and point Becca toward the future.

Seizing on Becca's invitations to join the waiting list at Wesleyan, Cornell and Columbia, Sharon told her that she wouldn't have received such offers from each school unless "someone there loves you." Drawing on her years in the admissions office at Occidental, she assured Becca that people did come off the waiting list. "Find out where you want to go," she advised, "and push."

Becca decided to channel her anger and frustration into a letter. Sitting down at her computer, she first typed, "To: Ralph Figueroa" and began to compose:

> Let me begin on behalf of all the applicants who will never get the chance—but THANK YOU for lobbying for our cause . . .

a thankless job in which you get to try to shuffle the fate of name-less, shapeless, amorphous, unabridged teenage versions of people pleading with you to buy their soul. I am lucky to have you rooting for me and I am grateful.

After briefly considering mourning the loss of my self-confidence by painting my toenails a hideous shade of black (rejection can be so demeaning), my resilient spirit wondered what could be done to catapult myself to Middletown ASAP.

It's back to pen and paper, in the same way I sat down a year ago, trying to come up with an all-encompassing statement to capture seventeen years and hypothesize about the four to come. And what rang true one year ago was the experience so controversial yet so honest—

I want you to hear my voice. I want to give you ammunition to fire at the committee—but I assure you there are inconsistencies and there are mistakes; there is arrogance and there are B minuses (even with hard work) . . . there is messiness and there are triumphs . . . such is my life, my adolescence. . . .

"Though it is a cliché," Becca wrote, she hoped that Ralph would "hear my voice and judge whether or not that voice will blend with those admitted to the Class of 2004." And should he or the rest of the committee decide that her voice was dissonant, she wrote, "So be it." She would "trust that the class will be spectacular with or without me."

When she reread what she had written, Becca felt a sense of catharsis but also realized that she had been writing more to herself than to Ralph. She couldn't send so melodramatic and overwrought a note to a college admissions officer, however accurately it captured the pain she was feeling. Instead, she cleared her computer screen and drafted a generic letter to send to Wesleyan, Cornell and Columbia. She decided that she would risk another round of rejection and would take her chances on the waiting list.

This time, she kept her letter to two paragraphs. She thanked each admissions committee for its consideration thus far, assured its members that she remained interested if accepted, and reported that she continued to work hard in her studies and on an independent film she was making. She concluded: "I anxiously await your response in May!"

By April 13, three days after she had broken down in Sharon's arms, Becca's letter had arrived at the admissions office at Wesleyan, at which point her application was stamped: "WAITLIST YES."

Now if she had any hope of ascending to the top and moving into the class, she would probably have to fly to the East Coast, for she would still have to sell herself to her potential customers, Cornell and Wesleyan. (She had ruled out a trip to Columbia because she had visited friends there in the past, and was doubtful she would get in.) With her mother in tow, Becca began her trip on Monday, April 17, flying first to Atlanta, to visit Emory. This was the one institution outside of the California university system that had accepted her, and she knew that she had to see it, as it might well be where she ended up.

Becca wound up hating everything about Emory. "I didn't meet anyone I thought I could be friends with," she said later. "The campus was just so dead." Nothing else about the school made the slightest impression, but Becca had the presence of mind to realize this was less a reflection of her surroundings than her state of mind at the time. "I was just feeling really bad that I got rejected everywhere," Becca said. "And I know I didn't get rejected everywhere. I just felt like I did."

The following morning, the Jannols flew to an aunt's house in New Jersey, from where they embarked on the four-hour ride to Ithaca, in western New York, where Cornell had been founded in 1865. Cornell had been a last-minute addition to Becca's college wish list, after Georgetown deferred her early application. Sharon knew that Becca had wanted to add one more marquee name to a list that was otherwise quite balanced and believed that Ken Gabard, the admissions officer at Cornell who had been responsible for Harvard-Westlake's "account" for nearly a decade, would ensure that her application was treated fairly.

Becca arrived on campus at midday, in a driving rainstorm. Cornell's most dramatic features—the two deep gorges that divide the campus into rough quarters and are spanned by wooden foot bridges—were obscured by fog, as was the view of nearby Cayuga Lake, which measured forty miles across. She sprinted from her aunt's car into the vestibule of the Statler Hotel, operated by students in the university's hotel school. As she dried off in the lobby, Becca had just one thought: *I'm going here.* This was not a carefully reasoned calculation, but like so many seventeen-year-olds making a college decision, she was going with her gut. And she was hoping for the best.

The remainder of Becca's visit to Cornell was mostly unremarkable. She went to a fraternity party with a family friend that night and had fun; the following morning, she attended a German history class and found it interesting. But the one element of Cornell that really stood out was her visit with Ken Gabard. Just when she thought that no one could ever take Ralph Figueroa's place in her heart, here was Becca almost melting over Ken. He was over six feet tall, with a full head of brown hair. Becca figured he was in his thirties (he was actually about to turn fifty) and that he had the bearing of a "young dad." That part was true; he was the father of two elementary-school-age daughters.

After all she had been through, Ken's soft voice was as comforting as a campfire. What her ear had detected were the remnants of his upbringing in a rural North Carolina community, near Winston-Salem. Like Ralph and so many of his counterparts, Ken had had an entirely different life before admissions. A graduate of Duke, he had gone on to receive a Ph.D. at Berkeley and had arrived at Cornell in 1978 to do postdoctoral research on the molecular biology of plants. Over the next decade, he had been enlisted to assist in the admissions process. Unlike Wesleyan and most other colleges, Cornell believed that admissions should not be entrusted to a committee of lay evaluators alone. So that professors could weigh in on the students they'd eventually be teaching, Cornell paired each admissions officer with several faculty members, who together would decide whom to admit. Ken found he loved such work and eventually switched sides, leaving his research professorship to become an assistant dean in the college of arts and sciences. That was essentially an elevated way of saying that he would be an admissions officer, as well as a dean of the freshman class. Cornell also liked to make sure that its admissions officers stayed active in the lives of its students after they were admitted, for at least the first year they were on campus. Becca thought Ken was well suited to both his jobs.

As they sat down in his office, Ken told Becca what he had related to Sharon in an earlier conversation: that Becca had narrowly missed being admitted. He didn't discuss the specific reasons, and the brownie was never mentioned, so Becca had no idea whether it had been a factor. Instead, Ken talked about all the applications that Cornell had received that year (ninety-two hundred for about one thousand seats) and spoke of a housing crunch on campus. He said that coming off the waiting list remained a possibility, but barring that, Becca would have one last-ditch option: Cornell might consider admitting a group of students over the summer, with their enrollment effective the following January, when the Class of 2004 would be halfway through its freshman year. By then, more housing might become available. If Cornell decided to do so, Ken asked, would Becca want to be considered?

Becca was noncommittal. It wasn't only that Cornell seemed to have invented yet another hoop for her to go through in this seemingly endless process, but she was also mindful that she hadn't seen Wesleyan yet. She thought to herself, *You can't say, "If you take me, I will come," to two places.* A lot of teenagers, let alone adults, would have certainly hedged their bets and made multiple promises to multiple institutions in the hope of achieving a long-sought goal. But her conscience just wouldn't allow her to tell Ken that he had become her number one choice. She knew her emotions were running high, and she wanted to give Ralph, and Wesleyan, a fair rebuttal. Ken was left with the impression that she was grateful for his offer, but undecided.

The Jannols drove back to New Jersey that night and set out the following morning on the three-hour drive to Connecticut, and Wesleyan. As they turned right off Route 66 onto High Street in Middletown, they saw the same nineteenth-century campus buildings that Ralph had seen on his very first trip into town: the stately brownstone of North College and the majestic spire of old Memorial Chapel. The buildings were illuminated by a sun brighter than any light they had seen at Cornell. Again, Becca had a knee-jerk reaction. "Wesleyan was dirty," she recalled. "It was gross." The campus map suggested that some of the world's most famous architects had contributed buildings to the campus, but all Becca saw were bricks that needed scouring and grass in desperate need of watering. She felt no better when she walked over to Foss Hill and saw some students trying to get a spring tan and others tossing a Frisbee. She was simply unimpressed. After nearly a year's buildup, Wesleyan just didn't match the picture in her mind's eye.

As she had at Cornell, Becca met up with a high school friend and walked to her dorm, where she would be spending the night. By this point Becca knew from Sharon—and from a brief telephone conversation with Ralph—that the admissions committee had been concerned about her consumption of the pot brownie. There was the intimation, however faint, that she might be bringing a drug problem along with her to Wesleyan. Yet as she walked through the front door of her friend's dorm, Becca was overwhelmed by a singular sensation: "It smelled like weed everywhere," she recalled.

Becca was informed by some of the dorm's residents that this was her lucky day: she was visiting Wesleyan on April 20, which was unofficially celebrated on campuses across the country as "Stoners' New Year." (At Wesleyan it was often called "Zonker Harris Day," after a character in the Doonesbury comic strip.) Legend had it that young pot smokers had settled on that date in tribute to their compatriots at a California high school who used to gather to get high after school at 4:20 P.M. The holiday would become so ingrained in the youth counterculture that by 2001, *USA Today* would publish a glossary to assist clueless parents. "Let's 420," the article explained, translated to "Let's smoke pot." "I'm 420-ed" meant "I'm stoned." Throughout the smoky halls of her friend's dorm, Becca heard the sounds of unrestrained giggling, but all she felt was anger.

Ralph's colleagues had been hypocritical, she felt, to worry about those few bites she took from that pot brownie.

That night at a party, Becca wasn't offered any pot, but she was sure she wouldn't have accepted even if asked, she said later. She had learned her lesson two years earlier. "When you're a pre-frosh, some kids like to party," she said. "I was like, 'I have a job to do.'"

As much as she had felt at home at Cornell, she felt alienated at Wesleyan. Her visit also coincided with the start of Passover, so she and her mother arranged to attend a seder on campus. But what they experienced bore little resemblance to the traditional dinners they had experienced as a family. They were informed by their student hosts that this was "an environmental seder," which interspersed poems "about our earth as our mother" with the more familiar story of Moses and his people in exile in the desert. Becca, who had always considered herself among the least materialistic and most liberal students at Harvard-Westlake, nonetheless found the participants at the dinner "hippie-ish." That was part of the Wesleyan reputation, and Becca decided it was warranted.

Becca was reassured to see Ralph's familiar face the following morning as she stopped by the admissions office. But in contrast to Ralph's visit to Harvard-Westlake in the fall, when she had been brimming with nervous questions about how to structure her essay, she found she had nothing to say to him now. What she had wanted to tell him was, "I liked Cornell better," which she clearly couldn't do. If Cornell didn't come through for her and Wesleyan did, she might still end up at Wesleyan, so there was no reason to burn a bridge.

Ralph felt awkward, too. The applicants whom Wesleyan had already approved for admission still had another ten days to let the university know whether they were accepting its offer. Only then would the school know whether it could offer Becca or anyone else on the waiting list a place. And if Wesleyan did go to the waiting list, Ralph knew that he had little capital remaining to win a seat in the class for Becca. He seemed as relieved as Becca when, after just a minute or two, she said she had to go meet her mother, who was waiting outside in the car.

The following Monday, Becca was back in California, on the hillside campus of Harvard-Westlake. Before her first class, she ran to Sharon's office, just as she had two weeks earlier, and when she found it empty, scribbled a quick note. "OMIGOD," it began. "For the first time since this process began I feel like I really, honest-to-goodness know what I want, and it might surprise you." She signed her note, "♥Becca" and attached copies of two letters that she had composed on the flight west and had already mailed.

One letter was to Ralph, and its tone was carefully measured. "Dear Mr. Figueroa," the note began, "thank you very much for taking the time to meet with me last week. I enjoyed my visit to Wesleyan immensely, and am honored to be on the wait-list." After reiterating that she was working as hard as ever in her senior spring, Becca closed by saying, "Thank you for your time and I look forward to hearing from you!"

The second note, to Ken Gabard, opened with the same "thank you," but continued:

> I love Cornell more than any other school, and am fully committed to attending should an offer of admission become a reality. I love Cornell not only for its beautiful setting, obvious quest for academic excellence, and diverse student body, but because more than anywhere else I can visualize myself there. I see myself engaged intellectually in the classrooms, curiously poking around in the libraries, and making friends in the dorms or in Collegetown. I only hope now that you, together with the other members of the Admissions Committee can see me in Ithaca with you.

After assuring Ken, as she had Ralph, that she was continuing to work hard, Becca closed by answering Ken's question: Yes, if necessary, she'd be willing to take the first semester off and start in January, a half-year behind her potential classmates at Cornell. She signed her name and added a postscript: "Just a reminder: California girls bring the sunshine with them wherever they go!!" The line was so whimsical that it was almost out of character. But Becca couldn't help herself: She was giddy with the thought that for the first time since October, the college admissions process was officially out of her hands. There was nothing more she could do but wait.

Ten
UNNAMED GORGEOUS SMALL LIBERAL ARTS SCHOOL

Jordan Goldman turned on the computer at the small wooden desk in his bedroom. It was Monday, April 17, and he had just returned from a fact-finding mission to Wesleyan and Vassar. In only two weeks, his responses to the offers of acceptance that he received from those two colleges—as well as a half dozen others—were due. As a first step, he began to compose an e-mail message. On the recipient's line he typed: "ADMITTED STUDENT LISTSERV." He wanted to transmit his thoughts to as large an audience as possible: all the other applicants who had been offered acceptance into the Class of 2004 at Wesleyan.

To help ease the decisions of those students, Wesleyan had established an electronic bulletin board, or Listserv, so that they could communicate with one another directly, via mass e-mail. Each posting was automatically sent to every other applicant who had registered on the Wesleyan website. In the two weeks since the school had mailed out its acceptances, the bulletin board had already received more than two thousand postings. By summer's end, the number would reach nearly seven thousand.

Some applicants asked straightforward questions, such as whether dogs were permitted in dorm rooms. (No, someone responded, Wesleyan only allowed animals that were in cages.) Others asked if Wesleyan fostered a tolerant environment for gay students. (An overwhelming yes was the general consensus.) The questions were answered by fellow applicants and current Wesleyan students, as well as by Ralph and his colleague Rod Bugarin, who were assigned by the admissions office to monitor the postings.

But most applicants who logged on to the bulletin board did so to announce where they had decided to attend college. "Don't attack me, I'm going to Vassar," someone had written early one morning. Around the same time, another correspondent proclaimed: "Ladies and gentlemen, it is now official. I'll be moving to beautiful Middletown come this August. I'm soooooooo excited. I filled out all of my rejecting school forms today (so now there's no going back)."

Jordan had been monitoring these postings closely, and he concluded that the Listserv offered the perfect forum to broadcast his decision. There was only one problem: as he sat down to write, he had yet to decide what he wanted to say. Like so many other writers, he did his best thinking when he was typing, and so he started to hash out his dilemma on the fifteen-inch screen in front of him. He began:

College.
    This decision is, I have to say, hands-down, the single most intimidating, scary-assed dilemma I've ever been faced with. And I've been doing quite a lot of deliberation these past few days. . . .
    I went to WesFest. And was impressed by a helluva lot of things I saw there—but, to be honest, let down by a few things too.
    So I did what any reasonable guy would do. I visited some other college campuses. To get a well-rounded perspective, to make sure I wasn't being overly influenced by any one factor or another. And to get a clearer view of Wesleyan in light of these other schools.

Jordan identified the other schools vying for his acceptance as follows: Big City U., Ivy U. and Unnamed Gorgeous Small Liberal Arts School. He would later explain that he had obscured the names of his choices publicly because he did not want to risk alienating a graduate school to which he might someday apply, which was certainly consistent with how Jordan approached life, his mind always racing a step ahead. But he had other motivations for cloaking his choices, as well.

After finishing his introduction, Jordan raised the question of whether he should attend Big City U. Unbeknownst to Jordan's readers, Big City U. was an amalgam of two universities that had admitted him: Boston University (which had accepted him into its honors program) and New York University (which had accepted him into its prestigious Tisch School of the Arts). In his mass e-mail message, Jordan wrote:

> Big City U. was good, but lacked a campus feeling completely, which is something that I feel is pretty important. . . . Move wherever you want, live wherever you want. But you have few times in your life to learn from PEOPLE, to be in a position where everyone is so uniformly intelligent.

Jordan had ultimately decided that he didn't want to go to college in a city, and by the time he sat down to write his message had indeed ruled out NYU and BU. His choices were narrowing.

Returning to his e-mail, he next tackled the question of whether he should attend Ivy U. At this point, a narrative that was otherwise grounded in reality drifted into territory that was decidedly fictional. Jordan had, of course, been rejected by the only Ivy League colleges to which he had applied, Brown and Penn. Asked later to reveal the identity of Ivy U., he answered that it, too, was a combination of two colleges: Brown and Johns Hopkins. Jordan said he was well aware that unlike Brown, Hopkins was not part of the Ivy League football conference. But he considered this a technicality: Hopkins, which had accepted him, was widely believed by many observers to be on par with the Ivies, at least academically. Jordan said he had even read somewhere that Hopkins had once been invited to be "the ninth Ivy," but that it had refused, preferring to remain in its own football conference. Thus, Jordan reasoned, it wasn't much of a stretch to label Hopkins as Ivy U. (Asked later if Hopkins had ever received an offer to join the Ivy League, a university spokesman said it had not.)

But Jordan had more pressing reasons for wanting to introduce the notion of "Ivy U." into his e-mail. First, he had been careful not to reveal any of his acceptances or rejections to the students he met at WesFest, having been too embarrassed. With this e-mail he could begin to stoke the myth that he had indeed been accepted by at least one Ivy. Like those of the exalted top 20 students at his high school, the opinions of the prefrosh whom he had met at Wesleyan meant a lot to him, whether he would be attending college with them or not. They'd surely be impressed that he was weighing an Ivy League acceptance.

But by inventing Ivy U., Jordan was ultimately giving himself a much-needed opportunity to work through the pain of having been rejected. Like a man whose girlfriend had turned down his proposal of marriage, he wanted to enumerate all the reasons why he never should have fallen in love with Brown or Penn in the first place:

> I went to visit Ivy U., good faculty, good rep. First thing I noticed, though, was that the kids were unbelievably pretentious. A lot of them had come from extremely rich families, took their acceptances into the ivys as a given, not something they'd worked for, deserved.
>
> It seemed they weren't there because they chose the school, but because their parents told them to go there, it had a good name, because they didn't really think things through, but Ivy U.'s prestige made the choice for them. Like they hadn't looked into the school at all, instead looking only at name and how highly it was listed at US NEWS AND WORLD REPORT. . . .
>
> It's funny, if you stripped an ivy of its name and prestige, and took a bunch of kids over to see it, they wouldn't be nearly as enthusiastic about going there. Most of the ivys have huge classes, irrelevant work, no personal attention, huge core curriculums (which I'm extremely against)—and yet people flock there because of the bumper sticker that they get to put on their car. . . .
>
> Sense any resentment? In my school alone, the three most brilliant kids I've ever met—honestly, mind-blowing brilliant—all got turned down from the Ivys in favor of these two girls that stay up all night, every night, memorizing textbooks word for word. . . . Yeah, they both got into princeton, brown, upenn, yale and columbia—and from what I've heard, this isn't the exception, it's the norm. So while schools like Wes accept kids that would be a fit to their philosophy, reputation-minded ivys admit SAT scores rather than people. . . .

To anyone who really knew Jordan, most of these thoughts—with the exception of his genuine envy of his high school classmates—represented a 180-degree turn from what he had been saying in the months leading up to his rejection from Brown. He, of course, had been one of the very people who "flock" to schools like Brown "because of the bumper sticker that they get to put on their car," and no one read the *U.S. News* rankings more closely.

In order to accept Brown's rejection, Jordan decided, *he* would have to reject *Brown,* even if it was after the fact. Around the country, countless other high school seniors were having similar conversations with themselves at the same time. Just as a record number of applicants had reached for the Ivies that fall and winter, a record number had been turned down in the spring. Jordan may not have been completely honest with his readers, but he was beginning to level with himself, taking the first real steps toward realizing how empty his reasons for attending Brown had been. He was just too emotional at this point to share that particular insight with a wider audience.

Whether the decision was his or Brown's, the end result was the same: as he wrote to the electronic bulletin board, he wouldn't be attending Ivy U. (His actual decision for turning down Hopkins, which he did not visit, had little to do with the preceding analysis. He had been skeptical about the strength of its writing program and had read in one of the guidebooks that Hopkins students were often conservative in their politics.)

Jordan now told his readers that his decision had come down to a choice between Wesleyan and only one other college: Unnamed Gorgeous Small Liberal Arts School or, as he referred to it on subsequent reference, UGSLAS. This part, by all accounts, was true, and the unnamed school was Vassar. Jordan admitted in his message that, after WesFest, he "didn't leave Wesleyan falling head-over-heels-I-can-see-my-own-ass in love." With an open mind, he wrote, he had next traveled to UGSLAS with his best friend, who had been admitted early. Here was Jordan's report of his trip to Poughkeepsie in early April:

> Let me start by saying that the U.G.S.L.A.S. campus is amazingly, extraordinarily, mind-blowingly beautiful. . . . You see this sprawling, classic, tree-lined campus and old buildings, and the classic architecture and you say: "Now THIS is college."
>
> No kidding, I've visited half the ivys and about 20 other schools. U.G.S.L.A.S. was, hands down, the nicest campus I've yet to see. . . . I went to its dining hall, and when I say gourmet style food, it doesn't even do the stuff justice. It was amazing.

> So at that point, I'm sold by the aesthetics. I'm saying hey, rep-wise it's solid, and the place is beautiful, and my parents will be happy, and my friends will come visit and be envious . . . and huuuuuuuge dorm rooms, bigger than my room at home, no joke. . . .

"My decision's been made," he wrote, "off to U.G.S.L.A.S. I go." And indeed he was. Jordan had picked Vassar over Wesleyan.

His decision, he wrote, had lasted for all of ten minutes.

At Vassar, Jordan had ended his visit by meeting with an English professor, and something about her had just rubbed him the wrong way. "She talked to the air above my head," he wrote, and hadn't made any attempt to get to know him. And, at least as he recounted it, she told him that he "couldn't possibly have the talent, or understanding, to write well as a freshman." That, she explained, was why certain English classes were reserved only for sophomores, juniors and seniors.

At this point in his visit to Vassar, Jordan wrote, he recalled that "at Wesleyan, almost all courses are open to frosh." He also began to think about how kindly he had been treated by the creative writing professor at Wesleyan, who had set aside time to talk to him. "I don't know," he wrote, "I guess I just felt at Wes, the faculty really listened to me." He also recalled for his readers how impressed he had been that "free expression"—in the form of those posters and sidewalk scrawls he had seen around campus, many poking fun at the university president—had been allowed during WesFest.

By now, Jordan's e-mail had run to its eighth printed page, which he was determined would be his last. He concluded:

> My visits to other campuses helped me to get a perspective on the things about Wes that I really loved. And sometimes . . . the things you really loved ARE subtle, almost so subtle that they don't even register—sometimes it's best when a school doesn't slap you so hard it leaves a mark. . . . The quality of students, teachers, etc.—that's what stays with you. . . .
>
> When I left Wes, I said, "if this place was on a better campus, a nicer town, I'd go here in a second."
>
> And now—I've realized that the campus and town parts aren't so important after all.

But that I'd go there in a second??? Yeah, that part still stands:)

—Jordan Goldman

It was nearly seven P.M. and he had been at his computer for more than three hours. Scrolling back up to the subject line of his message, he now wrote: "you MUST read—why wesleyan is ABSOLUTELY the school for you." However messy the process, however much it had been out of his hands, he had made his decision. So that no one missed it, he scrolled back down to the first page of his text and inserted two sentences: "Wesleyan is my clear first choice. I'll give ya a breakdown of why." And then, he pushed SEND.

Jordan slept well that night, the best he had in a while. When he awoke, he shared his e-mail message with his mother. Now, for the first time in memory, she and Jordan's stepfather could truly relax again, at least until Jordan began preparing to leave the nest. Melanie hugged her only son and told him that she was pleased with his choice. She had liked Wesleyan a lot, and still remembered how thoughtful the admissions staff had been to her mother, and how much the family had enjoyed drinking those cute bottles of mineral water with the Wesleyan label. But she would have been happy wherever Jordan chose to go. Yes, Wesleyan's $35,000 tuition and fees—minus the $5,000 loan he had received—would be impossible to afford on a teacher's salary. But not only would her husband (a floor covering salesman) and her ex (Jordan's father) be chipping in, so would other relatives.

Jordan's uncle Jay endorsed his nephew's choice as well, telling Jordan that, based on what he had heard in the business world, Wesleyan was by far the best of his options. "Any employer will instantly know what Wesleyan is," Jay asserted, as Jordan later recalled. Jordan's father had counseled Jordan from his home in Florida to ignore the relative prestige of his choices and consider the best deal. Not only was NYU offering a big scholarship, but so were BU and Emerson. But when Jordan called his dad to tell him his decision, his father said he was happy and proud.

On the morning after he had sent off his message, Jordan felt a sense of peace, though he realized he still wasn't "bouncing off the walls excited." While he had no intention of revisiting his decision, he had to admit that he still had reservations about Wesleyan. His lingering regrets began to melt away when he logged on to America Online and checked the mailbox on his account. He was stunned to see more than a dozen responses to what he had written. Like his own message, all of the responses had been e-mailed to everyone else on the bulletin board.

Among the first responses had been one posted by Rod Bugarin, whom Jordan had never met. Rod wrote that he had returned to his office at about nine P.M. on Monday, after a thirty-minute swim, to find Jordan's opus. He began his response by assuring Jordan of "guaranteed employment at the Wesleyan admissions office," and then predicted the course of the rest of Jordan's freshman year:

> Jordan will replace our fabled cardinal as the University's Mascot . . . and will be leading you all in singing our Fight Song during orientation . . . He will be the first student to become a senior interviewer in his freshman year.
> Jordan, just see Ralph/me when you come back to campus. We'll make sure that your room will be decorated and that we'll be ready to bottle your fragrance so we can market it to every intellectual/creative/independent/athletic/way-cool student in the country . . .

Rod signed off by writing: "Welcome to the family, Jordan. I know Wesleyan will be great because you are in the student body."

A fellow applicant wrote that she had been "trying to decide between Amherst and Wesleyan" and was "leaning toward Amherst." But then she read Jordan's posting. "To tell you the truth," she wrote, "my biggest qualm to saying no to Amherst is that the school is generally considered to be more 'prestigious' than Wesleyan, with better academics and whatnot. But after reading your letter I am so much more sure that I am going to choose Wesleyan." Another woman who had already been accepted to Wesleyan early decision wrote that she had been "having second thoughts" about having applied only to Wesleyan. But, she reported, Jordan's message had "stopped them in their place and reminded me why I wanted to go to Wesleyan in the first place."

Ralph hadn't gotten a chance to read his e-mail until late the following morning, and it was only after he got to the bottom of Jordan's message and saw his name that he finally made the connection: this was one of the kids he had met in the cafeteria during WesFest. Ralph then logged on to the admissions office database to see which admissions officer had read Jordan's application, and discovered not only that it had been he, but that he had been so impressed that he had crossed out the space for the second reader. Now Ralph remembered: this was the kid from Staten Island who wrote about X-Men and his friend in the wheelchair. *I'm glad I liked him so much,* Ralph thought to himself. He then posted his own response to the electronic bulletin board, which he titled, "The Book of Jordan," and in which he wrote: "OK, Jordan is my absolute favorite. No one else need apply. That's it. Amen." He signed his missive: "Ralph, the awestruck."

Ralph then sent a copy of Jordan's message to all of his colleagues in the admissions office, several of whom replied, privately, to express their suspicions that the boy was an invention of Ralph's imagination. No one in the office could recall a better case having been articulated for Wesleyan. Ralph was grateful that whatever else he accomplished that year, he would always be known as the guy who had brought Jordan Goldman to Wesleyan.

Jordan's remark had struck an obvious chord in such a competitive year, and as his e-mail raced across the campus—even President Bennet was sent a copy—he became a Wesleyan folk hero, five months before he would even matriculate. Not a bad introduction for a guy still carrying a bit of a torch for Brown.

Whatever doubts Jordan had been feeling, though, were allayed by the reaction his words had touched off. A week before his decision was due, he mailed off a $250 deposit and his official response to Wesleyan: a form that had "YES" preprinted in large type at the top. Jordan then went out to his mother's car and pressed a clear Wesleyan decal against the inside of the back window.

Three days after Jordan posted his message, Julianna Bentes and her mother left Wesleyan for the short drive south to New Haven. With memories of the unsettling club visit still rattling in her head, Julianna was waiting under a long gothic archway for her host, a Yale freshman, to pick her up, when she noticed a statue of a former president of the university, bathed in a ray of sunlight so bright it appeared to be emanating from a celestial source. "The entire courtyard was golden," she recalled.

"It was just short of voices crying out to me from the sky." The moment seemed to be such a divine portent that she actually started to laugh out loud.

That night, Julianna, one of the most heavily recruited applicants to American colleges that year, experienced another heavenly vision. The moon was out as she gazed into a granite-topped fountain commemorating the number of women who had been enrolled at Yale throughout its history. The fountain had been designed by Maya Lin, herself a Yale alumna, who had also designed the Vietnam veterans' memorial in Washington. Julianna saw that there was a stream of water tracing the institution's history of coeducation. As she looked into the fountain, she realized that there was just enough moonlight for her to see her own reflection staring back. "This was beyond laughing out loud," Julianna recalled. "I could actually see myself there."

After she awoke the next morning in the third-floor dorm room where she had been staying, Julianna sat alone on a couch for ten minutes, looking at the wood floors and the paneling and the cozy fireplace. Outside the window an oversized magnolia tree was in full bloom. For all the disparate locations that her college search had taken her—from Goucher in Maryland to the University of Chicago, from Kenyon in rural Ohio to Wesleyan—Julianna realized that Yale was "the one place I didn't want to leave."

All the students on the New Haven campus seemed to want to meet her and asked if there was anything they could do for her. Her host alone must have introduced her to thirty new friends. Though there were dozens of other applicants visiting at the time, no doubt weighing similar options, Julianna spent two uninterrupted hours with an admissions officer. Sharon would later tell Julianna that almost no applicant could command that kind of face time at such a frenetic point in the admissions process, when applicants' decisions were due in just ten days. But that was how badly Yale wanted Julianna Bentes.

The officer, who had graduated from Yale in the mid-1990s and had worked there for only a few years, told Julianna that she had begun keeping her own file of favorite essays, in which Julianna's had now found a place. They spent most of their time discussing Yale's nationally recognized history department and a theater program that offered Julianna a menu of at least five different dance groups. She didn't need to hear any more; Yale seemed without a blemish.

As she prepared to depart the next day, Julianna reviewed the itinerary for the final leg of her last college tour. She would take Amtrak three hours north to Boston, to see Harvard, and then another train south from Massachusetts to Pennsylvania, to see Swarthmore. From Pennsylvania, she'd hop a flight to Northern California, to visit Stanford.

This, she decided, was a good time to rank her choices thus far. Wesleyan, she now knew, just couldn't compete with Yale. It wasn't just that Yale was so architecturally rich—Julianna had left Yale, like so many who came before her and since, feeling as if she was in England—and it wasn't necessarily that Yale was friendlier and much less "out there" socially than Wesleyan. Yale was also bigger; its freshman class would have more than a thousand students, compared to about seven hundred at Wesleyan. There'd be more people to meet, more classes to take, more organizations to join. That Yale was part of the Ivy League and Wesleyan was not, Julianna insisted, was not the primary factor in her decision. Sharon, who knew her better than almost anyone, was sure that this was true.

Julianna wouldn't reveal her thinking to Sharon or anyone else for several more days, but from this point forward, she had resolved that Wesleyan was out. And so, for that matter, was Swarthmore, since Julianna imagined it to be similar—in size and location—to Wesleyan. Julianna would now travel to Harvard, and then, instead of enduring a six-hour train ride to Pennsylvania, fly to Stanford a day earlier than planned.

Harvard had always been the only school that her father had wanted her to attend. Having grown up in the Amazon in Brazil, he had heard about Harvard long before he had heard of any other American college. It was the ultimate symbol of the American Dream, and he was thrilled when his only child was admitted. But after visiting Yale and then Harvard Yard, Julianna decided that Harvard just didn't appeal to her as strongly as had Yale. An admissions officer there had met with her, and, recalling her essay in similarly vivid detail, urged, "I hope you do something with writing." And there was no denying Harvard's colonial beauty, with red brick bordering the Charles River and a bonafide quadrangle. But just as at the University of Chicago, there were little things at Harvard that bothered her. No one, for example, seemed to want to get out of the way when she attempted to pass through a crowded doorway. And when Julianna told her host at Harvard that she was uninterested in attending a lecture on Irish history that had been put on her schedule, the host replied: "We *have* to go." The students at Harvard, as at the University of Chicago, just seemed so much more uptight than at Yale.

By the time she headed to Logan Airport for her flight to Northern California, Julianna had decided that if she went to school on the East Coast, Yale would be it. Her father would have to understand. But still, two major obstacles lay in Yale's path. One was out of Yale's control: Julianna had no idea what she'd think of Stanford, which she had never seen. It certainly had the advantage of being closer to Los Angeles than New Haven, and Julianna had a strong relationship with her parents. But there was a more serious hurdle for Yale, at least as far as Catherine Bentes was concerned: Yale's offer of financial aid was perhaps the least generous of the thirteen colleges to which her daughter had been admitted.

Sharon had urged Catherine to become well acquainted with the financial aid officers at the colleges that had admitted her daughter, advising her, "No school would want to see Julianna turn them down for financial reasons." There was sometimes room for bargaining, particularly for the most sought-after applicants.

That had not always been the case. For four decades, Yale had been part of an organization of more than twenty colleges—including the seven other Ivies, and Wesleyan—that met annually to discuss their financial aid offers to the thousands of applicants who had been accepted at more than one member of the organization. The group had wanted to ensure that each institution's offer was consistent, and that none of them could gain an unfair financial advantage over another. But those meetings came to an abrupt end in 1991, after the Justice Department charged that this particular organization was a cartel that violated federal antitrust law, not unlike that of oil-producing nations that met to fix the price of their product. From that point onward, according to a consent decree that the universities signed with the Justice Department, the free market would reign.

Almost nine years to the day since the signing of that consent decree, Catherine Bentes camped out in the financial aid office at Yale while her daughter surveyed the campus. Catherine, a compact, heavyset woman who concedes she can come on a little strong, had been trying to reach the office by phone for days but had only been able to get a recorded message. When she walked through the actual door, she did not fare any better. Standing behind a counter that reminded her of one at the department of motor vehicles, a financial aid officer motioned her to take a seat in the reception area and promised that someone would be with her momentarily. After an hour passed, and no officer had appeared, Catherine had had enough. "I have one day to see someone," she blurted out, to no one in particular but loud enough that she could be heard behind the counter. "Someone needs to see me, or you're not going to want to deal with me when I get really upset!" Within seconds, she later recalled, an officer was standing in front of her and ushering her to the counter.

Catherine was characteristically blunt and told the officer that Stanford and Harvard had given her daughter better financial aid offers, and that money might dictate her daughter's decision. The tuition and fees at all three institutions were about the same—$36,000—and each had offered Julianna at least $1500 in federal loans. But while Stanford had promised her $8000, and Harvard was offering a more modest but still welcome $5000, Yale had offered no direct aid.

Because Yale's philosophy was that its scholarships should be set aside for the exclusive benefit of those who needed the money most, Catherine was told that for her to win Julianna a bigger award, she would have to demonstrate extenuating circumstances. Otherwise, the income that the family had reported on its income tax forms the previous year (more than $50,000 but less than $100,000) would be deemed simply too large to justify a need-based scholarship, at least as calculated by Yale.

As it turned out, Catherine informed the officer, she had faxed Yale just such a letter the previous month, laying out the family's financial difficulties. In the four-page document, Catherine described her chronic health problems and the leaves of absence she was often forced to take from her part-time job. The letter was so long that Catherine had divided it into chapters. Under the heading, "Medical-Dental," Catherine detailed the money that her husband sent home to Brazil each year. He did so to care for the eighty-seven-year-old aunt who had raised him, who had recently suffered a stroke. Under the heading "Downsizing, Earthquake, Restructuring in California," Catherine talked about the $10,000 insurance deductible that the family was still struggling to pay off, after an earthquake did $60,000 worth of damage to their small home five years earlier. In her conclusion, she wrote: "We live very simply. We eat at home, dining out very occasionally (4 times per year)." These were the sorts of personal details that Catherine had not included in Julianna's financial aid forms.

The Yale officer, who had not seen the letter, listened intently as Catherine recounted its contents, and then she asked that she fax the letter again. The officer would make no promises, other than that she would agree to review Julianna's case. That was all Catherine could ask, and she thanked the officer for her time.

That conversation had taken place on a Friday; on Monday morning the Benteses arrived in Palo Alto. As she took the measure of Stanford's sprawling campus for the first time—with its stucco-covered walls, Spanish-style roofs and palm trees—Julianna felt as if she had come home. "I was off the East Coast," she recalled. "I was back in my California sun." It was Yale versus Stanford. This, Julianna knew, was going to be a tough call.

The history professor whom Stanford had designated as Julianna's contact person had invited her several days earlier to visit a seminar he was teaching that afternoon. Julianna had initially responded that she'd be at Swarthmore that day, and not arriving at Stanford until Tuesday. The professor had then sent back an e-mail with a coy lament: if she had only been able to attend the class, then she would have been able to meet Chelsea Clinton, who was one of his students. After she had canceled her trip to Swarthmore, Julianna had excitedly written back informing the professor that she would be attending his class after all.

Sure enough, as Julianna took her seat in the fifteen-student seminar, there was Chelsea, sitting across the conference-style table. Julianna could see that the president's daughter, a junior, was stylishly dressed in a pink top, a black sweater and black capri pants. Julianna was certain that several of the "students" flanking Chelsea were Secret Service agents. Once the class began, Chelsea was among three or four people who carried much of the discussion.

During a break in the nearly two-hour class, Julianna rose to go to the bathroom, as did Chelsea, and the two women struck up a conversation. Chelsea said she assumed that Julianna was a prospective freshman and asked what her choices were. With a week to go before her decision was due, Julianna said that it had come down to Yale and Stanford. Chelsea smiled. Those schools, she said, had been her finalists, too.

Chelsea then told Julianna something that she had not heard before: that virtually until the moment her decision was due, she intended to go to Yale. Julianna already knew that both Bill and Hillary Clinton had been law students at Yale, where they met. Yale was comfortably familiar to the family, but, as Julianna later recalled, Chelsea said that she ultimately gravitated toward the adventure that Stanford represented. Having lived half her life in Arkansas and the other half in Washington, she decided she "wanted to see what it was like on the West Coast."

At this point, Chelsea asked Julianna where she lived. When Julianna replied Los Angeles, Chelsea had an immediate response: "If I grew up on the West Coast, I'd have probably gone to Yale." After her mystical experiences in New Haven, Julianna had been on the lookout for one final sign that would seal her decision. She was sure she had just received it, from the daughter of the president of the United States, of all people. Chelsea, who had been dispatched to make the case for Stanford, had instead wound up inadvertently helping one of its top recruits choose Yale. Julianna felt certain that Chelsea was right, that a more dramatic change of scenery might be good for her. If the money could be worked out, she decided, she wanted to go to Yale.

Julianna didn't have to wait long to hear Yale's response to her mother's plea. Soon after the Benteses returned to Los Angeles, they received a fax from the Yale office of financial aid. The letter, which was unsigned, began: "The Undergraduate Financial Aid staff has adjusted your financial aid package"; the annual loans it was offering had remained about the same, $3,500, as had the $1,600 Julianna would earn from a work-study job, but the school, which had initially offered her no direct aid, was now awarding her a scholarship of $6,500. Yale characterized its scholarship as need-based, and the amount was only a little less than what she was being given by Stanford. Whatever Yale's formulas, the college had managed to adjust them to make its offer even with that of a competitor. And just to complicate matters, Harvard had sent Catherine a fax at around the same time saying that it, too, had raised its scholarship offer—to $6,550 from about $5,000—after hearing Catherine make an appeal similar to the one she had made at Yale. At each institution, the Benteses would now be responsible for providing about $24,000 annually for an education that would otherwise cost $36,000.

Julianna now had her mother's blessing to pick Yale. While Goucher and Kenyon would have given her a free ride, Catherine agreed with her daughter that Yale would offer a superior education. And while the University of Chicago, which was arguably Yale's academic equal, would have also completely underwritten Julianna's education, Catherine knew her daughter didn't want to go there. Even if the Benteses, like so many parents, had to mortgage their small house again, they would find the money.

Only a year ago, Julianna's wish list of colleges had included fifty-four names. Now there was only one. The pitched competition for the privilege of educating Julianna Bentes, which had lasted almost as long as a presidential campaign, was finally over.

For all his efforts on behalf of Harvard, Ray Bentes would smile with pride when told of his daughter's decision. Yale was still a long way from the rubber plantation in the jungle where he had spent much of his childhood. Since they had returned from the East Coast, Ray had heard all the stories from his wife and daughter about their trip. "I very much respected their findings," he said later. "Harvard was not the best option." Sharon applauded Julianna's choice as well—not so much for the decision itself as the way that Julianna had gone about making it. Sharon couldn't remember another student from Harvard-Westlake who had been accepted at Harvard and Yale and yet still made time to visit Goucher and Kenyon, which registered nowhere near the Ivies on the meter of *U.S. News*. Julianna had known all along that Yale was among the most prestigious universities in the world, yet she had given every other college the benefit of the doubt.

Around the time that she made her decision, Julianna got an e-mail from Stanford. "So," that professor asked, "will we see you here in the fall, or did you opt for New Haven?" He had apparently decided that he couldn't wait for the official word from the Stanford admissions office. Julianna wrote back: "I opted for New Haven, because I need to try to check out the East Coast." She decided to omit the role that his prized student, Chelsea, had played in the decision, and closed her message by telling the professor: "Thank you so much for all of your help and availability—it made my choice decidedly more difficult."

Telling the professor had been relatively easy, Julianna thought, but she couldn't bear the thought of notifying Ralph. It wasn't just that he was her college counselor's good friend. She genuinely liked him. "He was a cool person," Julianna said. "I was always telling myself not to associate the admissions officer with the school." But that had proved impossible, and Julianna knew she had hung on to Wesleyan so long largely because of her admiration for Ralph.

To her relief, Ralph would hear the news from elsewhere. On April 28, the Friday before Julianna's decisions were due, Ralph was in the midst of his annual spring visit to Los Angeles. The previous night, he had helped lead a seminar for parents and kids from Harvard-Westlake and four other L.A. prep schools. He presented his audience with several mock applications and asked it to assess them as if it were an admissions committee, voting on whom to accept and why. Afterward, the audience members compared their choices to Ralph's.

The following afternoon, he was relaxing in Sharon's office when he couldn't stand the suspense any longer. As soon as they got a moment alone, Ralph wanted to ask Sharon about Julianna's college plans. As far as he knew, Wesleyan was still alive, for he had seen Julianna only a few days earlier. As he sat making small talk, he almost jumped when he heard a colleague of Sharon's ask his very question: "So what's Julianna doing?" Sharon pretended to cover Ralph's ears with her hands as she stage-whispered the news: "She's going to Yale."

Ralph had a quick response that was just as melodramatic: "Oh. . . . break . . . my . . . *heart*," he cried, trying to sound as anguished as Tony in that production of *West Side Story* all those years ago. Despite their attempts at making light of this news, Sharon could tell that her old friend was crushed. "I felt for him," she said later. "Julianna had genuinely considered Wesleyan as an option. I knew Ralph had followed her for so long. When you let yourself believe there's the chance you might get them, and you don't, it hurts. And then they're out of your life."

A few days later, Ralph was feeling better, consoling himself with the fact that Wesleyan had been in the race from Julianna's last year of middle school until the final week of her college tour. That was remarkable, given her choices, he decided. But he later learned about the club meeting that she had been taken to—an experience that she had reported to neither Ralph nor Sharon—and he immediately buried his head in his hands.

Typical of Wesleyan, with its penchant for openness, the only students who were barred from hosting prospective freshmen were those who were on academic probation. Otherwise, the school made no regular attempt to screen its hosts. Wesleyan's philosophy was that it wanted its applicants to have an unobstructed view of the campus. Ralph had read about the club in the school newspaper and wasn't especially bothered by its existence or mission. What had irritated him, he admitted, was that Julianna had wound up getting such a limited glimpse of the Wesleyan experience. "That's a part of Wesleyan," he said, "but not all of it."

Had Julianna not attended the meeting, Ralph acknowledged, she probably would have picked Yale over Wesleyan, anyway. It was hard for Wesleyan to compete with Yale's prestige, its endowment, its course offerings. But he still regretted that, in the end, Wesleyan had not given Yale as strong a fight as it could have. In any other year, given how important Julianna was to him, he might have at least chatted in advance with the student who hosted her, as he had with the student who gave Mig his tour. For that matter, Ralph could have had a preliminary conversation with the judge who had been assigned to conduct her alumni interview, before there had ever been a disagreement over the date. He would have seen to it that the judge knew to handle her with great care, that Julianna was at the top of Wesleyan's wish list. As it turned out, Ralph hadn't even called the judge after he sent Julianna out of his courtroom, and had failed to make sure that his instructions to send a plane ticket to Julianna—"Fly her out"—had been seen in the office and executed. Julianna had received no such offer.

Until recently, this sort of attention to detail would have been a realistic goal. But the assembling of the Class of 2004 had been like no other Ralph could remember. At times, it seemed to Ralph that he and his colleagues were buckling under the strain of the record number of applications. Trying to decide where to direct his attention in those final, critical weeks of March had sometimes made him feel like a trauma surgeon assigned to triage in a M.A.S.H. unit. He was meeting with his colleagues and voting in the final committee round during the day, while trying to finish reading all of those essays late into the night. All the while, he was supposed to be devising and executing strategies to get the best applicants to come to Wesleyan. That Ralph had been patiently tracking Julianna since she was a high school freshman had ultimately counted for little in the last, frenzied days of the admissions season. There had been too many applications, and too few people to read them.

"She definitely deserved to have more attention paid to her," Ralph said. "Each year we remind ourselves to do more follow-up with the applicants. We know it's the hardest piece. We drop the ball in many cases. It's frustrating. It's aggravating. But you almost have to laugh that Julianna had that experience, despite all your other plans."

"But for time," he said. "I would have done more."

As Julianna celebrated the end of one journey and anticipated the beginning of another, Becca Jannol was still at sea. Although Becca and Julianna had been classmates for four years, they didn't know each other well, given their different interests. Still, Becca knew by late April that the college plans of Julianna and almost all of the 274 other seniors at Harvard-Westlake were now set. Julianna was one of 14 going to Yale. Another 12 were bound for Harvard, and 11 to Stanford. Of more immediate relevance to Becca was the fact that 5 would soon be on their way to Cornell, while 7 others would be joining Ralph at Wesleyan.

When May 1 arrived, Becca sent in a small deposit to Emory. She did so with little enthusiasm, considering the money an insurance policy that she hoped she would never have to cash. Her father assured her that if Wesleyan or Cornell came through with an offer, he'd happily consider the money a write-off. Becca, knowing she'd have to wait weeks, if not months, for a decision telling her whether she'd be moving to Georgia, Connecticut or New York, had entered a parallel reality that Sharon liked to call "wait-list limbo."

As Becca began her wait, the responses flowing back to Wesleyan from around the country and the world were slowing to a trickle. By the middle of May, the final tally did not bode well for Becca or the six hundred other applicants who had accepted Wesleyan's offer to reserve a spot on the waiting list.

In addition to the 300 students admitted to Wesleyan in the early rounds, 431 other applicants who were accepted in the main round in the spring had reserved seats in the Class of 2004. The class now had a total of 731 students, which was about all that Wesleyan could accomodate, and more than had been anticipated. Part of the reason, Wesleyan was sure, was that its competitors in the Ivy League, and at Williams and Amherst, had rejected more applicants than ever this year, as had Wesleyan itself.

For a while it seemed that Wesleyan might not be able to take a single applicant off the waiting list for the incoming class. But then Greg Pyke, the office's chief statistician, wedged open the front gate again, however slightly. In the past, Greg explained to Nancy, Wesleyan usually lost about ten of its admitted students during the period between May and September. These were usually students who put in a deposit at Wesleyan but ultimately came off the waiting list at a college that they had ranked higher, a process Greg and others liked to call the "summer melt." Anticipating that ten students who had accepted Wesleyan's offer would drop out over the summer, Greg and Nancy decided that they would make room in the new class for ten students on the waiting list—ten, out of the six hundred who had expressed interest.

With so few slots available, Greg was relieved that there were no real imbalances in the new class that needed to be corrected, in contrast to previous years. The percentage of men, which had been 44 percent on the eve of the committee hearings, was now 49 percent, certainly close enough to the ideal of 50 percent. The median SAT score—1430 in early March—had since fallen, because some of Wesleyan's highest-scoring applicants chose to go elsewhere, as had been expected. But the damage was minimal. At 1360, the median SAT score of the Class of 2004 was only 10 points lower than that of the current freshman class. *Wesleyan would still look fine in* U.S. News, Greg thought.

The percentages of minority students in the Class of 2004 had also held since March. In a virtual mirror of the Class of 2003, the new freshman class was 11 percent African American, 12 percent Asian or Asian American, and 7 percent Latino. Those numbers would play well at high schools with high minority populations, as well as with any observer committed to affirmative action. The new class also had delegates from forty states, the District of Columbia and more than two dozen foreign countries, which gave it the geographic diversity that colleges prized. But as in years past, it was dominated by students from the Mid-Atlantic states (41 percent) and New England (27 percent). These broad statistics would be well received by Wesleyan's alumni and trustees.

Months before the students would arrive on campus, professors, administrators and coaches in individual departments had been getting a more detailed briefing on the actual individuals themselves. And the admissions office was getting good feedback. The cross-country team had landed a prized distance runner from Washington State, among the fastest ever to attend Wesleyan. Nearly three-quarters of the students in the new class had taken biology, chemistry and physics, which pleased the science faculty. One out of three of the incoming freshmen was either the president of his or her student body, the captain of a sports team or editor of the newspaper. Wesleyan would not suffer for leadership.

In mid-May, Nancy and Greg sent out an e-mail to the admissions officers, asking them to help narrow the choices of those who might come off the waiting list. Working in pairs, they were to identify twelve to fifteen applicants from each of the four main regions of the country, for a total of no more than sixty. These were the applicants whom Nancy and Greg would consider admitting into the class, with the assumption that if fifteen of these sixty were ultimately offered admission to Wesleyan, ten would probably accept.

There were no overriding criteria that would guide the officers' search, but perhaps more than at any other time during the year, an applicant's passion for attending Wesleyan would actually count for something as the officers made their wish lists. For that reason, each applicant placed on the waiting list had been given the option to write a page-long essay on why he or she wanted to come to the school.

With the odds against acceptance now staggeringly high, some applicants always took the directive of demonstrating their ardor to the extreme. In 1993, for example, the Wesleyan admissions committee had placed Carter L. Bays, an aspiring playwright from Shaker Heights, Ohio, on the waiting list. He was convinced that the committee had made a terrible mistake in not accepting him immediately, and wrote, "To prove that I am worthy of attending your school and that you are worthy of having me as a student, I'm going to send you a postcard every day until you accept me."

The first day, a postcard arrived that was titled, "Reason No. 1 why Carter L. Bays belongs at Wesleyan University." That reason, Carter wrote, was that he had recently won a local playwriting festival. The next day, "Reason No. 2" promised that he would "take full advantage of the millions of volumes in Olin Library."

Before long, Judy Goodale, the office manager, and Charlotte Lazor, the office's longtime systems manager, were racing each other to the mailbox to retrieve Carter's latest note. Each wanted to be the first to read aloud that Carter was "an excellent singer" or that he could "chew gum and ride a bike at the same time." They then decorated their bulletin boards with the photographs on the opposite side of the card, as if the cards had been sent by a daffy uncle on vacation. There was one with a collection of dogs playing poker, another with a svelte Elvis, and a third that displayed a replica of Stonehenge made out of toothpicks. Without fail, a card arrived every day for nearly a month.

When the deans asked Judy to send up the workcards of those applicants whom they would consider accepting off the waiting list that year, she and Charlotte decided to cast a rare vote: they put Carter's card on the very top. "He was our personal case," Charlotte recalled. When an admissions officer telephoned Carter a few days later to notify him that he had indeed been accepted, she added that she was calling over the objection of the assistants in the office, who had begged her to delay the call, wanting more mail. That day, Carter dashed off a final postcard containing only a two-word message: "Thank you."

But the relationship didn't end there. Once enrolled at Wesleyan, Carter became a regular contributor to the student newspaper, and Judy and Charlotte clipped his articles like proud parents. Though they were eager to meet him, they could never summon the courage to invite him for a visit to the office. But they never forgot him. After Carter graduated, they logged on to the alumni database to learn of his first job out of college and were hardly surprised at what flashed on the computer screen: "*Staff Writer, The Late Show with David Letterman.*" Applying to Wesleyan, as it turned out, had prepared Carter L. Bays well for his chief responsibility on the Letterman show: writing the on-air responses to Dave's viewer mail. "It was almost poetic," Charlotte said.

Greg was quick to caution that for every applicant who succeeded by mounting a "stupid applicant trick" like Carter's, hundreds of others failed. As usual, boxes of candy and fresh-baked cookies descended on the back office of the admissions building in the spring of 2000 from those seeking to move up the waiting list for the Class of 2004. But while those offerings were eagerly consumed, they never seemed to gain the sender any sway. The life-size doll that was an apparent dead-ringer for one applicant was promptly shipped off to a local nursery school, while the glitter that filled some envelopes only served to irritate those in the office who made the mistake of opening the letters over their computer keyboards.

Toward the end of May, Ralph and Rod met in a conference room to assemble their waiting list nominees. The men shared responsibility for the West and for the State of New Jersey, and they would make their picks together. The general understanding was that no applicant from their regions would be sent to Nancy's desk unless they had each signed off on him or her.

To Rod's surprise, the meeting was brief: Ralph just sat back as Rod made almost all the picks himself, and merely said, "Whatever you want." Ralph did make a few recommendations but did not even bother to suggest Becca Jannol. "I knew it was a longshot," Ralph acknowledged, "and that Rod would say no," for he had been one of the eight officers who had voted against Becca in that heated committee hearing in which the issue of the brownie had been raised. When the pair had finalized their choices, Ralph offered to deliver the pile of a dozen or so ballots to Nancy, which Rod said would be fine; he was happy to be done with it.

It was only after Ralph had made a stop at his own office that he made one final selection of his own. Flipping through a stack of files on his desk, he located Becca's application and laid her workcard on the bottom of the group that he and Rod had compiled. "I didn't want Rod to see," Ralph admitted later. It was an almost Machiavellian maneuver, the type of thing that Ralph would almost never undertake, but he reasoned that he was justified because he had worked in the Wesleyan admissions office four years longer than Rod, who was still in his first year, and because he was considered the senior dean for the region. Whatever the ground rules were that he and Rod had agreed upon, Ralph figured he had earned a wildcard of his own. He was determined that Becca receive one final look, for she was simply too good a candidate. In time, Rod would probably understand. And if Becca wasn't taken off the waiting list, Rod would probably never discover what Ralph had done.

The following morning, as he prepared to deposit their recommendations in Nancy's office, Ralph made two other changes: he moved Becca's card from the bottom of the pile to the top. To Greg and Nancy, Becca would now appear to be Ralph and Rod's lead nominee. Ralph then attached a bright yellow Post-it to Becca's workcard that couldn't be missed: "Still very, very interested. Lots of support from everybody at school." And in case anyone had forgotten, Ralph added: "Great leader."

Nancy and Greg announced their picks to the staff, via e-mail, a few days later. One lucky winner was a prep school student whose uneven grades had troubled Ralph but whose poetry had ultimately won over Greg. Another had made no strong impression in the main round but had ultimately come to the attention of President Bennet, though he, as usual, had made no request to the committee for special treatment.

Ralph saw that there were five other names on the list, but Becca's was not one of them. It was over. Ralph felt sorry for Becca, but he had no regrets about how he had handled her case. "I did everything I could, and then some," he said later. He didn't even bother to call Sharon, for he had already made it clear to her how tough the odds had been.

But then, a few weeks later, a funny thing happened. Though the Class of 2004 was now effectively closed, Greg and Nancy had waited before officially disbanding the waiting list. Sometimes, the summer melt was so intense that students were taken off the waiting list as late as August. Administrators at Dartmouth had been telling a story for years about a young woman from Long Island who was removed from the waiting list in August in the mid-1980s, and went on to win a Rhodes Scholarship.

In the middle of June of 2000, Greg Pyke, ever the number cruncher, had noticed a statistical anomaly in the Class of 2004. Usually, about fifteen students a year who had been accepted into a particular class had asked to defer their enrollment at Wesleyan until the following year's class. The idea of taking a year off between high school and college was becoming increasingly attractive, particularly as the pressure to get into college grew. As Wesleyan decided in March of 2000 how many students it could admit to the Class of 2004, it had always assumed that, once again, fifteen students would elect to start a year late, and it adjusted its offers accordingly. It also assumed that when it began its search for the Class of 2005, beginning in the fall, the class would already have fifteen students committed to it. But, as it turned out, only five applicants who were accepted for the Class of 2004 had asked Wesleyan to put off their enrollment a year. That, Greg reasoned, left room for another ten applicants to be accepted now for the Class of 2005, a year early. After all, Wesleyan had already set aside those early seats.

Wesleyan had never initiated such an offer before, leaving it to the applicants themselves to sort out whether they wanted to put off college for a year. But Greg and Nancy had regretted that there were so many good applicants who remained on the waiting list for the Class of 2004, and this would be a way to get a few of them to Wesleyan after all.

Toward the end of June, Ralph received an e-mail message explaining their surprise decision to start stocking the Class of 2005 more than a year in advance. "In part," Nancy wrote to her colleagues, "this is to address a small number of political cases—alumni/trustee interest, school relations, etc.—that we were unable (unwilling?) to include in the small group we took a couple of weeks ago."

One applicant who had been designated to receive an offer of this early-early acceptance was a student at a top New York City prep school. A powerful alumnus knew the applicant well and had expressed regret that there had been no room for him at Wesleyan in the Class of 2004. Barbara-Jan, as Wesleyan's chief fund-raiser, had passed that complaint on to Nancy, who had been receptive. Another applicant now being offered admission to the following year's freshman class had written movingly of herself as both an observant Jew and a practicing Buddhist. No one who read her file had been able to forget her, but it didn't hurt that her father and sister were Wesleyan alumni. Now, long after the game seemed over, she had won admission to Wesleyan.

Becca Jannol had no family connections to Wesleyan, but she did fall into the category that Nancy's e-mail described as "school relations." Ralph was stunned to learn from Nancy's message that Becca was being invited to join the Class of 2005 as well. Nancy had remembered that Sharon, her friend from that conference years earlier, had been especially disappointed with the way Becca's application had been treated. And Nancy still recalled being impressed with Becca. Ralph hadn't needed to remind her, and indeed, she hadn't even given him the opportunity to; this was her pick. Ralph felt as if he had received a Christmas present in the middle of summer. *What a perfect way to end this,* he thought.

Because time was short, an assistant from the admissions office had already been dispatched to call Becca at home to gauge her interest, before Ralph would ever have the chance to pick up the phone. Becca's answer was polite, and swift: the call from Wesleyan had come too late.

Several days earlier, Becca had been sitting in a small audio-visual studio at Harvard-Westlake, editing a short film, when the phone rang. "It's for you," her teacher told her. The voice on the line was Sharon's.

"He called!" she said.

Sharon didn't even have to say Ken Gabard's name. At least twice a day for the past few weeks, Becca had been asking Sharon if she had received any word from their favorite admissions officer at Cornell. And now, finally, Sharon had.

Sharon told Becca that she had been accepted into the Class of 2004 at Cornell, in the School of Arts and Sciences. But there was a catch: as Ken had predicted during her visit to Cornell, there was not enough housing left on campus for Becca to start in the fall. But she and about sixty other candidates were being invited to join the Class of 2004 in January, for the second semester. He had pushed for Becca and his colleagues were receptive. Her response was instantaneous.

"Wuh-hoo!" she said to her college counselor. "This is awesome!"

Anyone eavesdropping would have been hard-pressed to tell who was more excited, Sharon or Becca. Becca's application had been among the toughest that Sharon had ever shepherded. But her initial strategy had won out, even if it took a few extra weeks to do so. Sharon had advised Becca to apply to Wesleyan, and later to Cornell, in part because she was confident that Becca would find a sympathetic reader and a champion at each school, which is precisely what had happened.

While the admissions committee at Wesleyan had reached a consensus, at least initially, to reject Becca resoundingly, she had faced no such committee at Cornell, a factor that had helped her. Instead, Cornell paired an admissions officer with a faculty member and assigned the pair responsibility for making the call on everyone who had applied to Cornell from a particular geographic region. That could work against a candidate, of course, for if he or she failed to win over the first two readers of his or her application, there was little recourse, as there was at Wesleyan. But if those two readers liked an applicant, and there was room in the class, he or she was in.

When he had first read Becca's application in late winter, Ken had reacted to the story of the pot brownie as Ralph had. "The way we've always approached stuff like that," Ken explained later, "is that if the student has faced up to the problem, writes to us about it, and the school supports her application, then as far as we're concerned she's fine." Drawing on the letter from Becca's dean, Mr. Sal, Ken concluded that Becca had grown from the experience. The professor who was reading alongside Ken—they were sitting together at a desk in Ken's office—concurred. "We felt she redeemed herself," Ken said.

Moreover, Ken and the professor agreed that if they had rejected Becca based on an ultimately harmless brush with drugs, they would be nothing if not hypocritical. "We all have been young," Ken said. "We all have made mistakes. It's not something that should ruin your life." That Becca had narrowly missed admission to Cornell during the main round was more a factor of her SAT scores. Of the 1000 Californians who applied in the main round for admission to the College of Arts and Sciences at Cornell, Ken could make offers to about only 270, and he felt there were too many other applicants from California who had scored better than Becca. But once he received permission from Cornell, in late spring, to offer about 10 more Californians a chance to start at midyear, he made sure he could find room for her.

After hearing this good news from her college counselor, Becca told Sharon immediately that she wanted to accept Ken's offer. Even if Wesleyan admitted her over the summer—which, of course, it subsequently would—she preferred to go to Cornell. In contrast to Julianna's case, Sharon felt no disappointment for Ralph in losing this candidate. Wesleyan had had its chance to land Becca in April and had passed on her. That wasn't Ralph's fault, but he would surely understand that the girl's feelings for Wesleyan had changed in the interim. "I love the fact that Becca ended up someplace that didn't appear on her list until mid-December," Sharon said later.

As the euphoria of Sharon's call faded, Becca grew a bit anxious, as did her parents, who were concerned about how she would fare, socially and academically, by arriving on the Cornell campus three months after almost everyone in her class. Becca began to daydream about working on a sheep farm in New Zealand and perhaps, if there was time, trekking in Nepal, before departing for Cornell in January. She reasoned that her father, a successful lawyer, could afford it, and she had earned it. But he vetoed her initial choices, explaining that he wanted her to go easy on the expenses and confine herself to the Western Hemisphere.

Becca ultimately decided she would spend the summer and fall in Costa Rica, living with a rural family and teaching English. And to prove to her father that she was aware of the dent she was putting in his wallet, she sent a mass mailing to "family, friends and potential sponsors." After disclosing her plans, she asked that "those interested in supporting me" send a donation to her home address. Even Sharon received a copy. Becca had meant the line as a joke, but the letter prompted a flurry of phone calls to her father to see if she was serious. No, he explained, this was his treat; he couldn't be prouder of his daughter.

Until recently Becca had never imagined having an Ivy League name attached to her own, and she was amazed at how good it made her feel. She was now, officially, the "best of the best," she said. And no matter what she chose to do in life, she felt certain that Cornell would surely open doors for her that Emory or UC Santa Cruz or even Wesleyan might not. Still, as she prepared to embark on her Costa Rican adventure, her excitement was tempered by two competing emotions. One was an uncharacteristically smoldering anger. She felt her college application had taken an unnecessary pounding, at Wesleyan and elsewhere, and her self-esteem had suffered as a result. "I'm sorry so many kids have to go through this process," she said. "It makes you feel really bad about yourself at times." There had to be a better way, she said, but she was hard-pressed to suggest one.

Becca was also experiencing a sense of loss, for after months of imagining Ralph as the white knight who would come to her rescue, she now found it difficult even to think about him. It wasn't that she was ungrateful for his efforts; to the contrary, she was contemplating what she'd be missing. Students who had gone on to Wesleyan from Harvard-Westlake in previous years told her that Ralph made them feel like part of his family. He and his wife even opened their home to the students he had brought to campus. Ralph not only felt responsible for their well-being but enjoyed their company.

"My only regret about not going to that school," Becca finally decided, "is that I don't get to hang out with Ralph."

EPILOGUE

The following winter, the mailroom at the back of the Wesleyan admissions office filled with more applications for the Class of 2005 than it had for the Class of 2004, breaking through what had once been the unimaginable psychological barrier of seven thousand. Many of Wesleyan's competitors also received more mail in that winter of 2001. While the piles of envelopes weren't collecting at the same rate as during the frenzy of the late 1990s, Wesleyan and its competitors still anticipated growing in popularity for another decade, at which point enrollment at high schools across the country was projected to begin leveling off and to eventually drop. But early in the new century, there were already indications that applications to elite colleges might continue to rise even as the number of high school graduates decreased. Neither the slowing economy of 2001 — which shrank colleges' bank accounts, as well as parents' — nor the terrorist attacks of September 11 were powerful enough factors to deter record numbers of American teenagers from seeking to attend marquee colleges. The opportunity to compete for the privilege of receiving such an education remained too enticing.

In the spring of 2002, two years after the Class of 2004 had been admitted, Harvard, Yale, Dartmouth, Kenyon and Vassar, among other institutions, reported yet again shattering the previous year's total number of applications. Columbia and NYU were among the few highly selective universities that experienced decreases, but those losses were thought to be largely attributable to the skittishness of some high school seniors to relocate to New York City so soon after the collapse of the World Trade

Center. That, however, did not explain why Wesleyan, situated one hundred miles north of Manhattan, received about five hundred fewer applications for the Class of 2006 than it had for the Class of 2005—its first drop in four years.

As concerned as she was curious, Nancy placed phone calls that spring to a number of guidance counselors and quickly calculated that about half of the loss could be traced to those public and private high schools like Harvard-Westlake that had been Wesleyan's most reliable feeders. The counselors reported to Nancy that some seniors who might have been expected to apply to Wesleyan in past years had decided on their own not to even try that year because they had learned how competitive the university had become—and because they feared that their SAT scores or grades might not be up to par. In previous years, other premier colleges had experienced similar plateaus for similar reasons. And yet while Wesleyan had not received applications that winter from some of the lower performing seniors at its top feeder schools, it had continued to draw the highest rated applicants. Indeed, the median SAT scores of its applicant pool for the Class of 2006 were actually higher than in any other year.

The drop in applications, however much it may have eased the reading workload in the admissions office, did not dissuade Nancy from continuing to pursue a change in policy that she had instituted in the fall of 2000, as the Class of 2004 had taken its place on campus and she had approached her one-year anniversary as dean of admission and financial aid. Nancy decided then that the crush of applications for the Class of 2004 had pushed her and her nine-member staff to the breaking point. With the fresh perspective of an outsider who now had a sense of how Wesleyan worked, she decided that the procedures that had served the university so well in the past would have to be amended. Wesleyan, for example, had long taken great pride in the notion that the dean—or, in the case of the past year, the new dean working with an interim director—had made the final decision on every applicant whose case was not voted on by the committee. That meant judging nearly six thousand applications, and she and Greg had made most of those calls in the span of just a few weeks at the end of the reading season. Now that Nancy had a year's experience under her belt, she would be on her own.

To apportion that burden, Nancy initiated a new policy: beginning with the selection of the Class of 2005, the four members of her staff with the most seniority—including Ralph—would be responsible for recommending a final decision on each application submitted from within their geographic regions. The senior officer would have to consult the junior officer in the region—in Ralph's case, that was Rod—but the final recommendation was the senior officer's, including whether he or she felt the committee should be consulted. While an officer chosen at random would still read each application first, and Nancy would review all the decisions, she would change a decision only in the most extraordinary circumstances. (One reason Nancy might intervene would be if she perceived that the students in one region were being held to a different standard than those in another.) The sheer number of applications that Wesleyan was receiving dictated that the dean could no longer give each application the same scrutiny she had in the past. And because Wesleyan spent so much time and money trying to woo more applicants every year, the admissions office was at least partly responsible for putting in motion the events that forced the change.

There was no way to predict in advance whether a particular applicant would benefit or suffer as a result of the new policy, as compared to the old. But now more than ever, an applicant's fate at Wesleyan hinged on the personality, interests and judgment of the senior admissions officer assigned to his or her high school. Had the new system been in place when Becca Jannol applied to Wesleyan, for example, she probably would have been admitted in the main round, since her champion, Ralph Figueroa, would have had the power to make it happen.

But with new opportunities to say yes, Ralph also had more authority to say no, and to recommend that someone who might have been accepted by the committee under the old system now never made it past the front gate. Indeed, the number of applicants referred to the committee round in the selection of the Class of 2005 was lower than the previous year. Like his colleagues, Ralph relished the new responsibility. Because he was more familiar with his territory than Nancy and more likely to have met the applicants, he felt he was in a better position to make such calls.

In fall 2001, Nancy oversaw the adoption of another new policy, when President Bennet, along with his counterparts at Amherst and Williams (the so-called Little Three), agreed to decrease the number of students in their freshman classes who were admitted primarily for athletic ability. (As if describing an arms-control agreement between the Americans and Russians, a *New York Times* editorial reported that the reduction would be as much as 20 percent.) In addition, Wesleyan committed to improve the academic quality of all student athletes admitted to future freshman classes. Both initiatives were intended to address the increasing gap in the academic credentials of athletes and nonathletes. The admissions process, though, would remain the same: all student athletes would continue to be run through the same gantlet as nonathletes. Each application would be read by at least two admissions officers, and the various strengths and weaknesses of each would be weighed, often in the committee round.

There would be other, more noticeable changes inside the cozy house that was home to the admissions office. Bozoma Arthur and Lyllah Martin, each having graduated from Wesleyan a little over a year earlier, decided to leave their jobs in the summer of 2000, before the freshmen whom they had helped select had even arrived on campus. Lyllah moved only a few miles north, to Trinity College, where she enrolled in a master's program in public policy. Bozoma, by contrast, had decided to move to an advertising agency owned by Spike Lee in New York City. She had achieved her personal goal of experiencing how the whole process worked, so much so that after participating in the rapid-fire debates and votes of the committee round, she had been tempted to ask her veteran colleagues if they had argued over her own case five years earlier. But she decided she didn't want to know. And now it was time to move on.

The most surprising departure, though, was Rod's. He had stayed on at Wesleyan a second year, participating in the selection of the Class of 2005 and again playing a critical role in flagging Asian American applicants whom he thought worthy of consideration. And then he had decided he had had enough. At age twenty-seven, he was eager to do something different with his life, having spent the previous three years as an admissions officer at Hampshire and feeling burnt out after all that reading and agonizing. After much contemplation—all of it transpiring in the dead of night, of course—he decided that he had found his next calling: he would become a flight attendant for a commercial airline.

Rod had always loved to fly but had never thought he had the right stuff to become a pilot, even if he had managed to graduate from the University of Rochester, with its heavy emphasis on the sciences. Early in 2001, at the outset of the reading season and nine months before the terrorist attacks would decimate the airline industry, he was one of fifteen thousand people who sent off applications to United Airlines seeking these positions. Soon, he received word that he had made the first cut: he had been invited to the airline's Chicago headquarters for an interview.

No one at United could understand why someone would give up an annual salary of $37,000 for one that would barely break $20,000, at least initially. But United was impressed and agreed to put Rod through the final round of the application process. While the airline didn't ask its applicants to write an essay, he had to undergo a battery of psychological tests and participate in several team-building exercises. In April, just as the applicants for the Class of 2005 were receiving their decisions from Wesleyan, Rod went to his own mailbox and saw that he had received an envelope from United. It was thin. "My first reject letter in a long time," he commented. Ultimately, United had been able to place fewer than 350 applicants in its flight attendant training program. "Some of these people were unemployed and truly wanted to be in the air," he said. "I'm glad I didn't take the place away from them."

Not long after he heard from United, Rod saw a posting on a bulletin board at Wesleyan from Brown University, which was seeking an assistant director of financial aid. The job had two main attractions to him. Not only would it be a change of pace—he would be helping to give away $7 million annually to people who had already been accepted to Brown— but he would also be able to move in with his boyfriend, who worked for an environmental laboratory in Rhode Island. Rod was offered the job but then grew conflicted over whether to leave Wesleyan. What ultimately made the difference, he said, were his ongoing concerns about how the school considered Asian American applicants. "The pressure to admit those kids just isn't there," Rod said, after eventually moving to Providence. "There were way too many Asian American kids from Andover and Exeter and Stuyvesant who were on our waiting list at Wes and should have gotten in." While the Class of 2005 was 11 percent black, and 11 percent Asian or Asian American, a higher percentage of blacks who had applied had been accepted than Asians. When told of Rod's comments, Ralph said that his former colleague's concern was justified.

"It's not an institutional thing," Ralph explained. "It's each individual admissions officer having a little less sympathy toward the Asian American experience. Society makes us feel that Asian students aren't quite as disadvantaged. Sometimes it's true, sometimes it's not." He said that everyone was aware of Rod's dissatisfaction, and that one of Rod's successors, a first-generation American whose parents were from India, had immediately taken up where Rod had left off. After the officers had completed the early-decision process for the Class of 2006, Rod's successor had reviewed the data and persuaded Nancy to admit several Asian American applicants who had initially been denied, Ralph said.

While Rod had pushed Ralph and his colleagues to include Asian Americans more prominently in their definition of affirmative action, the will of the rest of the nation on race-conscious admissions—or at least the will of its judiciary branch—grew more muddled. In the months after the Class of 2004 was admitted, federal judges in several states issued contradictory rulings about the constitutionality of affirmative action policies in university admissions offices. The most striking of them were in Michigan. In 2000, one federal judge, citing Justice Powell's argument in *Bakke,* upheld an undergraduate policy at the University of Michigan that automatically added 20 points—on a 150-point scale—to the scoring of applications of black and Hispanic applicants, as well as the applications of white applicants from poor backgrounds. Because of Michigan's size, these numbers were far more important than the ratings of 1 to 9 at Wesleyan, which merely served as guideposts as the admissions officers thought about their decisions. Michigan, by contrast, had a rough-cut score for admission, and the extra 20 points often brought many students over the line and into Ann Arbor. But in 2001, another federal judge, also citing *Bakke,* ruled that the University of Michigan Law School had violated the Constitution by targeting a "critical mass" of minorities for its incoming class, much as Wesleyan had done in seeking to ensure that the percentage of minorities in its freshman class did not diminish from year to year. In May 2002, a federal appeals court reversed the lower court ruling and upheld the law school policy. By then, constitutional scholars were arguing that the Michigan cases—and the overall confusion about affirmative action—could be reconciled only by the Supreme Court. But it was not known whether the Court was interested in taking those cases on, nor was it clear whether a reversal of *Bakke* by the Supreme Court, if it came to pass, would apply to private colleges like Wesleyan, which receive only a small percentage of their income from the federal government. Still, Ralph was watching the national developments like an anxious sentry, for if it was the will of the Supreme Court that Justice Powell had been mistaken about considering race "a plus" in admitting a class, then Ralph was sure that Wesleyan would have to change its policies.

"It's not a fight anyone wants to be in," Ralph said. "We'd have to go back and look at how we talk about race, how we talk about diversity. Could we talk in the same way? Could we even think the same way we used to think?" But for all the concerns in the admissions offices of liberal arts colleges that a conservative court might roll back affirmative action, Ralph was more optimistic. He was hoping that the current justices would endorse Justice Powell's doctrine in a way that the justice's colleagues never had, at least not publicly. "The court could confirm that in the field of higher education, diversity does constitute a compelling state interest," he explained. "That would be all you'd need. Boom. What an effect that would have."

Affirmative action was hardly the only aspect of selective college admissions that was under fire in 2000 and 2001. So were colleges' reliance on the SAT, early-notification programs and even the rankings of *U.S. News & World Report*. Perhaps not since the 1960s were so many different questions being raised about how selective colleges were deciding who would gain access to their campuses.

The most dramatic challenge was being mounted from within the University of California, among the largest and most influential public college systems in the nation. The university president, Richard Atkinson, proposed in 2000 that the university trustees no longer require the main SAT exam as a condition of admission. Dr. Atkinson complained that the exams, with their emphasis on problem-solving over achievement, were not an appropriate measure for college admission. Moreover, he lamented that the anxiety surrounding the tests, and their outsized role in teenage life, were disrupting the high school experience. While more than a few teenagers and parents had been making such arguments for years, only to have them fall on deaf ears, Dr. Atkinson was easily the most prominent and powerful educator to challenge the status quo. In the spring of 2001, it appeared likely that the university faculty and Board of Regents would approve the policy by year's end and that several other states might soon follow suit. It was a stunning setback for an exam whose use had grown unchecked and largely unquestioned for more than a half century. In response, the College Board began to draft plans to add an essay section to the main SAT exam, to broaden what it measured.

As he watched California wrestle with its policies regarding the SAT, Ralph was less concerned than he was about affirmative action. Like its other Ivy League brethren, Harvard, whose influence among smaller private colleges was comparable to California's among public universities, had not wavered in its basic endorsement of the exams. Like Wesleyan, it believed that at a time when it was more difficult than ever to compare the A of a student at one school to the A of a student at another, the SAT offered the prospect of a common yardstick, however imperfect. Still, Ralph could sympathize with the plight of the public universities: while Wesleyan had the time and resources to put a student's SAT score in context, the big public universities often had to choose many of their students by feeding a combination of grades and test scores into a computer. For the foreseeable future, though, the SAT would continue to be a reality, at least for anyone who had set his or her sights on Wesleyan or most of the nation's other highly selective private colleges. Ralph himself continued to support its use.

The assault on early-notification programs was joined, less than thirty miles southwest of Middletown, in New Haven. In an interview with *The New York Times* in late 2001, Yale's president Richard Levin said that his school would be willing to consider giving up its binding early-decision program—like Wesleyan, it accepted more than a third of its incoming freshman class before April—provided other highly selective colleges joined him in laying down their arms. Just as others worried about the damage that the SAT was doing to teenagers, Levin said he was concerned that an increasing number of applicants felt pressure to make a binding commitment to their first-choice college in the fall, rather than preserving their options for the spring. To Ralph, the gesture seemed disingenuous and unlikely to go far. Less than ten years earlier, Yale, which had one of the last nonbinding early-notification programs in the country, decided it would change its policy and compel all applicants admitted early to attend.

None of Levin's counterparts in the Ivy League rushed to endorse this proposal that early notification be eliminated entirely. But even if the Ivy presidents eventually decided to pull the plug on such programs, Ralph was sure that Wesleyan would not. While Yale and Harvard could always be certain that many of the best college applicants in the country would still apply in the winter if they were not permitted to do so in the fall, Wesleyan, with a reputation that was not as prestigious as that of the Ivies, could not be so confident. "I agree philosophically with Mr. Levin," Ralph said. "I think early decision is too prevalent and I think the potential for harm is as great as the potential for good. But we need to have that base in the class."

As critics raised concerns in 2000 and 2001 about the many perceived shortcomings of selective college admissions, Ralph joined the chorus on only one: he said he would be willing to bar Wesleyan from providing data to *U.S. News & World Report* for its annual fall rankings. But this was Wesleyan's call, not his. In September 2001, as the members of the Class of 2005 took their seats at Wesleyan, Amy Graham, who had worked as a research director for *U.S. News*, co-authored an article in *The Washington*

Monthly in which she questioned what such rankings really measured. She wondered, for example, what students' high school SAT scores really indicated about the quality of their colleges. Ralph, reading the article at his desk in the admissions office, nodded in concurrence. "It's just ridiculous how much weight is put on something that is manipulated constantly," he said. "Not only do all the colleges play, they play by different rules. They manipulate the data they submit. They lobby *U.S. News.*" Still, he knew as well as anyone that Wesleyan could ill afford to lose the marketing boost that *U.S. News* provided. While it had long ago conceded the race to Amherst (number 1 on the liberal arts list in 2001) and Williams (number 3), Wesleyan could count on receiving dozens, if not hundreds, of applications later that fall as a result of its ranking: a respectable number 11. The magazine put Wesleyan in a tie with Grinnell and ranked it ahead of such formidable competition as Vassar (tied for 14), Bryn Mawr (tied for 17), Bates (tied for 22) and Barnard (tied for 28). Those rankings had been based, in large part, on the profile of the Class of 2004. Despite his reservations, Ralph, who had invested so much in assembling that class, felt no small amount of pride that Wesleyan had beaten out those other schools.

So did Jordan Goldman, whose high SAT scores had contributed, however minimally, to Wesleyan's high standing in that fall's survey. Once arriving on the Wesleyan campus, Jordan had had little trouble putting Brown out of his thoughts. For one thing, his roommate—in the dorm with the clothing-optional policy—told him something on the first day that Jordan found astonishing: he had been accepted to Brown and Wesleyan, but had chosen Wesleyan. Jordan's roommate liked the fact that Wesleyan was more intimate and low-key. The same day, Jordan met a girl on the same floor who had been accepted to Princeton but chose Wesleyan for similar reasons. "It makes me feel good that other kids realized Wesleyan's just as good as other schools, if not better," Jordan said at the time. "It validates me."

True to their word, Ralph and Rod, who had been so taken by Jordan's e-mail opus the previous spring, found Jordan a work-study job in the admissions office. He could not have been more qualified for his assignment: he was responsible for monitoring the e-mails posted on the electronic bulletin board by applicants for the following year's class. Ralph and Rod even sent out Jordan's message again that year, as if it were a rerun of a Charlie Brown Christmas special that had gotten high ratings the first time it was shown. Jordan became such a big booster of Wesleyan that Ralph recommended him for a job in Barbara-Jan's fund-raising operation. Jordan was now responsible for training teams of Wesleyan athletes to make phone calls to alumni asking them for donations.

When he had visited Wesleyan as a prospective freshman, Jordan had been impressed that the college permitted so many students to speak their minds on so many issues. After the terrorist attacks of September 11, he would marvel at how the entire campus was seemingly caught up in trying to make sense of the attacks and to evaluate the merits of the American response. As they had at the height of the Vietnam War, Wesleyan students and faculty staged candlelight vigils on Foss Hill, teach-ins at the student center and marches past the nineteenth-century brownstone buildings on College Row. The graffiti artists were out in force, too—armed with colored chalk, rather than paint, as always.

As he watched some of those protests from the floor-to-ceiling windows of the admissions office that fall, Ralph would be struck by one thought related to his job: he was disappointed that so few applicants for the Class of 2006, at least those applying for early decision, had chosen to write about their views of September 11. Still, he knew exactly why that was the case. They were trying to outthink the admissions process, just as he had always warned them not to do. They were sure that everyone would write about 9/11 and that their essays would all blend together, giving no one an edge. But Ralph, who was usually on the lookout for essays that were unique, felt that many applicants had erred by writing about other matters. "They missed the point," Ralph said. "It's probably the most important event of their lifetimes. I want to know what they thought about it."

As he had hoped, Jordan received plenty of opportunities to write essays and short stories at Wesleyan and to have them critiqued. He even applied to teach his own English seminar during his freshman spring. He called the course "Experimental Fiction," and among the novels in his syllabus was *The Wanderers,* by Richard Price. Wesleyan, always progressive, permitted students to apply to teach courses that would be offered pass/fail. Jordan's was accepted—the first by a freshman that anyone could remember—and he proved to be a tough teacher, assigning three hundred pages of reading and a ten-page paper every week. As a backstop, a creative writing professor reviewed all of his grades. In the end, all twelve students passed, including Jordan's roommate.

By the middle of his sophomore year, Jordan said he could not imagine himself anywhere but at Wesleyan. But when he learned that Wesleyan had a one-year study-abroad program at Oxford, he felt he had to apply. He relished the prospect of living in England and experiencing Oxford's tutorial system, in which, for example, he might spend a week reading everything Mark Twain had ever written and then meet with a professor to discuss it for three hours. But there was, of course, another reason. As happy and challenged as he was at Wesleyan—and there was every indication that those sentiments were genuine—Jordan had never stopped thinking about how he might improve his résumé, for he still worried about how book editors or graduate schools would judge the name "Wesleyan." Around the time that he applied for the Oxford program, he had seen a book written by a graduate of the University of Pennsylvania whose author's note made reference to the year he had spent at Oxford. Jordan was certain that such a distinction would help his own author's note someday. In late winter of 2002, Jordan learned he had been accepted to the program. In October, he would be on his way to England.

Although they didn't get to know each other, beyond saying a casual hello once in a while, Jordan Goldman and Migizi Pensoneau were among the 150 students who had ended up in the same film class, "History of World Cinema, World War II to the Present," in the fall of their freshman year. Perhaps feeling inspired by the course, Mig had decided to decorate his first-floor dorm room, a single, with black-and-white photos of some of his favorite film stars: Greta Garbo, Vincent Price, the Marx Brothers, Jack Nicholson in *The Shining,* Humphrey Bogart in *Casablanca.* He found the photos, along with the fuzzy lion slippers that a young cousin had given him, comforting, and throughout that fall, he had needed a little comforting.

Ralph had certainly been honest: Mig had yet to meet another Native American student or even a faculty member at Wesleyan. For the first time in his life, he was the only person for miles who knew firsthand that a pipe was a sacred religious object and not something smoked by some movie-western Indian to celebrate peace. Mig found he missed little things, like hearing snippets of Ojibwa (his mother's language) or Lakota (his stepfather's). "I'd really like to have other native kids here," Mig admitted on a Sunday morning that fall. He was wearing a sleeveless white tank top that revealed a tattoo of an eagle—the translation of his name, in Ojibwa—that he had gotten the day before leaving Minnesota for Middletown. "As far as my religion, my spirituality, I can't relate to these guys," he said, gesturing down a dank dorm hallway that looked like a motel. Ralph had told him that, at least initially, that's how he should expect to feel.

But before long, another part of Ralph's pitch to Mig at NAPS had also come to pass. There were indeed so many people from so many different backgrounds at Wesleyan that Mig didn't feel like an outsider for long. He knew that there were people in his class from nearly every state and more than two dozen foreign countries, and soon found that he enjoyed learning about the disparate lives of his classmates. He even discovered someone he "could really relate to" in conversations about religion: another freshman, named Benny, who lived next door, was an Orthodox Jew. "He doesn't break Shabbat," Mig said, smiling as he used a word for the Jewish Sabbath, which he heard for the first time only several weeks earlier. Mig, who was often tempted to drink alcohol but who said he was prohibited by his religion from doing so, said he drew strength from his Jewish friend's discipline.

Having turned his C's and D's in Bemidji into A's and B's at NAPS, Mig vowed throughout his freshman year at Wesleyan that he would not fall back on old habits. "I feel really grateful," he said at one point. "I feel like I owe a lot to a lot of people. I don't want to let anyone down. I always keep in mind that being here isn't enough." During the fall semester, he had managed a B in a drama class and a C in that movie course. "Not exactly up to par," he had to concede, but he succeeded in passing both. He was less successful in physics, which he failed, but it was just one course. In the spring, though, he wound up failing another: Greek drama, which surprised him. Mig put none of the blame on Wesleyan. A dean had reached out to him, and he had met with her, but he had ultimately just given up. "The support was there," he said, "I just wasn't." He was at a loss to explain why. As was the case in high school in Minnesota, he felt certain he was intelligent enough to understand the work. He just lacked the desire.

Because of his grades, Mig would have to leave Wesleyan, at least for a semester, at which point he would be permitted to apply for readmission. He would miss his new friends—and there were many more besides his Jewish neighbor—but he found himself wanting to return to Bemidji, the northern Minnesota town he had worked so hard to escape three years earlier. He had always taken the presence of so many Native Americans in Bemidji for granted, and hadn't missed them at NAPS. But now he couldn't wait to hear familiar voices. "I just realized how much of it was a part of me," he said, speaking by phone from home the following Christmas.

Mig never told Ralph that he was in academic trouble, or that he wasn't returning to Wesleyan. It wasn't that he was embarrassed, Mig explained; it just never occurred to him. During his freshman fall and spring, he had occasionally seen Ralph on campus, and they had waved to each other or said hello. Ralph had invited Mig to at least one party at his home, one that Jordan had wound up attending. But Mig hadn't shown up, and Ralph had decided not to push him. "A lot of it has to be done by him," Ralph said.

At some point in the fall of 2001, which would have been the beginning of Mig's sophomore year, Ralph decided to look up Mig's phone number on the campus website, but the computer kept informing him that no listing for the name "Pensoneau" was available. Ralph had no idea what had happened to Mig and scribbled himself a note to call the registrar, but he never did. When he traveled to NAPS again that fall on a recruiting trip, he didn't mention Mig. "I knew I couldn't find him," Ralph said. "I think they didn't know at NAPS he had left."

When I ran into the same problem with the website at around the same time, I called Mig's mother, and Mig eventually called back. I then spoke to Ralph, who said he certainly knew it had been risky to bring Mig to Wesleyan, and he had acknowledged as much to Mig and to his colleagues in the admissions office. Ralph remembered hearing that one of the first Hispanic students who had attended Wesleyan, someone who had even founded a Hispanic student organization there in the 1960s, wound up transferring elsewhere to graduate. But because he spent so much time away from the school itself, either traveling to meet applicants or reading their applications, Ralph had to set boundaries for what he could do for a freshman, no matter how great his needs. He did not have the time to hold Mig's hand, nor would Mig have necessarily wanted him to. "It does highlight an underlying frustration of the job," Ralph said. "Once they get here, we kind of have to hand them over to somebody else. Sometimes the university does a good job picking up where we left off. Sometimes it doesn't." Knowing how this case had turned out, Ralph said he would have still recruited Mig, if given the chance. "It's a shot worth taking," Ralph said, just after Christmas.

Several weeks later, in January 2002, Mig called me to say he had news. He had enrolled in several classes at Bemidji State, including one in physics, and he had already been in touch with a dean at Wesleyan. Mig told her he wanted to come back in the fall, and she indicated that Wesleyan would have him, as long as he did well in his classes at Bemidji. He might have to take some extra credits at Wesleyan, too, but Wesleyan would help him on that score. Feeling suddenly refreshed, Mig said, "I'm confident I'll do a lot better."

By late spring, Mig had completed his courses at Bemidji. He said he knew already that he had passed, but was awaiting his final grades before contacting Wesleyan to request his reinstatement. (His alma mater, the Native American Preparatory School, had not fared as well. That same spring, as it completed its sixth year of operation, the school shuttered its doors, a victim, according to an article in the *Albuquerque Journal,* of insufficient fund-raising, administrative turnover and lingering concerns among some Native Americans that its philosophy, however well intentioned, had been set down primarily by non-Natives.)

Ralph's response to Mig's plans was measured, but hopeful. "There is still potential," he observed. "The fact that he hasn't given up is important. It's not over." Wesleyan might well succeed in recruiting and graduating its first Native American student in years.

Early in her freshman year at Muhlenberg College, two hundred miles south of Wesleyan, in Allentown, Pennsylvania, Aggie Ramirez was wrestling with a different issue. She was burned out. In Aggie's case, grades were not the main problem. Oldfields, where she had had a rocky senior fall with that D and those C's, had actually prepared her quite well for Muhlenberg, she felt. She took an introduction to sociology course that focused a lot on race and ethnicity, and took its lessons to heart. "Now I know the difference between race and ethnic groups," Aggie said at the time. "Like I'm part of the black race and white race, and my ethnic groups are Latino. That's pretty neat that I fit."

Even Aggie would come to conclude, though, that Wesleyan had probably made the right call on her by not accepting her. In this case, it was Greg Pyke's instincts, and his concerns that Aggie might not be able to handle the work at Wesleyan, that had been on target. Many of the guidebooks indicated that Wesleyan's courses were often rigorous, probably more challenging than at a school like Muhlenberg. And Aggie herself had already picked up signs that she was beginning to struggle to do her work at Muhlenberg. A writing class, for example, met at nine A.M., and as an incentive to lure sleepy students, 20 percent of its grade was based on participation. If a student was late, he or she would lose points, and Aggie estimated she had missed at least six classes. Part of the reason was that she was staying up working in the theater at Muhlenberg, just as she had vowed when she had seen the rehearsal for *West Side Story* on the day she had first visited campus. She was now acting as the property manager on a production of *Little Shop of Horrors,* a position for which she was a natural. But, while still dreaming of a career as an actress, she was reluctant to step on stage herself. "You have to be free to act," she said. "I'm not sure if I'm ready."

One of the reasons Aggie was hesitant to step out on that stage was that Muhlenberg was overwhelmingly white. She had known this going in, of course, and was aware that she had been recruited, at least in part, as someone who might make the school more hospitable for those who followed her. To that end, she joined the executive board of the black students association, which had fewer than twenty members. Because the Hispanic students association, which was even smaller, met at a time that conflicted with her other activities, she passed on joining, for the moment. But she felt very alone. Her friend from New York, who had been her campus tour guide, was there, but Aggie admitted, "I feel like there are very few people I can completely connect with."

One of the few new friends she had made at Muhlenberg was Melissa Falk, the admissions officer who had been her champion. They had grown close, and Aggie sometimes did her laundry at Melissa's home, which was near campus, and went out to dinner with her and her husband, also a Muhlenberg alumnus who was working as a lawyer in the district attorney's office. One night in December of her freshman year, Aggie stunned Melissa and her husband by telling them she would be taking a leave of absence from Muhlenberg after concluding her final exams. She needed a break, and she didn't know if she'd be back.

"I want to spend some time at home," Aggie explained, reminding Melissa that she had been away at boarding school for four years, and pushing to get herself into boarding school for many years before that. "I love the opportunities I've been given. I'm really grateful. I think I need some time where I'm not living in a community where everyone's my age."

Melissa offered words of encouragement and support, urging Aggie to follow her heart, but she could feel the tears welling up in her own eyes as she said them. Aggie kept insisting that her departure had nothing to do with Muhlenberg, but Melissa couldn't help feeling that her best work over the last year, the wooing of Aggie Ramirez to Muhlenberg, was crumbling before her eyes. Melissa's "water walker," as she had so often described Aggie to her colleagues, was sinking.

"If she doesn't come back, it's meant to be," Melissa would recall saying to her husband later that night. "But she got this far here. I can't imagine she's going to disappear."

After returning to Washington Heights for Christmas, Aggie spent a lot of time lying on the couch in her parents' apartment, eating junk food and watching movies. But soon, feeling lazy, she found part-time work tutoring, and helped an elderly relative clean her home. Before long, Aggie, who had been such a spark plug throughout so much of her young life, was energized. She was rested. Her head felt clear. And she was surprised to discover that she was homesick for Allentown. In what would have been the spring of her freshman year, she returned to Muhlenberg for a visit with only one purpose in mind. She hadn't called Melissa in advance, so Melissa was startled to pass her on campus that day. Melissa could see that she was in a rush, and Aggie didn't even stop to say hello, though she did blow Melissa a kiss. A few moments later, Aggie had accomplished her mission: she had registered for fall classes. She was going back to Muhlenberg, and resuming her education.

In the fall of her sophomore year, Aggie did indeed return, and she and Melissa were again spending time together. Melissa was struck by how "recentered" Aggie seemed. She had even refrained from signing on to work on any fall theater productions. "I'm easing myself back in," Aggie explained; her studies now came first. The year that followed would be among the most successful of Aggie's academic career. Melissa would decide that Aggie was even more of an inspiration than she had ever imagined when she was lobbying her colleagues for Aggie's admission. As Mig had learned, one's education didn't necessarily proceed in a straight line. There were very often stops and starts, and though many people could get through college in four uninterrupted years, others could not. "Aggie is courageous," Melissa said that fall. "Another kid, without her strength and resilience, wouldn't have had the courage to take a break or then to come back." Melissa had brought a role model to Muhlenberg after all.

Tiffany Wang, whom Ralph had met on paper the same day he met Aggie, found that whatever concerns she had had about dorm life at New York University were quickly overcome. On arriving on campus in the fall of 2000, she was given the keys to a fifteenth-floor double with views of the Empire State and Met Life Buildings. More than ever, she was glad she had not settled for a rural school. The dorm life was far more social than Tiffany had been led to believe, and the late-night chat sessions she hosted in her room—under posters of Brad Pitt and Enriqué Iglesias— were evocative of those late-night escapes from the window of her parents' home.

Yet Tiffany proved she could be a far more serious student than she had been in high school. She worked hard to earn an A in a tough economics course that fall, and was proud of it. She had recently read an essay by the nature writer and onetime Wesleyan professor Annie Dillard entitled "Living Like Weasels." Dillard's piece described a weasel as living "as he's meant to, yielding at every moment to the perfect freedom of single necessity." After reading that passage, Tiffany found herself thinking about "how exactly are we supposed to live life to achieve the greatest satisfaction?" She had no ready answers, but she felt she was beginning to search for a way to give her life meaning, that was clear.

At least at the beginning of her freshman year, Tiffany had not made a great effort to get involved in the NYU campus life. She was still adjusting. A political or business career, and maybe law school, was still on the horizon. And there were certainly opportunities at the school to find kindred spirits in her opposition to the death penalty. But she would give herself time before wading in.

As she had prepared to leave California for NYU in late summer, Tiffany had sought to bring one familiar aspect of home with her. She had given her inmate pen pal her new address. But as of late October, she had not heard from him, which was not like him. A visitor asked Tiffany, gingerly, if it was possible that the man had been executed. For all her concern that the lives of death row inmates be spared, Tiffany said she had never stopped to think that her pen pal might actually die. "The way he always talks," she said, "it doesn't sound like it's urgent." Tiffany had never done any research on her pen pal, or his crime, and she said she wasn't going to start now. She would simply hope for a letter and pray that one arrived. As of late spring 2002, nearly two years later, none had.

By then, Tiffany was in Prague, where she spent the spring semester studying history and politics, which was now her major. "Two of my teachers were senators!" she said in a telephone interview at the time. "One was the former foreign minister." Her time abroad had also been restorative emotionally. While walking to class on September 11, she had been able to see the World Trade Center burning. "I don't really like to talk about it," she said, eight months later. "I don't want to go down there, even now."

In contrast to Tiffany, Julianna Bentes arrived on the Yale campus in a rush, eager to dive into the full range of activities that had kept her so busy at Harvard-Westlake. By the fall of her sophomore year, she had become a leader in no fewer than five organizations. She served, for example, as the copresident of the Black Student Alliance, where she took an active role in disseminating a report on the role of slave traders at Yale two centuries earlier. She also became a leader in another group, United Students at Yale, a fledgling organization that patterned itself on a labor union and sought to serve as a student voice on a range of issues. One was the students' desire that Yale pay a "living wage" to its maintenance staff. Another issue, near to Julianna's mother's heart, was that all Yale students on financial aid be permitted to graduate debt free, with no loans to pay back. In reflecting on her mother's experience at the financial aid office, where she had only achieved her goals by bulldozing her way through the front door, Julianna said: "I can't help but think of the students who took one look at Yale and said, 'There's no way I'm going to be able to do this' and gave up. The inaccessibility of the financial aid process in general makes it hard for us to make a truly genuine claim of trying to get economic diversity on campus." Julianna was asked by the group concerned with that topic to deliver the closing remarks at one of its rallies. After much thought, she decided to lead the two hundred or so students gathered in front of Phelps Gate in a chant that she had learned in a dance class many years earlier. "We are one!" she began. "We are one!" At first her voice was soft, and then, slowly, it built to a scream. Later, she was still smiling about the response: "Everyone was pumped."

After September 11, Julianna, like Jordan, became caught up in the many protests and teach-ins that were organized at Yale. Her position was unequivocal: as terrible a thing as had happened to America at the World Trade Center, the obliteration of Afghanistan was not a just response. "I don't trust the government when it comes to things like this," she remarked. On top of all of those activities, as well as a job as the business manager of a dance company, Julianna was coping with the breakup of her parents' marriage. In the end, her father, born and raised in the Amazon, and her mother, a native of Pasadena, had grown apart. Her mother was even leaving Los Angeles and moving to Northern California, near where her brother lived. On the one hand, Julianna wondered if she would have done better to have stayed on the West Coast, perhaps at Stanford, where she could be nearer to her parents. But she also acknowledged it was easier, being so far from home, to put her parents' separation out of her head.

Still, the turmoil in her personal life had made concentrating a challenge. She received a B minus in organic chemistry, far below her average at Harvard-Westlake, and was elated, all things considered. "I've never been so proud of a B minus in my life," she insisted. Still, she was wondering if she was cut out to be a pediatric surgeon, which was the career she had in mind when she arrived. She was still keeping an open mind, but she was majoring in history. Of one thing, though, she was certain: the full breadth of her life at Yale was exactly what she had imagined for herself. She was more involved in extracurricular activities than she would have been at the University of Chicago, she said, and more challenged academically than she would have been at Wesleyan. "There's no other place I'd rather be," she said.

While Julianna and every other senior from Harvard-Westlake was adjusting to their new campuses in the fall of 2000, Becca Jannol was in Costa Rica, keeping busy until Cornell had a bed available for her in January. For three months, she lived in a rural pueblo, two hours from the nearest supermarket or telephone. She lived with a family, taught English to local schoolchildren, helped build a library—and, as she lay awake at night, reflected on her wild ride through the college admissions process, including her disappointments and triumphs at both Cornell and Wesleyan. She felt ashamed that she had come to care so much about attaining such a prize, considering it now took her half a day just to go into town and get a tube of toothpaste. The goal of obtaining an elite education seemed suddenly empty.

"Obviously the people there didn't have e-mail, they'd never seen a computer, they rarely talked on the telephone," Becca said, once back in her parents' home near Beverly Hills, on the eve of her departure for Cornell. "Their way of life was so conducive to walking slow and talking slow. It's not like I'm going to burn my clothes and rage against my family. But I'm definitely going to simplify my life."

Before leaving for Cornell in early January 2001, Becca returned to Harvard-Westlake to visit with younger friends who were now in the throes of the process that had consumed her only a year earlier. "They're just where I was," she said afterward. "They've lost whatever sense of self they had. They're saying, 'I'm not going to get in anywhere. My SAT's aren't high enough. So and so already got in early.'"

Asked what advice she had offered them, considering her newfound perspective, Becca said she had put it like this: "Applying to college is about trying to control all these things you couldn't control even if you tried." Whenever he visited Harvard-Westlake or any other high school, Ralph always hit that message hard. But now this was one of their own talking. They should all just relax and let the process run its course. Becca was much more blunt when talking to a visitor. "It just seems so stupid now," she said.

As she flew to Ithaca, she worried that she had lost the ability "to relate to kids my own age." Once on campus, she was sure that was the case. She was miserable most of her first semester, and it wasn't simply that more than a thousand of her new classmates had been there for months, and that she was one of only several dozen who were newly arrived. "I really didn't see the usefulness of my being there," she recalled. "I hated it." Where once she had thrown herself into student government at Harvard-Westlake, she spent her free time at Cornell working in a vintage clothing shop. "I've lost that passion to do good," she said. "I'm that typical lazy college student."

That was not entirely true, though. That spring, she summoned her courage and submitted yet another application to Cornell. She was one of a hundred freshmen who applied for an honors program that would release them from all of Cornell's graduation requirements—except the swimming test, which was still mandatory—so that they might have as much time as possible to nurture a special project. The applicants needed to have more A's than B's, and to craft a proposal that the honors committee found interesting. Becca's idea, drawn on her experience in Costa Rica, was that she would study agricultural, economic and social development in Latin America.

In June of her truncated freshman year, Becca received word of the committee's decision: she was one of forty people who had been accepted. The bearer of those good tidings was again Ken Gabard, who was not only her admissions officer and class dean but also the director of the program. "Rebecca," he told her, "you're a success story."

After the fall of 2001, in which her work on her honors courses made her feel as if she had found a place for herself at Cornell, she flew to Costa Rica once again—this time to do fieldwork as a Cornell student. When classes ended the following spring, she traveled to Rome for a month with twenty other Cornell students and two professors. "I am here to write and draw," she reported in an e-mail message, "This morning I got a great tan sketching at the Forum and in an hour I'm off to the Keats-Shelley House. Not bad."

Around that same time, unbeknownst to any of his colleagues, Ralph Figueroa was thinking about making a big change in his life, as well. He was considering leaving Wesleyan. He had recently been reflecting on the last few years and had calculated that he would be marking his seven-year anniversary at Wesleyan during the summer of 2002. "The seven-year itch," he said, "is as real in admissions as in a marriage." Unlike Rod,

Ralph had no particular dissatisfaction. He felt appreciated at Wesleyan, as well as respected by his colleagues. Disagreements like the one over Becca had been extremely rare, and everyone had moved on soon afterward. But for all his one-liners and practical jokes, Ralph sometimes had an air of melancholy about him. Lately, he had thought that he was a bit homesick, having been away from the West Coast for so long. His parents and most of his siblings still lived in California, and they remained a close-knit family. At one point a few years earlier, he had even applied for the dean of admissions job at his alma mater, Stanford. He assumed he wouldn't get it—he was only in his midthirties, which was young for so important a job at a big university—and indeed he hadn't, losing out to a woman who was then the dean of admissions at Swarthmore. He figured the experience of putting his name forward couldn't hurt, and it hadn't. He had also applied for the dean's job at Colorado College, but had been turned down for that, as well.

Now, in early 2002, Ralph had been encouraged by an acquaintance to apply for another position, this time as a college counselor at a private school in New Mexico, Albuquerque Academy. If he got it, he would be the director of college guidance and he would also be closer to his parents, only a day's drive from Los Angeles. And, like Sharon, he would be able to take everything he had learned on the admissions level and use it to counsel high school students. When Ralph discovered in the course of his interview that nearly a third of the students were on scholarship, and many of them were Mexican American, he couldn't help but see the parallel to his mother's work with Expanded Horizons. There was a chance that his life was about to come full circle. As of late January 2002, he had not yet gotten a sense of how the school's search was going. He was an applicant now; he could do nothing but wait. But even if he got the job, there was still the possibility that Natalie would balk at the move. She was very much enjoying teaching high school in Connecticut and was reluctant to leave.

In early March, Ralph received the offer from Albuquerque. He was told he would get a substantial raise (his current Wesleyan salary was $43,000), have a two-person staff (for a senior class of 150) and control a travel budget of $20,000 annually. *Cool!* Ralph thought. The ball was now in his wife's court. As much as she liked her work, Natalie began to think about how nice it would be to live closer to her own mother and sister, who were also in California. And she could tell that her husband was burned out. "It's a very demanding job," Ralph said at the time. "I'm starting to feel like I'm not being challenged." And so Natalie said yes, and they spent the spring making preparations to pack up their home and relocate to New Mexico in late June.

Nancy had known that Ralph was being interviewed for the New Mexico post, and when he told her that he was leaving Wesleyan, she hugged him and told him that his would be big shoes to fill. "I'll definitely miss the place and the people," Ralph told her. "I don't think I was that eager to switch schools. It's the opportunity."

Once arriving in New Mexico, Ralph and Natalie would have little time to unpack their belongings. On July 20, they were due in Los Angeles for a wedding. Nearly two decades after Raucous Ralph had first met Scared Sharon at Stanford, she was getting married. After becoming engaged, Sharon had called Ralph to ask him to participate in the ceremony. She wanted him to read aloud from the New Testament, as she had at his.

The wedding was to be held on the Occidental campus, where the groom, Vince Cuseo, was the dean of admissions. Ralph's sister Dina, still rising up the ranks in the admissions office at Caltech, was going to be there, too. Suddenly, this was sounding more like a NACAC convention than a wedding. But it seemed a fitting ceremony for Sharon, who was the Kevin Bacon of the admissions world, with only one or two degrees of separation from seemingly every guidance counselor and college dean in the country. Vince had not arrived at Occidental until after Sharon and Ralph had left for other jobs. But Ralph's career, like Sharon's, had crossed paths with Vince's at least once before. When Ralph traveled to Grinnell in 1994, it was Vince who was the dean of admissions, and who conducted Ralph's interview. Ralph had not liked Grinnell much at all, of course; there had been too many farms. But now, as he prepared to marry off his close friend, he was seized by a fresh thought: Grinnell, or at least its former dean, had finally passed The Tortilla Test.

ACKNOWLEDGMENTS

I would not have been able to report and write this book without the extraordinary assistance I received from Wesleyan University and *The New York Times,* as well as from the half dozen applicants who permitted me to tell their stories in such depth.

At Wesleyan, Barbara-Jan Wilson was immediately receptive when, in the fall of 1999, I pitched her my proposal for a newspaper series. Barbara-Jan went on to clear many paths for me, including the one leading to the university president, Douglas J. Bennet, whose energetic support was crucial. When Ralph Figueroa and I met for the first time, neither of us could have known that we would be spending so much of the next three years together, or that the few articles I imagined writing about him and his colleagues would mushroom into a work nearly twenty times as long. As I followed Ralph around, pelting him with questions, I felt sure he would eventually announce that he had had enough. But he never did. I am grateful for his patience, openness and humor. Ralph's wife, Natalie, always made me feel welcome, as did his parents, Bertha and Bill, and his baby sister, Dina. Sharon Merrow re-created the many serendipitous moments in her long friendship with Ralph and later guided me through the college preparation process at Harvard-Westlake. Her colleague Harry Salamandra reassembled the fragments of the day that Becca Jannol bit into the fateful brownie.

It could not have been easy for Nancy Meislahn to arrive at Wesleyan on her first day to find a *New York Times* reporter at the conference table. Nonetheless, her office door was always open to me. In addition to Greg

Pyke, who crunched many numbers and then spent hours on the phone explaining them, his colleagues Bozoma Arthur, Rod Bugarin, Amin Abdul-Malik, Chris Lanser, Lyllah Martin and Terri Overton graciously sat for extended interviews. It was essential to the integrity of this project that someone at Wesleyan gather supplemental information on the applicants I was following, but without tipping off the particular admissions officers to my interest. That role was played by Jed Hoyer, and he not only kept my confidences but also became a good friend. I enjoyed hearing the rollicking stories of Judy Goodale, Charlotte Lazor and Diane Crescimanno of the back office, and am grateful, too, for the assistance of Justin Harmon, Bill Holder, Kirstin Fearnley, Suzy Taraba, John Driscoll, Stephen Porter, Leilani Kupo, Jonathan Miller, Annette LeBoeuf, Joan Adams and Carter L. Bays. Samantha Smith and James Jacobus, two work-study students at Wesleyan, spent hours at the copy machine on my behalf, asking only for a "really cool shout-out in the book."

I don't know how I can properly thank Julianna Bentes, Jordan Goldman, Becca Jannol, Migizi Pensoneau, Aggie Ramirez and Tiffany Wang. They readily agreed to lay bare their young lives without any cover of anonymity, saying they were hopeful that they might ease the burden of those teenagers applying to college after them. I am indebted to them, and to their families, for their courage, their time and their trust. Other applicants who related their stories to me included Jannely Almonte, Albert Dixon, Daniela Gesundheit, Frank Lionetti, Katie Stockhammer and Amelia Walling.

At *The New York Times,* my editor, Ethan Bronner (a 1976 graduate of Wesleyan), was a terrific sounding board, and Joseph Lelyveld, Dean Baquet, Carolyn Lee and Luisita Lopez Torregrosa, among others, made sure those pieces found their way into print. Wallace Schroeder, Syd Bodnick and Jimmy Barden backed me up on the national copy desk, and Ozier Muhammad's photographs were stunning companions to my words. I also learned much from my partner on the national education beat, Jodi Wilgoren, as well as from my other colleagues in *The Times's* education department during this time: Karen Arenson, Abby Goodnough, Anemona Hartocollis, Lynette Holloway, Jane Karr, Tamar Lewin, Richard Rothstein, Diana Jean Schemo, Ed Wyatt, Kate Zernike and Yilu Zhao. Once the series was completed, Bill Schmidt permitted me to explore what more I might do with the notes I had taken, which grew into this book. And every author should have a friend with the marketing savvy of Felice Nudelman.

I would never have attempted a longer work had it not been for the persistent prodding of two of my literary heroes: Joseph Berger, who was then *The Times*'s deputy education editor, and Samuel C. Freedman, whose first book, *Small Victories,* served as a role model. Sam provided essential guidance on my book proposal, and Joe, having written two books in his spare time, persuaded me that I could and should do the same. Two dogged researchers, Kai-Ming Cha and Peter Valdina, helped me assemble the materials that would put this story in context. And Amy Hsieh filed a valuable dispatch from Northern California. I also want to thank Chiara Coletti at The College Board; Shanda Ivory and Judy Hingle at NACAC; Laura Freid and Mark Nickel at Brown University; Ken Gabard at Cornell; Melissa Falk at Muhlenberg College; Laurel Stavis and David Klein at Dartmouth; André Phillips at the University of Chicago; Josh Plaut at New York University; Marlyn McGrath Lewis and Andrea Shen at Harvard; Ron Ozio and Robert Zemsky of the University of Pennsylvania; Robin Mamlet at Stanford; Bruce Poch at Pomona; Anne Weeks at Oldfields; Chris Johnson at the Native American Preparatory School; Stephen Singer at Horace Mann School and Scott White at Montclair High School.

The consistent enthusiasm of my literary agent, Kris Dahl at I.C.M., was reassuring, as was that of her assistants, Jud Laghi and Sean Desmond. My editor at Viking, Rick Kot, not only provided a strong safety net but was also terrific company, both in his comments in the margins and in person. Also at Viking, Rick's assistant, Brett Kelly, always found time to answer my many questions; John Justino was an exacting copy editor; and Alex Gigante and Jeff Miller provided sensible legal advice. The firm of Pavia & Harcourt not only gave me legal assistance but also the occasional space to gather my thoughts and to write. At Pavia, I am grateful to Jordan Ringel, John Firestone, Linda Aro, Phyllis Barr, John Davis, Jenny Pointer, Gabriela Streat, Elizabeth Girodes, Frankie Almanzar and Safi Bowman.

In writing this book, I was fortunate to be tutored on matters both scholarly and literary by James O. Freedman, who spent hours reading several drafts and then discussing them with me. I also received constructive criticism, and no small amount of cheerleading, from Raymond Hernandez and Jon Danziger. I am thankful for the good counsel of Cynthia Marshall, Carlos Briceno, Steve Cohen, J. J. Hornblass, Sarah Jackson-Han, Robert Victor, Andy Watkins, Bill Berkeley, Jayson Blair, Walt Bogdanich, David Corcoran, Christopher Drew, Nick Fox, Jack Kadden,

Randy Kennedy, Diana Henriques, Adam Nagourney, Andy Revkin, John Schwartz, Nancy Sharkey, Steve Weisman and Monique Yazigi.

Because this book was written during vacations and on two years' of Sundays, my daughter, Alexandra, and son, Jordan, had to make sacrifices on which they were too young to be consulted. I look forward to the time when they are old enough to read these words of thanks. Pinch-hitting for me at home at various times were Marinel Rivera; Marilyn and Len Weinstock; Allison Steinberg; Mary Raffalli; Eric and Anne-Marie Schondorf; Alec Bokman; Jill and Jon Ames; Mark and Robin Weinstock; and Tony and Wendy Fisher.

My wife, Sharon, listened patiently to each word in this book on our many walks home after work, and her love and support, as well as her gentle editing, always kept me pushing forward. Last, I want to express my love and gratitude to my brother, A.J., and my parents, Barry and Edythe.

SELECTED BIBLIOGRAPHY

"America's Best Colleges," *U.S. News & World Report,* September 11, 2000, 90–133.

"America's Best Colleges," *U.S. News & World Report,* August 30, 1999, 62–75+.

"America's Best Colleges," *U.S. News & World Report,* November 25, 1985, 46–49.

Arenson, Karen W., "As Applications to Some New York Colleges Drop, Officials Cite Sept. 11," *New York Times,* March 22, 2002, p. B1.

———, "Study Faults Advanced-Placement Courses," *New York Times,* February 15, 2002, p. A14.

———, "Yale President Wants to End Early Decisions for Admissions," *New York Times,* December 13, 2001, p. D1.

———, "Youths Seeking Early College Entry Are More Likely to Get In, Study Says," *New York Times,* December 24, 2001, p. A12.

Associated Press, "Dean Says He's Leaving Wesleyan," *New York Times,* June 10, 1990, 12CN, p. 15.

———, "Defendant Put on Probation in Firebombing at Wesleyan," *New York Times,* August 7, 1991, p. B3.

———, "Office of Wesleyan's President Is Firebombed," *New York Times,* April 8, 1990, 1, p. 29.

———, "Wesleyan Unit Urges Six Be Disciplined," *New York Times,* January 30, 1987, p. B5.

Baker, Russell, "Sunday Observer: You Are Your Number," *New York Times,* October 23, 1983, 6, p. 29.

Bowen, William G., and Derek Bok, *The Shape of the River: Long-term Consequences of Considering Race in College and University Admissions* (Princeton: Princeton University Press, 1998).

Bronner, Ethan, "College Applicants of '99 Are Facing Stiffest Competition," *New York Times,* June 12, 1999, p. A1.

"Commencements; Wesleyan Senior Leaves a Bit of Himself Behind: His Hair," *New York Times,* May 27, 1996, 1, p. 26.

"The Disappearing Scholar-Athlete," *New York Times,* April 6, 2002, p. A14.

289

DePalma, Anthony, "Ivy Universities Deny Price-Fixing but Agree to Avoid It in the Future," *New York Times,* May 23, 1991, p. A1.

Dowd, Maureen, "Days of Reckoning: Picking the Class of '90," *New York Times,* March 19, 1986, p. B1.

———, "For Some Applicants, Student Essay Unlocks or Seals the Door to College," *New York Times,* January 13, 1986, p. B1.

———, "For Student and School, Admission Proves a Rich Source of Ever-Mounting Anxiety," *New York Times,* December 9, 1985, p. B1.

———, "Getting the Word: Elation, Frustration and Reflection," *New York Times,* April 26, 1986, p. 29.

———, "In Student Interviews, Pressure's on to Shine," *New York Times,* December 23, 1985, p. B1.

———, "Of Sneakers, Haircuts and Selecting Colleges," *New York Times,* December 16, 1985, p. B1.

Fallows, James, "The Early-Decision Racket," *Atlantic Monthly,* September 2001, 37–52.

Fetter, Jean H., *Questions and Admissions: Reflections on 100,000 Admissions Decisions at Stanford* (Stanford: Stanford University Press, 1995).

Fiske, Edward B., and Bruce G. Hammond, *The Fiske Guide to Getting into the Right College* (New York: Times Books, 1997).

Fiske, Edward B. et al., *The Fiske Guide to Colleges*, 13th ed. (New York: Times Books, 1996).

Freedman, James O., *Idealism and Liberal Education* (Ann Arbor: The University of Michigan Press, 1996).

Freedman, Samuel G. *Small Victories: The Real World of a Teacher, Her Students, and Their High School* (New York: HarperPerennial, 1991).

Golden, Daniel, "Glass Floor: How Colleges Reject the Top Applicants—and Boost Their Status," *Wall Street Journal,* May 29, 2001, p. A1.

Graham, Amy, and Nicholas Thompson, "Broken Ranks," *Washington Monthly,* September 2001, 9–13.

Heil, Diana, "The Last Class," *Albuquerque Journal,* May 26, 2002, p. 1.

Hernández, Michele A., *A Is for Admission: The Insider's Guide to Getting into the Ivy League and Other Top Colleges* (New York: Warner Books, 1997).

Holder, William L., "The Hedden Agenda: Wesleyan Buys a Press," *Wesleyan: The University Magazine,* fall 2000, 11–17.

Horowitz, Harvey, "No Indians at Wes Next Year," *Wesleyan Argus,* May 7, 1974, p. 1.

Johnson, Kirk, "Education; At Wesleyan, a Day to Reflect on Racial Tension," *New York Times,* May 9, 1990, p. B10.

Kauffman, Matthew, "Friend Sentenced to 33 Years in Death of Wesleyan Activist; Friend Sentenced in Shooting Death," *Hartford Courant,* January 9, 1993, sec. Connecticut, p. E1.

Kinkead, Katharine T., *How an Ivy League College Decides on Admissions* (New York: W. W. Norton and Company, 1961).

Kolata, Gina, "Admissions Test Courses Help, But Not So Much, Study Finds," *New York Times,* March 25, 2001, 1, p. 16.

Kranhold, Kathryn, "Campus Bombing Trial Left Its Mark; Wesleyan Case Left Defendant Changed," *Hartford Courant,* January 10, 1993, sec. Connecticut, p. B1.

———, "Firebombing Sentence Suspended," *Hartford Courant,* January 12, 1993, sec. Connecticut, p. C5.

———, "Images in Photos May Play Role in Wesleyan Bomb Trial," *Hartford Courant*, December 3, 1992, sec. Connecticut, p. B11.

Lemann, Nicholas, *The Big Test: The Secret History of the American Meritocracy* (New York: Farrar, Straus and Giroux, 1999).

Lewin, Tamar, "College Board to Revise SAT After Criticism by University," *New York Times*, March 23, 2002, p. A10.

MacFarquhar, Neil, "Naked Dorm? That Wasn't in the Brochure," *New York Times*, March 18, 2000, p. A1.

Madden, Richard L., "Wesleyan Cites 6 for Harassment," *New York Times*, December 14, 1986, 1, p. 55.

Mayher, Bill, *The College Admissions Mystique* (New York: Noonday Press, 1998).

Mercer, William, photographer, *Wesleyan: A Living Portrait* (Arlington: Royalston Press, 1990).

"110 Protesters to Face Charges at Wesleyan U," *New York Times*, May 3, 1988, p. B2.

Paul, Bill, *Getting In: Inside the College Admissions Process* (New York: Addison-Wesley Publishing Company, 1995).

Peterson, Karen S., "Pot Code '420' Burns into Pop Culture," *USA Today*, January 29, 2001, p. D1.

Potts, David B., *Wesleyan University, 1831–1910: Collegiate Enterprise in New England* (New Haven: Yale University Press, 1992).

Princeton Review, *The Best 311 Colleges*, 1999 ed. (New York: Times Books, 1998).

Raff, Lily, "John Waters Shares Life Anecdotes," *Wesleyan Argus*, April 14, 2000.

Ravo, Nick, "Commencements; Tutu Tells Wesleyan Its Help Paves the Way for Liberation," *New York Times*, June 4, 1990, p. B4.

Regents of the University of California v. Bakke, 438 US 265, 1978.

Rich, Eric, "ACLU Chief Praises Course," *Hartford Courant*, October 1, 1999, sec. Town News, p. B1.

———, "Learning Stripped Bare; For Some Students, Wesleyan a Pornographic Experience," *Hartford Courant*, May 8, 1999, p. A1.

———, "Porn-Free Curriculum Returns to Wesleyan—For Now; Professor Hope Weissman May Try to Reintroduce Her Controversial Course 'Pornography: Writing of Prostitutes' When She Returns from Sabbatical," *Hartford Courant*, September 1, 1999, p. A3.

Schemo, Diana Jean, "Head of U. of California Seeks to End SAT Use in Admissions," *New York Times*, February 17, 2001, p. A1.

Shulman, James L., and William G. Bowen, *The Game of Life: College Sports and Educational Values* (Princeton: Princeton University Press, 2001).

Smith, Nancy, "The Route to Diversity," *Wesleyan: The University Magazine*, fall 1999, 1–24.

Steinberg, Jacques, "Challenge Revives SAT Test Debate," *New York Times*, November 19, 2001, p. A14.

———, "College Gatekeepers Read Between the Lines," *New York Times*, April 3, 2000, p. A1.

———, "Court Says Law School May Consider Race in Admissions," *New York Times*, May 15, 2002, p. A16.

———, "For Gatekeepers at Colleges, a Daunting Task of Sorting," *New York Times*, February 27, 2000, p. A1.

———, "In the Admissions Process, a Bit of Horse-Trading," *New York Times*, September 29, 1999, p. B9.

——, "Role Reversal Time for College Supplicants," *New York Times,* May 3, 2000, p. A1.

——, "U.S. Appeals Court Hears Debate on Race-Based Admissions," *New York Times,* December 7, 2001, p. A27.

——, "Usefulness of SAT Test Is Debated in California," *New York Times,* November 17, 2001, p. A11.

Suskind, Ron, *A Hope in the Unseen: An American Odyssey from the Inner City to the Ivy League* (New York: Broadway Books, 1999).

Taraba, Suzy. Unpublished lecture delivered May 16, 2000 at the visit to Wesleyan University by the New England and New York Conference Commissions on Archives and History of the United Methodist Church.

Thernstrom, Stephan, and Abigail Thernstrom, *America in Black and White: One Nation, Indivisible* (New York: Simon & Schuster, 1997).

Wilgoren, Jodi, "Affirmative Action Plan Is Upheld at Michigan," *New York Times,* December 14, 2000, p. A16.

——, "Judge Rebuffs Law School at Michigan," *New York Times,* April 4, 2001, p. A12.

——, "Law School Wins Reprieve on Admission Policy," *New York Times,* April 6, 2001, p. A16.

——, "U.S. Court Bars Race as Factor in School Entry," *New York Times,* March 28, 2001, p. A1.

Wilgoren, Jodi, and Jacques Steinberg, "Under Pressure: A Special Report; Even for Sixth Graders, College Looms," *New York Times,* July 3, 2000, p. A1.

Yale Daily News, ed., *The Insider's Guide to the Colleges*, 25th ed. (New York: St. Martin's Griffin, 1998).

Zernike, Kate, "Fortunes of Colleges Are Shown to Rise, Fall with Rankings," *Boston Globe*, February 7, 2000, p. A1.

Zhao, Yilu, "Many Ride Out the Recession in a Graduate School Harbor," *New York Times,* January 24, 2002, p. A1.